PUTTING AUCTION THEORY TO WORK

This book provides a comprehensive introduction to modern auction theory and its important new applications. It is written by a leading economic theorist whose suggestions guided the creation of the new spectrum auction designs. Aimed at graduate students and professionals in economics, the book gives the most up-to-date treatments of both traditional theories of "optimal auctions" and newer theories of multi-unit auctions and package auctions, and shows by example how these theories are used. The analysis explores the limitations of prominent older designs, such as the Vickrey auction design, and evaluates the practical responses to those limitations. It explores the tension between the traditional theory of auctions with a fixed set of bidders, in which the seller seeks to squeeze as much revenue as possible from the fixed set, and the theory of auctions with endogenous entry, in which bidder profits must be respected to encourage participation. It shows how seemingly different auction designs can lead to nearly identical outcomes if the participating bidders are the same – a finding that focuses attention on (1) attracting bidders and (2) minimizing the cost of running the auction and bidding in it. It shows how new auction designs can accommodate complicated procurement settings and sales with many interrelated goods.

Paul Milgrom is Leonard and Shirley Ely Professor of Humanities and Social Sciences and Professor of Economics at Stanford University. He has also taught at Harvard University and MIT. A Fellow of the American Academy of Arts and Sciences and the Econometric Society, Professor Milgrom has served on the editorial boards of the *American Economic Review, Ecometrica*, the *Journal of Economic Theory*, the *Journal of Economics and Management Strategy*, and *Games and Economic Behavior*. He is coauthor with John Roberts of the 1992 landmark text *Economics, Organization, and Management*.

Professor Milgrom's research has been published in the leading journals in economics, including the *American Economic Review, Econometrica*, the *Journal of Political Economy*, the *Quarterly Journal of Economics*, the *Journal of Economic Theory*, the *Journal of Economic Perspectives*, and the *Journal of Mathematical Economics*. His current research interests are in incentive theory, planning, and auction market design. Professor Milgrom is internationally known for his work in spectrum auction designs.

CHURCHILL LECTURES IN ECONOMICS

The Churchill Lectures in Economics was inaugurated in 1993 to provide a series of public lectures on topics of current interest to students and researchers in the discipline. The lectures will be selected from the top echelon of leading scholars in the profession. Although they will always be acknowledged specialists in their field, they will be encouraged to take a broad look at their chosen subject and to reflect in a way that will be accessible to senior undergraduates and graduate students.

Peter Diamond, *On Time*, 1994
Douglas Gale, *Strategic Foundations of General Equilibrium: Dynamic Matching and Bargaining Games, 2000*
Ariel Rubinstein, *Economics and Language*, 2000

PUTTING AUCTION THEORY TO WORK

PAUL MILGROM
Stanford University

CAMBRIDGE
UNIVERSITY PRESS

CAMBRIDGE UNIVERSITY PRESS
Cambridge, New York, Melbourne, Madrid, Cape Town, Singapore,
São Paulo, Delhi, Dubai, Tokyo

Cambridge University Press
32 Avenue of the Americas, New York, NY 10013-2473, USA

www.cambridge.org
Information on this title: www.cambridge.org/9780521536721

First published 2001
Reprinted 2004, 2005, 2006, 2007, 2008

A catalog record for this publication is available from the British Library

Library of Congress Cataloging in Publication data

Milgrom, Paul R. (Paul Robert), 1948–
 Putting auction theory to work / Paul Milgrom.
  p. cm – (Churchill lectures in economics).
  ISBN 0-521-55184-6 (hard) – ISBN 0-521-53672-3 (pbk.)
  1. Auctions – Mathematical models. I. Title. II. Series.
 HF5476.M55 2003
 381'.17'01 – dc21   2003051544

ISBN 978-0-521-55184-7 Hardback
ISBN 978-0-521-53672-1 Paperback

Transferred to digital printing 2010

Contents

Preface

This book synthesizes the insights I have found from my teaching, research, and consulting about auction design. For me, the three have long been intertwined. I wrote my Ph.D. thesis about auction theory under the guidance of Robert Wilson, who was then already advising bidders about how to bid and governments about how to design auctions. Fifteen years later, Wilson and I together made proposals that became the basis for the design of the Federal Communications Commission (FCC) spectrum auctions – the most influential new auction design of the twentieth century. The FCC design was copied with variations for spectrum sales on six continents. In the intervening years, I had often taught about auction theory, though not yet as the practical subject that it was to become.

Work on this book began in spring of 1995, when I delivered the Churchill lectures at Cambridge University. Those lectures emphasized the history and design of the spectrum auctions run by the FCC beginning in 1994, as well as the bidders' experiences in the auctions. Wilson and I had only a few weeks in which to form our design and make recommendations, and my "Churchill project" was to complete the analysis of those recommendations by identifying the kinds of environments in which our new design was likely to be effective. Events caused the project to be delayed, but the project received a boost and a twist when I delivered lectures about auction theory in courses at Stanford in 1996 and 2000, in Jerusalem in 1997, and at Harvard and MIT in 2001 and 2002.

In my 1978 dissertation, I had written that there were seven main results of auction theory. Two decades later, there are many more and many views about what is most important and how best to synthesize this exceptionally beautiful theory. What is distinctive about my synthesis here and what makes it both more encompassing and more practical than earlier attempts is that it is rooted both in traditional demand theory and in real-world experiences.[1] I unify auction theory with demand theory partly by using familiar techniques and concepts: the envelope theorem, comparative statics methods, and demand theory concepts like substitutes and complements.

My perspectives on auction theory differ in emphasis and method from those of several recent contributors. In chapter 1, I describe how one can use the stylized results of auction theory in practical design. Chapter 2 presents my distinctive treatment of the Vickrey auction, which explains how the striking theoretical advantages of the auction are offset by equally striking disadvantages, which too often go unremarked.

Chapters 3 and 4 develop the classical results of auction theory using the tools of ordinary demand theory: the envelope theorem and the comparative statics techniques. This is in sharp contrast to graduate microeconomics textbooks that emphasize the distinctive "revelation principle" as the basic tool of mechanism design theory (Mas Colell, Whinston, and Green (1995)) – a tool that has no analog in or relevance for demand theory.

In chapter 5, I revisit the models of auctions with interdependent values and correlated information to recast them in the same terms. These new treatments show that parts of auction theory that had seemed difficult can be treated simply by using the same methods.

My experience in auction consulting teaches that clever new designs are only very occasionally among the main keys to an auction's success. Much more often, the keys are to keep the costs of bidding low, encourage the right bidders to participate, ensure the integrity of the process, and take care that the winning bidder is someone who will pay or deliver as promised. Chapter 6 emphasizes those considerations. It particularly emphasizes the consequences of free entry and the instruments available to the designer to encourage entry of the right kinds.

Chapters 7 and 8 deal with an area of auction design in which scholarly input can add enormous value. This is in the area of multi-unit

---

[1] In the years after the first FCC auctions, I contributed to spectrum auction designs in the United States, Germany, Australia, and Canada, electricity auction designs in New Jersey and Texas, asset sales in the United States and Mexico, and internet procurement auctions. My suggestions were also the principal basis of the FCC's design for auction #31 – its first package or "combinatorial" auction design.

auctions. Such auctions have been used for radio spectrum, electrical power, Treasury bills, and other applications. The design problems for these auctions include not just the usual ones about getting incentives and allocations right, but also limiting the complexity so that costs incurred by bidders are not too high and the reliability of the system is maintained. Unlike auctions for a single object, in which efficiency and revenue objectives are usually at least roughly aligned, multi-item auctions can involve radical trade-offs between these two objectives. Chapter 8, especially, highlights such trade-offs and explains how the new Ausubel–Milgrom design tries to reach a practical compromise.

I owe debts to many people not only for their help in preparing this book, but for helping me to reach this point in my understanding of auctions. Robert Wilson introduced me to auction theory in graduate school, directed my Ph.D. research, and joined me in the work of creating the FCC auction for our joint client, Pacific Bell. I have dedicated this book to him. The folks at Pacific Bell, particularly James Tuthill, had the patience and courage to support my applied research and to help me advocate it to the FCC. Evan Kwerel and the FCC team repeatedly showed the courage to be innovators, trying out radical new ideas. The colleagues with whom I have consulted on auction designs – Larry Ausubel, Peter Cramton, Preston McAfee, John McMillan, Charles Plott, and again Robert Wilson – inspired me with their ideas, enthusiasm, and inspiration.

Many people have directly supported my efforts in writing this book. I am especially grateful to five students and colleagues who read the entire manuscript and made helpful suggestions. Professor Valter Sorana's detailed and very thoughtful comments are reflected throughout the book. My research assistant, Hui Li, often sat next to me at my computer, insisting that certain passages or arguments needed further detail and prodding me to make the text, as she would say, "easy enough for me." The Harvard graduate students Parag Pathak and Siva Anantham and the Stanford graduate student Paul Riskind all read the entire manuscript and made hundreds of suggestions. The undergraduate Dan Kinnamon read and commented on parts of the manuscript and provided research assistance for the buy-price model of chapter 6. I also had invaluable discussions about particular parts of the subject matter with many colleagues, including Susan Athey, Larry Ausubel, Jeremy Bulow, Peter Cramton, Paul Klemperer, Evan Kwerel, Benny Moldovanu, Noam Nisan, Motty Perry, Leo Rezende, John Roberts, Al Roth, David Salant, Ilya Segal,

Padmanhabhan Srinagesh, Steve Tadelis, Bob Wilson, Lixin Ye, and Charles Zheng.

The period since I began this work was an especially difficult one for me personally and for my family, and I thank them, too. Without the love and support of my wife, Eva Meyersson Milgrom, and my children, Joshua and Elana, I could not have finished this book.

Foreword

Paul Milgrom has had an enormous influence on the most important recent application of auction theory for the same reason you will want to read this book – clarity of thought and expression. In August 1993, President Clinton signed legislation granting the Federal Communications Commission the authority to auction spectrum licenses and requiring it to begin the first auction within a year. With no prior auction experience and a tight deadline, the normal bureaucratic behavior would have been to adopt a "tried and true" auction design. In 1993, however, there was no tried and true method appropriate for the circumstances – multiple licenses with potentially highly interdependent values. I had been advocating the use of auctions to select FCC licensees since 1983, when I joined the staff of the FCC's Office of Plans and Policy. When auction legislation finally passed, I was given the task of developing an auction design.

One of the first auction design issues the FCC considered was whether to use an ascending bid mechanism or a single round sealed bid. The federal government generally used sealed-bid auctions, especially for high-valued rights such as offshore oil and gas leases. FCC staff felt reasonably confident that we could implement a sealed-bid auction – keep the bids secure, open the bids, and select the high bids. There were doubts whether we could do anything more complex. In the end, the FCC chose an ascending bid mechanism, largely because we believed that providing bidders with more information would likely increase efficiency and, as shown by Milgrom and Weber (1982a), mitigate the winner's curse.

The initial design the FCC proposed in September 1993 was a hybrid of an ascending bid and a first-price sealed-bid auction. It was intended to address the contentious policy issue of the appropriate geographic scope of the licenses for broadband personal communications services (PCS). Some companies argued that the FCC should issue nationwide licenses. Other companies, especially incumbent cellular providers that were barred from holding both a cellular and a PCS license in the same geographic area, argued for regional licenses. For each of two nation-wide spectrum blocks, the FCC proposed conducting a single round sealed-bid auction for all 51 licenses as a group, followed by a series of open outcry auctions for the same licenses individually. The sealed bids would be opened at the conclusion of the open outcry auctions, and the spectrum awarded to the highest sealed bid only if it exceeded the sum of bids on the individual licenses.

The initial FCC proposal also discussed the possibility of a simul-taneous auction mechanism. Had AirTouch, a large cellular operator, not advocated this approach, it might not have been mentioned in the FCC's September *Notice of Proposed Rule Making*. In a meeting with me, AirTouch pointed out that in my 1985 FCC working paper written with Lex Felker I had suggested a simplified system of simultaneous bid-ding where parties simultaneously placed independent bids on several licenses.

In 1985 I had no idea how to run such a simultaneous auction, and in 1993 I was very skeptical of the possibility of anyone developing and the FCC implementing a workable simultaneous auction within the one year provided by the legislation; but Paul Milgrom and Bob Wilson (working for Pacific Bell) and Preston McAfee (working for AirTouch) completely changed my thinking. Both the Milgrom–Wilson and the McAfee propos-als were mindful of the limits on the complexity of any proposal that the FCC could or would implement. Both proposed simultaneous ascending bid auctions with discrete bidding rounds. This approach promised to provide much of the operational simplicity of sealed-bid auctions with the economic efficiency of an ascending auction.

The 1993 legislation required that the FCC develop auction rules within 7 months and begin auctions within another 4 months. The FCC could have met the legislative mandate by beginning a sealed-bid auc-tion or an oral outcry auction. So why was it so important to begin a simultaneous auction within the legislative deadline? It was my view that whatever method was used in the first FCC auction, if it appeared successful, would become the default method for all future auctions, including broadband PCS. So I spent considerable effort looking for a set of licenses for our first auction that the FCC could successfully auction using the simultaneous multiple round design. I proposed to senior FCC staff that we auction 10 narrowband PCS licenses. This was a small enough number that we could successfully implement a simultaneous auction, and the licenses were valuable enough that a success would be considered important, but not so valuable that a failure would impose an unacceptably large loss.

The closing rule was one of the major design issues for a simultaneous auction. McAfee proposed a market-by-market closing rule with adjustments in bid increments to foster markets closing at approximately the same time. In contrast, Milgrom and Wilson proposed a simultaneous closing rule whereby the auction closes on all licenses only after a round has passed with no bidding on any license. Until then, bidding remains open on all licenses. McAfee proposed the market-by-market closing rule because of its operational simplicity. The FCC could surely run a number of separate ascending bid auctions in parallel. Milgrom argued however, that market-by-market closing could potentially foreclose efficient backup strategies. (For example, you might be the high bidder on a license for several rounds while a license that is a substitute for you closed. If you were then outbid on your license, you would not have the opportunity to place a bid on the substitute.) Milgrom's argument prevailed, and the FCC adopted a simultaneous closing rule, but not before addressing a closely related issue.

Would an auction with the simultaneous closing rule proposed by Milgrom and Wilson ever end? This was the worst case scenario that troubled me when I first met Paul Milgrom. He had come to the FCC to explain their auction design. The simultaneous multiple round auction with a simultaneous closing rule struck me as the most elegant solution I had seen for auctioning multiple licenses that could be both substitutes and complements. But might bidders each have an incentive to hold back while observing the bids made by others? If so, how could the FCC be sure that the auction would close in a timely fashion? I asked Milgrom this question. He clearly had thought about the problem and responded that with no loss of efficiency, bidders could be required to be active on at least one license in every round. Any serious bidder must either have a high bid or place an acceptable new bid. With only 20 days between Comments and the deadline for Reply Comments, Milgrom and Wilson developed this insight into the activity rule that the FCC has used in all its simultaneous multiple round auctions. The Milgrom–Wilson activity rule was an elegant, novel solution to a difficult practical auction design issue. It imposed a cost on holding back by tying a bidder's level of eligibility in future rounds to its activity level in the current round. If a bidder is not active on a minimum percentage of the quantity of spectrum for which it is eligible to bid, it suffers a permanent loss of eligibility. This discourages bidders from holding back, whether to "hide in the grass" or to collusively divide up the market.

The activity rule was critical to the FCC adopting the Milgrom–Wilson auction design. The FCC could not tolerate the risk that the auction would drag on indefinitely with little bidding. The activity rule, with the ability to increase the activity requirement during the action, provided the FCC with a mechanism to promote a reasonable auction pace without subjecting bidders to the risk of an unanticipated close when they still wished to make additional bids. Without this feature the broadband PCS auction might have ended after only 12 rounds with revenue at 12% of the actual total. Because of less than anticipated initial eligibility in the auction, the initial level of the activity requirement put little pressure on bidders to make new bids once there were bids on most licenses. Bidding almost ended after 10 rounds but dramatically increased after the FCC raised the activity requirement in round 12.

The elegance and the coherence of the proposal were not sufficient to make it an easy sell at the FCC. Many staff had little taste for taking the chance on an auction design that had never been used and seemed far more complex than any auction they had heard of. Chairman Reed Hundt's legal advisor, Diane Cornell, argued that the mechanism, especially the activity rule, was much too difficult for bidders to understand. I promised her that we would develop bidding software that would automatically calculate activity requirements and make it easy for bidders to participate. At the time, no such software existed, but fortunately we were able to develop user friendly interfaces in time for the first auction. A more serious concern was that the auction might be an operational fiasco. If that happened, the argument that the design had theoretical beauty would not carry much weight in a congressional oversight hearing. My boss was quite frank when he told me that he did not want the FCC to be a "beta test site" for new auction designs.

Why did the FCC adopt the basic Milgrom–Wilson auction design despite these concerns? First, it was good policy. It seemed to provide

bidders sufficient information and flexibility to pursue backup strategies to promote a reasonably efficient assignment of licenses, without
so much complexity that the FCC could not successfully implement it
and bidders could not understand it. Just having a good idea, though, is
not enough. Good ideas need good advocates if they are to be adopted.
No advocate was more persuasive than Paul Milgrom. He was so persuasive because of his vision, clarity and economy of expression, ability
to understand and address FCC needs, integrity, and passion for getting
things right. He was able to translate his theoretical vision into coherent
practical proposals and explain in plain English how all the pieces fit together. He took the time to learn relevant institutional facts and to listen.
He was willing and able to modify his proposals to address FCC concerns about auction length and destructive strategic behavior. He never
used hard sell or oversold his results, and thus he engendered the trust of
FCC staff. He was always responsive to the frenetic time pressures under
which the FCC often operates – willing to talk about auction rules while
he was on vacation, take desperate calls late at night, and visit the FCC
on very short notice during that first year it was developing its auction
design.

As persuasive as Milgrom was, the FCC might not have been willing
to risk adopting such a novel auction design without additional outside
supporters. One was John McMillan, whom the FCC hired as a consultant
to provide independent analysis of alternative auction designs. His report to the FCC (a revised version published in the *Journal of Economic
Perspectives* in 1994) provided strong support for the Milgrom–Wilson
design. And his calm manner and articulate explanations were reassur-
ing to FCC staff that we were going in the right direction.

Another ally was Preston McAfee, who helped solidify support for the
Milgrom–Wilson design when he said that he preferred it to the simpler
simultaneous design he had developed at a time when he underesti-
mated the FCC's ability to implement anything but the simplest auction
design. More important was his suggestion to modify the Milgrom–
Wilson proposal to permit bid withdrawals subject to a penalty. In a
conference organized by Barry Nalebuff in January 1994 to help the FCC
sort out alternative auction designs, McAfee proposed a simple way to
reduce the exposure risk faced by bidders for licenses with strong complementarities. To discourage strategic insincere bidding, the Milgrom–
Wilson design had not allowed for any bid withdrawals. However, when

a collection of licenses is worth more than the sum of the licenses individually, bidders face the risk of paying too much for part of a package of licenses when the rest of the package is won by other bidders. The National Telecommunications and Information Administration (NTIA), whose role includes advising the White House on telecommunications policy, had proposed combinatorial auction mechanism to address this concern. The design, based on the work of Banks, Ledyard, and Porter (1989) and developed in a NTIA staff paper by Mark Bykowsky and Robert Cull, seemed far too complex for the FCC to implement in the time available. As an alternative, McAfee proposed permitting bid withdrawals subject to a payment equal to the difference between the withdrawn bid and the subsequent high bid.

Though the FCC did not adopt the NTIA proposal, the fact that the NTIA proposed a simultaneous auction design was helpful in building support for the Milgrom–Wilson design. It made that mechanism look like a reasonable middle ground between sequential ascending bid auctions and simultaneous ascending auctions with package bidding. In addition to their written comments, in January 1994, the NTIA jointly sponsored with Caltech a PCS auction design conference that brought FCC staff together with academic experimentalists as well as game theorists. Proposed and organized by Mark Bykowsky and John Ledyard, the conference provided additional support for the use of a simultaneous auction mechanism. The demonstration by David Porter of the combinatorial auction mechanism proposed by NTIA helped show the feasibility of some form of electronic simultaneous auction. Perhaps most important was a presentation by Charles Plott of experimental evidence on the relative performance of sequential, simultaneous, and combinatorial auction designs. This research sponsored by PacTel at Paul Milgrom's suggestion, offered experimental evidence that when there were strong synergies among items, simultaneous auctions were better than sequential auctions, and combinatorial bidding was even better. Based on both the theory and experimental evidence, Ledyard persuasively argued that though it would be nice if the FCC implemented the combinatorial mechanism he had helped design, the FCC could achieve most of the benefits with a simpler simultaneous design along the lines proposed by Milgrom and Wilson.

Part of the explanation for the successful collaboration between outside economists and the FCC in designing spectrum auctions was that the initial responsibility for a design was given to the FCC's Office of Plans and Policy (OPP), which has a tradition of applying economics to public policy and tends to be far more open to new approaches than the operating bureaus. The OPP had been advocating the use of auctions for more than 10 years prior to the passage of the auction legislation, and was a logical home for a small team drawn from throughout the agency.

One of the pillars of that team was Karen Wrege, an auction project manager, whom the FCC recruited from the Resolution Trust Corporation. In 1993, it was not enough to convince FCC Chairman Reed Hundt that simultaneous multiple round auction was the best auction design. He had to be convinced that the FCC could implement it with the year mandated by Congress. Karen was able to visualize how the auction might work, convince Don Gips on Hundt's staff that it could work, and – as part of a remarkable FCC team – make it work. Jerry Vaughan led the team with indomitable courage through many harrowing moments, such as a complete system failure the night before the start of FCC auction #3. The team was too large for me to mention here all who deserve credit, but some who deserve particular mention for making the Milgrom–Wilson auction design proposal a reality are the lawyers Kent Nakamura, Jonathan Cohen, and Jackie Chorney, the information technology specialist John Giuli, the contracting officer Mark Oakey, and the economist Greg Rosston.

Much credit for implementing the FCC auctions goes to the contractors and consultants. Most of the programming for the electronic auction system was performed by outside contractors. After the first auction, the FCC hired a second economic theorist, Peter Cramton, to provide advice on refining the auction design and to develop a tool to help bidders and the FCC track the progress of the auction. We also contracted with a team of experimental economists from Caltech: Charlie Plott, John Ledyard, and Dave Porter. Without the help of Plott and Antonio Rangel, a first year graduate student, the contractor for the FCC's first auction might not have succeeded in translating the FCC auction rules into software code. Caltech also tested the software used in the first and second FCC narrowband PCS auctions. As part of their "torture testing" they paid experiment participants a bonus for any error they could find in the software. Caltech also developed a clever method for manually checking all the calculations during the first FCC auction. Run by Rangel in parallel with the electronic auction system, this also provided a manual backup that could have been put into service if the electronic system had failed. Fortunately it did not.

The first FCC simultaneous multiple round auction began on July 25, 1994 in the Blue Room of the Omni Shoreham Hotel in Washington, DC. Bidding was conducted electronically on site. Despite the testing of the software, there was some trepidation about whether it would work. There was particular concern about the software for stage II of the activity rule. The chief programmer for the contractor that developed the software and would run it during the auction said, in essence, "I am completely confident that the software will work properly in stage II, but do not try it." We never found out, because the auction closed successfully in stage I. Every round, the FCC decided on how to set the bid increments on each license. We had a committee of three consultants to advise us: John McMillan, a theorist; Charlie Plott, an experimentalist; and Bill Stevenson, an auctioneer. We had five days to complete the auction before we would be kicked out of the ballroom so it could be used for a wedding. There was vigorous discussion about how large to make the bid increments, how long to make the rounds, and whether to deploy stage II of the activity rule. As it turned out, with few licenses, vigorous competition, and bidders on site, the auction closed after 47 rounds and five days, in time for the wedding in the Blue Room.

Perhaps the biggest hero of the story of putting auction theory to work is FCC Chairman Reed Hundt. He defied the traditional tendency of government bureaucracies to do the safe thing even if it is not the best thing. He always wanted to know: "What does economic theory tell us?" He always tried to put into practice his favorite motto, "Do the right thing." But without economic theorists like Paul Milgrom, he would not have known what that was.

Evan Kwerel
January 2003

PUTTING AUCTION THEORY TO WORK

CHAPTER ONE

Getting to Work

The era of putting auction theory to work began in 1993–1994, with the design and operation of the radio spectrum auctions in the United States. Although the economic theory of auctions had its beginnings in the 1960s, early research had little influence on practice. Since 1994, auction theorists have designed spectrum sales for countries on six continents, electric power auctions in the United States and Europe, CO_2 abatement auctions, timber auctions, and various asset auctions. By 1996, auction theory had become so influential that its founder, William Vickrey, was awarded a Nobel Prize in economic science. In 2000, the US National Science Foundation's fiftieth anniversary celebration featured the success of the US spectrum auctions to justify its support for fundamental research in subjects like game theory. By the end of 2001, just seven years after the first of the large modern auctions, the theorists' designs had powered worldwide sales totaling more than $100 billion. The early US spectrum auctions had evolved into a world standard, with their major features expressed in all the new designs.

It would be hard to exaggerate how unlikely these developments seemed in 1993. Then, as now, the status of game theory within economics was a hotly debated topic. Auction theory, which generated its main predictions by treating auctions as games, had inherited the controversy. At the 1985 World Congress of the Econometric Society, a debate erupted between researchers studying bargaining, who were skeptical that game theory could explain much about bargaining or be useful for improving bargaining protocols, and those investigating in auctions and industrial organization, who believed that game theory was illuminating their studies. Although game theory gained increasing prominence throughout the 1980s and had begun to influence the leading graduate textbooks by the early 1990s, there was no consensus about its relevance in 1994, when the Federal Communications Commission conducted the first of the new spectrum auctions.

The traditional foundations of game theory incorporate stark assumptions about the rationality of the players and the accuracy of their expectations, which are hard to reconcile with reality. Yet, based on both field data and laboratory data, the contributions of auction theory are hard to dispute. The qualitative predictions of auction theory have been strikingly successful in explaining patterns of bidding for oil and gas[1] and have fared well in other empirical studies as well. Economic laboratory tests of auction theory have uncovered many violations of the most detailed theories, but several key tendencies predicted by the theory find significant experimental support.[2] Taken as a whole, these findings indicate that although existing theories need refinement, they capture important features of actual bidding. For real-world auction designers, the lesson is that theory can be helpful, but it needs to be supplemented by experiments to test the applicability of key propositions and by practical judgments, seasoned by experience.

Whatever the doubts in the academy about the imperfections of game theory, the dramatic case histories of the new auctions seized public attention. An article in 1995 in the New York Times hailed one of the first US spectrum auctions[3] as "The Greatest Auction Ever."[4] The British spectrum auction of 2000, which raised about $34 billion, earned one of its academic designers[5] a commendation from the Queen and the title "Commander of the British Empire." In the same period, game theorists were plying their trade on another important application as well. The National Resident Matching Program, by which 20,000 US physicians are matched annually to hospital residency programs, implemented a new design in 1998 with the help of the economist–game theorist Alvin Roth. By the mid-nineties, thirty-five years of theoretical economic research about fine details of market design was suddenly bearing very practical fruits.

---

[1] See Hendricks, Porter, and Wilson (1994).

[2] See Kagel (1995).

[3] The design was based on suggestions by Preston McAfee, Paul Milgrom, and Robert Wilson.

[4] William Safire, "The Greatest Auction Ever," *New York Times*, March 16, 1995, page A17, commenting on FCC auction #4.

[5] The principal designers were Professors Ken Binmore and Paul Klemperer. They give their account of the auction in Binmore and Klemperer (2002). It was Binmore whom the Queen of England honored with a title.

1.1 Politics Sets the Stage

To most telecommunications industry commentators, the main significance of the US spectrum auctions was that a market mechanism was
used at all. Spectrum rights (licenses) in the United States and many other
countries had long been assigned in *comparative hearings,* in which
regulators compared proposals to decide which applicant would put the
spectrum to its best use. The process was hardly objective: it involved
lawyers and lobbyists arguing that their plans and clients were most de-
serving of a valuable but free government license.[6] With its formal procedures and appeals, a comparative hearing could take years to complete.
By 1982, the need to allocate many licenses for cellular telephones in
the US market had overwhelmed the regulatory apparatus, so Congress
agreed to allow licenses to be assigned randomly among applicants by
lottery.

The lottery sped up the license approval process, but it created a new
set of problems. Lottery winners were free to resell their licenses, encouraging thousands of new applicants to apply for licenses and randomly
rewarding many with prizes worth many millions of dollars. Lottery winners were often simple speculators with no experience in the telephone
industry and no intention of operating a telephone business. Economic
resources were wasted on a grand scale, both in processing hundreds
of thousands of applications and in the consequent need for real wireless operators to negotiate and buy licenses from these speculators. The
lotteries of small licenses contributed to the geographic fragmentation
of the cellular industry, delaying the introduction of nationwide mobile
telephone services in the United States.

A better process was needed, and in 1993, Congress authorized auctions as the answer. The question of how an auction market for radio
spectrum should be designed was left to the Federal Communications
Commission (FCC).

1.2 Designing for Multiple Goals

Congress did provide some instructions to the FCC governing the new
spectrum auctions. One was that the first auctions were to be begun
by July 1994. A second called for the auctions to promote wide participation in the new industry. The FCC initially responded to the second

---

[6] The process was once characterized by an FCC Commissioner as "the FCC's equivalent of
the Medieval trial by ordeal" (as quoted by Kwerel and Felker (1985)).

mandate by introducing bidding credits and favorable financing terms for small businesses and woman- and minority-controlled businesses, to reduce the cost of any licenses acquired by those businesses. The statute also specified that the auction process should promote "efficient and intensive use" of the radio spectrum, in contrast with the fragmented use promoted by the lottery system. The meaning of the word "efficient" was initially subject to debate, but it was eventually read in economic terms to mean, in the words of Vice President Albert Gore, "putting licenses into the hands of those who value them the most."[7]

There is a powerful tradition in economics claiming that individuals and firms, left to their own devices and operating in a sound legal framework, tend to implement efficient allocations. The argument is that when resources are allocated inefficiently, it is possible for the parties to get together to make everyone better off. So, following their mutual interests, the parties will tend to eliminate inefficiencies whenever they can. This traditional argument has its greatest force when the parties can all see what is required and have no trouble negotiating how to divide the gains created by the agreement. For radio spectrum, with thousands of licenses and hundreds of participants involved, computing just one efficient allocation can be an inhumanly hard problem, and getting participants to reveal the information about their values necessary to do that computation is probably impossible. Compared to the development of a universal standard (GSM) for mobile telephones in Europe, the more fragmented system that emerged in the United States highlights that the lottery system did not lead to efficient spectrum allocations. With so many parties and interests involved, the market took many years to recover from the initial fragmentation of spectrum ownership. During those years, investments were delayed and consumer services degraded. Getting the allocation right the first time does matter. Achieving that with an auction system called for a different and innovative approach.

The FCC, which the law had charged with designing and running the spectrum auctions, had no previous auction experience. Within the FCC, the design task was assigned to a group led by Dr. Evan Kwerel, an economist and long-time advocate of using auctions to allocate spectrum licenses.[8]

---

[7] Quoted from Vice President Gore's speech at the beginning of FCC auction #4.
[8] Kwerel's initial advocacy is explained in Kwerel and Felker (1985).

Like any other important FCC decision, the auction design decision would need to be based on an adequate public record – a requirement that would force the FCC to go through a long series of steps. It would need to write and issue a proposed rule, allow a period for Comments and another for Reply Comments, meet with interested parties to discuss and clarify the points of disagreement, resolve those disagreements, issue a ruling, consider appeals, and finally run the auction. Steps like these often stifle innovation, but that is not what happened on this occasion. With no political guidance about what kind of auction to use, no in-house experts lobbying to do things their way, and no telecom with an historically fixed position about how an auction should be run, Dr. Kwerel had unusual freedom to evaluate a wide range of alternatives.

Kwerel drafted a notice that proposed a complex auction rule. Industry participants, stunned by the novel proposal and with little experience or expertise of their own, sought the advice of academic consultants. These consultants generated a flood of suggestions, and the FCC hired its own academic expert, John McMillan, to help them evaluate the proposed designs. In the end, Kwerel favored a kind of simultaneous ascending auction, based in large part on a proposal by Robert Wilson and me and a similar proposal by Preston McAfee. The Milgrom–Wilson–McAfee rules called for a simultaneous multiple round ascending auction.[9] This is an auction for multiple items in which bidding occurs in a series of rounds. In each round, bidders make sealed bids for as many spectrum licenses as they wish to buy. At the end of each round the *standing high bid* for each license is posted along with the minimum bids for the next round, which are computed by adding a pre-determined bid increment, such as 5% or 10%, to the standing high bids. These standing high bids remain in place until superseded or withdrawn.[10] An *activity rule* limited a bidder's ability to increase its activity late in the auction, thus providing an incentive to bid actively early in the auction. For example, a bidder that

[9] The principal difference was that the Milgrom–Wilson design proposed the now standard features that bidding on all licenses would remain open until the end of the auction, with progress ensured by Milgrom's activity rule. McAfee's design had no activity rule, and ensured the progress of the auction by closing bidding on each license separately after a period with no new bids on that license.

[10] A bidder that withdraws its bid pays a penalty equal to the difference, if positive, between the eventual sale price for the license and the amount of its withdrawn bid. If the eventual price exceeds its bid, then no penalty is payable.

has been actively bidding for ten licenses may not, late in the auction, begin bidding for eleven licenses.

The theory of simultaneous ascending auctions is best developed for the case when the licenses being sold are substitutes. During the course of the auction, as prices rise, bidders who are outbid can switch their demands to bid for cheaper licenses, allowing effective arbitrage among substitute licenses. One of the clearest empirical characteristics of these auctions is that licenses that are close substitutes sell for prices that are also close – a property that is not shared by most older auction designs.

The initial reception to Kwerel's recommendation was skeptical. The proposed auction was unexpectedly complicated, and FCC Chairman Reed Hundt sought the advice of other FCC staff. He asked the economics staff: If you could pick any design you want, would this be it? He asked those who would have to run it: Can this really work? Even in the short time available to set it up? With the endorsement of his staff, Chairman Hundt decided to take the risk of adopting a new auction design.

1.2.1 Substitutes and Complements

Auctions are processes for allocating goods among bidders, so the challenge of auction design can only be understood by studying the demands of the participants. In the initial PCS auction, there were three groups of potential bidders. The first group included long-distance companies with no existing wireless businesses. These companies, including MCI and Sprint, were making plans to enter the wireless business on a national scale. Each wished to acquire a license or licenses that would cover the entire United States, allowing it to make its service ubiquitous and to combine wireless with its own long distance service to offer an attractive and profitable package to consumers.

A second group comprised the existing wireless companies, including AT&T, some regional Bell operating companies, and others. The companies in this group already owned or controlled licenses that enabled them to offer services to parts of the country. Their objectives in the auction were to acquire licenses that filled in the varying gaps in their existing coverage and to expand to new regions or perhaps the entire nation. These companies posed a regulatory challenge for the FCC, which wanted to allow them to meet their legitimate business needs without gaining control of enough of the spectrum to manipulate market prices. To avoid this outcome, the FCC imposed limits on the amount of spectrum that any company could control in any geographic area. These existing wireless operators would be ineligible to bid for a nationwide PCS license of the sort that had typically been awarded in European countries. From MCI's perspective, this meant that a nationwide license might be bought cheaply at auction, so it lobbied the FCC to structure the new licenses in this way.

The last group consisted mainly of new entrants without wireless businesses. Some of these companies, like Pacific Bell in California, were quite large. These companies typically sought licenses or packages covering large regional markets, but not licenses covering the entire nation.

One of the first lessons to take from this description is that the auction game begins long before the auction itself. The scope and terms of spectrum licenses can be even more important than the auction rules for determining the allocation, because a license can directly serve the needs of some potential bidders while being useless to others. For the actual PCS auctions, a license provided its owner the right to transmit and receive radio signals suitable for mobile telephone service in a particular band of radio frequencies and in a particular geographic area. These license specifications constrained the possible spectrum allocations. For example, suppose three separate licenses covering areas A, B, and C were put up for sale. If one bidder wanted a license covering A and half of B while the other wanted a license covering C and the other half of B, the license specifications would prevent each bidder from acquiring its optimal allocation. One task of the auction designer was to promote the best (most "efficient") possible allocation, subject to such constraints.

Achieving efficiency involves various subtle complications. A certain license may be valuable to one bidder because it helps exclude entry and increase monopoly power, but be valuable to another because the buyer will use it to create valuable services. In comparing the efficiency of allocations, only the second kind of value counts, but bidders do not respect that difference when placing their bids. The value of a license to a bidder may depend not only on the license itself, but also on the identities of other licensees and the technologies they use. For example, the licensee identities can affect their "roaming arrangements" – which allow their customers to use another company's services when they roam to the other company's license area. A third complication is that the bidders may need to pool information even to determine their own likely profits from various arrangements, for example because the bidders have different information about the available technology or forecasted demand.

But the fundamental barrier to efficiency that was most debated among the FCC auction designers concerned the *packaging problem*. The value of a license to a bidder is not fixed; it generally depends on the other licenses the bidder receives. For example, a bidder might be willing to pay much more per license for a package of, say, five or six licenses than for smaller or larger packages.[11] Until such a bidder knows all of the licenses it will have, it cannot say how much any particular license is worth.

Consider a situation with just two licenses. If acquiring one license makes a bidder willing to pay less for the second, then the licenses are *substitutes*. If acquiring one makes the bidder willing to pay more for the second, then the licenses are *complements*. With more than two licenses, there are other important possibilities, and these add considerable complexity to the real auction problem. For example, if there are three licenses – say A, B, and C – and a certain bidder anticipates needing exactly two of them to establish its business, then A and B are complements if the bidder has not acquired C, but they are substitutes if the bidder has already acquired C. Nevertheless, most economic discussions of the auction design are organized by emphasizing the two pure cases.

Recent auctions devised by economic theorists differ from their predecessors in the ways they deal with the problems of substitutes and complements. Our later analyses will show that some of the new designs deal effectively with cases in which the items to be traded are substitutes, but that all auctions perform significantly worse when licenses might either be substitutes or complements. The impaired performance may take various forms including a loss of efficiency of the outcomes, uncompetitively low revenues to the seller, vulnerability to collusion, complexity for the bidders, and long times to completion.

---

[11] An instance of this sort arose in the Netherlands spectrum auction in 1998, where most of the licenses were for small amounts of bandwidth. New entrants were expected to need five or six such licenses to achieve efficient scale and make entry worthwhile.

To illustrate how value interdependencies affect proper auction design, we turn to a case study in which the matter received too little attention.

1.2.2 New Zealand's Rights Auction

New Zealand conducted its first auctions of rights to use radio spectrum in 1990. Some of the rights took the traditional form of *license rights* to use the spectrum to provide a specific service, such as the right to broadcast television signals using those frequencies. Others consisted of *management rights* according to which the buyer may decide how to use the spectrum, choosing, for example, television broadcasts, wireless telephones, paging, or some other service. In theory, when management rights are sold, private interests have an incentive to allocate spectrum to its most profitable uses, but the problem of coordinating uses among licensees can also become more complex.

Acting on the advice of a consulting firm – NERA – the New Zealand government adopted a *second-price sealed-bid auction* for its first four auction sales. As originally described by Vickrey (1961), the rules of the second-price auction are these: Each bidder submits a sealed bid. Then, the license is awarded to the highest bidder for a price equal to the *second* highest bid, or the reservation price if only one qualifying bid is made. The auction gets its name from the fact that the second highest bid determines the price.

The idea of a second-price sealed-bid auction strikes many people as strange when first they hear about it, but on closer analysis, the auction is not strange at all. In fact, it implements a version of the ascending (English) auction[12] similar to the one used at Amazon.[13]

In an ascending auction, if a bidder has a firm opinion about what the item is worth, then he can plan in advance how high to bid – an amount that we may call the bidder's *reservation value*. At sites like eBay and

---

[12] The most common form of an ascending (English) auction is one in which the auctioneer cries out increasing bids and the bidders drop out when they are no longer willing to pay above the current price. The auction ends when there is just one remaining bidder. As the winning bidder is required to pay the current high price, it is optimal for each bidder to stay in the auction only until the current price is equal to his valuation ("reservation value") of the item and not thereafter.

[13] eBay also runs a similar auction, but its fixed ending time involves additional gaming issues as described by Roth and Ockenfels (2000).

Amazon, the bidder can instruct a *proxy bidder* to carry out a *reservation value strategy*. The proxy keeps beating the current highest bid on the bidder's behalf so long as that bid is less than the specified reservation value. If everyone bids that way, then the outcome will be that competition ends when the price rises to the second highest reservation value, or thereabouts (with differences due to the minimum bid increment). If everyone adopts such a reservation value strategy, then the ascending auction is almost the same as a second-price auction.

Strategic considerations in a second-price auction are easy: each bidder should set his reservation value to what the object is worth to him. If it happens that the highest bid among the other bidders is greater than this value, then he cannot do better than to bid his reservation value, because there is no bid he could make that would win the auction profitably. If, instead, it happens that the highest competing bid is less than his value, then setting his reservation value in this way wins and fixes the price at what the competitor bid, which is the best outcome that any bid could achieve. Thus, regardless of the bids made by others, setting a reservation value equal to the bidder's actual value always earns at least as much as any other bid.

The second-price sealed-bid auction has two advantages over most other designs. First, it duplicates the outcome of an ascending bid auction with small bid increments, but without requiring the bidders to be assembled together or to hire agents to represent them in their absence. Second, it presents each bidder with a simple strategic bidding problem: each merely has to determine his reservation value and bid it. This also means that there is no need for any bidder to make estimates of the number of other bidders or their values, for those have no bearing on a rational bidder's optimal bid.

The second-price auction has a simple extension to sales of multiple identical items, and it, too, can be motivated by considering a particular ascending auction. For example, suppose there is such an auction rule with seven identical items for sale, to be awarded to the seven highest bidders in an ascending outcry auction. Again, bidders might sensibly adopt reservation value strategies, bidding just enough to be among the top seven bidders and dropping out when the required bid finally exceeds the bidder's value. An analysis much like the preceding one then leads to the conclusion that the items will be awarded to the seven bidders with the highest values for prices approximately equal to the eighth highest value. To duplicate that with a sealed-bid auction, the rule must award items at a uniform price equal to the highest rejected bid. In such an auction, the right advice to bidders is simple: "Bid the highest price you are willing to pay." A similar uniform-price rule has sometimes been used in the sale of U.S. Treasury bills.[14]

In New Zealand, the government was selling essentially identical licenses to deliver television signals. On the advice of its consultants, it did not adopt this highest-rejected-bid rule, but chose instead to conduct simultaneous second-price sealed tender auctions for each license. New Zealand's second-price rules would work well in one case only: when the values of the items were independent – neither substitutes nor complements. In the actual New Zealand auction, it would have been difficult to give bidders good advice. Should a bidder bid for only one license? If so, which one? If everyone else plans to bid for just one license and picks randomly, perhaps there will be some license that attracts no bids. Bidding a small amount for every license might then be a good strategy. On the other hand, if many spread around small bids like that, then bidding a moderate amount for a single license would have a high chance of success. With licenses that are substitutes or complements, independent auctions inevitably involve guesswork by the bidders that interferes with an efficient allocation.

The actual outcome of the first New Zealand auction is shown in Table 1. Notice that one bidder, Sky Network TV, consistently bid and paid much more for its licenses than other bidders. The Totalisator Agency Board, which bid NZ$401,000 for each of six licenses, acquired just one license at a price of NZ$100,000, while BCL, which bid NZ$255,000 for just one license, paid NZ$200,000 for it. Without knowing the exact values of various numbers of licenses to the bidders, it is impossible to be certain that the resulting license assignment is inefficient, but the outcome certainly confirms that the bidders could not guess one another's behavior. If Sky Network, BCL, or United Christian had been able to guess the pattern of prices, they would have changed the licenses on which they had bid. The bid data shows little connection between the demands expressed by the bidders, the numbers of licenses they acquired, and the prices they eventually paid, suggesting that the outcome was inefficient.

---

[14] The Treasury rule sets a uniform price equal to the lowest accepted bid.

Table 1. Winning Bidders on Nationwide UHF Lots: 8 MHz License Rights

Lot	Winning Bidder	High Bid (NZ$)	Second Bid (NZ$)
1	Sky Network TV	2,371,000	401,000
2	Sky Network TV	2,273,000	401,000
3	Sky Network TV	2,273,000	401,000
4	BCL	255,124	200,000
5	Sky Network TV	1,121,000	401,000
6	Totalisator Agency Board	401,000	100,000
7	United Christian Broadcast	685,200	401,000

Source: Hazlett (1998).

A second problem was even more embarrassing to New Zealand's government officials.[15] McMillan (1994) described it as follows: "In one extreme case, a firm that bid NZ$100,000 paid the second-highest bid of NZ$6. In another the high bid was NZ$7 million and the second bid was NZ$5,000." Total revenue, which consultants had projected to be NZ$250 million, was actually just NZ$36 million. The second-price rules allowed public observers to get a good estimate of the winning bidders' profits, some of which were many times higher than the price. To avoid further embarrassment, the government shifted from the second-price sealed-bid format to a more standard *first-price* sealed-bid format, in which the highest bidder pays the amount of its own bid. As we will see later in this book, that did not guarantee higher prices. It did, however, conceal the bidders' profits from a curious public.

The change in auction format still failed to address the most serious auction design problems. Unlinked auctions with several licenses for sale that may be substitutes or complements force a choice between the risks of acquiring too many licenses and of acquiring too few, leaving a guessing game for bidders and a big role for luck. Allocations are unnecessarily random, causing licenses to be too rarely assigned to the bidders who value them the most.

---

[15] For a detailed account, see Mueller (1993).

1.2.3 Better Auction Designs

In the New Zealand case, alternative auction designs could have performed much better. For example, the government could have mimicked the design of the Dutch flower auctions. The winner at the first round would be allowed to take as many lots as it wished at the winning price. Once that was done, the right to choose next could be sold in the next auction round, and so on. No bidder would be forced to guess about which licenses to bid on with such an auction. Each bidder could be sure that, if it wins at all, it will win the number of lots or licenses anticipated by its business plan at the bid price it chose.

There are other designs, as well, that limit the guesswork that bidders face. A common one in US on-line auctions allows bidders to specify both a price and a desired quantity. The highest bidders (or, in case of ties, those who bid earliest) get their orders filled in full, with only the last winning bidder running the risk of having to settle for a partial order. As with the Dutch design, efficiency is enhanced because bidders do not have to ponder over which licenses to bid on, and such rules reduce the *exposure* risk that a bidder may wind up acquiring licenses at a loss, because it buys too few to build an efficiently scaled system.

1.2.4 The FCC Design and Its Progeny

In the circumstances of the FCC's big PCS auction, it was obvious that some licenses would be substitutes. For example, there would be two licenses available to provide PCS service to the San Francisco area. Because the two licenses had nearly identical technical characteristics and because, for antitrust reasons, no bidder would be allowed to acquire both, these licenses were necessarily substitutes. The argument that some licenses were complements was also made occasionally, but the force of the argument was reduced by the large geographic scope of the licenses.[16]

As in the New Zealand case, the main design issue was to minimize guesswork, allowing bidders to choose among substitute licenses based

---

[16] Dr. Mark Bykowsky of the National Telecommunications and Information Administration (NTIA) was a forceful advocate of the view that licenses could be complements and proposed a complex package auction design to accommodate the possibility. His case that complementarity was important is more convincing for the later auctions in which smaller licenses were sold. Nonetheless, the short time available to run the first auction led to a near-consensus that the package auction proposal involved too many unspecified details and unresolved uncertainties for it to be evaluated and adopted immediately.

on their relative prices. When substitute goods are sold in sequence, either by sealed bids or in an ascending auction, a firm bidding for the first item must guess what price it will have to pay later if it waits to buy the second, third, or fourth item instead. Incorrect guesses can allow bidders with relatively low values to win the first items, leading to an inefficient allocation. With this problem in mind, the final rules provided that the licenses would be sold all at once, in a single open ascending auction, during which bidders could place bids on any of the licenses and track bids on all the licenses. The openness of the process would eliminate the guesswork, allowing bidders to switch among substitute licenses, and promote equal prices for licenses that are perfect substitutes.

In order for the auction to work in this idealized way, bidding on all licenses would need to remain open until no new bids were received for any license, but that raised a new issue. In a worst case scenario, the auction might drag on interminably as each bidder bid on just one license at a time, even when it was actually interested in eventually buying, say, 100 licenses. To mitigate this risk, the FCC adopted my *activity rule*. The general application of an activity rule involves two key concepts: eligibility and activity. A bidder's activity in any round is the *quantity* of licenses on which it has either placed new bids in the round or had the high bid at the beginning of the round. In the example cited earlier, the quantity is just the number of licenses on which a bid is placed, but other quantity measures, including the total bandwidth of the licenses bid or the bandwidth multiplied by the population covered, have also been used. The rule specifies that a bidder's total activity in a round can never exceed its eligibility. A bidder's initial eligibility, applicable to the first round of the auction, is established by filing an application and paying a deposit before the bidding begins. Its eligibility in each later round depends on its recent bidding activity. One simple form of the rule specifies that a bidder's eligibility in any round after the first is equal to its activity in the preceding round. Thus, bidders that are not active early in the auction lose eligibility to place bids later in the auction. This rule speeds the auction and helps bidders to make reliable inferences about the remaining demand at the current prices.

The FCC rules have evolved since the original 1994 design, but larger changes have been made to adapt the simultaneous ascending auction to other applications. One common variation arises when there are many units of each kind of item, such as auctions involving the sale of electricity contracts. In these auctions, for each item, each bidder bids its quantity demanded at the current price indicated on a *clock* visible to all bidders. The clock starts at a low price and keeps raising the price at any point at which the current total demand of all bidders exceeds the supply of that item. When demand equals supply on all items, the auction ends. A series of such clocks record the current prices for the various goods, and the rate of movement in these clocks determines the progress of the auction. A similar clock auction was used in March 2002 by the British government to buy 4 million metric tons of CO_2 emission reductions proposed by British businesses.

Clock auctions share several key characteristics with their FCC ancestor. Bidding on all items takes place simultaneously, so bidders can respond to changing relative prices. Prices rise monotonically, ensuring that the auction progresses in an orderly and predictable way. All bids are serious and represent real commitments. There is an activity rule that prevents a buyer from increasing its overall demand on all items as prices increase. Finally, bidding ends simultaneously on all the lots, so that opportunities for substitution do not disappear during the auction until all final prices are set.

New variations based on the same principles continue to be created to solve a wide range of economic problems. Electricité de France (EDF) used a particularly interesting one in 2001 in a sale of electrical power contracts. The sale involved power contracts of different lengths, ranging from three months to two years, but all beginning at the same time – January 2002 for the first sale. Because different buyers wanted different mixes of contract lengths and because all contracts covered the first quarter of 2002, EDF regarded the different kinds of contracts as substitutes.

Lawrence Ausubel and Peter Cramton developed the auction design. The first step was to assist EDF in developing a standard for "scoring" bids on contracts of different lengths. Bids expressed a price per megawatt per month that the buyer would pay for the right to acquire power. For the initial auction, EDF specified that the price for a three month contract for base-load power would always be €2139 higher than the corresponding price for a six month contract. Similarly, price differences were specified between the three-month contract and contracts lasting ten, twelve, twenty-four or thirty-six months. During the auction itself, the price clocks were controlled to maintain these price relationships, for example, the price of a three-month contract was at all times €2139 higher than the price of a six-month contract. Prices for contracts of all lengths continued to rise until the total remaining demand exhausted the total power available for the initial three-month period.[17] Such an auction creates competition among bidders for contracts of different lengths, increasing both efficiency and sales revenue compared to more traditional auction designs. Recently, the EDF auction has been further modified to include a "supply curve," so that total quantity of power sold depends on the price level.

1.3 Comparing Seller Revenues

The question most frequently asked of auction designers is: What kind of auction leads to the highest prices for the seller? The answer, of course, depends on the particular circumstances, but even the thrust of the answer surprises many people: There is no systematic advantage of either sealed bid over open bid auctions, or the reverse.

A particular formal statement of this conclusion is known as the *payoff equivalence theorem*. It holds that for an important class of auctions and environments, the average revenues and the average payoffs of bidders are exactly the same for every auction in the class. To illustrate the logic of the idea, suppose you are selling an item that is worth $10 to bidder A and $15 to bidder B. If you sell the item using an ascending bid auction with both bidders in attendance, then bidder A will stop bidding at a price close to $10 and B will acquire the item for that price. If you use sealed bids instead and sell the item to the highest bidder, then the outcome will depend on what the bidders know when they bid. If they know all the values, then in theory B will bid just enough to ensure that it wins – around $10 or $10.01 – and A will likely bid close to $10. If they behave that way, the price will be just the same as in the ascending auction.

The argument in this simple form was first made by Joseph Bertrand (1883). Nearly a century later, William Vickrey observed, that a similar conclusion holds on average for a much wider class of auction rules and in a more realistic set of situations than the one described here. For

---

[17] For example, in the sale of power beginning January 2002, when the total demand exceeded the power available for the first quarter of 2002, the auction ended. Any remaining unsold power for, say, the second quarter of 2002 was then included in subsequent sales.

forecasting average revenue, it is irrelevant which auction is used, within a certain class of standard auction designs.

Experienced auctioneers often contest this irrelevance conclusion. Those who advocate ascending auctions argue that they generate more excitement and more competition than sealed bids. After all, they claim, no bidder is willing to bid close to its value unless pushed to do so by the open competition of the ascending auction design. Those who favor sealed bids counter by arguing that ascending auctions never result in more being paid than is absolutely necessary to win the auction; there is no money "left on the table." Sealed bids frequently result in lots of money left on the table. For instance, in the December 1997 auction for licenses to provide wireless telephone services in Brazil, an international consortium including Bellsouth and Splice do Brazil bid $2.45 billion in that auction to win the license covering the Sao Paulo concession. This bid was about 60% higher than the second highest bid, so 40%, or about $1 billion, was left on the table.[18]

Similar arguments among practitioners arise quite frequently, sometimes with variations. In the United States, the staff of the Treasury Department have periodically argued the relative merits of two alternative auction schemes for selling bills. In one scheme, each bidder pays the amount of its own bid for each bill it buys; in the other, all bidders pay the same *market-clearing price*, identified by the lowest accepted bid. Advocates of the first ("each pays its own bid") scheme say that the government will get more money from the auction, because winning bidders are by definition people who have bid more than the lowest acceptable bid. Advocates of the second ("uniform price") scheme counter that bidders who know they must pay their own bid when they win will naturally bid less, reducing the market-clearing price and leading to lower revenues.

Informal arguments like these show that the matter is subtle, but they do not settle the issue. A formal analysis based on the *payoff equivalence theorem* discussed in chapter 3 helps to cut through the confusion. Under certain idealized conditions, if the allocation of lots among bidders is the same for two different designs, then the average payoffs to all parties, including the average prices obtained by the seller, must also be exactly

---

[18] Although the 60% overbid may be atypical, the ordinary amounts of money left on the table are still impressive. For example, in the Brazilian band A privatization, the median overbid was 27%. That is, for half the licenses, the winning bidders bid *at least* 27% more than the second highest bid.

the same. One cannot conduct a meaningful analysis of average prices alone, without also studying how the designs affect the distribution of the lots among the winning bidders.

The practical uses of the payoff equivalence theorem are similar in kind to the uses of the Modigliani–Miller theorems in financial economics, the Coase theorem in contract theory, and the monetary neutrality theorems in macroeconomics. All of these theorems assert that under idealized conditions, particular effects cannot follow from identified causes.[19] For example, according to the Modigliani–Miller theorems, if decisions about debt–equity ratios and dividend policies merely slice up the total returns to a firm's owners without affecting the firm's operations, then those decisions cannot affect the firm's total market value. Today, financial economists explain financial decisions by focusing on how financial decisions might affect a firm's operations – its taxes, bankruptcy costs, and managerial incentives. Similarly, according to the Coase theorem, if there were no costs or barriers to transacting, then the default ownership of an asset established by the legal system could not affect value. Today, economic theorists explain features of organization in terms of costs and barriers to transacting, including incomplete information and incomplete contracts. The payoff equivalence theorem is similar: the payment terms of an auction do not affect the seller's total revenue unless they are associated with a change in the allocation of the goods. Today, analysts focus more attention on how assumptions of the theorem are violated and the consequences of those violations or, for government regulators, about the implied trade-offs between their allocation and revenue objectives.

The planning for a sale of electrical power in Texas in 2002 illustrates how the payoff equivalence theorem has been applied in practice. According to the planned auction design, the auctioneer would gradually raise the prices for any products with excess demand and would accept quantity demands from the bidders, in much the fashion that Leon Walras once described. The auctioneer would not tell the bidders the

---

[19] According to the Modigliani–Miller theorems, under its idealized frictionless-markets conditions, a firm's financial structure and dividend policy cannot affect its market value. According to the Coase theorem, under other idealized conditions, the initial allocation of ownership rights cannot alter the efficiency of the final allocation. Monetary neutrality theorems hold that under yet other idealized conditions, monetary policy cannot change real outcomes in an economy. The payoff equivalence theorem holds that under its idealized conditions, changing payment rules cannot affect the participants' final payoffs.

quantities demanded by others. The rules called for the auctioneer to stop raising the price for a product when its total demand falls to the level of available supply. Texas ratepayers benefit from the revenues of this power sale, and the ratepayers' advocate argued that the auctioneer should continue to raise prices until demand is actually *less than* supply, and should then roll back the price by one increment. The idea was to sell power for the *highest* market clearing price, rather than the lowest one. This rule was problematic for a variety of reasons relating to the details of the auction, and the design team cited the payoff equivalence theorem to argue that there was little reason to expect that the proposed change would lead to higher prices on average, because bidders would bid differently if the payment rules were changed. A bidder that knows it may acquire power at a lower price if it withdraws demand early will be more inclined to do so than a bidder that knows it cannot cause a price rollback. The net effect on revenues is hard to predict, because it depends on how the proposed new rule changes the allocation. Eventually, the ratepayer advocate agreed not to oppose the auction design.

1.4 The Academic Critics

Economists who are putting auction theory to work encounter a dazzling array of issues, from ideological to theoretical to practical. Recognizing the complexity of the problems and the short times available to solve them, the engineering work for auctions sometimes entails guesses and judgments that cannot be fully grounded in a complete economic analysis. Auction designers generate ideas using theory, test those ideas when they can, and implement them with awareness of their limitations, supplementing the economic analysis with worst case analyses and other similar exercises.

The idea that economic theorists can add value through this mixture of auction theory and practical judgment has come under attack from some members of the economics profession. Some of the more frequent attacks, and my responses to them, are expressed below.

1.4.1 Resale and the Coase Theorem

One of the most frequent and misguided criticisms of modern auction design comes in the form of the remarkable claim that the auction design does not matter at all. After all, say the critics, once the licenses are issued, parties will naturally buy, sell, and swap them to correct any inefficiencies in the initial allocation. Regardless of how license rights are distributed initially, the final allocation of rights will take care of itself. Some critics have gone even farther, arguing on this basis that the only proper objective of the government is to raise as much money as possible in the sale, because it should not and cannot control the final allocation.

To justify this argument, the critics relied on the Coase theorem, which holds that if there are no costs to transacting after the auction, then the initial allocation of property rights cannot affect the final allocation, which will necessarily be efficient. Coase reasoned that so long as the allocation remains inefficient, the parties will continually find it in their interests to buy, sell, and swap as necessary to eliminate the inefficiency.[20]

The "zero transaction cost" assumption on which the Coasian argument is based, however, is not one that Coase ever advocated as a description of reality. Rather, it was advanced as part of a thought experiment to emphasize the importance of understanding actual transaction costs. Assuming that actual transactions costs are zero when they are not can lead to serious errors in one's conclusions. The history of the US wireless telephone service offers direct evidence that the fragmented and inefficient initial distribution of rights was not quickly correctable by market transactions. Despite demands from consumers for nationwide networks and the demonstrated successes of similarly wide networks in Europe, such networks were slow to develop in the United States.

As I argued during the deliberations at the FCC, the conclusion that initial allocations do matter follows by juxtaposing two well-known propositions from economic theory.[21] The first is that, as explained in chapter 2, auction mechanisms exist that achieve efficient license allocations for any number of available licenses, provided the government

---

[20] The Coase theorem includes a variety of assumptions that may fail in this application, such as the assumption that the parties' values reflect social value, not market power; the assumption that the parties have unlimited budgets, so spending on spectrum rights does not impair the ability to invest in infrastructure; and the assumption that rights have no *externalities*, that is, that bidders do not care about which competitors get license rights. The importance of the last assumption is analyzed by Jehiel and Moldovanu (1999).

[21] The theory described here applies to *private values* models, in which a bidder's maximum willingness to pay for any good or package of goods is independent of what other bidders know about that good.

uses the auction from the start. With just one good for sale, the English auction is such a mechanism. The generalized Vickrey auction, which works even in the case of multiple goods, is introduced in chapter 2. The second proposition is that, even in the simplest case with just a single license for sale, there exists *no* mechanism that will reliably untangle an initial misallocation. Intuitively, in any two-sided negotiation between a buyer and seller, the seller has an incentive to exaggerate its value and the buyer has an incentive to pretend its value is lower. These misrepresentations can delay or scuttle a trade. According to a famous result in mechanism design theory – the Myerson–Satterthwaite theorem – there is no way to design a bargaining protocol that avoids this problem: delays or failures are inevitable in private bargaining if the good starts out in the wrong hands.

1.4.2 Mechanism Design Theory

A second line of criticism emerges from a part of game theory called *mechanism design theory*. A *mechanism* is essentially a set of rules to govern the interactions of the parties. For example, it may specify the rules of an auction. Are there to be sealed or ascending bids? If sealed bids, how will the winner and price be determined? And so on.

Once the rules of the mechanism and the designer's objective have all been specified, the designer applies some criterion, or *solution concept*, to predict the outcome and then evaluates the outcome according to the objective. In the theory's purest and most elegant form, the aim is to identify the mechanism that maximizes the performance according to the specified objective. For example, one might try to find the auction that maximizes the expected selling price or the expected efficiency of the outcome. We will treat parts of this theory at length later in this book.

Mechanism design theory poses this challenge to practical auction designers: how can you incorporate the use of theory without, at the same time, applying the mechanism design approach? If you believe the theory accurately describes the behavior of players, you should use it to optimize the mechanism performance.

There is a longstanding joke about the arbitrage theory in financial economics that applies equally to mechanism design theory. Two people are walking along a street when one spots a $100 bill on the ground. "Pick it up," says one. "Why bother?" replies the other. "If it were real, someone would have picked it up already!"

Like arbitrage theory, the equilibrium analysis of game theory is an abstraction based on a sensible idea. Just as arbitrage theory implies that people do not leave real $100 bills lying on the street, equilibrium theory says that players in a game do not overlook ways to increase their payoffs. Both theories are useful idealizations – not reasons to leave $100 bills lying on the ground. Theories like these, based on ubiquitous awareness and thoroughly rational calculations, are obviously inexact models of real behavior, and one should be especially careful about applying them to choices that are complex and subtle, even when the players are sophisticated and experienced. In real auctions, where some players are unsophisticated, inexperienced, or lacking the time and other resources to support effective decision-making, equilibrium theory is still less reliable.

Despite their drawbacks, equilibrium models can be very valuable to real-world mechanism designers. Just as a mechanical engineer whose mathematical model assumes a frictionless surface treats those calculations as inexact, an economic designer whose model assumes that the players adopt equilibrium strategies can treat the predictions as approximations. Just as the real-world mechanical engineer pays attention to factors that increase friction and builds in redundancy and safety margins, the real-world mechanism designer pays attention to timing and bidder interfaces to make rational decisions easier, and plans to accommodate worst case scenarios, in case bidders make mistakes or simply behave contrary to expectations.

In the present state of the art, academic mechanism design theory relies on stark and exaggerated assumptions to reach theoretical conclusions that can sometimes be fragile. Among these are the assumptions (i) that bidders' beliefs are well formed and describable in terms of probabilities, (ii) that any differences in bidder beliefs reflect differences in their information, (iii) that bidders not only maximize, but also cling confidently to the belief that all other bidders maximize as well. These assumptions are extreme, and they are typically compounded in practice by the use of additional simplifying assumptions. Mechanisms that are optimized to perform well when the assumptions are exactly true may still fail miserably in the much more frequent cases when the assumptions are untrue. Useful real-life mechanisms need to be robust. Those that are too fragile should be discarded, whereas a robust mechanism can sometimes be confidently adopted even if, in the corresponding mechanism design model, it is not provably optimal.[22]

Besides the very demanding behavioral assumptions that characterize the theoretical mechanism design approach, the existing formal models of mechanism design theory capture and analyze only a small subset of the issues that a real auctioneer faces. Some of the important issues that are usually omitted from mechanism design models are listed below. Although none of these are incompatible with mechanism design theory in principle, accounting for all in a single optimization model is far beyond the reach of present practice.

- *What to sell?* If a farmer dies, should the entire farm be sold as a unit? Or should some fields be sold to neighbors? The house and barn as a holiday and weekend home? How should the FCC cut up the radio spectrum? Should power suppliers be required to bundle regulation services, or should they be priced separately?
- *To whom and when?* Marketing a sale is often the biggest factor in its success. Bidders may need to study the opportunity and line up partners, financing, regulatory approvals, and so on. Conditions may change: financing may be more easily available at one time than another; uncertainties about technology or demand may become partly resolved; etc. Bidders may actively try to discourage others from bidding, hoping to get a better price.[23] Auctioneers may seek to screen bidders to encourage participation by those who are most qualified, or may subsidize some participants to increase competition.
- *How?* For example, if the deal is complicated and needs to be individually tailored for each bidder, a seller might prefer to engage in a sequence of negotiations to economize on costs. If an auction is to be used, the right kind can depend, as we have already seen, on whether the items are substitutes or complements.

---

[22] The view expressed here is a variation of the *Wilson doctrine*, which holds that practical mechanisms should be simple and designed without assuming that the designer has very precise knowledge about the economic environment in which the mechanism will operate. Here, we further emphasize that even given a very complete description of the economic environment, the behavior of bidders cannot be regarded as perfectly predictable.

[23] On the eve of the FCC PCS spectrum auction #4, the author made a television appearance on behalf of Pacific Bell telephone, announcing a commitment to win the Los Angeles telephone license, and successfully discouraging most potential competitors from even trying to bid for that license.

- *Interactions?* Decisions about what to sell, to whom, when, and how
  are not independent ones. What to sell depends on what buyers want,
  which depends on who is bidding, which may depend on how and
  when the auction is conducted.
- *Mergers and Collusion?* The European spectrum auctions of 2000,
  with their very high stakes, provided some interesting examples of
  before-the-auction actions to reduce competition. In Switzerland,
  last minute mergers among potential bidders resulted in only four
  bidders showing up for four spectrum licenses. The auction was post-
  poned, but the licenses were eventually sold for prices close to the
  government-set minimum. Similar problems of valuable spectrum
  attracting few bidders and resulting in prices near the minimum occurred in Germany, Italy, and Israel.
- *Resale?* Most of the theory of mechanism design starts with a given set
  of bidders that keep whatever they buy. The possibility of resale not
  only affects auction strategy, it may also attract speculators that buy
  with the intention of reselling. Should the seller encourage speculators, because additional bidders create more competition in the auction? Or should the seller discourage them, because value captured
  by speculators must come from someone else's payoff – possibly the
  seller's?

The mechanism design purist's view, which holds that the only consistent approach is to develop theoretically "optimal" mechanisms, is not
useful in practice. Even if we could incorporate all the features described
above, our models of human behavior are not nearly accurate enough for
use in optimization. Behavior is neither perfectly stable over time, nor
the same across individuals, nor completely predictable for any single
individual. Useful analyses must be cognizant of these realities.

Despite these limitations, a large portion of this book focuses on
mechanism design and related analyses. The theory is especially useful in practice for identifying issues and effects. Among the decisions
that the theory can illuminate are ones about *information policy* (what
information to reveal to bidders), how to structure *split awards* (in which
a buyer running a procurement auction splits its business between two
or more suppliers), how to create *scoring rules* (in which bids are evaluated on dimensions besides price), and when and how to implement
handicapping (in which the auctioneer treats bids unequally in order

to encourage more effective competition, for example, promote small businesses or those run by women and minorities). The mechanism design approach also helps answer important questions about when to use auctions at all. Purchasing managers sometimes pose this question by asking whether particular goods and services are "auctionable," that is, whether the most effective procurement process is to run a formal bidding process.

1.4.3 Theory and Experiment

In sharp contrast to mechanism design purists, some economic experimenters raise an opposite objection: why should any attention be paid to auction theory at all, now that we have the capability to test alternative auction designs in experimental economics laboratories? Theories sometimes fail badly. The rest of the time, they explain only some of the data. So why rely on theory at all?

The possibility of experimental tests has, indeed, fundamentally shifted the way auctions can be designed. In the FCC auction design, successful tests conducted by Charles Plott in his laboratory at Caltech helped convince the FCC to adopt the theoretically motivated Milgrom–Wilson design. Working software demonstrating the design was another important element.[24] Yet, the experiments to date have been very far from replicating the actual circumstances of high-value auctions.

In practice, it is unlikely that anyone will ever test a range of actual proposals in a completely realistic setting. The amounts at stake in experiments are necessarily much smaller, and the preparation time for bidders will normally be much less. Because experimental settings differ so much from the auctions they simulate, the role of theory is indispensable. Theory guides the design of experiments, suggests which parts of any experimental results might be generalized, and illuminates the economic principles at work, enabling further predictions and improvements upon the original design.

---

[24] Working software demonstrating the feasibility of the new design was another important element. Implementation issues also played a huge role in the debate. The very possibility of running the computer implemented simultaneous auction raised the hackles of critics in 1994. To rebut the critics, my assistant, Zoran Crnja, programmed a flawless small-scale version of the software in a set of linked Excel spreadsheets. His software convinced the FCC that a reliable system could be created using our proposed rules even in the short time available.

The philosopher Alfred North Whitehead, when asked whether theory or facts was more important, answered famously: "theory about facts." Indeed, theories that are incompatible with facts are useless, but there can be no experimental designs and, indeed, no reporting of experimental results without a conceptualization of the issues. Theory will always play a key role in answering engineering questions, including questions about auction design.

1.4.4 Practical Concerns

The final criticism is that, in the real world, the whole mechanism design approach is irrelevant for several reasons. First, the auction rules themselves are subject to bargaining: there is no single mechanism designer. Second, the rules are rarely even a first-tier concern in setting up and running a complex auction. Several other issues are more important.

One such issue is marketing: an auction cannot succeed without participants. This interacts with the first observation: bidders may simply refuse to participate in designs that they consider strange or unfair.[25] This very observation, however, emphasizes that good design can be an affirmative way to attract more and better participants.

There are many examples of auctions and other competitions that get poor results because the rules are rigged to favor particular bidders and so discourage others from participating. One is the earlier description of MCI's attempts to rig the US spectrum auctions in its favor by making the "lot" a single national license. When different bidders want different kinds of lots, a package auction design, such as the ones often used in bankruptcy sales, may enable wider participation.

Another example is the initial public offering (IPO) of shares in a young company. In the past, the investment banks that organize the IPOs have often reserved shares in "hot" offerings for the bank's biggest and best customers, and that discourages small investors from participating. Trying to buck this trend, the investment bank WR Hambrecht has introduced its Open IPO product, which is a uniform price auction in which large and small investors are all subject to the same auction rules. The company tries actively to attract small investors to increase demand for

---

[25] My own experience designing a procurement auction system for Perfect Commerce, Inc., revealed the seriousness of this concern. Sellers do often refuse to participate in auctions that are not structured to their liking.

shares and create an alternative to the existing auction system, although its success will also depend on attracting larger investors, too, and companies willing to experiment with a new system.

A second important practical issue concerns the property rights being allocated. For example, if auctions are to be used to allocate takeoff and landing rights at a congested airport, then the rights themselves need to be carefully defined. What is to happen to a plane that is delayed for mechanical reasons and cannot depart in its assigned slot? What are the airline's rights if weather delays decrease the capacity of the airport? No sophisticated auction rule can lead to a good outcome unless these practical issues are resolved, and an auction system that fails to coordinate all the resources needed by the airlines – takeoff slots, landing slots, rights through en route choke points, gate access, and so on – cannot succeed regardless of how well rights are defined. Real problems require comprehensive solutions, and the auction rules are a partial solution whose importance varies across applications.

Another important practical detail for electronic auctions is the interface used by bidders. The original FCC auction software made it easy for bidders to make mistakes. On several occasions, bidders made what came to be called "fat finger bids." For example, when trying to bid $1,000,000, a bidder might accidentally enter a bid of $10,000,000 – an error encouraged by the fact that the early interfaces could not accept commas in the bid field.

The FCC's solution for this problem, however, was one that considered more than the ease of bidding. Under the FCC's initial rules, bidders found it easy to communicate messages, including threats, with their bids in the auction. Suppose, for example, that bidder A wished to discourage competitor B from bidding on a particular license, say #147, in a particular auction. If B bid on that license, A might retaliate by raising the price of another license on which B had the current high bid of, say, $9,000,000 by bidding $10,000,147, where the last three digits send a none-too-subtle message about its motivations. Such bids were frequently observed in some of the early FCC auctions.

Both the "fat finger" and the signaling problems were solved when the FCC changed the auction interface to require that a bidder select its bid from a short dropdown menu on its bidding screen. All bids on the menu used round numbers, being the minimum bid plus one or more increments. This system eliminated typos involving one or more extra digits and simultaneously made it much harder for bidders to encode messages in their bids.

Some critics respond to such anecdotes with the claim that although they do show that rules matter, they mainly show the dangers in electronic auctions or auctions using novel rules. However, even familiar, low-tech auctions can perform badly on account of problematic rules. In 1998, the Cook County, Illinois, tax collector conducted a traditional oral outcry auction to sell the right to collect certain 1996 property taxes that were two years overdue. In that 1996 *tax sale* auction, a bid specified the *penalty rate* that the winning bidder could charge in addition to the taxes due, as compensation for its collection services. The auction was conducted in an ordinary meeting room, with the auctioneer sitting in the front. The auctioneer would read a property number, and the bidding instantly began, with the bidders shouting penalty amounts. The maximum opening bid was 18%, and successively lower bids were shouted until a winning low bidder was determined.

The trouble occurred when several bidders simultaneously opened with bids of the maximum amount. Under the Cook County rules for that year, in the event of such a tie, the auctioneer was to assign the properties to winning bidders essentially at random. A bidder tied with, say, five others at 18% then faced a simple choice. He could bid less than 18%, having roughly a one in six chance to win the auction at a much lower rate than 18%. Or he could sit quietly and enjoy a one in six chance to win at a rate of 18%. Most bidders chose to sit quietly, and about 80% of the properties sold at the maximum rate of 18%.

How can we be sure it was the faulty rules, rather than collusion among (more than a dozen) bidders, that accounted for this outcome? A few days after the auction began, the county auctioneer announced a change in the rules. In the future, a tie bid at 18% would result in withdrawal of the property from the auction. After the change, penalty rates quickly collapsed to a lower level, providing some initial evidence that the treatment of ties does matter. Immediately after the rule change, some bidders sought a court order to restrain the auctioneer from changing its rules during the auction. The court agreed and issued the order. After the order was issued and the original rules restored, the winning bids quickly returned to 18%.

Understanding auction theory is helpful for more than just avoiding obviously bad designs. Well-designed auctions that link the allocation of related resources can perform much better than traditional auction sales. In the New Zealand case described earlier, if the novel second-price auction rules had been replaced with more traditional pay-as-bid rules, any simultaneous sealed-bid auction would still be prone to misallocation, because bidders would still need to guess about which TV licenses to bid on. Computational experiments suggest that 25–50% of the value might have been lost simply because the allocation was so poorly coordinated. In similar circumstances, the current world standard for spectrum auctions, the simultaneous ascending auction, can theoretically lead to a more efficient outcome and higher revenues as well.

The simultaneous ascending auction has limitations too, which can be particularly important when the items for sale are ones that different bidders prefer to package in different ways, or when there are complicated constraints on the collection of acceptable offers. In such cases, a package auction design can both attract a wider set of bidders and vastly increase the likelihood that the right packages emerge from the auction. The design of these auctions is, however, subject to many pitfalls, to which we return in part II of this book.

There are many more examples of the importance of the detailed auction rules. One is from a Mexican sealed-bid auction for a road construction contract, in which the bidders were asked to submit a total bid and to divide the total bid into three sub-parts in case part of the project was delayed or canceled. Although each bidder was required to specify four numbers (a price for each part and a total price), the project was to be awarded based only on the total price. The winning bidder submitted a bid in which the "total" was less than the sum of the prices for the three parts. As matters transpired, the sum of the three was low enough to win, and the winner claimed that he had simply made an "arithmetic mistake" and that the price must, of course, be the sum of the three component parts. It seems more likely that this device was used to place two bids, allowing the bidder to withdraw the lower bid if the higher one was a winner. That could be a useful option in a competitive setting, but even more so if the bidders were colluding, because the low "total price" bid would prevent a deviator from cheating on the agreement and placing a lower than expected bid. Indeed, if the auctioneer intended to facilitate collusion in the bidding, this was quite an effective design!

Another example of how the details matter is drawn from the German experience in a 1999 spectrum auction. In that auction, Mannesmann and T-Mobil managed to divide the market between themselves without engaging in intense price competition. With ten licenses for sale and a 10% price increment, Mannesmann opened the bidding by jumping to prices of DM20 million for five licenses and DM18.18 million for the other five, effectively suggesting to T-Mobil that the ten licenses be divided five-and-five at a price of DM20 million. In the event, T-Mobil bid DM20 million for the five lower-priced licenses and that ended the auction. The facts that equal division was possible and that the bidder could make such jump bids are design elements that contributed to this outcome. The risk was predictable. Indeed, the danger that such rules posed had been previously been pointed out in a 1997 report commissioned by the US spectrum authorities.[26]

In the US electricity markets, ill-considered market rules frequently contributed to high prices by making it too easy for power suppliers to manipulate the system. In a famous example, energy traders at the Enron Corporation manipulated the California power market by scheduling transmissions on congested links that were far in excess of those Enron had actually planned. That led the California Power Exchange to try to mitigate the expected congestion by paying the company to reduce its transmissions, resulting in massive profits for the company. Only after repeated failures did these designs evolve to produce more reasonable results, yet all of these defects could have been anticipated by a simple game theoretic analysis of the market designs.

The most careful statistical evidence of the importance of design comes not from auction markets per se but from the closely related *matching* markets, such as the ones by which most new US doctors are matched to hospital residency programs. Roth (1991) provides evidence that a particular characteristic of the matching rules – whether the rules lead to a *stable* match – is an important determinant of whether organized markets succeed in attracting participants over a long period of years. A match is stable if no medical student strictly prefers to be matched to another program rather than the one he is currently matched with while that other program simultaneously strictly prefers that medical student to one of those with whom it is matched. The analogous criterion for auctions is that no group of participants should be able to do better by rejecting the auction outcome and making a side deal of

---

[26] See Cramton, McMillan, Milgrom, Miller, Mitchell, Vincent, and Wilson (1997).

their own. Auctions that do not have this theoretical property are likely to run into trouble in practice, as some participants try to void the auction outcome to reach a better deal among themselves.

Successful auction programs need to be well designed in all important respects, of which auction rules are one. Applying the perspective of auction theory can be valuable in many ways. It can enable an auctioneer to avoid mistakes like those that marred the 1993 spectrum auction in New Zealand, the 1996 tax auction in Cook County, the California electrical power markets and the 1999 German spectrum auction. It can help the auctioneer to pursue multiple objectives, like promoting minority participation, encouraging alternative suppliers, and enhancing competition among bidders with diverse advantages. Finally, rules can be designed to accommodate complicated preferences and constraints for the bidders and the auctioneer. We will see some examples of this later in this book.

1.5 Plan for This Book

This book integrates two projects, which are presented in the two main parts. The first part gives a review of traditional auction theory and is based on courses that I have given over a period of years at Stanford, Jerusalem, Harvard, and MIT. Traditional auction theory is based largely on the theory of mechanism design and the chapter organization follows certain principles of that theory. Much of the analysis is focused on auctions in which each buyer wants only a single object – a condition called *singleton demand*.

My treatment of the material differs from other treatments in two ways. First, it emphasizes practical applications where possible and makes an effort to include the issues that are most important in practice. Second, the treatment reflects my view that incentive theory is not best viewed as some entirely new part of economics; it is best viewed as an evolutionary development of traditional demand theory. Rather than treating it from its own specialized perspective that obfuscates connections with older theories, I use general perspectives and techniques that not only unify the theories but also prove their worth by reducing the lengthy and difficult proofs of incentive theory to shorter, more intuitive ones.

The second part of the book differs from the first in its questions and methods. The questions mainly concern the design of auctions for environments in which there are multiple heterogeneous goods. These environments are fundamentally more complex than ones with singleton demand. One reason is that the number of possible allocations is exponentially larger, which leads to serious issues about the practical feasibility of auction algorithms and bidder strategies. For example, in an auction with five bidders and one item, there are only five theoretically possible allocations of the item, and each bidder bids over just a single item. However, in an auction with five bidders and five items, there are $5^5 = 3125$ theoretically possible allocations. A second way in which singleton demand is special is that it eliminates much of the tension between promoting efficient allocations and ensuring competitive revenues for the seller. In the general case of part II, where multiple heterogeneous goods are sold with complementarities among the items, that tension can be severe. For example, the Vickrey auction, noted for its ability to promote efficient outcomes, can lead to zero or low revenues in relevant examples. A third difference concerns the problem of *value discovery*. With singleton demand, bidders have only one allocation to evaluate, but in the general case the exponentially larger number of allocations can force a bidder to reduce its valuation activities, which can limit both efficiency and price competition.

Because the Vickrey mechanism plays a significant role in both parts of the theory, we begin by studying this mechanism in the next chapter.

Auction theory has grown into a huge area of research, and this book reports on only those parts of the theoretical research that are relatively settled and that, in my opinion, have promise to be helpful to auction designers. With these criteria in mind, I have given only light coverage to some of the elegant formal treatments of how auctions perform when there are very many bidders[27] as well as much of the recently developing literature about one or more of these topics: auctions with interdependent valuations, collusion among bidders, corrupt auctioneers, purchases for resale, and information processing during auctions. Readers who wish to follow the frontiers of auction theory are encouraged to read about these subjects in the new auction literature.

---

[27] This research begins with Wilson (1977) and includes Milgrom (1979) and the especially beautiful results by Pesendorfer and Swinkels (1997, 2000) and Swinkels (2001).

REFERENCES

Bertrand, Joseph (1883). "Théorie Mathématique de la Richesse Sociale." *Journal des Savants* **69**: 499–508.

Binmore, Ken and Paul Klemperer (2002). "The Biggest Auction Ever: The Sale of the British 3G Telecom Licenses." *Economic Journal* **112**: C74–C96.

Cramton, Peter, John McMillan, Paul Milgrom, Brad Miller, Bridger Mitchell, Daniel Vincent, and Robert Wilson (1997). "Auction Design Enhancements for Non-Combinatorial Auctions." Report 1a: Market Design, Inc. and Charles River Associates, www.market-design.com/files/97cra-auction-design-enhancements-for-non-combinatorial-auctions.pdf.

Cremer, Jacques and Richard P. McLean (1985). "Optimal Selling Strategies Under Uncertainty for a Discriminating Monopolist When Demands are Independent." *Econometrica* **53**(2): 345–361.

Dasgupta, Partha and Eric Maskin (2000). "Efficient Auctions." *Quarterly Journal of Economics* **95**: 341–388.

Hazlett, Thomas (1998). "Assigning Property Rights to Radio Spectrum Users: Why Did FCC License Auctions Take 67 Years?" *Journal of Law and Economics* **XLI**(2, pt 2): 529–575.

Hendricks, Kenneth, Robert Porter, and Charles Wilson (1994). "Auctions for Oil and Gas Leases with an Informed Bidder and a Random Reservation Price." *Econometrica* **63**(1): 1–27.

Jehiel, Philippe and Benny Moldovanu (1999). "Resale Markets and the Assignment of Property Rights." *Review of Economic Studies* **64**(4): 971–991.

Kagel, John H. (1995). Auctions: A Survey of Experimental Research. *The Handbook of Experimental Economics*. J. H. Kagel and A. E. Roth. Princeton, Princeton University Press. Chapter 7: 501–585.

Kwerel, Evan and Alex Felker (1985). "Using Auctions to Select FCC Licensees," Federal Communications Commission Working Paper 16.

McMillan, John (1994). "Selling Spectrum Rights." *Journal of Economics Perspectives* **8**: 145–162.

Milgrom, Paul (1979). "A Convergence Theorem for Competitive Bidding with Differential Information." *Econometrica* **47**: 670–688.

Mueller, Milton (1993). "New Zealand's Revolution in Spectrum Management." *Information Economics and Policy* **5**: 159–177.

Perry, Motty and Philip Reny (2002). "An Efficient Auction." *Econometrica* **70**(3): 1199–1212.

Pesendorfer, Wolfgang and Jeroen Swinkels (1997). "The Loser's Curse and Information Aggregation in Common Value Auctions." *Econometrica* **65**: 1247–1281.

Pesendorfer, Wolfgang and Jeroen Swinkels (2000). "Efficiency and Information Aggregation in Auctions." *American Economic Review* **90**(3): 499–525.

Roth, Alvin E. (1991). "A Natural Experiment in the Organization of Entry-Level Labor Markets: Regional Markets for New Physicians and Surgeons in the United Kingdom." *American Economic Review* **81**(3): 415–440.

Roth, Alvin E. and Axel Ockenfels (2000). "Last Minute Bidding and the Rules for

Ending Second-Price Auctions: Theory and Evidence from a Natural Experiment on the Internet." *NBER* Working Paper: 7299.

Swinkels, Jeroen (2001). "Efficiency of Large Private Value Auctions." *Econometrica* **69**(1): 37–68.

Vickrey, William (1961). "Counterspeculation, Auctions, and Competitive Sealed Tenders." Journal of Finance **XVI**: 8–37.

Wilson, Robert (1977). "A Bidding Model of Perfect Competition." *Review of Economic Studies* **44**: 511–518.

PART ONE

THE MECHANISM DESIGN APPROACH

The five chapters of Part I apply mechanism design theory and related methods to problems of auction design. We begin with informal descriptions of the main concepts of mechanism design theory. Although these descriptions correspond closely to the formal ones, they conceal technical details that are occasionally important, so the mathematical development is indispensable for a full understanding of the theory.

Mechanism design theory distinguishes sharply between the apparatus under the control of the designer, which we call a *mechanism*, and the world of things that are beyond the designer's control, which we call the *environment*. A mechanism consists of rules that govern what the participants are permitted to do and how these permitted actions determine *outcomes*. An environment comprises three lists: a list of the participants or potential participants, another of the possible outcomes, and another of the participants' possible *types* – that is, their capabilities, preferences, information, and beliefs.

In a political mechanism model, the participants could be legislators, and an outcome the set of bills that are enacted. Or the participants could be voters, and the outcome a set of elected officials. The mechanism analyst might investigate how a particular legislative process affects the likelihood of stalemate or how the electoral system distorts choices by politicians concerned with reelection. In economic mechanism models, the participants could be workers, or the members of a family, or departmental managers. The analyst would model how mechanisms determine job assignments, the distribution of household chores or the family budget, or the levels of funding of departments within a firm. Indeed, the most commonly studied mechanisms in economics are *resource allocation mechanisms* in which the outcome is an allocation of resources.

Mechanism theory evaluates alternative designs based on their comparative *performance*. Formally, performance is the function that maps environments into outcomes. The function "When it rains, we distribute umbrellas; when the sun shines, we distribute bathing suits" gives better performance than the opposite distribution pattern.

The goal of mechanism design analysis is to determine what performance is possible and how mechanisms can best be designed to achieve the designer's goals. Mechanism design addresses three common questions: Is it possible to achieve a certain kind of performance, for instance a map that picks an efficient allocation for *every* possible environment in some class?[1] What is the complete set of performance functions that are *implementable* by some mechanism? What mechanism *optimizes* performance (according to the mechanism designer's performance criterion)?

Mechanism design theory is outcome-oriented. A central assumption of the theory is that people care only about outcomes, not how they are achieved. In the real world, processes sometimes succeed or fail based on whether they are perceived as fair, simple, or open – attributes that are hard to evaluate in a formal model. Setting aside these considerations facilitates a formal but partial analysis. Once that analysis is complete, the omitted issues and criteria can be examined.

Two categories of problems plague mechanism designers. *Information problems* are the first category. Consider the problem of an airline regulator trying to respond to bad weather around a major airport that requires delaying or canceling some flights. Which flights? The regulator might ask the airlines to cooperate by identifying which flights can be canceled with only moderate disruptions to passengers and the schedule, but then airlines that honestly identify those flights will bear most of the cost of cancellations. Canceling flights could even make passenger service problems worse. For example, when flights on large planes are canceled or delayed, some wealthy passengers may hire private jets that use the same runway capacity to serve fewer customers. In this example, the regulator might be able to alleviate the information problems by

---

[1] In applying the theory, one needs to be cautious about the definition of "efficiency" used in the theory. These formulations focus only on the payoffs to participants in N. If some outcome has value to a participant because it allows him to extract rents through the application of monopoly power, then the identified allocations are generally not efficient in the economist's usual sense of Pareto optimality.

paying any airline that voluntarily sacrifices a runway slot and charging a fee to an unscheduled airline seeking an extra slot. In practice, cash compensation may not be allowed. What can be achieved then? What additional performance is possible if cash payments are possible?

Problems caused by inadequate information can be found throughout the economy. An architect who requires use of materials of a certain quality may not know that the builder has actually used a less costly and less durable substitute. Black marketeers who conceal their transactions or people who misreport income may thwart a government's tax system. A business manager may find a system of performance-related pay frustrated by inaccurate or intentionally distorted performance measures.

The second kind of problem facing mechanism designers is a *commitment problem*, in which participants do not trust the designer to keep his promises. For example, suppose the workers in a certain factory are paid a certain amount, called a *piece rate*, for each unit they produce. The manager of a factory promises not to change a piece rate, regardless of how much workers earn. Suppose the workers believe the manager and increase their output, but it turns out that some workers' piece rates are much too high relative to others, allowing them to earn much higher incomes. The manager's superiors and the workers whose piece rates are relatively low are likely to pressure the manager to reduce the higher rates and increase the lower ones. Anticipating such a reaction, the factory workers in the easy jobs may try to make their jobs look hard by limiting their production to avoid a reduction in their piece rates. In this example, the manager's inability to commit not to change rates reduces the factory output.

Both kinds of problems play a role in mechanism design theory and in its application to the *economic theory of contracts*. We will focus on information problems, however, because these are the most relevant ones for auction theory. They arise for the simple reason that bidders know more about their values than the auctioneer.

An *auction* is a mechanism to allocate resources among a group of bidders. An auction model includes three major parts: a description of the potential bidders (and sometimes the seller or sellers), the set of possible resource allocations (describing the number of goods of each type, whether the goods are divisible, and whether there are legal or other restrictions on how the goods may be allocated), and the values of the various resource allocations to each participant.

Values may be determined in subtle ways. For example, when a bottle of fine wine is sold at auction, the winning bidder's payoff may depend on how much she likes the particular wine, likes the prestige of winning the bottle, or likes keeping the bottle away from a certain competing collector. Losers, too, may care about the outcome, for example because they expect that if a certain friend wins the bottle, he will serve it at an upcoming wine tasting party. The mechanism designer's problem is to choose the rules of the auction – what bids are allowed, how the resources are allocated, and how prices are determined – to achieve some objective, such as maximizing the seller's proceeds.

Three important early contributions to mechanism design deserve special mention. The next chapter reviews the first of these contributions, William Vickrey's design of auctions that allocate resources efficiently in a wide range of circumstances.

The second important contribution was the Vickrey–Mirrlees design of an optimal income tax and welfare system given a utilitarian objective. Vickrey built the basic model, which gave structure to the question. The model incorporated the ideas that individual utility depends on income and leisure, that different people have different opportunities to generate income by sacrificing leisure, that the taxing authority can only observe total income, and that the tax system affects labor supply. The problem was to create a tax-and-transfer system to maximize the total utility of everyone in society. The utilitarian optimal solution would tax those with high earning ability and pay transfers to those with low earning ability, but would be limited by the incentive problem that entails. James Mirrlees later revisited and solved the optimization problem implied by Vickrey's formulation. Subsequent researchers have often mimicked Mirrlees' methods. For their contributions to the theories of efficient auctions and optimal taxation, Vickrey and Mirrlees shared the 1996 Nobel Prize in economic science.

The third important contribution was the Clarke–Groves analysis of the optimal provision of public goods. For example, a condominium association may need to decide whether to improve its common areas, perhaps by installing a faster elevator in the building, renovating the exterior, or building a children's playground. Improvements are costly and must be funded out of association funds and by an assessment levied on the association members. In these circumstances, the association board may want to know how much various improvements are worth to its members. Depending on exactly how the information is used and how costs are shared, association members might be inclined to misstate their preferences. Clarke and Groves analyzed how to arrange affairs to make truthful reporting consistent with individual interests. Their methods and conclusions are quite similar to Vickrey's; we treat the two together in chapter 2.

In the years that followed, mechanism design techniques were applied to problems in the public sector, e.g. the optimal state regulation of public utilities to maximize consumer welfare, and the private sector, e.g. the optimal design of contracts to maximize the welfare of the contracting parties. Roger Myerson's work on designing auctions to maximize revenue was the first to apply mechanism design to auction theory.[2]

Formalities of the Mechanism Design Model[3]

The model we shall study has two parts: an environment and a mechanism. In the simplest case, an *environment* is a triple (N, Ω, Θ). The first element of the triple, $N = \{1, \ldots, n\}$, is the list of *participants* (or potential participants) in the mechanism. When it is convenient to include the mechanism designer among the participants, we may instead write $N = \{0, \ldots, n\}$. The second element, Ω, is the set of possible outcomes over which the participants and the mechanism designer have preferences. The third element is the most abstract one: $\Theta = \Theta^1 \times \cdots \times \Theta^N$ is the set of *type profiles* $\vec{t} = (t^1, \ldots, t^N)$, which includes a type for each participant. Participant i's *type* (t^i) indexes the participant's information, beliefs, and preferences. For example, we may say that bidder 1 is of type A if the item for sale is worth $100 to that bidder and the bidder believes that the item is worth $150 to bidder 2, and of type B if the item is worth $200 to the bidder and the bidder believes it is worth $175 to bidder 2. The set of types lists all the possibilities that the modeler considers.

The type profile and the outcome combine to determine individual payoffs: $u^i : \Omega \times \Theta \to \mathbb{R}$. Thus, $u^i(\xi, \vec{t})$ denotes the payoff or utility that participant i gets when the outcome is $\xi \in \Omega$ and the type profile is $\vec{t}$.

In much of economic theory, a player's payoff depends only on the outcome and his own type, but the general formulation allows a broader dependence than that. An example in which payoffs depend on others'

---

[2] See Myerson (1981).
[3] The first general mechanism design model was formulated by Hurwicz (1973).

types comes from George Akerlof, who shared the 2001 Nobel Prize in economic science. In his famous *lemons* model of the market for used cars,[4] there are two kinds of participants: buyers and sellers. A seller's type describes the car's condition, which only the seller knows. A buyer's utility depends on both the buyer's tastes and the car's condition. Market models in which some participant has quality information that affects other participants' payoffs are called *adverse selection* models. The name reflects the idea that the selection of cars being sold in this model is not a random cross section of all cars but instead is overweighted by cars that are in bad condition, because owners of bad cars are more eager to sell them.

Although the treatment of adverse selection in auction models has a long history,[5] the largest part of auction theory sets adverse selection aside to focus on the *private-values* case, in which each participant's utility depends only on its own type: $u^i(\xi, \vec{t}) = u^i(\xi, t^i)$. In this case, others' information cannot influence a participant's ranking of the outcomes in Ω. Except where specifically noted, all the models in this book deal with the private-values case.

Most mechanism models assume that participants are uncertain about what other participants know. In *Bayesian* models, the conditional probability distribution $\pi^i(\vec{t}|t^i)$ describes a participant's beliefs, which depend on the participant's own type. Throughout most of this book, we employ the *Harsanyi doctrine* that the beliefs are derived from a *common prior* distribution π.[6] Although this doctrine is restrictive and rules out certain interesting and realistic phenomena, it does have one important advantage. It rules out *betting pathologies*, which are models in which participants can make themselves much better off simply by betting against one another based on the differences in their beliefs.[7] The Harsanyi doctrine is popular in mechanism design models,

---

[4] Akerlof (1970).

[5] There were auction models with adverse selection even before the pioneering work of Akerlof (1970). See Ortega-Reichert (1968) and Wilson (1969).

[6] Harsanyi (1967–1968).

[7] Legend has it that the betting pathology was first discovered in the coffee room of the Stanford University economics department, when Professors Joseph Stiglitz and Robert Wilson disagreed about whether a certain uncomfortable seat cushion was stuffed with foam or feathers. They agreed to bet $10 on the issue and to cut open the cushion, with the loser to pay for a new cushion. Alas, the department administrator stopped them before they could execute their agreement. The pathology is that this agreement, from which both participants

because it eliminates such bets and focuses attention on other aspects of the design problem.

It is sometimes convenient to write a type profile as $\vec{t} = (t^i, t^{-i})$, where t^{-i} lists the types of the participants other than i. A (*strategic form*) *mechanism* is a pair (S, ω) where $S = S^1 \times \cdots \times S^N$ is the set of possible *strategy profiles* (S^j is the set of possible strategies of a typical player j) and $\omega : S \to \Omega$ maps strategy profiles to outcomes.[8]

For each mechanism and each realization $\vec{t}$ of the type vector, we can define a corresponding strategic form *game*. The game $(N, S, U(\cdot|\vec{t}))$ is a triple consisting of a set of players, a set of strategy profiles, and a *payoff function* U mapping strategy profiles into payoffs. The arguments of the payoff function are strategies, but these matter to the players only insofar as they determine the outcomes that the participants care about: $U^i(\sigma^1, \ldots, \sigma^n, \vec{t}) = u^i(\omega(\sigma^1, \ldots, \sigma^n), \vec{t})$. If the players are Bayesians, adding the beliefs as described above completes the description of a Bayesian game.

Given a mechanism (S, ω), if the game theoretic solution concept forecasts that a particular strategy profile $\sigma = (\sigma^1(t^1), \ldots, \sigma^n(t^n))$ will be played, then one can use that forecast to predict and evaluate the performance of the mechanism. The forecasted outcome will be $\xi(\vec{t}) = \omega(\sigma^1(t^1), \ldots, \sigma^n(t^n))$. The function $\xi(\cdot)$ mapping type profiles to outcomes is the *performance function* corresponding to the mechanism (S, ω). Many game theoretic solution concepts are not single-valued; for example, many games have multiple Nash equilibria. There are several ways to accommodate multiple equilibria, but for part I we focus on

---

expected to benefit, required the destruction of real resources. It would have been possible to buy a new cushion without destroying the old one first, but that would not have allowed the professors to benefit from the bet. When the Harsanyi doctrine does not hold and parties with the same information nevertheless have different beliefs, side bets like that between Wilson and Stiglitz are quite generally beneficial. According to the *no trade theorem* (Milgrom and Stokey (1982)), the Harsanyi doctrine precludes mutually beneficial side bets, so adopting the doctrine focuses the analysis on other, more economically plausible aspects of the mechanism design problem. This resolution is unsatisfying, however, because it is contradicted by evidence about human beliefs. Moreover, we will see later that even with the Harsanyi doctrine, side bets still arise in optimal mechanisms when the participants' types are statistically correlated (Cremer and McLean (1985)).

[8] This is a *strategic form* description of the mechanism. One can also describe a mechanism in *extensive form*, by completely describing the succession of possible moves (the *game tree*), the information available to each player when she moves (the *information sets*), and the outcome that follows each possible sequence of moves. The difference between the two descriptions is potentially significant when one applies an extensive form solution concept, such as sequential equilibrium or perfect equilibrium.

the following one. When a game has multiple solutions, we define the *augmented mechanism* (S, ω, σ) to be the mechanism plus a selected solution. The idea is that the solution σ represents a recommendation made by the mechanism designer to the participants. If the recommendation is consistent with a solution concept that adequately captures the participants' incentives, then no participant will have any incentive to deviate from the recommendation, and σ is therefore a reasonable prediction of how the participants will behave.

When σ is a solution according to some solution concept, we say that the mechanism (S, ω) or the augmented mechanism (S, ω, σ) *implements* the performance $\xi = \omega \circ \sigma$. In other words, the equilibrium outcome of the mechanism is ξ, which is obtained from the outcome function ω when each participant plays according to σ_i. Sometimes, we attach the name of the solution concept, saying that a mechanism *implements in dominant strategies* or *Bayes–Nash implements* the particular performance.

The Chapters of Part I

We develop the mechanism design approach to auction theory in a series of steps. In chapter 2, we review the Vickrey analysis of auctions and the related Clarke–Groves analysis of public decisions. The Vickrey–Clarke–Groves (VCG) design establishes a useful benchmark with which subsequent analyses of resource allocation mechanisms must be compared.

Chapter 3 introduces the envelope theorem and some of its most important consequences, including Holmstrom's lemma and Myerson's lemma, which are incentive theory analogs of the famous demand theory lemmas of Hotelling and Shepard. Using the envelope theorem allows short proofs of many famous results and reveals their close relationship. Among these are the Green–Laffont–Holmstrom theorem that the VCG mechanisms are the only efficient dominant strategy mechanisms, the Myerson–Satterthwaite theorem about the inescapable inefficiencies of bargaining with incomplete information, the Jehiel–Moldovanu theorem about the impossibility of implementing efficient outcomes with adverse selection, the celebrated payoff and revenue equivalence theorems, the Myerson–Riley–Samuelson optimal auctions theorem, and the McAfee–McMillan weak-cartels theorem.

Chapter 4 introduces the *single crossing properties*, the *constraint simplification theorem*, and the *ranking lemma*. Together, these facilitate analyses of standard auction designs, the characterization of implementable performance functions, the ranking of standard auctions in various different environments, and a fuller development of optimal auction theory.

The models explored in chapters 2–4 are simplified by the assumptions that bidders know their own values and know nothing about others' values. In chapter 5, we explore models in which these assumptions no longer hold, including models in which bidders or the seller invest in additional information and conceal or reveal it. A seller can benefit in several ways by revealing valuation information. The information can avoid inefficiencies caused by mistaken evaluations, reduce the risk premia that bidders deduct in valuing uncertain assets, and decrease the information rents that bidders earn. All of these changes can increase expected revenues.

Chapter 6 sets a larger context for auctions by treating entry decisions and post-auction performance. These larger considerations are extremely important in practice: an auction can hardly be considered optimal if no bidders choose to participate or if the winner defaults on his obligations. They also shift the focus of auction design in several important ways. First, when participation is costly, unless enough profit is left for the bidders, they will not choose to participate, damaging both efficiency and revenues. Maximizing efficiency can involve pre-screening of potential bidders, so that only the most qualified incur the cost of learning their types and preparing bids. Pre-screening and other devices can also help ensure that the selected bidder is able to perform. When bidders differ in their qualifications, evaluating bids becomes more complicated as well, as the seller balances whether to accept a higher bid from a weak buyer who may default or a lower bid from a qualified buyer.

REFERENCES

Akerlof, George (1970). "The Market for 'Lemons': Quality Uncertainty and the Market Mechanism." *Quarterly Journal of Economics* **84**: 488–500.

Cremer, Jacques and Richard P. McLean (1985). "Optimal Selling Strategies under Uncertainty for a Discriminating Monopolist When Demands Are Independent." *Econometrica* **53**(2): 345–361.

Harsanyi, John (1967–1968). "Games with Incomplete Information Played by Bayesian Players (Parts I–III)." *Management Science* **14**: 159–182, 320–334, 486–502.

Hurwicz, Leonid (1973). "The Design of Mechanisms for Resource Allocation." *American Economic Review* **63**(2): 1–30.

Milgrom, Paul and Nancy Stokey (1982). "Information, Trade and Common Knowledge." *Journal of Economic Theory* **26**: 17–27.

Myerson, Roger B. (1981). "Optimal Auction Design." *Mathematics of Operations Research* **6**(1): 58–73.

Ortega-Reichert, Armando (1968). *Models for Competitive Bidding under Uncertainty.* Stanford, CA: Stanford University.

Wilson, Robert (1969). "Competitive Bidding with Disparate Information." *Management Science* **15**(7): 446–448.

CHAPTER TWO

Vickrey–Clarke–Groves Mechanisms

This chapter describes the important contributions of Vickrey, Clarke, and Groves (VCG) to the theory of mechanism design. Vickrey (1961) analyzed a situation in which bidders compete to buy or sell a collection of goods. Later, Clarke (1971) and Groves (1973) studied the public choice problem, in which agents decide whether to undertake a public project – e.g. construction of a bridge or highway – whose cost must be borne by the agents. This latter analysis formally includes any choice from a finite set. In particular, it includes the Vickrey analysis for the case of discrete assets. We limit attention in this chapter to the case of finite choice sets, to bypass technical issues associated with infinite choice sets, particularly issues associated with the existence of a best choice.

The VCG analysis has become an important standard. It is the work by which nearly all other mechanism design work is judged and in terms of which its contribution is assessed. As we will see in later chapters, there are deep and surprising connections between the VCG theory and many other parts of auction theory.

2.1 Formulation

We begin the theoretical development in this section by introducing notation and defining direct mechanisms and VCG mechanisms.

Thus, let $N = \{0, \ldots, n\}$ denote the set of participants, with participant 0 being the mechanism operator. Let X denote the set of possible decisions with typical element x. For chapters 2–5, we assume that the set of participants is exogenously given and omit any analysis of the incentives to participate. An outcome is a pair (x, p) describing a decision x and a vector of positive or negative payments $p = (p^0, p^1, \ldots, p^n)$ by the participants. For example, in a first-price sealed-bid auction, the decision x is a vector where $x^i = 1$ if agent i gets the object and 0 otherwise. The associated vector of payments is p, where $p^i = b^i = -p^0$ if i bids b^i and wins, and in that case, $p^j = 0$ for the other bidders.

For most of our analysis, we also assume that each participant i values outcomes according to $u^i((x, p), \vec{t}) \equiv v^i(x, t^i) - p^i$, that is, i's payoff corresponding to outcome (x, p) is i's value of the decision x, which depends only on i's own type t^i, minus the payment that i must make. This *quasi-linear* specification of the utility function plays an indispensable role in the formal analysis of this chapter. The assumption of quasi-linearity implies that bidders are able to make any cash transfers described by the mechanism, that there exists a cash transfer that exactly compensates any individual for any possible change in outcomes, and that redistributing wealth among the participants would not change this compensatory transfer. These assumptions represent better modeling approximations for some situations than for others. For example, if the bidders are firms with ample liquidity, the assumptions might be a very good approximation of reality, but if they are consumers with significant credit constraints that apply to the transactions, then the assumptions might be an unacceptably bad fit.

Recall that "performance" means the function that maps environments into outcomes. Given our assumptions about the two-part description of outcomes, the performance of any mechanism can be also described in two parts. The *decision performance* maps types into decisions x, whereas the *transfer performance* maps types into payments or transfers. When the decision x allocates goods, we sometimes also call x the *allocation performance*.

The VCG analysis sometimes attempts to achieve efficient performance subject to the constraint that transfers add up to zero. Given the assumptions described above, a decision x is efficient if it maximizes the total value $\sum_{i \in N} v^i(x, t^i)$. For example, in an auction of a single good, the final allocation is efficient if it awards the good to the bidder who values it the most. In the models studied here, by construction, net payments always add up to zero, because the seller (or mechanism designer) receives any sums that the buyers (or bidders) pay.

In some publicly run auctions, the design objective is efficiency as defined above, although revenues (the total transfer to the mechanism designer) may also be an important goal. In private-sector auctions, revenues are always an important goal and often the only one.

Sometimes, the designer wants to run an auction in which $p^0 \equiv 0$, that is, in which there is never any net transfer to the auction designer. These *balanced-budget mechanisms* are useful, for example, in regulatory contexts where the regulator is not authorized to contribute or collect money from the regulated parties. They also arise in the theory of the firm, where the mechanism operator is similarly restricted. As we will see later, there is often a tension in mechanism design between achieving efficient outcomes and ensuring a balanced budget.

The VCG mechanisms are *incentive-compatible direct mechanisms*. This means that (1) $S = \Theta$ and that (2) the strategy profile $(\sigma^i(t^i) = t^i)_{i \in N}$ is an equilibrium. In words, the first condition means that each participant is required to report a possible type to the mechanism operator. We will sometimes speak of direct mechanisms as being pairs (x, p), leaving the strategy set implicit. The second condition, *incentive compatibility*, means that reporting one's type truthfully is an equilibrium according to whatever solution concept we have chosen. For VCG mechanisms, we focus on *dominant-strategy implementation*, so the relevant solution concept is that each participant plays a dominant strategy.

One appeal of incentive-compatible direct mechanisms is that they spare participants the need for elaborate strategic calculations: truthful reporting serves each participant's individual interest. Choosing dominant strategies as the solution concept, an incentive-compatible direct mechanism is one for which truthful reporting leads to as high a payoff as any other strategy for all possible types of opponents and all possible actions that these opponents may take. For example, as discussed in chapter 1, it is always optimal for a bidder in a second-price sealed-bid auction for a single good to bid his valuation. Moreover, this *truthful* bidding strategy is the only strategy that is always optimal, so it is a *dominant strategy*. Thus, the second-price auction is a dominant-strategy incentive-compatible direct mechanism.

The operator of a VCG mechanism uses the reported types to compute the maximum total value $V(X, N, \vec{t})$ and a corresponding total-value-maximizing decision $\hat{x}(X, N, \vec{t})$ as follows:

$$V(X, N, \vec{t}) = \max_{x \in X} \sum_{j \in N} v^j(x, t^j), \tag{2.1}$$

$$\hat{x}(X, N, \vec{t}) \in \arg\max_{x \in X} \sum_{j \in N} v^j(x, t^j). \tag{2.2}$$

One might think that such a direct approach would be doomed to failure, because each participant seems to have an incentive to misrepresent his preferences to influence the decision in his favor. However, the participants' incentives depend not only on the decision but also on the cash transfer, which is the clever and surprising part of the VCG mechanism.

The VCG mechanism eliminates incentives for misreporting by imposing on each participant the cost of any distortion he causes. The VCG payment for participant i is set so that i's report cannot affect the total payoff to the set of *other* parties, $N - i$. Notice that $0 \in N - i$, that is, the set includes the mechanism designer whose payoff is the mechanism's net receipts.

With this principle in mind, let us derive a formula for the VCG payments. To capture the effect of i's report on the outcome, we introduce a hypothetical *null report*, which corresponds to bidder i reporting that he is indifferent among the possible decisions and cares only about transfers. When i makes the null report, the VCG mechanism optimally chooses the decision $\hat{x}(X, N - i, t^{-i})$. The resulting total value of the decision for the set of participants $N - i$ would be $V(X, N - i, t^{-i})$, and the mechanism designer might also collect a payment $h^i(t^{-i})$ from participant i. Thus, if i makes a null report, the total payoff to the participants in set $N - i$ is

$$V(X, N - i, t^{-i}) + h^i(t^{-i}).$$

The VCG mechanism is constructed so that this same amount is the total payoff to those participants regardless of i's report. Thus, suppose that when the reported type profile is $\vec{t}$, i's payment is $\hat{p}^i(X, N, \vec{t}) + h^i(t^{-i})$, so that $\hat{p}^i(X, N, \vec{t})$ is i's additional payment over what i would pay if he made the null report. The decision $\hat{x}(X, N, \vec{t})$ generally depends on i's report, and the total payoff to members of $N - i$ is then $\sum_{j \in N-i} v^j(\hat{x}(X, N, \vec{t}), t^j) + \hat{p}^i(X, N, \vec{t}) + h^i(t^{-i})$. We equate this total value with the corresponding total value when i makes the null report:

$$\hat{p}^i(X, N, \vec{t}) + h^i(t^{-i}) + \sum_{j \in N-i} v^j(\hat{x}(X, N, \vec{t}), t^j)$$

$$= h^i(t^{-i}) + V(X, N - i, t^{-i}). \tag{2.3}$$

Using (2.1), we solve for the extra payment as follows:

$$\hat{p}^i(X, N, \vec{t}) = V(X, N - i, t^{-i}) - \sum_{j \in N-i} v^j(\hat{x}(X, N, \vec{t}), t^j)$$

$$= \sum_{j \in N-i} v^j(\hat{x}(X, N - i, t^{-i}), t^j)$$

$$- \sum_{j \in N-i} v^j(\hat{x}(X, N, \vec{t}), t^j). \qquad (2.4)$$

According to (2.4), if participant i's report leads to a change in the decision $\hat{x}$, then i's extra payment $\hat{p}^i(X, N, \vec{t})$ is specified to compensate the members of $N - i$ for the total losses they suffer on that account.

We now introduce some definitions:

Definition
1. A *Vickrey–Clarke–Groves (VCG) mechanism* $(\Theta, (\hat{x}, \hat{p} + h))$ is a direct mechanism in which $\hat{x}$ satisfies (2.2), $\hat{p}$ satisfies (2.4) (for all N, $X, \vec{t}$, and $i \in N$), and payments are determined by $\hat{p}^i(X, N, \vec{t}) + h^i(t^{-i})$.
2. A participant is *pivotal* if $\hat{x}(X, N, \vec{t}) \neq \hat{x}(X, N - i, t^{-i})$.
3. The *pivot mechanism* is the VCG mechanism in which $h^i \equiv 0$ for all $i \in N$.

In words, a participant is pivotal if consideration of his report changes the decision, compared to excluding the participant or attributing the null report to him. According to (2.4), if participant i is not pivotal, then $\hat{p}^i(X, N, \vec{t}) = 0$. In the pivot mechanism, the only participants who make or receive non-zero payments are ones who are pivotal.

Vickrey first introduced the pivot mechanism in a model where the decision x allocated a fixed quantity of a single divisible good. In the auction context, a bidder is not pivotal if he acquires a zero quantity. So the pivot mechanism in the Vickrey model is an auction in which losing bidders neither make nor receive payments.

2.2 Always Optimal and Weakly Dominant Strategies

In this section, we verify that the VCG rules do indeed ensure that it is always optimal for the participants to report truthfully, regardless of the reports made by others. We also demonstrate that reporting truthfully is often a *dominant strategy*, that is, it is the only strategy that is always optimal.

There are circumstances in which reporting truthfully, although always optimal for the VCG mechanism, is not a dominant strategy. For example, suppose that two parties are considering sharing the rental of a boat, which costs $200. One party values the rental either at $300 or at $0, and his reported value is restricted to lie in the set {$0, $300}. The other party's value is some amount between $0 and $150, and his report is restricted to lie in the interval [$0, $150]. In this example, the pivot mechanism prescribes that the boat is rented if and only if the first party's value is $300, and in that case the first party pays $200. The second party always pays $0, and his report does not affect the outcome. Consequently, any report by the second party is always optimal, and any report of $200 or more by the first party is always optimal when his value is at least $200.

The preceding example is constructed so participants can sometimes predict that certain reports will be irrelevant. In less contrived examples, one expects that truthful reporting will be a dominant strategy.

We formalize these claims using the following definitions. Truthful reporting is an *always optimal* strategy if condition (i) below holds, and it is a *dominant strategy*[1] if, in addition, condition (ii) holds:

(i) for all t^{-i}, $t^i \in \arg\max_{\tilde{t}^i}\{v^i(\hat{x}(X, N, \tilde{t}^i, t^{-i}), t^i) - \hat{p}^i(X, N, \tilde{t}^i, t^{-i})\}$.

(ii) if $\tilde{t}^i \neq t^i$, then for some t^{-i}, $\tilde{t}^i \notin \arg\max_{\tilde{t}^i}\{v^i(\hat{x}(X, N, \tilde{t}^i, t^{-i}), t^i) - \hat{p}^i(X, N, \tilde{t}^i, t^{-i})\}$.

To rule out contrived examples like the boat rental example, we will use the following condition:

All reports are potentially pivotal: For all $i \in N$ and t^i, $\tilde{t}^i \in \Theta^i$, there exists $t^{-i} \in \Theta^{-i}$ such that $\sum_{j \in N} v^j(\hat{x}(X, N, \tilde{t}^i, t^{-i}), t^j) < V(X, N, \vec{t})$.

This condition asserts that for any false report $\tilde{t}^i$ by bidder i, there is some type profile t^{-i} of the other participants such that the false

---

[1] A strategy for a player in a normal form game is *dominant* if (1) it is a best reply to every opposing strategy profile and (2) there is no other strategy with the same property. The definition in the text specializes this definition to the direct revelation games we are studying.

report leads the mechanism to choose a suboptimal outcome. When this condition holds, no participant can be sure that a false report is harmless.

Theorem 2.1. In any VCG mechanism, truthful reporting is an *always optimal* strategy. If all reports are potentially pivotal, then truthful reporting is a *dominant* strategy.

Proof. To show that truthful reporting is always optimal, fix the profile $\vec{t}$ of actual types. When bidder i reports type $\tilde{t}^i$, the decision chosen is $\hat{x}(X, N, \tilde{t}^i, t^{-i})$. So, given the formula for i's payment, his payoff is $\Pi^i(\tilde{t}^i | \vec{t}) = v^i(\hat{x}(X, N, \tilde{t}^i, t^{-i}), t^i) - \hat{p}^i(X, N, \tilde{t}^i, t^{-i}) - h^i(t^{-i})$. Using (2.4), the gain that i enjoys from the deviation is therefore

$$\Pi^i(\tilde{t}^i | \vec{t}) - \Pi^i(t^i | \vec{t})$$
$$= [v^i(\hat{x}(X, N, \tilde{t}^i, t^{-i}), t^i) - \hat{p}^i(X, N, \tilde{t}^i, t^{-i}) - h^i(t^{-i})]$$
$$- [v^i(\hat{x}(X, N, \vec{t}), t^i) - \hat{p}^i(X, N, \vec{t}) - h^i(t^{-i})]$$
$$= \sum_{j \in N} v^j(\hat{x}(X, N, \tilde{t}^i, t^{-i}), t^j) - \sum_{j \in N} v^j(\hat{x}(X, N, \vec{t}), t^j)$$
$$= \sum_{j \in N} v^j(\hat{x}(X, N, \tilde{t}^i, t^{-i}), t^j) - V(X, N, \vec{t}) \leq 0.$$

This proves that truthful reporting is always optimal.

By the assumption that all reports are potentially pivotal, for all $\tilde{t}^i \neq t^i$, there exists t^{-i} such that

$$\Pi^i(\tilde{t}^i | \vec{t}) - \Pi^i(t^i | \vec{t})$$
$$= \sum_{j \in N} v^j(\hat{x}(X, N, \tilde{t}^i, t^{-i}), t^j) - V(X, N, \vec{t}) < 0.$$

Hence, by definition, truthful reporting is a dominant strategy. ∎

The formal proof implements the following simple intuitive argument. The VCG payments are defined so that i's report cannot affect the total payoff of the other participants. If i reports truthfully, the mechanism maximizes the total actual payoff. If i reports falsely in any way that changes the decision, then the change in total payoff must be negative and must be equal to the change in i's own payoff. So reporting truthfully is optimal. Moreover, if every false report is sometimes pivotal, then it is sometimes suboptimal, so it is dominated by reporting truthfully.

The most widely known example of a pivot mechanism is the *second-price* auction. In the private-values auction model, a bidder's value for any decision depends only on the goods the bidder acquires, and not on the goods acquired by the other bidders: $v^i(x, t^i) = v^i(x^i, t^i)$, where $x^i = 1$ if the bidder acquires the good and $x^i = 0$ otherwise. The value of not acquiring the good is normalized to zero: $v^i(0, t^i) = 0$. Let us simply write v^i for $v^i(1, t^i)$.

Since losing bidders are not pivotal (because their presence does not affect the allocation), they pay zero in the pivot mechanism. According to (2.4), the price a winning bidder pays in this mechanism is equal to the difference between two numbers. The first number is the maximum total value to the other participants, including the seller, when i does not participate in the auction, which is $\max_{j \neq i} v^j$. The second number is the total value to the other bidders when i wins, which is zero. Thus, when bidder i wins, he pays $\max_{j \neq i} v^j$, which is equal to the second highest bid. For this reason, the pivot mechanism for the one good case is called the *second-price auction*.

Vickrey originally introduced the second-price auction as a model of ascending auctions, such as those now commonly used at internet auction sites. To develop the connection, we take special notice of the fact that auction sites like eBay and Amazon Auction encourage bidders to use a *proxy bidder* facility. The bidder tells the proxy a maximum price that it is willing to pay – its *maximum bid*. The proxy keeps this information secret and bids on the bidder's behalf in the ascending auction. Whenever it does not have the high bid, it raises the bid by one increment, provided that does not exceed the specified maximum bid. If every bidder were to use a proxy, then the result would be that the bidder who has specified the highest maximum price acquires the item and pays a price (approximately) equal to the second highest such price. If we replace the phrase "maximum price" with "bid price," then this is precisely the same rule that describes the outcome of a Vickrey auction for a single good. In the language of game theory, the English auction with proxy bidders and the second-price auction are *strategically equivalent*: there is a one-to-one mapping between the strategy sets such that corresponding strategy profiles lead to identical outcomes.[2]

---

[2] This theoretical account fairly describes Amazon Auction, but the rules are slightly different at eBay. eBay uses a fixed ending time after which no more bids are accepted. The ordering

We will henceforth use the term *Vickrey auction* to refer to the pivot mechanism in auction environments. By inspection of (2.4), the price paid by any participant $i \neq 0$ is equal to the loss imposed on other participants by adjusting the decision to account for i's values. This price is always non-negative. In contrast, prices paid in the more general VCG mechanism can be negative if h^i is sometimes negative. The possibility of negative payments to some participants raises a question about whether the sum of the payments to participants $i \neq 0$ is positive, negative, or zero.

2.3 Balancing the Budget

In public goods applications, the designer may want to ensure that the total payments to and from the participants *excluding the mechanism operator* add up to zero. This is called *balancing the budget*. If the mechanism designer is a public authority, this means that the authority runs neither a surplus nor a deficit on this project. In such cases, the mechanism designer typically has no independent value for the decision, so we formulate the model with $N = \{1, \dots, n\}$, excluding the designer from the set of participants.

Definition. A direct mechanism (x, p) satisfies *budget balance* if for all finite Θ and all $\vec{t} \in \Theta$, the sum of all transfers is zero:

$$\sum_{i \in N} p^i(X, N, \vec{t}) = 0.$$

Summing the required payments reveals that the possibility of budget balance implies a restriction on the maximum value function, as follows:

$$
\begin{aligned}
0 = \sum_{i \in N} p^i(X, N, \vec{t}) &= \sum_{i \in N} (\hat{p}^i(X, N, \vec{t}) + h^i(t^{-i})) \\
&= \sum_{i \in N} (V(X, N - i, t^{-i}) + h^i(t^{-i}))
\end{aligned}
$$

---

and timing of bid submissions can be relevant in an eBay auction. Indeed, "sniping" (waiting until the last few seconds to bid) is a common and viable strategy at eBay, but is almost totally absent at Amazon Auction, where an auction cannot end until there have been no new bids for ten minutes. See Ockenfels and Roth (2002).

$$-\sum_{i\in N}\sum_{j\in N-i} v^j(\hat{x}(X, N, \vec{t}), t^j)$$

$$= \sum_{i\in N}(V(X, N-i, t^{-i}) + h^i(t^{-i}))$$

$$-\sum_{i\in N}(V(X, N, \vec{t}) - v^i(\hat{x}(X, N, \vec{t}))$$

$$= (n-1)\left(\sum_{i\in N} f^i(t^{-i}) - V(X, N, \vec{t})\right), \tag{2.5}$$

where

$$f^i(t^{-i}) = \frac{V(X, N-i, t^{-i}) + R^i(t^{-i})}{n-1}. \tag{2.6}$$

So a necessary condition for budget balance is that there exist functions f^i such that for all $\vec{t}$,

$$V(X, N, \vec{t}) = \sum_{i\in N} f^i(t^{-i}). \tag{2.7}$$

Holmstrom (1977) has observed that the same condition is actually necessary and sufficient for the existence of a budget-balancing VCG mechanism.

Theorem 2.2. There exists a VCG mechanism that satisfies budget balance if and only if there exist functions f^i such that (2.7) holds for all $\vec{t}$.

Proof. The necessity of (2.7) was established above. For sufficiency, given the functions f^i, take $h^i(t^{-i}) = (n-1)f^i(t^{-i}) - V(X, N-i, t^{-i})$ and observe that this implies (2.6) and hence (2.5). ∎

To establish that the form (2.7) is restrictive, we use a simple two-player auction example with $N = \{1, 2\}$, a formulation that excludes the mechanism designer from the set of participants. There is a single good to be allocated, whose values to participants 1 and 2 are $v^1 \in \{1, 3\}$ and $v^2 \in \{2, 4\}$, respectively. There exists no way to represent $\max(v^1, v^2)$ as a sum $f^1(v^2) + f^2(v^1)$, so there can be no VCG mechanism in this setting that satisfies budget balance. To verify that directly, we tabulate the payments:

Participants' VCG Payments for the Four Value Profiles

	(1, 2)	(3, 4)	(1, 4)	(3, 2)
Participant 1	$h^1(2)$	$h^1(4)$	$h^1(4)$	$2 + h^1(2)$
Participant 2	$1 + h^2(1)$	$3 + h^2(3)$	$1 + h^2(1)$	$h^2(3)$
Total	$1 + h^1(2) + h^2(1)$	$3 + h^1(4) + h^2(3)$	$1 + h^1(4) + h^2(1)$	$2 + h^1(2) + h^2(3)$

Notice that, for any choice of h^1 and h^2, the sum of the total payments in the first two columns minus the corresponding sum in the last two columns is 1. Consequently, there is no choice of h^1 and h^2 such that all the column totals are zero: no balanced-budget VCG mechanism exists.

Theorem 2.2 still allows that there are some environments in which the VCG mechanism does always balance the budget. An important class of these are the ones in which the mechanism designer is treated as a participant who has just one possible type. In that case, the maximum value depends only on t^{-0} and so satisfies (2.7); indeed, $V(X, N, \vec{t}) \equiv f^0(t^{-0})$ for all $\vec{t}$. A VCG mechanism that works in this case specifies the pivot mechanism payments for all participants except participant 0 and balances the budget by having participant 0 receive the net proceeds of the mechanism. In situations where the mechanism designer is a regulator, a committee, or another entity with decision authority, the designer is frequently not allowed to receive or make payments from or to those over whom it has authority. Such restrictions might be imposed, for example, to prevent corruption in the system. In such cases, the budget-balance condition arises naturally and imposes restrictions on what can be implemented.

2.4 Uniqueness

Can another mechanism besides the VCG mechanism implement efficient decisions with dominant strategies? The answer depends on additional assumptions about the environment. For example, if there is a buyer whose value lies in the set $\{0, 10\}$ and a seller whose cost of supplying a good is 5, then the following direct mechanism implements an efficient outcome in dominant strategies. In the mechanism, each party must report a value from its set of possible types. The seller has no choice but to report a cost of 5. If the buyer reports a value of 10, trade occurs at a price of 8; otherwise, there is no trade and no transfers occur. By inspection, it is a dominant strategy for both sides to report truthfully, and the outcome is always efficient. A VCG mechanism that makes no transfers when there is no trade is a pivot mechanism, and the pivot mechanism in this case sets a price of 5. It follows that the suggested mechanism is not a VCG mechanism.

The preceding example relied on the discrete nature of the type space. According to the next theorem, when the type space is smoothly connected, only the VCG mechanisms can implement efficient outcomes in dominant strategies.

Theorem 2.3. Suppose that for each i, $\Theta^i = [0, 1]$ (or simply that Θ^i is smoothly path connected[3]) and that for each decision outcome x, $v^i(x, t^i)$ is differentiable in its second argument. Then any efficient, incentive-compatible direct mechanism is a VCG mechanism.   ■

The version of theorem 2.3 stated here was first proved by Holmstrom (1979), generalizing earlier work by Green and Laffont (1977), who had employed more restrictive assumptions about the type space. We postpone the proof to the next chapter, which contains several other closely related analyses.

2.5 Disadvantages of the Vickrey Auction

Despite its attractive features, the Vickrey auction has important disadvantages that make it unsuitable for most applications. In this section, we illustrate these disadvantages. We give a more detailed analysis of certain of the disadvantages in chapter 8, where the Vickrey design is pitted against certain leading alternatives.

The disadvantages of the Vickrey auction are divided into three kinds: practical disadvantages, monotonicity problems, and merger-investment disadvantages.

2.5.1 Practical Disadvantages

In this subsection, we discuss certain practical difficulties of implementing a Vickrey auction on account of factors that are omitted from the formal model.

---

[3] A set Θ is *smoothly path connected* if for every two points $\theta, \theta' \in \Theta$ there is a differentiable function $f : [0, 1] \to \Theta$ such that $f(0) = \theta$ and $f(1) = \theta'$.

One such problem is that a Vickrey auction can severely tax bidders' computational abilities. For example, consider a Vickrey auction to sell twenty spectrum licenses. In principle, each bidder must submit bids on every combination of licenses he might win, but there are more than one million such combinations. If the bidders must incur even a small cost to determine a value for each distinct combination of licenses, then the cost of running the Vickrey auction makes it impracticable. For some applications, this cost is not too onerous. For example, if the licenses are sufficiently similar, then a bidder might simply specify a value for each different number of licenses, or might adjust that for differences in the licenses. At least for the general case, allowing bids on all packages imposes costs that are too high for a realistic design.

A second practical problem is that real bidders often face serious budget limitations, which the Vickrey design does not take into account. In the presence of such constraints, a bidder in a Vickrey auction may have no always optimal strategy. For example, consider an auction with two identical goods and a bidder with values of 20 for one unit of a good and 40 for the package, but with a total budget of 10. This bidder has no always optimal strategy in the Vickrey auction. If there are credit restrictions or large penalties for default, then bids exceeding the bidder's budget can be ignored. If bidder 1's sole competitor bids 10 for one unit and 19 for two, his best reply is to bid 10 for one unit (and 10 for two units as well). However, if the competitor bids 9 for one unit only, then the best reply is to bid 0 for one unit and 10 for two units.

A third practical problem is that the Vickrey design may force the winning bidder to reveal too much information. A bidder might fear that its value information could be leaked, disadvantaging it in subsequent negotiations with the auctioneer or other buyers or suppliers (Rothkopf, Teisberg, and Kahn (1990)).

2.5.2 Monotonicity Problems

A different set of disadvantages of the Vickrey auction arises from the fact that payments are determined by a non-monotonic function of the bidders' values. We illustrate the problems that raises with a series of examples, borrowed from Ausubel and Milgrom (2002). A formal analysis that identifies the set of auction environments in which these disadvantages are relevant is presented in chapter 8, as part of a comparison of the advantages of several multi-object auction designs.

Here, we provide a series of examples illustrating the monotonicity problems that the Vickrey auction can suffer. In the Vickrey auction, (1) *adding* bidders can *reduce* equilibrium revenues, (2) revenues can be zero even when competition is ample, (3) even losing bidders can have profitable joint deviations in which they *increase* their bids in concert to win items while creating *lower* prices for themselves, and (4) bidders can profitably use shill bidders, intentionally increasing competition in order to generate lower prices.

Consider a Vickrey auction of two identical spectrum licenses. Bidders 1 and 2 are new entrants, which each need two licenses to establish a business of economic scale. Bidder 1 is willing to pay up to $1 billion for the pair of licenses, and bidder 2 is willing to pay up to $900 million. If these are the only bidders in the auction, then the auction is effectively a second-price auction for the pair of licenses. Bidder 1 will acquire the two licenses for a price of $900 million.

Now, suppose instead that there are two additional bidders. Bidders 3 and 4 are both incumbent wireless operators. Each seeks just a single additional license to expand the capacity of its network. Suppose each incumbent is willing to pay up to $1 billion for a single license. If the Vickrey auction is used and all bidders play their dominant strategies, then the two incumbents will acquire the licenses. Because the licenses are given to those who value them the most, this outcome is efficient and results in a total value of $2 billion.

One might expect that increasing the number of bidders and their maximum total value for the pair of licenses would increase the seller's revenue, but that is not the case: the total price paid by the winning bidders is *zero*. To see why, let us compute the price paid by bidder 3. According to (2.4), this price is the opportunity cost to the other bidders of the license that bidder 3 wins. More specifically, it is the maximum value of the two licenses to the other three bidders, which is $1 billion, minus the maximum value of a single license to those bidders, which is also $1 billion. The difference of zero is bidder 3's price and bidder 4's price is determined in the same way.

Notice that the declining revenue problem vanishes if the first two bidders regard the licenses as substitutes. For example, suppose that instead of bidding only $1 billion for two licenses, bidder 1 is also willing to pay $500 million for one license, and similarly bidder 2 is willing to pay

$450 million for one license. Then bidders 3 and 4 must each pay $500 million for a license, and the seller's revenue climbs from $900 million to $1 billion.

The next two variations exploit the feature of the Vickrey auction that, when goods are not substitutes, prices may decrease as the bids increase or the set of bidders expands.

First, we modify the preceding example. As before, bidders 1 and 2 each want only a pair of licenses and are willing to pay $1 billion or $900 million for the pair, respectively. In the modified example, however, each of the incumbents, bidders 3 and 4, has a value of $400 million for a single license. If the incumbents play their dominant strategies, they win no licenses and earn payoffs of zero. If, however, they act in concert, both raising their bids to $1 billion for a single license, then the prices are determined just as above, and the situation is the one we have already examined: bidders 3 and 4 win the two licenses for a total price of zero. Thus, the Vickrey auction provides opportunities and incentives for collusion among the low-value, losing bidders.

Next, we consider another variation. In this one, there are only three bidders, with the first two described just as above. In this variation, the third bidder is also a new entrant and also has value only for the pair of licenses, but its value is lower than that of the first two bidders. It is willing to pay just $800 million for the pair of licenses, compared to $900 million and $1 billion for the other two bidders. Still, the third bidder can win the licenses profitably by entering the auction with two identities, as bidders 3 and 4, and having 3 and 4 each bid $1 billion for a single license. The result, just as before, is that bidders 3 and 4 win, each acquiring a single license for a price of zero. Thus, by combining the tactics of shill bidding and loser collusion, a bidder in the Vickrey auction whose values are too low to be assigned any licenses at the efficient allocation can profitably win both licenses and force the seller to accept a zero price.

Standard auctions do not suffer the monotonicity problems plaguing the Vickrey auction. For example, if the seller simply takes sealed bids and awards licenses to the highest bidders at prices equal to the winning bids, then none of the monotonicity problems occur: Adding bids and bidders cannot reduce prices; introducing shill bids cannot reduce anyone's price, and losers cannot become winners except by paying higher prices.

These monotonicity problems are significant practical defects. In section 2.5.3 below, we reexamine these examples to see whether they are in some sense exceptional, that is, whether they are unlikely to arise in practice. We find that, to the contrary, monotonicity problems can only be ruled out in cases where goods are likely to be substitutes, which is a small subset of the possible cases.[4]

2.5.3 The Merger–Investment Disadvantage

The Vickrey auction also suffers another important disadvantage, distinct from those described above. This one arises even when the auctioneer's objective is efficiency rather than revenue, and when shill bidding and collusion are impossible. The problem is that the Vickrey design can distort the bidders' investment and merger incentives *ex ante* (before the auction),[5] leading to inefficiency.[6]

To illustrate, we return to the first example of the previous section, in which bidders 1 and 2 value only the pair of licenses and have values of $1 billion and $900 million, respectively. Suppose that, before the auction, bidders 3 and 4 could merge and, by coordinating, increase the total value of the licenses by 25% from $2 billion to $2.5 billion. Even though such a merger would increase the maximum total value, the parties would not profit by merging. Recall that the unmerged firms paid a total of zero and enjoyed net profits of $2 billion. The merged firm, however, would pay $1 billion in a Vickrey auction, leaving it a net profit of just $1.5 billion.

In this example, the Vickrey auction discourages a merger by reducing the joint profits of the merging parties. Thus, even by the standard of efficiency, the Vickrey mechanism can have significant disadvantages.

---

[4] In an unpublished result, Daniel Lehmann has shown that with more than two items, the restriction that items must be substitutes fails generically. That is, treating the valuation functions as a vector, for any valuation v where goods are substitutes, almost every valuation in any neighborhood of v fails to satisfy the substitutes condition.

[5] Several authors have developed analyses based on the observation that there are no such distortions for single item auctions. With the set of bidders fixed, because any bidder's profit is equal to his contribution to social surplus, the bidder has correct incentives for any investments that affect only his own values. The same applies to bidders' decisions about how much information to acquire about their own values (Bergemann and Valimaki (2002)).

[6] Economists typically emphasize market power issues when analyzing mergers, and those issues are excluded entirely from this analysis. As discussed earlier, the term "efficiency" as used in mechanism design theory is narrower than the economic idea of Pareto optimality, because here it takes into account only the interests of the mechanism participants.

In analyzing merger incentives, as in studying collusion and shill bidding, whether the assets being auctioned are substitutes proves important. In the Vickrey auction, if the bidders regard the goods as substitutes, then winners generally can reduce their prices by merging. Thus, Vickrey auctions tend to favor mergers when goods are substitutes. For example, suppose that there are four bidders for three items. Each of the first three bidders has a value of 2 for a single item and the fourth bidder has a value of 1. The Vickrey outcome is that the three high-value bidders acquire single items for a price of 1. If the first two bidders merge, the allocation of goods is the same: the merged bidder gets two units and bidder 3 gets one unit. Bidder 3's price is unchanged – it pays a price of 1 for its unit – but the merged bidder pays a total of 1 for its *two* units, so its average price is $\frac{1}{2}$ per unit. This price reduction is typical for the case when goods are substitutes.

If the government is to auction assets to an industry in which it wishes to promote competition or encourage entry, e.g. electrical power generation, it may properly view with suspicion rules that promote mergers and favor larger bidders.

As our examples have shown, however, Vickrey auctions do not always promote mergers. In our telecommunications auction example, we found that merged firms may pay relatively high prices and may even find it profitable to use shills to divide demand between two smaller bidders. If shills are impossible, then the Vickrey auction may discourage profitable and welfare-enhancing mergers. Taken together, the various examples establish that Vickrey auctions can be too favorable to mergers or too discouraging.

2.6 Conclusion

The Vickrey–Clarke–Groves theory provides important insights into what mechanism design can achieve. In the class of environments with quasilinear preferences, the VCG mechanisms provide every participant with a dominant strategy, which is to reveal his type truthfully. When bidders do report honestly, the decision selected is the total-value-maximizing one. Moreover, the VCG mechanisms are the *only* mechanisms that exhibit these two properties without restrictions on the possible set of values.

Offsetting these advantages of the VCG mechanisms are certain problems. Using the VCG mechanism to decide how much of a public good to produce may prevent balancing the budget. Budget balance presents no obstacle to using the VCG mechanism to conduct an auction, however, for the auctioneer is quite happy to pocket any surplus that the mechanism generates.

Besides the budget balance problem, the Vickrey auction suffers a variety of other drawbacks. Some of these are practical, associated with the complexity of the auction, its inability to accommodate budget constraints, and the information it demands from the bidders. Another set of drawbacks are the *monotonicity problems*, which include the possibility that increased competition can lead to reduced seller revenues, that revenues can be very low or zero even when competition is substantial, that losing bidders may have profitable ways to collude, and that a single bidder can sometimes benefit by pretending to be several independent bidders. The third set of drawbacks concern distortions in merger and related investment decisions.

We return to the monotonicity problems in chapter 8, where we will find that they are potentially present in a wide range of environments. They are reliably absent only if all bidders regard all the goods being sold as substitutes. In chapter 8, we will identify an alternative mechanism that matches the advantages of the Vickrey design when goods are substitutes but avoids some of the disadvantages.

In the chapters between, the VCG mechanism plays a very different role – as a benchmark for assessing the performance of alternative mechanisms.

REFERENCES

Ausubel, Lawrence and Paul Milgrom (2002). "Ascending Auctions with Package Bidding." *Frontiers of Theoretical Economics* **1**(1): Article 1.

Bergemann, Dirk and Juuso Valimaki (2002). "Information Acquisition and Efficient Mechanism Design." *Econometrica* **70**(3): 1007–1033.

Clarke, E.H. (1971). "Multipart Pricing of Public Goods." *Public Choice* **XI**: 17–33.

Green, Jerry and Jean-Jacques Laffont (1977). "Characterization of Satisfactory Mechanisms for the Revelation of Preferences for Public Goods." *Econometrica* **45**: 427–438.

Groves, Theodore (1973). "Incentives in Teams." *Econometrica* **61**: 617–631.

Holmstrom, Bengt (1977). *On Incentives and Control in Organizations*: Doctoral thesis, Stanford University.

Holmstrom, Bengt (1979). "Groves Schemes on Restricted Domains." *Econometrica* **47**: 1137–1144.

Ockenfels, Axel and Alvin E. Roth (2002). "Last Minute Bidding and the Rules for Ending Second-Price Auctions: Evidence from eBay and Amazon Auctions on the Internet." *American Economic Review:* **92**(4): 1093–1103.

Rothkopf, Michael, Thomas Teisberg, and Edward Kahn (1990). "Why Are Vickrey Auctions Rare?" *Journal of Political Economy* **98**: 94–109.

Vickrey, William (1961). "Counterspeculation, Auctions, and Competitive Sealed Tenders." *Journal of Finance* **XVI**: 8–37.

CHAPTER THREE

The Envelope Theorem and Payoff Equivalence

Mechanisms are defined very generally and can take a wide variety of forms. The sheer size and variety of the set of mechanisms would seem to make it intractable for use in an economic analysis. Yet such uses are now routine, largely following the pattern set in the early analyses by Myerson (1981) and Holmstrom (1979).

Myerson had posed the following question: which mechanism should a seller use to sell a single indivisible good to maximize his expected revenue, if he can choose among *all* possible augmented mechanisms? To answer this question, known as the *optimal auction problem*, Myerson derived a lemma establishing that a certain payoff formula holds for all feasible augmented mechanisms at Bayes–Nash equilibrium and bounds the expected revenues associated with any mechanism. He demonstrated that standard auction designs with a well-chosen reserve price sometimes achieve the bound.[1]

Holmstrom asked whether any mechanisms besides the Vickrey–Clarke–Groves mechanisms could implement efficient decisions in dominant strategies. He, too, derived a lemma establishing that a certain payoff formula holds for all feasible mechanisms at a dominant strategy solution. He then demonstrated that only the VCG payment scheme prescribes payments consistent with that formula.

The two payoff formulas, which we will sometimes call *Myerson's lemma* and *Holmstrom's lemma*, are closely analogous to Hotelling's

---

[1] Myerson derived the formulas using the so-called *revelation principle*, which holds that any performance that can be Bayes–Nash implemented using any mechanism can also be Bayes–Nash implemented using an incentive-compatible direct revelation mechanism. This extra conclusion, however, has no independent significance for the study of auctions. As we shall see, it is the payoff formula of Myerson's lemma that lies at the heart of auction theory and its various extensions.

lemma and Shepard's lemma from demand theory. All four lemmas are derived from the envelope theorem. Each can be stated as either a restriction on a derivative or as a restriction on an integral.

Myerson's treatment of the optimal auction problem made secondary use of a *single crossing condition* that arises naturally in the auction problem, but that is not needed to derive many of the main results of the theory. This chapter explores the implications of the envelope theorem and its related lemmas for a variety of incentive problems, without relying on single crossing. The next chapter explores the additional conclusions that can be derived when the assumption of single crossing is added.

3.1 Hotelling's Lemma

To emphasize the close connection between incentive theory and ordinary demand theory, we begin our analysis by reviewing *Hotelling's lemma*.[2] This lemma relates the supply behavior of a price-taking firm to its maximum profits.

Let X denote the firm's set of feasible choices, and let $\pi(p) = \max_{x \in X} p \cdot x$ denote the firm's maximum profits as a function of the market price vector $p \in \mathbb{R}_+^L$. In its usual textbook form, Hotelling's lemma asserts that if π is differentiable at p, then the firm's net supply for product j satisfies $x_j^*(p) = \partial \pi / \partial p_j$.[3] So, if the firm makes its choices to maximize profits, then one can recover its choices from knowledge of the maximum profit function π.

One can also reverse this relationship and write the formula as expressing the firm's profits in terms of its supply choices. For, suppose the firm produces good 1 and buys the other goods as inputs. Using the fundamental theorem of calculus, if π is differentiable,

$$\pi(p) = \pi(0, p_{-1}) + \int_0^{p_1} \pi_1(s, p_{-1}) \, ds$$
$$= \pi(0, p_{-1}) + \int_0^{p_1} x_1^*(s, p_{-1}) \, ds. \tag{3.1}$$

---

[2] In general, incentive problems are quite close to various problems that arise in traditional demand theory and the theory of the firm. Other examples are emphasized by Bulow and Roberts (1989) and Klemperer (2002), who underline the connections between auction theory and monopoly pricing theory.

[3] For example, see Mas Colell, Whinston, and Green (1995), Simon and Blume (1994), or Varian (1992).

Price

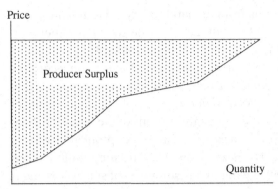

Quantity

Figure 1. The shaded area between a firm's supply curve and the vertical is the firms's producer surplus.

Graphically, this corresponds to the familiar statement that the *producer surplus* is the area between the supply curve and the vertical axis, as shown in Figure 1.

Combining both forms of the statement, we have the following:

Hotelling's lemma. If π is absolutely continuous, then $\pi(p) = \pi(0, p_{-1})$ $+ \int_0^{p_1} x_1^*(s, p_{-1}) \, ds$. If π is differentiable at p, then for each product j, $x_j^*(p) = \partial\pi/\partial p_j$.

Note well that the first conclusion of Hotelling's lemma relies only on the assumption that π is absolutely continuous. It does not require that the production set be convex or that x_1^* be differentiable or continuous, or even that it exist everywhere. A sufficient condition for π to be absolutely continuous is given immediately below.

3.2 The Envelope Theorem in Integral Form

Results similar to Hotelling's lemma play a central role in mechanism design analysis. In graduate economics texts, the envelope theorem is traditionally reported in differentiable form and often relies on assumptions about the convexity or topological structure of the choice set X. Such assumptions are not satisfactory for applications to the theory of mechanism design, because a participant's choice problem may not have the necessary structure. For example, the participant may have to choose a message to send to the mechanism operator from a set of messages X

that lacks a "nice" structure. Moreover, even if the structure of X is not a problem, the maximum value function V may not be differentiable everywhere. For our applications, what is needed is a theorem that verifies a formula like (3.1) without restrictive assumptions on the choice set.

We derive such a formula by studying a family of maximization problems, parameterized by $t \in [0, 1]$, by studying the related functions, as follows:

$$V(t) = \sup_{x \in X} u(x, t), \tag{3.2}$$

$$X^*(t) = \{x \in X | u(x, t) = V(t)\}, \tag{3.3}$$

$$x^*(t) \in X^*(t) \qquad \text{for all } t \text{ such that } X^*(t) \neq \emptyset. \tag{3.4}$$

The function V is the *value function*. It is also sometimes called the "envelope function" because of its graphical representation. If, for each x, one plots the function $u(x, \cdot) : [0, 1] \to \mathbb{R}$, then V is the upper envelope of these functions.

The function $X^*(t)$ is the set of optimal solutions for problem (3.2). For some values of the parameter, this set may be empty. Any function $x^* : [0, 1] \to X$ satisfying (3.4) is a *selection* from X^*. Envelope theorems establish a relation between the value function V and any selection x^* from X^*. The integral form envelope theorem reported here is due to Milgrom and Segal (2002).

Theorem 3.1 (Integral form envelope theorem). Suppose that $u(x, \cdot) : [0, 1] \to \mathbb{R}$ has the properties that

1. there exists a real-valued function $u_2(x, t)$ such that for all $x \in X$ and every $[a, b] \subset [0, 1]$, $u(x, b) - u(x, a) = \int_a^b u_2(x, s)\, ds$, and
2. there exists an integrable function $b : [0, 1] \to \mathbb{R}_+$ (that is, $\int_0^1 b(s)\, ds < \infty$) such that $|u_2(x, t)| \leq b(t)$ for all $x \in X$ and almost all $t \in [0, 1]$.

Further suppose that that $X^*(t) \equiv \arg\max_{x \in X} u(x, t) \neq \emptyset$ for almost all $t \in [0, 1]$. Then for any selection $x^*(t)$ from $X^*(t)$,

$$V(t) = u(x^*(t), t) = u(x^*(0), 0) + \int_0^t u_2(x^*(s), s)\, ds. \tag{3.5}$$

Proof. First, we show that V is absolutely continuous. Let

$$B(t) = \int_0^t b(s) \ ds.$$

For any t', $t'' \in [0, 1]$ with $t' < t''$,

$$
\begin{aligned}
|V(t'') - V(t')| &\le \sup_{x \in X} |u(x, t'') - u(x, t')| \\
&= \sup_{x \in X} \left| \int_{t'}^{t''} u_2(x, t) \ dt \right| \\
&\le \int_{t'}^{t''} \sup_{x \in X} |u_2(x, t)| \ dt \\
&\le \int_{t'}^{t''} b(t) dt = B(t'') - B(t').
\end{aligned}
$$

Notice that, by construction, B is absolutely continuous. Fix any $\varepsilon > 0$. Since b is integrable, there is some positive number M such that $\int_{\{|b(t)|>M\}} |b(t)| \ dt < \varepsilon/2$. Let $\delta < \varepsilon/2M$, select any non-overlapping intervals $[a_i, b_i]$, and let $x_i^* \in X^*(b_i)$ and $\tilde{x}_i \in X^*(a_i)$. If $V(b_i) - V(a_i) \ge 0$, then $|V(b_i) - V(a_i)| = u(x_i^*, b_i) - u(\tilde{x}_i, a_i) \le u(x_i^*, b_i) - u(x_i^*, a_i)$. Similarly, if $V(b_i) - V(a_i) \le 0$, then $|V(b_i) - V(a_i)| = -u(x_i^*, b_i) + u(\tilde{x}_i, a_i) \le -u(\tilde{x}_i, b_i) + u(\tilde{x}_i, a_i)$. Consequently, if $\sum_{i=1}^k |b_i - a_i| < \delta$, then

$$
\begin{aligned}
\sum_{i=1}^k |V(b_i) - V(a_i)| &= \sum_{i=1}^k |u(x_i^*, b_i) - u(\tilde{x}_i, a_i)| \\
&\le \sum_{i=1}^k \max \left(|u(x_i^*, b_i) - u(x_i^*, a_i)|, |u(\tilde{x}_i, b_i) - u(\tilde{x}_i, a_i)| \right) \\
&= \sum_{i=1}^k \max \left(\left| \int_{a_i}^{b_i} u_2(x_i^*, t) \ dt \right|, \left| \int_{a_i}^{b_i} u_2(\tilde{x}_i, t) \ dt \right| \right) \\
&\le \sum_{i=1}^k \max \left(\int_{a_i}^{b_i} |u_2(x_i^*, t)| \ dt, \int_{a_i}^{b_i} |u_2(\tilde{x}_i, t)| \ dt \right) \\
&\le \sum_{i=1}^k \int_{a_i}^{b_i} b(t) \ dt \\
&< \varepsilon/2 + M \sum_{i=1}^k |b_i - a_i| \\
&< \varepsilon.
\end{aligned}
$$

This establishes that V is absolutely continuous, and hence differentiable almost everywhere. Let t be a point of differentiability. Because $V(t) = u(x^*(t), t)$ and $V(t') \geq u(x^*(t), t')$, it follows that

$$\frac{V(t') - V(t)}{|t' - t|} \geq \frac{u(x^*(t), t') - u(x^*(t), t)}{|t' - t|}. \tag{3.6}$$

Because V is differentiable at t, letting $t' \downarrow t$ leads to $V'(t) \geq u_2(x^*(t), t)$, and letting $t' \uparrow t$ leads to $V'(t) \leq u_2(x^*(t), t)$. Hence, $V'(t) = u_2(x^*(t), t)$ at every point of differentiability of V. Equation (3.5) then follows from the fundamental theorem of calculus.   ∎

The integral form envelope theorem applies to problems in which the objective function $f(x, t)$ is parameterized but the set of feasible strategies X is not. In mechanism design problems, if the agent's action is to report information, then every type t chooses from the same feasible set. In that case, if an augmented mechanism design specifies a set of strategies S and an outcome function $x : S \to \Omega$, then the participant is effectively choosing an outcome from the feasible set $X = x(S) \subset \Omega$ to maximize his own payoff – a problem to which we can apply the theorem. Equation (3.5) then restricts the performance functions x that can be implemented on a $[0,1]$-type space.

The second condition of the integral form envelope theorem about the integrable bounding function b is indispensable.[4]

3.3 Quasi-linear Payoffs

In this section, we specialize our analysis to the most extensively analyzed set of mechanism design models – those in which participants have *quasi-linear preferences*. The various subsections explore the implications that can be derived using these models by applying Holmstrom's lemma and Myerson's lemma, which are the special forms of the envelope theorem for this class of mechanism design models.

---

[4] Here is an example to show that the conclusion of the theorem is not guaranteed if the bounding condition is dropped. Let $X = (0, 1]$ and $f(x, t) = g(t/x)$, where g is any continuously differentiable, single-peaked function with a maximum value of $g(1)$. In this example, for all $t \in (0, 1]$, $X^*(t) = \{t\}$ and $V(t) = g(1)$. For $t = 0$, however, $X^*(t) = (0, 1]$ and the value is $V(0) = g(0) < g(1)$, so the function V is not absolutely continuous, contrary to the conclusion of the theorem.

To see that the bounding condition fails in this example, define $B = \sup_{s>0} sg'(s)$. Then, the relevant bound is $b(t) = \sup_{x \in (0,1]} g'(t/x)/x = (\sup_{s>0} sg'(s))/t = B/t$, where we obtain the bound by substituting $s = t/x$. The bound $b(t) = B/t$ is not integrable.

Throughout this section, an outcome is a pair $\omega = (x, p)$, where x is a decision from some finite set $X = \{x_1, \ldots, x_K\}$ and $p = (p^1, \ldots, p^N)$ is a vector of cash payments from the participants to the mechanism operator, and any participant's payoff is given by

$$u^i(x, p^i, t^i) = v^i(x, t^i) - p^i. \tag{3.7}$$

In particular, each participant cares about his own cash payment, but not about payments made by other participants. To describe the full performance function in this context, it is convenient simply sometimes to omit the outcome function and write $\omega(\vec{t}) = (x(\vec{t}), p(\vec{t}))$ instead of $\omega(\sigma(\vec{t})) = (x(\sigma(\vec{t})), p(\sigma(\vec{t})))$. We will use these two notations interchangeably.

The outcome function $\omega = (x, p)$ in this setup comprises allocation and payment functions $x : S^1 \times \cdots \times S^N \to X$ and $p : S^1 \times \cdots \times S^N \to \mathbb{R}^N$. If we suppose that ω is implemented by some always optimal strategy for participant i, then the strategy is optimal when the others are playing equilibrium strategies corresponding with their true types. Suppose that u^i_2 has the integrable bound b required by the envelope theorem. Then, when agent i has type τ, its maximal value is

$$V^i(\tau, t^{-i}) = \max_{\sigma^i \in S^i} u^i(\omega(\sigma^i, \sigma^{-i}(t^{-i})), \tau). \tag{3.8}$$

For economy of notation, we sometimes describe outcomes in 0–1 vector form, as follows. We identify each possible outcome $x_k \in \{x_1, \ldots, x_K\}$ by a canonical basis vector $z_k \in \mathbb{R}^K$ with a 1 as its kth coordinate and all other coordinates zero, so the outcome set can be described by the 0–1 vectors $Z = \{z_1, \ldots, z_K\}$. We then describe the *decision performance function* of the augmented mechanism as a function of the types by $z(t)$, where $z : \Theta \to Z$. We represent the scalar-valued function $v^i(\cdot, t^i)$ by the vector $v^i(t^i)$, where the kth component is $v^i_k(t^i) = v^i(x_k, t^i) = z_k \cdot v^i(t^i)$. Also, just as we sometimes write $x(\vec{t}) = x(\sigma(\vec{t}))$, we may also write $z(\vec{t}) = z(\sigma(\vec{t}))$.

3.3.1 Holmstrom's Lemma

In this section we use the just-developed notation to obtain Holmstrom's lemma, which is a formula for the values and payments associated with any dominant strategy mechanism.

Holmstrom's lemma. Suppose that $v^i(\cdot)$ is continuously differentiable, and let V^i be participant i's full information maximum value, as defined by (3.8). Then

$$V^i(\tau, t^{-i}) = V^i(0, t^{-i}) + \int_0^\tau \left(z(s, t^{-i}) \cdot \frac{dv^i}{ds} \right) ds. \tag{3.9}$$

In particular, if V^i is differentiable at τ, then $\frac{\partial}{\partial \tau} V^i(\tau, t^{-i}) = z(\tau, t^{-i}) \cdot dv^i(\tau)/d\tau$. Participant i's payments must satisfy

$$p^i(\tau, t^{-i}) = -V^i(0, t^{-i}) + z(\tau, t^{-i}) \cdot v^i(\tau) - \int_0^\tau z(s, t^{-i}) \cdot \frac{dv^i}{ds} ds. \tag{3.10}$$

Proof. Applying the envelope theorem to (3.8) using the quasi-linear payoffs of (3.7),

$$V^i(\tau, t^{-i}) - V^i(0, t^{-i}) = \int_0^\tau u_2^i(\omega(\sigma^i(s), \sigma^{-i}(t^{-i})), s) \, ds$$

$$= \int_0^\tau z(s, t^{-i}) \cdot \frac{dv^i}{ds} \, ds. \tag{3.11}$$

Rearranging terms yields (3.9). Taking the derivative with respect to τ yields $\frac{\partial}{\partial \tau} V^i(\tau, t^{-i}) = z(\tau, t^{-i}) \cdot dv^i(\tau)/d\tau$. Substituting $V^i(\tau, t^{-i}) = z^i(\tau, t^{-i}) \cdot v^i(\tau) - p^i(\tau, t^{-i})$ into (3.9) and rearranging terms again leads to (3.10). ∎

3.3.2 The Green–Laffont–Holmstrom Theorem

In the study of dominant strategy mechanisms, one of the central questions is how to characterize the complete set of mechanisms that (1) satisfy the relevant incentive constraints and (2) implement efficient decision performance. In chapter 2, we found that the VCG mechanisms have both of these properties. Are there any others?

The Green–Laffont–Holmstrom theorem shows that, provided the set of preferences satisfies a certain connectedness property, the VCG mechanisms are the only dominant strategy incentive-compatible mechanisms to implement efficient outcomes. The connectedness condition is implicitly included in the statement of Holmstrom's lemma through the assumption that the valuation function v^i is differentiable. As we have seen, equation (3.10) necessarily holds for any mechanism that implements z using dominant strategies. That leads to the next theorem.

Theorem 3.2. Suppose that for each i, Θ^i is smoothly path connected[5] and that $v^i(t^i)$ is continuously differentiable. Then any direct mechanism such that

    (i) the decision outcome rule is the efficient rule $\hat{x}$ and
    (ii) truthful reporting is an always optimal reply, that is, $t^i \in \arg$
    $\max_{\bar{t}^i}(v^i(x(\bar{t}^i, t^{-i}), t^i) - p^i(\bar{t}^i, t^{-i}))$,

is a VCG mechanism. (That is, given the pivot mechanism payments $\hat{p}^i$, there exist functions h^i such that for all $\vec{t}$, $p^i(\vec{t}) = h^i(t^{-i}) + \hat{p}^i(\vec{t})$.) In particular, the Vickrey auction (pivot mechanism) is the unique such mechanism in which bidders who acquire no goods (*losing bidders*) pay zero.

Proof. Fix any two distinct points t^i, $\bar{t}^i \in \Theta^i$, and let $\tau^i : [0, 1] \to \Theta^i$ be a differentiable function satisfying $\tau^i(0) = t^i$ and $\tau^i(1) = \bar{t}^i$. Let $\hat{V}^i(0, t^{-i})$ be the payoff to player i of type t^i in the pivot mechanism. Let (1) $\hat{z}(s, t^{-i})$ express the VCG outcome $\hat{x}(\tau^i(s), t^{-i})$ in 0–1 vector form, (2) $\hat{p}(s, t^{-i})$ be the payment rule of the pivot mechanism when the types are $(\tau^i(s), t^{-i})$, and (3) $\hat{v}^i(s) = v^i(\tau^i(s))$. Then, according to Holmstrom's lemma,

$$\hat{p}^i(1, t^{-i}) = -\hat{V}^i(0, t^{-i}) + \hat{z}(1, t^{-i}) \cdot \hat{v}^i(1) - \int_0^1 \hat{z}(s, t^{-i}) \cdot \frac{d\hat{v}^i}{ds} \, ds.$$

$$(3.12)$$

Given any other dominant strategy mechanism that implements the efficient decision $\hat{x}$ with value function V, define $h^i(t^{-i}) = \hat{V}^i(0, t^{-i}) - V^i(0, t^{-i})$. Applying Holmstrom's lemma again,

$$p^i(1, t^{-i}) = -V^i(0, t^{-i}) + \hat{z}(1, t^{-i}) \cdot \hat{v}^i(1) - \int_0^1 \hat{z}(s, t^{-i}) \cdot \frac{d\hat{v}^i}{ds} \, ds$$

$$= h^i(t^{-i}) + \hat{p}^i(1, t^{-i}). \qquad (3.13)$$

Because $\bar{t}^i$ was arbitrary and $h^i(t^{-i})$ does not depend on $\bar{t}^i$, this payoff formula applies to all types. Hence, it is a VCG formula. Because $h^i(t^{-i}) = \hat{V}^i(0, t^{-i}) - V^i(0, t^{-i})$ is bidder i's payment in the mechanism when i loses, there is a unique VCG mechanism with $h^i(t^{-i}) = 0$, and the Vickrey auction is such a mechanism.   ∎

---

[5] This means that for any two distinct points t^i, $\bar{t}^i \in \Theta^i$, there exists a differentiable function $\tau^i : [0, 1] \to \Theta^i$ satisfying $\tau^i(0) = t^i$ and $\tau^i(1) = \bar{t}^i$. The function τ^i is the *path* connecting t^i to $\bar{t}^i$.

The use of the envelope theorem in this proof is typical, so it is worthwhile to build intuition by restating the argument in words. Holmstrom's formula (3.10) is the technical part. It establishes a *necessary condition* for how a bidder's cash payments can vary with his type, given the rule z specifying decision outcomes. Together, the decision outcome and the payoff of the lowest type fix a unique payment rule. For the Vickrey auction, the lowest type is a bidder that always loses the auction and has a payoff of zero. Generally, the VCG mechanism corresponding to the function h is the unique mechanism with properties (i) and (ii) in which a losing bidder i pays the amount $h^i(t^{-i})$.

Expressing the participant's maximal payoff as the integral of the partial derivative of the payoff function has long been an important step in optimal mechanism design problems. Mirrlees (1971), Holmstrom (1979), Laffont and Maskin (1980), Myerson (1981), Riley and Samuelson (1981), Fudenberg and Tirole (1991), and Williams (1999) all derived integral conditions in particular models by restricting attention to piecewise continuously differentiable choice rules or even narrower classes. However, it may be optimal to implement a choice rule that is not piecewise continuously differentiable. One example is the class of trading problems with linear utility described in chapter 6.5 of Myerson (1991). The integral form envelope theorem gives us the necessary tool for dealing with the full range of possibilities.

We next see that very much the same argument can be applied in the context of Bayesian equilibrium. As in the dominant strategies application, the formula sharply limits the payment rules that can apply at equilibrium.

3.3.3 Myerson's Lemma[6]

In practice, many designers, regulators, and observers of auctions have falsely high expectations about how changes in the rules can affect prices and payoffs. Many believe auction procedures can affect expected selling prices and bidders' payoffs without affecting the way the goods are allocated.

---

[6] Most expositions of incentive theory treat payoff equivalence and revenue equivalence as a single result, but that seems to me a mistake. That treatment not only obfuscates the close connections between incentive theory and demand theory, it also impedes applications to models with risk averse decision makers or in which outcomes are inefficient. The approach taken here makes it straightforward to treat these additional developments.

According to current economic theory, an auction designer's ability to manipulate prices and payoffs without changing allocations is much more limited. Here, we examine what the auction design can do when bidders play Bayes–Nash equilibrium strategies, bidding optimally given their beliefs about others' types and strategies.

Definition. A strategy profile σ is a *Bayes–Nash equilibrium* of the mechanism $\Gamma = (S, \omega)$ in environment $(\Omega, N, [0, 1]^N, u, \pi)$ if for all t^i,[7]

$$\sigma^i(t^i) \in \arg\max_{\tilde{\sigma}^i \in S^i} E^i[u^i(\omega(\tilde{\sigma}^i, \sigma^{-i}(t^{-i})), \vec{t})|t^i]$$

$$= \arg\max_{\tilde{\sigma}^i \in S^i} \int u^i(\omega(\tilde{\sigma}^i, \sigma^{-i}(t^{-i})), \vec{t}) \, d\pi^i(t^{-i}|t^i). \qquad (3.14)$$

In most of this chapter, we study a *standard independent private values* model. This entails the assumptions that

  (i) the types are $\Theta^i = [0, 1]$,
  (ii) payoffs are quasi-linear, as described above, and bidders are risk neutral,
  (iii) values are *private* $(v^i(x, \vec{t}) \equiv v^i(x, t^i))$,
  (iv) types are statistically independent, and
  (v) the conditions of the integral form envelope theorem (theorem 3.1) are satisfied.

With these assumptions, expected payoffs can be written as follows:

$$E^i[u^i(\omega(\tilde{\sigma}^i, \sigma^{-i}(t^{-i})), \vec{t})|t^i]$$

$$= E^i[z(\tilde{\sigma}^i, \sigma^{-i}(t^{-i})) \cdot v^i(t^i) - p^i(\tilde{\sigma}^i, \sigma^{-i}(t^{-i}))]. \qquad (3.15)$$

Let $V^i(t^i)$ denote the maximum expected payoff of player i of type t^i in the game. Then

$$V^i(t^i) = \max_{\tilde{\sigma}^i} E^i[z(\tilde{\sigma}^i, \sigma^{-i}(t^{-i})) \cdot v^i(t^i) - p^i(\tilde{\sigma}^i, \sigma^{-i}(t^{-i}))]. \qquad (3.16)$$

In close analogy to Holmstrom's lemma, we have the following:

Theorem 3.3 (Myerson's lemma; payoff equivalence theorem). Consider a standard independent private values model, and suppose that σ is a Bayes–Nash equilibrium of the game corresponding to

---

[7] In this expression E^i refers to an expectation computed with respect to the beliefs of player i.

$(\Omega, N, S, \omega, [0, 1]^N, v, \pi)$ with full performance (x, p). Then the expected payoffs satisfy

$$V^i(\tau) = V^i(0) + \int_0^\tau E^i[z(\vec{t})|t^i = s] \cdot \frac{dv^i}{ds}\, ds. \tag{3.17}$$

In particular, if V^i is differentiable at τ, then $\frac{\partial}{\partial \tau} V^i(\tau) = E^i[z(\vec{t})|t^i = \tau] \cdot dv^i(\tau)/d\tau$. Expected payments must satisfy

$$E^i[p^i(\vec{t})|t^i = \tau] = -V^i(0) + E^i[z(\vec{t})|t^i = \tau] \cdot v^i(\tau)$$
$$- \int_0^\tau E^i[z(\vec{t})|t^i = \tau] \cdot \frac{dv^i}{ds}\, ds. \tag{3.18}$$

Proof. Equation (3.17) follows directly from (3.16) and the envelope theorem. The derivative form of the theorem follows by differentiating (3.17) with respect to τ. At equilibrium, a player's expected payoff is $V^i(\tau) = E[z(\vec{t})|t^i = \tau] \cdot v^i(\tau) - E[p^i(\vec{t})|t^i = \tau]$. Substituting that into (3.17) and rearranging yields (3.18). ∎

If we compare two different auction mechanisms in which the lowest types of bidders always lose and pay zero, then $V^i(0) = 0$ for both. If the outcome function z is also the same for both, then according to the theorem, bidders' expected payoffs and payments are also the same. Provided our model of strategic bidders is right, this conclusion contradicts intuitive claims that one can change bidder payoffs by manipulating rules without reducing efficiency.

3.3.4 Revenue Equivalence Theorems

The (risk neutral) payoff equivalence theorem applies to bidder payoffs, but it also has immediate implications for the seller's expected revenues. The original theorem of this sort is Myerson's revenue equivalence theorem, which applies to auctions of a single good. We begin with a recent extension reported by Williams (1999).

As above, $(\hat{x}, \hat{p})$ denotes the VCG pivot mechanism.

Theorem 3.4. Consider a standard independent private values model, and suppose that σ is a Bayes–Nash equilibrium of the game corresponding to $(\Omega, N, S, \omega, [0, 1]^N, v, \pi)$ with full performance $(\hat{x}, p)$. Then the expected payment to the mechanism operator is the same as for the VCG mechanism $(\hat{x}, \hat{p} + h)$, where $h^i(t^{-i}) \equiv E^i[p^i(0, t^{-i})]$.

Proof. Because the always optimal equilibrium of the VCG mechanism is also a Bayes–Nash equilibrium, Myerson's lemma applies to it, with $p = \hat{p} + h$ and $V^i(0) = 0$. So the expected total revenue is $E[\sum_{i \in N} p^i(\vec{t})] = E[\sum_{i \in N} E[p^i(\vec{t})|t^i]] = E[\sum_{i \in N} E[\hat{p}^i(\vec{t})|t^i]] = E[\sum_{i \in N} \hat{p}^i(\vec{t})]$.   ∎

The famous revenue equivalence theorem of auction theory is a special case:

Corollary. Consider a standard independent private values model with a single indivisible good for sale and in which losers' payoffs are zero. Suppose that σ is a Bayes–Nash equilibrium of the corresponding game $(\Omega, N, S, \omega, [0, 1]^N, v, \pi)$. Suppose the full performance is $(\hat{x}, p)$. Let $v^{(1)}$, $v^{(2)}$, ... denote the order statistics of the bidder valuations for the single good, from highest to smallest. Then the total expected payment by participants in the mechanism is $E[v^{(2)}]$.

Proof. Observe that $v^{(2)}$ is the sales revenue associated with the Vickrey mechanism in this environment, and apply theorem 3.4.   ∎

The preceding version of the revenue equivalence theorem is the best-known theorem in auction theory. The history of the theorem begins with Vickrey, who computed equilibria for four different auction mechanisms and made the then surprising discovery that the expected revenues were exactly the same in each of them. Simultaneous contributions by Myerson (1981) and by Riley and Samuelson (1981) implicitly established the reason in terms of the envelope and payoff equivalence theorems, as described above.

Various extensions of the standard revenue equivalence theorem are possible by adapting the same argument to more general models. The following one is a version that applies to the interdependent values model of Milgrom and Weber (1982), provided the types are statistically independent.

Theorem 3.5. Consider a standard independent private values model with a single indivisible good for sale in which losers' payoffs are zero and the private values condition is replaced by the condition that each bidder i's value for the good satisfies $v^i = v(t^i, t^{-i})$, where v is continuously differentiable. Suppose that σ is a Bayes–Nash equilibrium of the corresponding game $(\Omega, N, S, \omega, [0, 1]^N, v, \pi)$. If the bidder with the highest type always wins the auction, then the expected payoff of each bidder i is $E[\int_0^{t^i} v_1(s, t^{-i})\, ds]$ and the seller's expected revenue is

$$E\left[v(t^{(1)}, t^{-(1)})\right] - N \cdot E\left[\int_0^{t^i} v_1(s, t^{-i})\, ds\right].$$

Proof. The bidder's payoffs are the ones determined in the now-familiar way from the envelope theorem formula. The total expected payoff is $E[v(t^{(1)}, t^{-(1)})]$, so the seller's expected payoff is the total minus the sum of the bidders' expected payoffs. ∎

One important use of the revenue equivalence theorems is as a benchmark for analyzing cases when the assumptions of the theorems do not hold. In the next chapter, we will see how budget constraints, risk aversion, endogenous quantities, and correlation of types all lead to systematic predictions comparing expected revenues from different kinds of auctions, even ones with the same decision performance. Of course, mechanisms with different decision performance will also have different levels of expected revenue. This is potentially important because standard auctions in asymmetric environments generally have different decision performance.

3.3.5 The Myerson–Satterthwaite Theorem

Another famous early problem of mechanism design theory is designing efficient exchange between a buyer and a seller when both have uncertain types. These situations are often known as the bilateral monopoly or bilateral trade problem. Earlier developments in transaction cost economics and bargaining theory had treated it as an axiom that exchange will take place whenever that is necessary for efficiency. This *efficiency axiom* is explicit in the derivations of the Nash bargaining solution, the Kalai–Smorodinsky solution, and the Shapley value, as well as in many treatments of the so-called Coase theorem.

Doubts about the efficiency axiom are based partly in concerns about bargaining with incomplete information. After all, a seller is naturally inclined to exaggerate the cost of his good, and a buyer is inclined to pretend that her value is low. Should we not expect these exaggerations to lead sometimes to missed trading opportunities? Is the problem of exaggeration in bargaining a fundamental one? Or can a bargaining mechanism or protocol be designed that eliminates the incentive to exaggerate? How would it work?

To evaluate the answers, we use a simple model with a single indivisible good for sale. There is one potential buyer and one potential seller with values $b = v^b(t^b)$ and $s = v^s(t^s)$, respectively. With quasilinear preferences, there are gains from trade precisely when $b > s$. Let $p^b(t)$ and $p^s(t)$ denote the payments made by the buyer and seller at equilibrium of some mechanism when the type profile is t. We assume that v^b and v^s are smooth and bounded, so that the envelope theorem applies.

Let us start with the observation that this environment is a special case where we can apply the VCG mechanism. In particular, the *pivot mechanism* (the VCG mechanism in which $h^s \equiv h^b \equiv 0$) might seem a plausible candidate to solve the problem. It specifies that trade should take place and transfers should be made only when the reported values satisfy $b > s$. When trade takes place, the seller receives a payment of b while the buyer pays s. With payments determined in this way, the buyer and seller both find it always optimal to report their values truthfully, regardless of what the other reports. When they do report truthfully, the efficient allocation decision is implemented with always optimal strategies, but there is a budget deficit because whenever trade takes place we have $b > s$. In chapter 2, we observed that, in general, there is no VCG mechanism that always exactly balances the budget. Is this a serious problem? Is there any mechanism that can both implement efficient outcomes and achieve budget balance at a Bayes–Nash equilibrium?

The Myerson–Satterthwaite theorem shows that, under certain conditions, there exists no mechanism for which the decision performance function always maximizes the total value. The theorem employs the solution concept of Bayes–Nash equilibrium.

Theorem 3.6. Suppose that, in addition to the assumptions of theorem 3.3, the participants and the designer have identical prior beliefs: $\pi^1 = \cdots = \pi^N = \pi$. Further suppose that the types are statistically independent, and v^b and v^s are continuously differentiable. Consider any trading mechanism and Bayes–Nash equilibrium at which (i) trade occurs at equilibrium exactly when $b > s$, (ii) sellers of type 1 and buyers of type 0 never trade, and (iii) no payments are made when no trade occurs. Then the mechanism incurs an expected payment deficit equal to the expected gain from trade, that is, the total expected payments satisfy $E[p^b(t) + p^s(t)] = -E[\max(0, b - s)]$.[8]

Proof. The Vickrey mechanism is a mechanism that satisfies the conditions of the theorem. It specifies that trade occurs when $b > s$, and that when trade occurs the seller receives a price of b and the buyer pays a price of s. For every (b, s) realization, each player enjoys a payoff of $(b - s)^+ \equiv \max(0, b - s)$ – the entire gain from trade. Any other mechanism with the same decision performance results in the same total expected gains $E[(b - s)^+]$ from trade and, by the payoff equivalence theorem, has the same total expected payoff of $2E[(b - s)^+]$ for the buyer and seller. The expected deficit $-E[p^b(t) + p^s(t)]$ is the excess of the total expected payoff over the total expected surplus: $E[(b - s)^+]$. ∎

3.3.5.1 Application: Auctions Versus Lotteries
Despite calls by Coase (1959) and others for the Federal Communications Commission (FCC) to allocate spectrum frequencies by auction, the US Congress did not give the FCC the authority to assign wireless operating rights by auction until 1993. Prior to 1993, Congress had granted the FCC the power to assign rights to the spectrum by lottery. Although allocating spectrum by lottery eliminated the long bureaucratic procedures and delays of the previous system of comparative hearings, it introduced various inefficiencies of its own.[9]

In the debates surrounding the initial spectrum auctions, some observers suggested that lotteries can be turned into an efficient mechanism by allowing winners to re-sell their rights to others who value the rights more. Citing the Coase theorem, they argued that once transferable licenses are in the hands of private parties, the parties themselves will negotiate to a jointly profit-maximizing ownership configuration. Therefore, they concluded, the form of the initial auction does not matter for efficiency.

---

[8] Notice that no assumptions are made here about the distributions of types. In their original treatment, Myerson and Satterthwaite imposed the weaker condition that trade occurs exactly when (i) $b > s$ and (ii) b and s are both in the supports of their respective distributions, and found that efficient trade without deficits could sometimes be achieved when supports are disjoint. For example, if the buyer's value is distributed on $[\frac{1}{2}, 1]$, the seller's cost on $[0, \frac{1}{2}]$, and each is restricted to reporting a type in the corresponding interval, then the VCG mechanism that always sets a price of $\frac{1}{2}$ implements efficient trade with zero deficit.

[9] Some of these were described in chapter 1.

Theoretical arguments can influence the FCC staff's recommendations to the Commission, which in turn help shape policy. Economists advocating auctions to the FCC staff countered the proponents of lotteries with an argument combining the Myerson–Satterthwaite and Vickrey theorems. If a single license is awarded at random by lottery to one of two symmetric applications, then the Myerson–Satterthwaite theorem implies that no feasible bargaining protocol can guarantee an efficient result. But the Vickrey theorem shows that an auction mechanism exists that guarantees an efficient result. Therefore, the initial allocation mechanism can affect the efficiency of the final allocation: auction design does matter. The FCC staff was influenced by this argument and was led to pay careful attention to the expected efficiency of the allocations created by the auctions.

3.3.6 The Jehiel–Moldovanu Impossibility Theorems

Jehiel and Moldovanu (2001) apply payoff equivalence to demonstrate limits on mechanisms' ability to implement efficient allocations when participants do not have private values. Without the private-values assumption, a bidder might know something that, if revealed, could affect another bidder's choices.

An example to illustrate the general possibilities is the classic used-car model of adverse selection, in which the owner of a used car has private information about the condition of the car. The seller's information could certainly affect the buyer's decision about whether to buy at some specified price. Partly for that reason, a seller may try to convince the buyer that his motive for selling the car is not that the car is in bad condition. For example, the seller's advertisement might include a phrase like "Moving, must sell."

For an auction-related example, suppose there is a certain piece of land for sale just outside of a city. Participant 1 is a developer planning to build a shopping center on the land to attract urban customers. Participant 2 is a mining company interested in a possible mineral deposit beneath the surface. The value of the land as a shopping center also depends on whether nearby properties will be used for noisy or dirty mining operations – something about which the mining company knows more than the developer. Given that the value of the land to the developer depends on information held by the mining company, is there any mechanism that allocates the land efficiently?[10]

One might think of many ways to try to achieve efficient allocation, for example by providing a cash bonus to the mining company depending on what information it acknowledges about the value to the developer. However, the spirit of the Jehiel–Moldovanu theorem is that, unless the mining company's information can be independently verified, there is no way that it can be used to implement efficient decisions.

Intuitively, the logic of the theorem is simple. Suppose some agent j has observed a signal s that does *not* bear on his own values but is relevant to determining the efficient allocation. Because the signal s does not affect either what j can report or j's preferences over allocations, it cannot affect his maximal payoff. As shown below, that implies that the signal cannot affect j's allocation. To illustrate, suppose that when s is higher, the efficient allocation always assigns less of certain valuable goods to j. Then, by the payoff formula of the envelope theorem, j's payoff must be lower when s is higher, which contradicts the conclusion that his maximal payoff cannot depend on s. Therefore, it is impossible to implement the efficient allocation. The formal account develops this sort of contradiction thoroughly for both *ex post* Nash equilibrium models and Bayesian equilibrium models, without any special assumption about how s affects the efficient allocation.

We begin with the *interdependent values model* in which there is a single item for sale. To allow the possibility that each bidder may have information that is relevant to each other bidder, we represent each bidder's type by an N-vector $t^i = (t^i_1, \ldots, t^i_N)$, where t^i_j represents any information that bidder i may have about how valuable the item will be to bidder j. We take the components of the type profile $\vec{t}$ to be jointly distributed according to a atomless distribution on $[0, 1]^{N \times N}$. Bidders' types are assumed to be statistically independent. For analytical simplicity, we specify that the full information value of the item to bidder i is $t^i_i + v^i(t^{-i}_i)$.

The first issue is to determine whether there is some clever payment scheme that results in efficient allocation performance in *ex post* equilibrium. This means that each player i's strategy should depend only

---

[10] It is quite common in auctions of business assets such as spectrum licenses that competitors' plans affect the value of a license or that losers are not indifferent about the identity of the auction winner.

on his own type t^i, but the strategy profile $(\sigma^i(t^i))_{i \in N}$ should be a Nash equilibrium for every realization of the type profile $\vec{t}$. The advantage of such a solution concept is discussed in chapter 5.

Thus, suppose that there is some allocation performance z that is implemented in *ex post* equilibrium, where $z^i(\vec{t})$ is the probability that the item is assigned to bidder i, and $p^i(\vec{t})$ is the corresponding payment. Then each bidder is playing a best reply to all the other bidders' strategies, given $\vec{t}$. Using the integral form envelope theorem applied to the one-dimensional parameter t_i^i, the equilibrium payoff achieved by bidder i when the type vector is $\vec{t}$ is

$$V^i(t^i, t^{-i}) = \max_{\hat{\sigma}^i} \left\{ z^i(\hat{\sigma}^i, \sigma^{-i}(t^{-i})) \left(t_i^i + v^i\left(t_i^{-i}\right)\right) - p^i(\hat{\sigma}^i, \sigma^{-i}(t^{-i})) \right\}$$

$$= V^i\left(0, \not{x}_i, t^{-i}\right) + \int_0^{t_i^i} z^i\left(\sigma^i\left(s, t_{-i}^i\right), \sigma^{-i}(t^{-i})\right) ds. \qquad (3.19)$$

Regard these expressions as functions of t^i with t^{-i} held fixed. Because the right-hand expression on the first line of (3.19) does not depend on t_{-i}^i, the expression on the second line must be a function of t_i^i alone. Hence, the integrand satisfies $z^i(\sigma^i(s, t_{-i}^i), \sigma^{-i}(t^{-i})) \equiv z^i(\sigma^i(s, 0), \sigma^{-i}(t^{-i}))$ almost everywhere. To summarize:

Theorem 3.7. In the interdependent values model with a single good for sale, suppose $\hat{z}^i(t)$ depends non-trivially on t_{-i}^i. Then, there exists no mechanism that implements the allocation performance $\hat{z}$ at an *ex post* equilibrium.

In particular, the theorem implies there exists no mechanism that generally implements the efficient allocation performance in *dominant* strategies. It does not imply that i's information t_{-i}^i cannot affect the decision at all. For example, if bidder 1 knows the values to bidders 2 and 3, then that information can be used in deciding how to allocate the good between bidders 2 and 3, but it cannot affect the allocation to bidder 1.

The preceding theorem deals with *ex post* equilibrium strategies. Jehiel and Moldovanu asked a related question: Does there exist an augmented mechanism that allocates efficiently when the solution concept is Bayes–Nash equilibrium?[11]

---

[11] In their original treatment, Jehiel and Moldovanu treat the case of many goods. Although the notation is more involved, that case can be treated by methods similar to the ones used here.

Theorem 3.8. Let $z(t)$ be an allocation performance function, and suppose that the function $E(t^i) \equiv E[z^i(t)|t^i]$ depends non-trivially on t^i_{-i}.[12] Then, no mechanism exists that implements z at any Bayes-Nash equilibrium.

Proof. Suppose that some augmented mechanism (S, Ω, σ) is specified such that σ is a Bayes–Nash equilibrium of the associated Bayesian game. Let the outcome function Ω consist of a decision outcome function z and a payment function p. The corresponding equilibrium payoff value for an individual i is

$$V^i(t^i) = \max_{\hat{\sigma}^i} E\left[z^i(\hat{\sigma}^i, \sigma^{-i}(t^{-i}))\left(t^i_i + v^i\left(t^{-i}_i\right)\right) - p^i(\hat{\sigma}^i, \sigma^{-i}(t^{-i}))|t^i\right]$$

$$= \max_{\hat{\sigma}^i} \left\{ E[z^i(\hat{\sigma}^i, \sigma^{-i}(t^{-i}))]t^i_i + E\left[z^i(\hat{\sigma}^i, \sigma^{-i}(t^{-i}))v^i\left(t^{-i}_i\right)\right. \right.$$

$$\left.\left. - p^i(\hat{\sigma}^i, \sigma^{-i}(t^{-i}))\right]\right\}, \quad (3.20)$$

where the last step uses the statistical independence of the types. Hence, $V^i(t^i) = V^i(t^i_i, 0)$ is actually a function of t^i_i alone. Using that and the integral form envelope theorem,

$$V^i\left(t^i_i, 0\right) - V^i(0, 0) = \int_0^{t^i_i} E[z^i(\sigma^i(s, 0), \sigma^{-i}(t^{-i}))]\, ds$$

$$= V^i\left(t^i_i, t^i_{-i}\right) - V^i\left(0, t^i_{-i}\right)$$

$$= \int_0^{t^i_i} E\left[z^i(\sigma^i\left(s, t^i_{-i}\right), \sigma^{-i}(t^{-i}))\right]\, ds. \quad (3.21)$$

Because these functions of t^i_i are equal everywhere, the integrands must be equal almost everywhere:

$$E\left[z^i\left(\sigma^i\left(s, t^i_{-i}\right), \sigma^{-i}(t^{-i})\right)\right] = E[z^i(\sigma^i(s, 0), \sigma^{-i}(t^{-i}))] \quad \text{a.e.} \quad (3.22)$$

This contradicts the hypothesis that $E(t^i) \equiv E[z^i(t)]$ depends non-trivially on t^i_{-i}. ∎

These two theorems establish some important limits on what mechanisms can achieve.

---

[12] For example, if the functions v^i are all increasing, then the efficient decision function $\hat{z}^i(t)$ is nonincreasing in t^i_{-i}. To this we add the non-degeneracy condition that that function is not constant.

3.3.7 Myerson and Riley–Samuelson

Revenue-Maximizing Auctions

In this subsection, we return to the optimal auction question posed by Myerson (1981), discussed in the introduction to this chapter. A similar theory of revenue-maximizing auctions was also developed independently at about the same time by Riley and Samuelson (1981), but it was limited to the case of bidders with symmetrically distributed values. Myerson's original proof relied on the revelation principle to limit attention to direct incentive-compatible mechanisms, but we simplify his analysis here by using the integral form envelope theorem.

Consider an auction for a single good whose value to individual i is $v^i(t^i)$. Each $v^i : [0, 1] \to \mathbb{R}_+$ is a strictly increasing, continuously differentiable function, and the types are independently and uniformly distributed. Note that these assumptions do not imply that the values $v^i(t^i)$ are identically distributed: the value distributions are given by the functions $(v^i)^{-1}$, which can be any strictly increasing, smooth, bounded distribution.[13]

Definitions

1. An augmented mechanism (S, ω, σ) is *voluntary* if for every player i and type t^i, the maximal expected utility satisfies $V^i(t^i) \geq 0$ (where the utility of non-participation has been normalized to zero).

2. The *expected revenue* from the augmented mechanism (S, ω, σ) is

$$R(S, \omega, \sigma) = E\left[\sum_{i=1}^{N} p^i(\sigma^1(t^1), \ldots, \sigma^N(t^N))\right].$$

3. The augmented mechanism (S, ω, σ) is *expected-revenue-maximizing* if for any other voluntary augmented mechanism $(\tilde{S}, \tilde{\omega}, \tilde{\sigma})$,

$$R(\tilde{S}, \tilde{\omega}, \tilde{\sigma}) \leq R(S, \omega, \sigma).$$

For the next theorem, it is convenient to write $x^i = 1$ in case individual i is awarded the item and $x^i = 0$ otherwise.

Theorem 3.9. Consider a standard independent private values model with a single good for sale. For each i, define $m^i(s^i) \equiv v^i(s^i) - (1 - s^i)$

---

[13] One can also dispense with the upper bound by taking the type spaces to be $[0, 1)$.

dv^i/ds^i (*the marginal revenue as a function of price*), and suppose that m^i is an increasing function.[14] Further suppose that $v^1(0) = \cdots = v^N(0)$. Then an augmented mechanism is a revenue-maximizing mechanism if it satisfies $V^i(0) = 0$ and has the following decision performance function:

$$x^i(\vec{t}) = \begin{cases} 1 & \text{if } m^i(t^i) > \max(0, \max_{j \neq i} m^j(t^j)), \\ 0 & \text{otherwise.} \end{cases} \tag{3.23}$$

Furthermore, at least one such mechanism exists.

Proof. Given any decision performance x, the probability that bidder i receives the good when its type is t^i is $E[x^i(\vec{t})|t^i]$. Hence, by the envelope theorem, bidder 1's maximal payoff when its type is $t^1 = \tau$ satisfies

$$V^1(\tau) - V^1(0) = \int_0^\tau E\left[x^1(s^1, t^{-1})|t^1 = s^1\right] \frac{dv^1}{ds^1} \, ds^1$$

$$= \int_0^\tau \int_0^1 \cdots \int_0^1 \frac{dv^1}{ds^1} x^1(s^1, \ldots, s^N) \, ds^2 \cdots ds^N ds^1. \tag{3.24}$$

So bidder 1's *ex ante* expected payoff must satisfy

$$E[V^1(t^1)] - V^1(0)$$

$$= \int_0^1 \int_0^\tau \int_0^1 \cdots \int_0^1 \frac{dv^1}{ds^1} x^1(s^1, \ldots, s^N) \, ds^2 \cdots ds^N ds^1 d\tau$$

$$= \int_0^1 \cdots \int_0^1 \int_{s^1}^1 d\tau \frac{dv^1}{ds^1} x^1(s^1, \ldots, s^N) \, ds^1 \cdots ds^N$$

$$= \int_0^1 \cdots \int_0^1 (1 - s^1) \frac{dv^1}{ds^1} x^1(s^1, \ldots, s^N) \, ds^1 \cdots ds^N$$

$$= \int_0^1 \cdots \int_0^1 (v^1(s^1) - m^1(s^1)) x^1(s^1, \ldots, s^N) \, ds^1 \cdots ds^N, \tag{3.25}$$

where the second equality follows from the first by changing the order of integration. A similar expression holds for the other bidders.

---

[14] This corresponds to the common condition in monopoly pricing theory that the marginal revenue is a decreasing function of the quantity offered for sale. An equivalent formulation that is common in the literature specifies the marginal revenue condition in terms of the distribution of values, $F^i = (v^i)^{-1}$. The condition then becomes that $v^i - (1 - F^i(v^i))/f^i(v^i)$ is increasing in v^i.

For any realized type profile $\vec{t}$, the total *ex ante* payoff to all bidders plus the revenue to the seller is $x(\vec{t}) \cdot v(\vec{t})$, so the seller's expected revenue must be

$$R(S, \omega, \sigma) = E[x(\vec{t}) \cdot v(\vec{t})] - \sum_{i=1}^{N} E[V^i(t^i)]$$

$$= \int_0^1 \cdots \int_0^1 \sum_{i=1}^{N} x^i(s^1, \ldots, s^N) v^i(s^i) \, ds^1 \cdots ds^N$$

$$- \sum_{i=1}^{N} E[V^i(t^i)]$$

$$= \int_0^1 \cdots \int_0^1 \sum_{i=1}^{N} x^i(s^1, \ldots, s^N) m^i(s^i) \, ds^1 \cdots ds^N$$

$$- \sum_{i=1}^{N} V^i(0)$$

$$\leq \int_0^1 \cdots \int_0^1 \max\left(0, \max_i m^i(s^i)\right) ds^1 \cdots ds^N. \tag{3.26}$$

The inequality follows because $x^i(t)$ is the probability the good is assigned to bidder i and hence satisfies $x^i(t) \geq 0$ and $\sum_{i=1}^{N} x^i(t) \leq 1$.

This proves that the specified performance, if feasible, gives an upper bound on the revenue. For feasibility, we display a mechanism that achieves that bound. It is the direct mechanism with decision performance (3.23) and these payment functions:

$$p^i(\vec{t}) = p^i(t^{-i}))$$
$$= \begin{cases} v^i\left((m^i)^{-1}\left(\max\left(0, \max_{j \neq i} m^j(t^j)\right)\right)\right) & \text{if } x^i(t) = 1, \\ \\ 0 & \text{otherwise.} \end{cases} \tag{3.27}$$

It is immediate that $V^i(0) = 0$ (type 0 never wins and never makes or receives a payment).

Finally, observe that for all types, truthful reporting is an always optimal strategy. Since m^i is increasing, for any report i may make, he can acquire the good only by paying a price $p^i(t^{-i})$, because the allocation rule specifies that i acquires the item precisely when $v^i(t^i) - p^i(t^{-i}) > 0$. Thus, by reasoning analogous to the second price-auction analysis, bidding truthfully is always optimal. ∎

An interesting corollary of this theorem is that certain standard auctions with reservation prices can sometimes be expected-revenue-maximizing auctions. Indeed, suppose that we add to the assumptions of the theorem the extra assumption that $v^1 = \cdots = v^N = v$, so that $m^1 = \cdots = m^N = m.$ Suppose that the seller sets a minimum price, or *reserve* in a second-price auction. If any bid exceeds the reserve, then the price is equal to the larger of the reserve or the second highest bid. If the seller sets a reserve of $r^* = v(t^*)$, where t^* solves $m(t^*) = 0$, then the Vickrey auction with reserve r^* achieves the decision performance specified in the theorem: bidder i wins if and only if its type is highest and $m(t^i) > 0.$ Moreover, type 0 bidders always lose: $V^i(0) = 0.$ So the Vickrey auction with reserve r^* is an expected-revenue-maximizing auction in this class of symmetric environments.

3.3.8 The McAfee–McMillan Weak-Cartels Theorem

McAfee and McMillan (1992) were among the first to study the theory of *bidding rings*, which are groups of bidders that make collusive agreements about how to divide the items for sale in an auction.[15] Ring members might try to agree before the auction which of them will be the winner, with the understanding that other bidders will make no bids or low bids in the auction. In that way, the winner may be able to get the item for a low price, possibly even at the reserve, enhancing its own profit.

Rings face a series of problems if they are to operate effectively. One is to enforce agreements, which might be done in a series of auctions by threatening to retaliate against those who violate the ring rules. A second problem is to prevent new bidders from entering when the prices in a series of auctions seem low. A third is how to divide the spoils. This can be a serious problem in that, as McAfee and McMillan state, most of the US Department of Justice's bid-rigging convictions begin when one of the cartel members turns in other members because he is unhappy with his share of the profits. To avoid leaving incriminating records, cartels often avoid making cash payments among their members, and that restriction limits what the cartel members can achieve.

We call a ring that cannot make cash payments among its members a *weak ring*. One might think that the members of the ring could hold discussions and tailor their dealings to take advantage of their information,

---

[15] See Graham and Marshall (1987) for a detailed description of ring operations.

allocating the goods most often to those with the highest values. What complicates the problem is that, with no side payments to use to divvy up the profits, bidders will have little incentive to reveal their information even to fellow ring members. McAfee and McMillan show that, under a certain condition, a weak cartel cannot extract *any* useful information from its members: it can do no better than to randomize the allocation among its members.

In our treatment of the McAfee–McMillan model, we assume that the seller sets a reserve price of r and that participants express interest if and only if their values are at least r. Types are statistically independent and uniformly distributed on $[0, 1]$, and i's value is given by $v^i(t^i)$, where $v^1(0) = \cdots = v^N(0) = r$. Given the augmented mechanism devised by the ring, let $x^i(t^i)$ denote the probability that bidder i of type t^i acquires the item, and let $\bar{x}^i = E[x^i(t^i)]$. The *corresponding random allocation* is the allocation that assigns the item to individual i with probability $\bar{x}^i$ regardless of the vector of types. This random allocation is certainly feasible, for the original mechanism is so. Because a player of type zero has no way to earn a positive profit, $V^1(0) = \cdots = V^N(0) = 0$.

As Vickrey first observed, $x^i(\cdot)$ is necessarily nondecreasing. If it were otherwise, then a bidder could "rectify" the relationship between its bids and types, leaving its expected payments unchanged but increasing $E[x^i(t^i)v^i(t^i)]$.[16]

Theorem 3.10. Consider a standard independent private-values model for a single good, and suppose that $(1 - t^i)\, dv^i/dt^i$ is a decreasing function. Then any mechanism by which the weak ring allocates the asset among its members that differs non-trivially from a random allocation is *ex ante* dominated for all bidders by its corresponding random allocation.

Proof. Let $V^i(t^i)$ and $\bar{V}^i(t^i)$ denote the expected payoff of type i from the proposed mechanism and the corresponding random allocation, respectively. Then the *ex ante* utility from the proposed mechanism is

$$E[V^i(t^i)] = \int_0^1 V^i(\tau)\, d\tau = \int_0^1 \int_0^\tau \frac{dv^i}{ds} x^i(s)\, ds\, d\tau$$

---

[16] This argument and related ones will be developed more fully in the next chapter.

$$
\begin{aligned}
&= \int_0^1 \int_s^1 d\tau \frac{dv^i}{ds} x^i(s)\, ds = \int_0^1 (1-s)\frac{dv^i}{ds} x^i(s)\, ds \\
&< \int_0^1 (1-s)\frac{dv^i}{ds}\, ds \int_0^1 x^i(s)\, ds \\
&= \int_0^1 (1-s)\frac{dv^i}{ds} \bar{x}^i ds = \cdots = E[\bar{V}^i(t^i)].
\end{aligned}
\tag{3.28}
$$

The second equality follows from the envelope theorem. After reversing the order of integration, the strict inequality follows from a *majorization* theorem (stating that the expected value of the product of an increasing function and a decreasing function of the same variable is less than the product of the expectations).[17] Then reversing the initial series of steps establishes that the right-hand side of the inequality is the expected payoff from the corresponding random allocation. ∎

Given the assumption that v^i is increasing and that types are uniformly distributed on [0, 1], the inverse function $v^i(\cdot)^{-1}$ is the distribution of bidder values, which we may also write as F^i with density f^i. The condition that $(1 - t^i)\, dv^i/dt^i$ is decreasing is thus equivalent to the condition that $(1 - F^i(v))/f^i(v)$ is decreasing. Accordingly, the condition is sometimes called the "increasing hazard rate" condition. As we have seen, a similar condition arises in the analysis of expected-revenue-maximizing auctions.

The McAfee–McMillan theorem expresses a clear limit on what a weak ring can accomplish. Without cash payments, the ring can do no better than to randomize the right to bid among its members and let one of them win at the reserve price.[18] To create greater profits by allocating the item more efficiently, the ring would need to require a member who claims a high value to pay more than the reserve price. In a weak ring, that extra payment would go to the seller. Hence, subject to the stated

---

[17] This is equivalent to the theorem that the covariance of an increasing function of a random variable with a decreasing function of the same random variable is negative.

[18] Athey, Bagwell, and Sanchirico (2003) amplify this conclusion using a repeated game model in which the bidders observe the price, but not the identity of the winner, after the auction. In their model, like the one in the text, the ring would like to promote the efficient outcome by arranging for the ring member with the highest value to win the auction. However, the ring's inability to identify the winner makes the ring weak despite the repeated game, so (subject to a condition on the distribution of values) the ring can do no better than to randomize the allocation among its members. This conclusion changes if the winning bidder's identity is revealed after each auction; see Athey and Bagwell (2001).

assumption about the distribution of values, this leaves the ring worse off than with a simple randomization.

3.3.9 Sequential Auctions and Weber's Martingale Theorem[19]

In this section, we investigate the pattern of prices that emerges when several identical items are sold one at a time, in sequence, and each bidder can buy only one item. We find that if the prices are announced after each sale, then the sequence of prices forms a martingale. This means that the expectation of the $n + 1^{st}$ price given the prior prices is equal to the nth price. This property of sequential auctions is especially interesting in that empirical tests suggest that actual prices in art and wine auctions contradict this prediction: they follow a declining pattern.[20]

To formulate the problem, suppose that there are k identical items for sale and N bidders, and each bidder is limited to receiving just one item. The items are to be sold in a sequence of auctions using a rule in which the highest bidder wins and only the winner pays. Let the auction rules be such that, given any information I_n that may become available after n items have been sold, there is a symmetric, increasing equilibrium bid function $\beta_{n+1}(\cdot | I_n)$ that applies to the bidding for item $n + 1$. Then, at equilibrium, the highest type bidder wins the first item, the second highest wins the second item, and so on.

Let p_n denote the price paid for the nth item, $t^{(1)}, \ldots, t^{(N)}$ denote the order statistics in decreasing order from among the bidder types, and I_0 denote null information.

Theorem 3.11. At any equilibrium $\beta = \{\beta_n\}_{n=1}^k$ of any auction game satisfying the conditions described above, the sequence of prices and information $(p_n, I_n)_{n=1}^k$ satisfies $E[p_n | I_{n-1}] = E[v(t^{(k+1)}) | I_{n-1}]$. If the auctions are first-price or second-price auctions and I_n is the sequence of past prices $\{p_1, \ldots, p_n\}$, then $(p_n, I_n)_{n=1}^k$ is a martingale.

Proof. We focus on bidder 1 and suppose he has not yet won an item when the first $m - 1$ items have been sold. We apply Myerson's lemma

---

[19] The analysis of sequential auctions originates with Weber (1983) and Milgrom and Weber (2000). Some additional results about the martingale property are reported in the original sources.

[20] See Ashenfelter (1989) and Ashenfelter and Graddy (2002).

to the game starting with the sale of item m, which has the same decision outcome as the Vickrey auction. Consequently, the expected total payments by bidder 1 given the information I_{m-1} must also be the same:

$$E\left[\sum_{n=m}^{k} p_n 1_{\{t^1=t^{(n)}\}} \big| I_{m-1}\right] = E\left[v(t^{(k+1)})1_{\{t^{(m-1)}>t^1 \geq t^{(k)}\}} \big| I_{m-1}\right]. \tag{3.29}$$

For $m = k$, bidder 1 wins at that round if $t^1 = t^{(k)}$ and then $E[p_k|I_{k-1}] = E[v(t^{(k+1)})|I_{k-1}]$. By symmetry, the identity of the winning bidder for the nth item is independent of the price p_n, so

$$E[p_n 1_{\{t^1=t^{(n)}\}} | I_{m-1}] = E[1_{\{t^1=t^{(n)}\}} | I_{m-1}] E[p_n | I_{m-1}]$$

$$= \frac{1}{N+1-m} E[p_n | I_{m-1}],$$

and similarly

$$E\left[v(t^{(k+1)})1_{\{t^{(m-1)}>t^1 \geq t^{(k)}\}} \big| I_{m-1}\right] = E\left[1_{\{t^{(m-1)}>t^1 \geq t^{(k)}\}} | I_{m-1}\right] E\left[v(t^{(k+1)}) | I_{m-1}\right]$$

$$= \frac{k+1-m}{N+1-m} E\left[v(t^{(k+1)}) | I_{m-1}\right],$$

so equation (3.29) becomes

$$\frac{1}{N+1-m} \sum_{n=m}^{k} E[p_n | I_{m-1}] = \frac{k+1-m}{N+1-m} E\left[v(t^{(k+1)}) | I_{m-1}\right]. \tag{3.30}$$

Using (3.30), we may conclude that $E[p_n|I_{m-1}] = E[v(t^{(k+1)})|I_{m-1}]$ for all $m \leq n \leq k$. For otherwise, there is some $\tilde{n}$ that is the largest value of n for which the equality fails. Then using (3.30) with $m = \tilde{n}$, $E[p_{\tilde{n}}|I_{\tilde{n}-1}] = E[v(t^{(k+1)})|I_{\tilde{n}-1}]$, so for $m \leq \tilde{n}$, $E[p_{\tilde{n}}|I_{m-1}] = E[E[P_{\tilde{n}}|I_{\tilde{n}-1}]|I_{m-1}] = E[E[v(t^{(k+1)})|I_{\tilde{n}-1}]|I_{m-1}] = E[v(t^{(k+1)})|I_{m-1}]$, which is a contradiction.

If the auction is a second-price auction (respectively, first-price auction), then by inverting the bid functions, the information I_n is $(t^{(1)}, \ldots, t^{(n-1)})$ (respectively, $(t^{(2)}, \ldots, t^{(n)})$), so $E[p_n|I_{m-1}] = E[v(t^{(k+1)})|I_{m-1}] = p_{m-1}$, by Myerson's lemma. ∎

3.3.10 Matthews' Theorem: Risk Averse Payoff Equivalence
In the models studied above, bidder payoffs are the expected value received minus the expected amount paid. This specification incorporates two kinds of assumptions about bidder preferences. The first is that there

are no *wealth effects* on choices under uncertainty: changing a bidder's wealth by taxing him or giving him a transfer before presenting him with a risky choice would not alter his most preferred choice. In particular, wealth transfers do not affect bidding decisions. The second is that each bidder is risk-neutral with respect to gambles involving money.

Matthews (1983) studied auctions with risk averse buyers whose preferences exhibit no wealth effects. As in the risk neutral case, the key to a simple analysis is to use the envelope theorem to obtain a simple restriction on the bidders' payoffs. In this case, we find that the bidder's expected utilities cannot vary among auction designs in a certain class, that is, the bidders are indifferent among the designs.

To simplify the analysis, we normalize the utility payoff of a losing bidder to be zero and denote bidder i's constant coefficient of absolute risk aversion by r^i. When i wins, his utility payoff is $1 - \exp[-r^i(v^i(t^i) - p^i)] = 1 - \hat{v}^i(t^i)u^i(p^i)$, where $\hat{v}^i(t^i) = \exp[-r^i(v^i(t^i))]$ and $u^i(p^i) = \exp[r^i p^i]$.

Theorem 3.12. Consider an auction game in which bidder payoffs display constant absolute risk aversion, as specified above. Suppose that σ is a Bayes–Nash equilibrium of a game with full performance (x, p) in which a bidder of type 0 always loses and losing bidders always pay zero. Define $X^i(t) \equiv E[x^i(t, t^{-i})]$. Then, the equilibrium expected utility of bidder i of type t is

$$V^i(t) = X^i(t) - \hat{v}^i(t)\left(X^i(0) + \int_0^t \frac{1}{\hat{v}^i(s)} dX^i(s)\right). \tag{3.31}$$

In particular, two auction games with the same decision performance function x specify the same expected utility $V^i(t)$ for each type of each bidder.

Proof. Given the strategies of the other bidders, when bidder i of type t plays strategy ("bids") b, his expected utility is $\pi(b, t) = E[x^i(b, t^{-i})(1 - \hat{v}^i(t)u^i(p(b, t^{-i})))]$.[21] Define $\varphi^i(t) = E[x^i(t, t^{-i})u^i(p(t, t^{-i}))]$. Then the bidder's equilibrium expected utility is $V^i(t) = E[x^i(t, t^{-i})(1 - \hat{v}^i(t)u^i(p(t, t^{-i})))] = X^i(t) - \hat{v}^i(t)\varphi^i(t)$. To establish (3.31), we will show that $\varphi^i(t) = X^i(0) + \int_0^t [1/\hat{v}^i(s)] dX^i(s)$.

---

[21] It is in this expression that we utilize the assumption that losing bidders always pay zero and so have a normalized utility of zero.

By the envelope theorem and using the boundary condition $V^i(0) = 0$, we obtain a second expression for the expected utility: $V^i(t) = \max_b \pi(b, t) = \int_0^t \pi_2(\sigma^i(s), s)\, ds = -\int_0^t \hat{v}^{i\prime}(s)\varphi^i(s)\, ds$. Equating the two expressions leads to $X^i(t^i) - \hat{v}^i(t^i)\varphi^i(t^i) = -\int_0^t (\hat{v}^i)'(s)\varphi^i(s)\, ds$. Differentiating with respect to t^i: $dX^i(t^i) - \hat{v}^i(t^i)d\varphi^i(t^i) = 0$, or $d\varphi^i(t^i) = dX^i(t^i)/\hat{v}^i(t^i)$. By assumption, $p(0, t^{-i}) = 0$ and $u^i(0) = 1$, so $\varphi^i(0) = X^i(0)$ and $\varphi^i(t^i) = X^i(0) + \int_0^t [1/\hat{v}^i(s)]\, dX^i(s)$. ∎

Several things about this analysis merit comment. First, although the result asserts that the expected payoffs are the same for different bidders in a class of auctions, it does not follow that the expected payoffs are the same for the seller. In the risk neutral case, the seller's expected revenue is equal to the expected total surplus minus the bidders' expected payoffs, but here that identity no longer applies. In fact, we will see in the next chapter that bidder risk aversion in this model creates a revenue advantage for the first-price auction over the second-price or ascending auction.

Second, the risk averse payoff equivalence result is more limited than the corresponding risk neutral version, because it applies only when losing bidders always pay zero. For example, the theorem typically applies to the expected payoffs in standard first- and second-price auctions, but it does not apply to lotteries and all-pay auctions, in which even losing bidders may pay something.

Finally, we emphasize again our view that this use of constant absolute risk aversion is merely an analytic technique, similar to ones that have been used to good effect elsewhere in auction theory and principal–agent theory.[22] This technique does not prejudge the importance of wealth effects, any more than calculating a pure substitution effect in consumer

---

[22] For example, Milgrom and Weber (1982) use constant absolute risk aversion to study the effects of revealing statistical information on auction prices. One effect is that such information tends to reduce risk on average. Abstracting from wealth effects, that always increases the average price that a bidder is willing to pay. For any smooth utility specification without constant absolute risk aversion, there always exist examples of gambles and statistical information such that the wealth effect of the revealing information works against, and is larger than, the risk reduction effect.

Similarly, Holmstrom and Milgrom (1987) introduce a principal–agent model with constant absolute risk aversion to abstract from the effect that an agent's past compensation may have on his current risk averseness. The optimality of linear compensation contracts such as commissions for sales agents or piece rates for factory workers hinges on a set of assumptions including that one.

theory prejudges the importance of income effects in that theory. Wealth effects can be studied separately, and the relative importance of the two effects will naturally vary across different applications.

3.4 Conclusion

This chapter organizes some of the major results of mechanism design theory using the envelope theorem and the related lemmas of Holmstrom and Myerson.

To emphasize the close connection between demand theory and incentive theory, we begin by presenting Hotelling's lemma in its two forms. Its integral form, which is the important one for our purposes, asserts that producer surplus is equal to a certain integral representing the area between the supply curve and the vertical axis.

The same kind of formula can be derived for the more abstract choice spaces of mechanism design theory, but this requires first introducing an extended envelope theorem. The theorem implies Hotelling's lemma when the parameter used is the *price* at which goods can be sold. It implies Holmstrom's lemma when the parameter is the mechanism participant's *type* and the participant maximizes his payoff knowing the opposing type profile t^{-i}. It implies Myerson's lemma when the parameter is the mechanism participant's type and the participant maximizes his *expected* payoff, *not* knowing the opposing type profile t^{-i}.

Holmstrom's lemma leads to the *Green–Laffont–Holmstrom theorem*, which holds that if the set of possible values is smoothly connected, then all augmented mechanisms that implement efficient outcomes in dominant strategies are VCG mechanisms.

Myerson's lemma leads to the famous *revenue equivalence theorem*, which holds that if the set of possible values is smoothly connected, then all augmented mechanisms that implement efficient outcomes in Bayes–Nash strategies lead to the same expected revenues as the Vickrey auction.

The remaining theorems of the chapter explore the restrictions on mechanism performance that the preceding results imply. We derive the *Myerson–Satterthwaite theorem* by examining the payoffs that bargainers must achieve if efficient bargaining outcomes are to be realized. Those payoffs add up to twice the surplus available for distribution. Accordingly, we conclude that efficient bargaining outcomes cannot generally be implemented (unless a donor is available to cover the cash shortfall).

Myerson's optimal auction theorem identifies the auction design that maximizes the seller's expected revenue in a class of environments. The analysis works by expressing the seller's expected revenue as the expected total surplus minus the bidders' total expected profits, using Myerson's lemma to obtain an expression for the latter. Maximizing the revenue expression identifies the decision performance associated with the highest possible expected revenue.

The *Jehiel–Moldovanu theorem* evaluates the possibility of implementing efficient performance in a different set of environments. Using the envelope theorem, we find that to implement efficient performance, each bidder's maximum profit function must depend on any unique information that bidder has about the value of the allocation to other bidders. By direct inspection, we find that the maximum payoff function cannot have that property, and the contradiction implies that implementing the efficient outcome must be impossible.

The *McAfee–McMillan weak-cartels theorem* examines what members of a cartel can achieve for themselves when the members are unable to make cash transfers among themselves. By the envelope formula, there is an exact correspondence between the allocation performance that the cartel implements and the payoffs that the members achieve. Examination of the payoff formula leads to a simple answer when a certain increasing hazard rate condition is satisfied. Then, the *random* mechanisms, in which the item is allocated to cartel members according to some pre-specified probabilities, form a Pareto-dominating class: any other mechanism leads to expected payoffs that are *weakly lower for every bidder* than the expected payoffs of some random mechanism.

Weber's martingale theorem examines a sequence of auctions when bidders want to acquire just one unit. By Myerson's lemma, at the start of each auction, the expected price for each item must be the expectation of the Vickrey price, given the bidders' information. This leads to the conclusion that the sequence of prices must form a martingale.

Matthews' risk averse payoff equivalence theorem establishes the indifference of bidders among a class of auctions in which losing bidders always pay zero, when the bidders exhibit constant absolute risk aversion. The theorem is proved by using the envelope theorem to derive a formula for bidder payoffs that is independent of the payment rule used in the auction. The revenue equivalence theorem does not apply to this model, which establishes that results about bidder-payoff equivalence are distinct from revenue equivalence results.

REFERENCES

Ashenfelter, Orley (1989). "How Auctions Work for Wine and Art." *Journal of Economic Perspectives* **3**: 23–36.

Ashenfelter, Orley and Kathryn Graddy (2002). "Art Auctions: A Survey of Empirical Studies." *Center for Economic Policy Studies.*

Athey, Susan and Kyle Bagwell (2001). "Optimal Collusion with Private Information." *Rand Journal of Economics* **32**(3): 428–465.

Athey, Susan, Kyle Bagwell, and Chris Sanchirico (2003). "Collusion and Price Rigidity." *Review of Economic Studies* (forthcoming).

Bulow, Jeremy and John Roberts (1989). "The Simple Economics of Optimal Auctions." *Journal of Political Economy* **97**(5): 1060–1090.

Coase, Ronald (1959). "The Federal Communications Commission." *Journal of Law and Economics* **2**: 1–40.

Fudenberg, Drew and Jean Tirole (1991). *Game Theory.* Cambridge, MA: MIT Press.

Graham, Daniel and Robert Marshall (1987). "Collusive Bidder Behavior at Single-Object, Second-Price and English Auctions." *Journal of Political Economy* **95**: 1217–1239.

Holmstrom, Bengt (1979). "Groves Schemes on Restricted Domains." *Econometrica* **47**: 1137–1144.

Holmstrom, Bengt and Paul Milgrom (1987). "Aggregation and Linearity in the Provision of Intertemporal Incentives." *Econometrica* **55**(2): 303–328.

Jehiel, Philippe and Benny Moldovanu (2001). "Efficient Design with Interdependent Valuations." *Econometrica* **69**(5): 1237–1259.

Klemperer, Paul (2002). "Why Every Economist Should Learn Some Auction Theory." http://www.paulklemperer.org/.

Laffont, Jean-Jacques and Eric Maskin (1980). "A Differentiable Approach to Dominant Strategy Mechanisms." *Econometrica* **48**: 1507–1520.

Mas Colell, Andreu, Michael Whinston, and Jerry Green (1995). *Microeconomic Theory.* New York: Oxford University Press.

Matthews, Stephen (1983). "Selling to Risk Averse Buyers with Unobservable Tastes." *Journal of Economic Theory* **30**: 370–400.

McAfee, R. Preston, and John McMillan (1992). "Bidding Rings." *American Economic Review* **82**(3): 579–599.

Milgrom, Paul and Ilya Segal (2002). "Envelope Theorems for Arbitrary Choice Sets." *Econometrica* **70**(2): 583–601.

Milgrom, Paul and Robert J. Weber (1982). "A Theory of Auctions and Competitive Bidding." *Econometrica* **50**: 463–483.

Milgrom, Paul and Robert J. Weber (2000). "A Theory of Auctions and Competitive Bidding, II." *The Economic Theory of Auctions*. P. Klemperer. Cheltenham: Edward Elgar Publishing, Ltd. **2**: 179–194.

Mirrlees, James (1971). "An Exploration in the Theory of Optimal Taxation." *Review of Economic Studies* **38**: 175–208.

Myerson, Roger B. (1981). "Optimal Auction Design." *Mathematics of Operations Research* **6**(1): 58–73.

Myerson, Roger B. (1991). *Game Theory*. Cambridge, MA: Harvard University Press.

Riley, John G. and William S. Samuelson (1981). "Optimal Auctions." *American Economic Review* **71**(3): 381–392.

Simon, C. and Larry Blume (1994). *Mathematics for Economists*. New York: W.W. Norton & Co.

Varian, Hal R (1992). *Microeconomic Analysis*. New York: W.W. Norton & Co.

Weber, Robert J. (1983). "Multiple-Object Auctions." *Auctions, Bidding, and Contracting: Uses and Theory*. R. Engelbrecht-Wiggans, M. Shubik, and R. M. Stark. New York: New York University Press. 165–191.

Williams, Steven R. (1999). "A Characterization of Efficient, Bayesian Incentive Compatible Mechanism." *Economic Theory* **XIV**: 155–180.

CHAPTER FOUR

Bidding Equilibrium and Revenue Differences

This chapter has two main purposes. The first is a technical one: showing how to identify candidate equilibrium strategies in a variety of auction forms and to verify whether the candidate strategies actually form an equilibrium. This part of the analysis uses various single crossing conditions extensively. Researchers have analyzed several different single crossing conditions; in this chapter we describe and relate these conditions and highlight their significance.

The second purpose is to investigate the comparative performance of different auctions when some of the assumptions of chapter 3 do not hold. For example, we show that in a standard symmetric single-good auction model, although expected revenues are the same for the first- and second-price auctions, revenues are riskier in the second-price auction. Consequently, a risk averse seller prefers a first-price auction. In the same model, introducing bidder risk aversion prevents application of the revenue equivalence theorem and leads to higher average prices in the first-price auction than in the second-price auction. Hence, bidder risk aversion also makes sellers favor the first-price auction design. In a procurement auction in which competitive bids determine prices but the buyer afterwards determines quantities, we show that first-price auctions yield lower prices than second-price auctions and that both bidders and buyers may favor the first-price design. On the other hand, introducing a certain type of positive statistical dependence (*affiliation*) among the buyers' types leads to the conclusion that prices are higher, on average, in a second-price or ascending auction.

This chapter has four main sections. The first explains and analyzes the single crossing conditions that are central to the entire chapter. The second uses these conditions to derive and verify equilibrium in different types of auctions. The third develops the most commonly used method for comparing revenues in auction models that depart from the standard model. The final section studies revenue-maximizing auctions in the one good case.

4.1 The Single Crossing Conditions

This section defines several kinds of single crossing conditions and shows the relationships among them.

The term "single crossing condition" can cause confusion because different authors use it to mean different things. In the three most commonly used definitions, the domain of the function is either $\mathbb{R}$, $\mathbb{R}^2$, or $\mathbb{R}^3$, but the range is always $\mathbb{R}$.

The most basic definition applies to one-dimensional domains. Let the domain be any set $X \subset \mathbb{R} \cup \{-\infty, +\infty\}$. Then the function $f : X \to \mathbb{R} \cup \{-\infty, +\infty\}$ satisfies the *single crossing condition* if for all $t > t'$, $f(t') > 0 \Rightarrow f(t) > 0$ and $f(t') \geq 0 \Rightarrow f(t) \geq 0$; it satisfies the *strict single crossing condition* if for all $t > t'$, $f(t') \geq 0 \Rightarrow f(t) > 0$. Intuitively, the strict single crossing condition holds when the function crosses zero only once, and only from below. The ordinary single crossing condition is similar, but it allows the possibility that the function intersects the x-axis along an entire interval, rather than just at a single point. Thus, nondecreasing functions and increasing[1] functions satisfy the ordinary and strict single crossing conditions, respectively. Figure 1 illustrates three other functions that satisfy strict single crossing.

In this book, we use the one-dimensional property only as a building block for the higher dimensional conditions. Higher dimensional versions of the property are useful for the exercise known as *sensitivity analysis* or *comparative statics analysis*.

We begin with the simplest kind of comparative statics analysis on a choice problem where the decision maker chooses a real variable x and the parameter is a real variable t. The objective is a function $g(x, t)$ mapping a subset of $\mathbb{R}^2$ to $\mathbb{R}$. We shall say that g satisfies the *single crossing differences* condition or the *strict single crossing differences* condition if, for any $x' > x$, the function defined by $f(t) = g(x', t) - g(x, t)$ satisfies the

---

[1] "Increasing" means the same thing as "strictly increasing," that is, $x > y \Rightarrow f(x) > f(y)$. If the domain of f is only partially ordered, then $x > y$ means that $x \geq y$ and $x \neq y$.

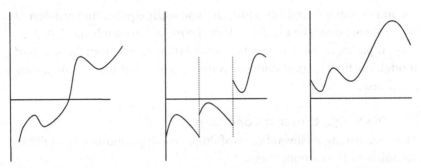

Figure 1. These three functions all satisfy the strict single crossing condition.

corresponding one-dimensional single crossing condition. Thus, g satisfies single crossing differences if for all $t > t'$ we have $g(x', t') - g(x, t') > 0 \Rightarrow g(x', t) - g(x, t) > 0$ and $g(x', t') - g(x, t') \geq 0 \Rightarrow g(x', t) - g(x, t) \geq 0$. Figure 2 illustrates these relationships for $x' > x$.

The following invariance property reveals some of the structure of the single crossing difference conditions. For any increasing function $h : \mathbb{R} \to \mathbb{R}$, the function $g(x, t)$ has the (ordinary or strict) single crossing difference property if and only if $h(g(x, t))$ has the same property. This fact suggests several ways to verify the property. For example, if $g(x, t)$ is differentiable, then if either one of the following two conditions holds for all (x, t), the single crossing differences property holds as well:

$$(i)\ \frac{\partial^2 g(x, t)}{\partial x \partial t} \geq 0 \quad \text{or} \quad (ii)\ g(x, t) > 0 \text{ and } \frac{\partial^2 \log g(x, t)}{\partial x \partial t} \geq 0.$$

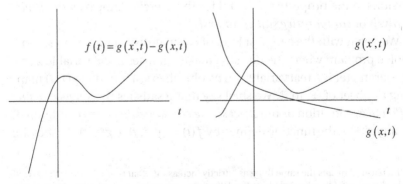

Figure 2. The function g satisfies single crossing differences because, for $x' > x$, the difference function f has the one-dimensional single crossing property.

Condition (i) implies single crossing differences because it implies that for any $x > x'$, the difference $g(x, t) - g(x', t) = \int_{x'}^{x} g_1(s, t)\, ds$ (where $g_1 = \partial g/\partial x$) is nondecreasing in t and so crosses zero only once and only from below. To show that condition (ii) also guarantees single crossing differences, just set $h(x) = \log x$.

Conditions (i) and (ii) are both commonly used in auction theory. If x is the probability that a bidder wins an item, $b(x)$ is what the bidder must bid to win with probability x, and t is his value for the item, then the bidder's expected payoff is $g(x, t) = xt - xb(x)$, which satisfies condition (i). If the bidder is not risk neutral, condition (i) does not apply, but condition (ii) does apply to a reformulated version of the bidder's problem in which x is the amount bid and $p(x)$ is the probability of winning. Then, the expected payoff is $g(x, t) = p(x)u(t - x)$. Without loss of generality, we may limit attention to bids for which $u(t - x) > 0$. On that domain, if the function $z \to \log u(z)$ is concave, then $g(x, t)$ satisfies the second of the conditions listed above.

Note that although the sufficient conditions cited are *symmetric* in the two arguments (x, t), the single crossing differences conditions are not. For example, the condition that g is strictly monotonic (either increasing or decreasing) in x implies single crossing differences, but the condition that g is strictly monotonic in t does not.

A slightly stronger version of the single crossing differences condition will help us conduct our analysis using integrals and derivatives. We use subscripts here to denote partial derivatives, letting $g_1(x, t) = \partial g/\partial x$ and $g_2(x, t) = \partial g/\partial t$. A function g satisfies the *smooth single crossing differences* condition if it satisfies the single crossing difference condition and, in addition, has the property that for all $x \in \mathbb{R}$, if $g_1(x, t) = 0$, then for all $\delta > 0$ one has $g_1(x, t + \delta) \geq 0$ and $g_1(x, t - \delta) \leq 0$. The single crossing differences condition implies that for $\varepsilon > 0$, if $g(x + \varepsilon, t) - g(x, t) = 0$, then for all $\delta > 0$ one has $g(x + \varepsilon, t + \delta) - g(x, t + \delta) \geq 0 \geq g(x + \varepsilon, t - \delta) - g(x, t - \delta)$. The smooth single crossing differences condition strengthens the ordinary condition by requiring that the preceding inequality hold even when ε is infinitesimal.

4.1.1 The Monotonic Selection Theorem
The next three theorems summarize important, general consequences of the single crossing differences conditions. The first is a theorem from Milgrom and Shannon (1994). Following our earlier practice, we limit the parameter space to [0, 1].

Theorem 4.1 (Monotonic selection).[2] The function $g : \mathbb{R} \times [0, 1] \to \mathbb{R}$ satisfies the strict single crossing differences condition if and only if for every finite[3] set $X \subset \mathbb{R}$, every optimal selection $x^*(t, X) \in \arg\max_{x \in X} g(x, t)$ is nondecreasing in t.

Proof. We first show that if g satisfies the strict single crossing differences condition, then every optimal selection is nondecreasing. Let x be a selection from $\arg\max_{x \in X} g(x, t)$; let $t_0 < t_1$; and take $x^*(t_0, X) = x_0$ and $x_1 = x^*(t_1, X)$. Optimality implies that $g(x_0, t_0) - g(x_1, t_0) \geq 0$ and $g(x_0, t_1) - g(x_1, t_1) \leq 0$. These two inequalities and strict single crossing differences imply that $x_1 \geq x_0$. Hence, the condition implies that the selection x^* is nondecreasing in t.

Next, we show that if g does not satisfy the strict single crossing differences condition, then there is some optimal selection that is not nondecreasing. Suppose that the strict single crossing differences condition does not hold. Then there is some $t_0 < t_1$ and $x_0 > x_1$ such that that $g(x_0, t_0) - g(x_1, t_0) \geq 0$ and $g(x_0, t_1) - g(x_1, t_1) \leq 0$. Because the statement of the theorem must hold for every finite set X, consider $X = \{x_0, x_1\}$, and let $x^*(t_0, X) = x_0 > x_1 = x^*(t_1, X)$. Then the optimal selection $x^*(\cdot, X)$ is decreasing. ∎

As we have seen, single crossing conditions sometimes hold in auction models. In a typical application, t will be the bidder's type and x will be some other variable, such as the probability of winning or the amount bid. The single crossing condition then implies that the probability of winning, or the bid itself, must be a nondecreasing function of the bidder's type.

4.1.2 The Sufficiency Theorem
The sufficiency theorem connects single crossing ideas with ideas used in the envelope theorem to provide a useful tool for the analysis of equilibria in auctions.

---

[2] There is also a version of the monotonic selection theorem establishing the equivalence between the *weak* single crossing condition and the existence of *some* monotonic selection. See Milgrom and Shannon (1994).

[3] We limit attention to finite sets to ensure that the maximum exists so that the selection is well defined.

The envelope theorem and the monotonic selection theorem imply that, under certain conditions, if $\bar{x}(t) \in x^*(t) = \arg\max_{x \in X} g(x, t)$, then (1) $g(\bar{x}(t), t)$ satisfies the envelope integral formula and (2) $\bar{x}$ is a nondecreasing function. The next theorem turns this around. Under a different set of assumptions, conditions (1) and (2) imply that $\bar{x}(t) \in X^*(t) = \arg\max_{x \in X} g(x, t)$.

One of these assumptions is a regularity condition. Recall that any nondecreasing function $\bar{x}$ can be discontinuous only at its jumps. So, $\bar{x}$ can be expressed as $\bar{x} = \bar{x}_J + \bar{x}_C$: the sum of a jump function and a continuous function. We denote the jump function by $\bar{x}_J(t) = \sum_{t \in J, s \leq t} \lambda_-(s) + \sum_{t \in J, s < t} \lambda_+(s)$, where J is the set of jump points and $\lambda_-(s)$ and $\lambda_+(s)$ are the sizes of the left- and right-hand jumps at s, and we denote the continuous function by $\bar{x}_C$.

Any nondecreasing function $\bar{x}$ is differentiable almost everywhere. It will be convenient below to let $\bar{x}'(t)$ denote the derivative where it exists and to set $\bar{x}'(t) = 0$ elsewhere. The regularity condition for the next theorem is that the continuous part of $\bar{x}$ is absolutely continuous. Therefore, for all t and $\hat{t}$, $\bar{x}_C(t) - \bar{x}_C(\hat{t}) = \int_{\hat{t}}^{t} \bar{x}'(s) \, ds$. Although the regularity condition excludes functions like the Cantor function that are continuous but not absolutely continuous, it covers all of the functions that we will encounter below.

Theorem 4.2 (Sufficiency). Suppose that $g(x, t)$ is continuously differentiable and has the smooth single crossing differences property. Let $\bar{x} : [0, 1] \rightarrow \mathbb{R}$ have range X, and suppose that $\bar{x} = \bar{x}_J + \bar{x}_C$, where $\bar{x}_J$ is a jump function and $\bar{x}_C$ is absolutely continuous. If

(1) $\bar{x}(t)$ is nondecreasing and
(2) the envelope formula holds: $g(\bar{x}(t), t) - g(\bar{x}(0), 0) = \int_0^t g_2(\bar{x}(s), s) \, ds$,

then $\bar{x}(t)$ is a selection from $X^*(t) = \arg\max_{x \in X} g(x, t)$.

Proof. Because $\bar{x}$ is nondecreasing, for all t we have $\lim_{\hat{t} \downarrow t} \bar{x}(\hat{t}) \equiv \bar{x}_+(t) \geq \bar{x}(t) \geq \bar{x}_-(t) \equiv \lim_{\hat{t} \uparrow t} \bar{x}(\hat{t})$. Recall that J is the set of jump points of $\bar{x}$, and consider $s \in J$. By (2), $g(\bar{x}(t), t)$ is continuous, so $g(\bar{x}(s), s) = g(\bar{x}_+(s), s) = g(\bar{x}_-(s), s)$. By single crossing, for all $t > s$ we have $g(\bar{x}_-(s), t) \leq g(\bar{x}(s), t) \leq g(\bar{x}_+(s), t)$, and for all $t < s$ we have $g(\bar{x}_-(s), t) \geq g(\bar{x}(s), t) \geq g(\bar{x}_+(s), t)$.

If $s \notin J$, then $\bar{x}$ is continuous at s. Hence, by condition (2) of the theorem, $\frac{d}{ds} g(\bar{x}(s), s) = g_2(\bar{x}(s), s)$. Applying the chain rule, $\frac{d}{ds} g(\bar{x}(s), s) = g_2(\bar{x}(s), s) + g_1(\bar{x}(s), s)\bar{x}'(s)$. So either $g_1(\bar{x}(s), s) = 0$ or $\bar{x}'(s) = 0$ (which includes, by convention, the possibility that $\bar{x}$ is not differentiable at s). In the former case, by smooth single crossing differences, for all $t > s$ we have $g_1(\bar{x}(s), t) \geq 0$, and for all $t < s$ we have $g_1(\bar{x}(s), t) \leq 0$. Because $\bar{x}'(s) \geq 0$, it follows that for $t > s$ we have $g_1(\bar{x}(s), t)\bar{x}'(s) \geq g_1(\bar{x}(s), s)\bar{x}'(s)$, and for $t < s$ the reverse inequality holds.

So, for $t > \hat{t}$,

$$g(\bar{x}(t), t) - g(\bar{x}(\hat{t}), t)$$
$$= \int_{\hat{t}}^{t} g_1(\bar{x}(s), t)\bar{x}'(s) \, ds + \sum_{s \in J, \hat{t} < s < t} (g(\bar{x}_+(s), t) - g(\bar{x}_-(s), t))$$
$$+ (g(\bar{x}(t), t) - g(\bar{x}_-(t), t)) + (g(\bar{x}_+(\hat{t}), t) - g(\bar{x}(\hat{t}), t))$$
$$\geq \int_{\hat{t}}^{t} g_1(\bar{x}(s), s)\bar{x}'(s) \, ds + \sum_{s \in J, \hat{t} < s < t} (g(\bar{x}_+(s), s) - g(\bar{x}_-(s), s))$$
$$+ (g(\bar{x}(t), t) - g(\bar{x}_-(t), t)) + (g(\bar{x}_+(\hat{t}), \hat{t}) - g(\bar{x}(\hat{t}), \hat{t})) = 0, \quad (4.1)$$

where the inequality holds for each term of the integrand and summand. Similarly, for $t < \hat{t}$,

$$g(\bar{x}(\hat{t}), t) - g(\bar{x}(t), t) = \cdots$$
$$\leq \int_{t}^{\hat{t}} g_1(\bar{x}(s), s)\bar{x}'(s) \, ds$$
$$+ \sum_{s \in J, t < s < \hat{t}} (g(\bar{x}_+(s), s) - g(\bar{x}_-(s), s))$$
$$+ (g(\bar{x}_+(t), t) - g(\bar{x}(t), t)) + (g(\bar{x}(\hat{t}), \hat{t}) - g(\bar{x}_-(\hat{t}), \hat{t}))$$
$$= 0.$$

Hence, $g(\bar{x}(\hat{t}), t) \leq g(\bar{x}(t), t)$ for all $t, \hat{t}$.   ∎

Necessity of Smooth Single Crossing Differences

This sub-subsection establishes that we can generally dispense with the extra assumption of smooth single crossing differences only when the choice set is discrete.

In the proof of theorem 4.2, we analyze the jump and continuous parts of $\bar{x}$ separately. The jump part corresponds to the sums in (4.1), and the continuous part corresponds to the integrals. The analysis of the jumps requires only the ordinary single crossing differences condition. Therefore, the conclusion of the theorem applies to discrete choice sets under this assumption, regardless of whether the objective function satisfies smooth single crossing differences.

We use an example to establish that the ordinary single crossing differences condition is not sufficient when the choice set is $[0, 1]$. Let $g : [0, 1]^2 \to \mathbb{R}$ be given by $g(x, t) = (x - t)^3$. Because g is increasing in x, it satisfies strict single crossing differences. Consider the function $\bar{x}(t) = t$, which is increasing and continuously differentiable. Observe that $g(\bar{x}(t), t)$ satisfies the envelope formula, because $g(\bar{x}(t), t) = 0 = g_2(\bar{x}(t), t)$. Moreover, because $\max g(x, t) = (1 - t)^3 > 0$ for $t < 1$, it follows that $\bar{x}(t) \notin X^*(t)$. So weakening the assumption of theorem 4.2 to strict single crossing would invalidate the theorem.

According to theorem 4.2, the fact that $\bar{x}(t) \notin X^*(t)$ must imply that some condition of the theorem fails, so the function g must not satisfy smooth single crossing. For completeness, we verify that, as follows: for $\hat{t} < t, g_1(\bar{x}(t), \hat{t}) = 3(t - \hat{t})^2 > 0 = g_1(\bar{x}(t), t)$.

4.1.3 The Constraint Simplification Theorem

In mechanism design, we sometimes want to identify as completely as possible the set of performance functions that can be implemented. If the payoff function satisfies the strict single crossing differences condition and the integrable bound condition, then the monotonic selection theorem and envelope theorem establish that conditions (1) and (2) above – monotonicity and the envelope formula – are necessary conditions for optimality. According to the sufficiency theorem, a different set of assumptions implies that they are sufficient. In models where all of the relevant assumptions hold, conditions (1) and (2) are necessary and sufficient for optimality. This fact characterizes the set of feasible performance functions.

Theorem 4.3 (Constraint simplification). Suppose that the function $g : \mathbb{R} \times [0, 1] \to \mathbb{R}$ is continuously differentiable and satisfies the strict and smooth single crossing differences properties. Further suppose that there is an integrable function $b(t)$ such that $\sup_x |g_2(x, t)| \leq b(t)$. Let $\bar{x} : [0, 1] \to \mathbb{R}$ have range X, and suppose that $\bar{x} = \bar{x}_J + \bar{x}_C$, where $\bar{x}_J$ is a jump function and $\bar{x}_C$ is absolutely continuous. Then $\bar{x}(t)$ is a selection from $x^*(t) = \arg\max_{x \in X} g(x, t)$ if and only if the following two additional conditions are satisfied:

(3) $\bar{x}(\cdot)$ is nondecreasing;
(4) the envelope formula holds: $g(\bar{x}(t), t) - g(\bar{x}(0), 0) = \int_0^t g_2(\bar{x}(s), s) \, ds$.

The constraint simplification theorem has been a workhorse of optimal mechanism design, because it characterizes the performance functions $\bar{x}(t)$ a mechanism can implement when the participants act optimally, in their own interests. We will see such applications later in the chapter.

4.1.4 The Mirrlees–Spence Representation Theorem

There is a long tradition in consumer theory of evaluating the change in a rational consumer's choice from a budget set as his preferences shift. For example, if the consumer's indifference curve becomes steeper, then he will generally elect to consume more of the good on the horizontal axis (Figure 3). Given a parameterized utility function $U(x, y, t)$ for a two-dimensional goods space, indifference curves are steeper with increases in t when their slope $dy/dx = -U_1(x, y, t)/U_2(x, y, t)$ is increasing in t.

Precisely the same mathematical condition arose again in the celebrated optimal taxation and signaling analyses by James Mirrlees (1971)

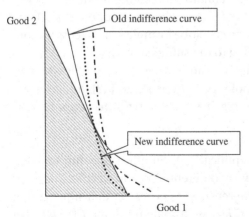

Good 2

Old indifference curve

New indifference curve

Good 1

Figure 3. In the traditional consumer theory, where the consumer has convex preferences and faces a straight line budget set, a steeper indifference curve leads to more consumption of the first good.

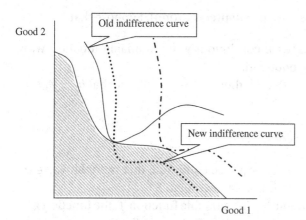

Figure 4. Even with the non-convex choice set, a steeper indifference curve still leads to more consumption of the first good.

and A. Michael Spence (1973). The main analytical difference between the Mirrlees and Spence models and their predecessors is that the choice set is not limited to a budget set – a line segment – but can take more general shapes, as shown above. Even so, a steeper indifference curve still induces greater consumption of the good on the horizontal axis (Figure 4).

This mathematical condition – that the indifference curve through any point becomes steeper with increases in t – implies that two indifference curves corresponding to different types can cross only once. Indeed, if an indifference curve for type $t > t'$ were to cross the t'-curve twice, then there would have to be one crossing from above and one crossing from below, violating the assumption that the t-curve is steeper than the t'-curve at any point of crossing. This property that indifference curves cross once is the reason that the Mirrlees–Spence condition is often called a "single crossing condition."

In simple bidding models, choice occurs in a one-dimensional space: the bidder chooses a bid. However, the bid determines a two-dimensional outcome – a price and allocation of the good. This fact creates a close connection between the single crossing conditions for one- and two-dimensional choice problems. The next result summarizes this connection.[4]

---

[4] For additional development of the relationship between single crossing conditions and the Mirrlees–Spence condition, see Milgrom and Shannon (1994), Edlin and Shannon (1998a, 1998b).

Theorem 4.4 (Mirrlees–Spence Representation). Suppose that

(i) $h: \mathbb{R}^3 \to \mathbb{R}$ is a twice continuously differentiable function with $h_2 \neq 0$ and $|h_1|$ bounded, and
(ii) for every $(x, x', y, t) \in \mathbb{R}^4$, there exists $y' \in \mathbb{R}$ such that $h(x', y', t) = h(x, y, t)$.

Then the following are equivalent:

(1) h satisfies the Mirrlees–Spence condition, that is, for all $x, y \in \mathbb{R}$, $h_1(x, y, t)/|h_2(x, y, t)|$ is nondecreasing in t.
(2) For every continuously differentiable function f, the function $g^f : \mathbb{R}^2 \to \mathbb{R}$ defined by $g^f(x, t) = h(x, f(x), t)$ satisfies the smooth single crossing differences condition.

Proof. To show (2) $\Rightarrow$ (1), fix $\hat{x}, \hat{y}, \hat{t} \in \mathbb{R}$. Set $f(z) = \hat{y} + \alpha(z - \hat{x})$, where $\alpha = -h_1(\hat{x}, \hat{y}, \hat{t})/h_2(\hat{x}, \hat{y}, \hat{t})$. Then, $g_1^f(\hat{x}, \hat{t}) = h_1 + \alpha h_2 = 0$. So smooth single crossing implies that

$$
\begin{aligned}
0 &\leq \frac{\partial}{\partial t} g_1^f(\hat{x}, t)|_{t=\hat{t}} \\
&= \frac{\partial}{\partial t} \left[h_2(\hat{x}, \hat{y}, t) \left(\alpha + \frac{h_1(\hat{x}, \hat{y}, t)}{h_2(\hat{x}, \hat{y}, t)} \right) \right]_{t=\hat{t}} \\
&= \left[h_2(\hat{x}, \hat{y}, t) \frac{\partial}{\partial t} \left(\alpha + \frac{h_1(\hat{x}, \hat{y}, t)}{h_2(\hat{x}, \hat{y}, t)} \right) + 0 \right]_{t=\hat{t}},
\end{aligned}
$$

which implies that h satisfies the Mirrlees–Spence condition.

To show (1)$\Rightarrow$(2), we first show that (1) implies g^f has single crossing differences. Let $f: \mathbb{R} \to \mathbb{R}$ be an arbitrary function. Suppose $\hat{x} > \tilde{x}$, $\hat{y} = f(\hat{x})$, and $h(\hat{x}, \hat{y}, \hat{t}) \geq h(\tilde{x}, \tilde{y}, \hat{t})$. We must show that for any $t > \hat{t}$ we have $h(\hat{x}, \hat{y}, t) \geq h(\tilde{x}, \tilde{y}, t)$.

Suppose not. Because h is continuous in t, there exists $\hat{t} \in [\hat{t}, t)$ such that $h(\hat{x}, \hat{y}, \hat{t}) = h(\tilde{x}, \tilde{y}, \hat{t})$. Let $\{(x(s), y(s))|s \in [\hat{t}, \hat{t}]\}$ satisfy $x(s) = \tilde{x} + \lambda(s - \hat{t})$ where $\lambda = (\hat{x} - \tilde{x})/(\hat{t} - \hat{t}) > 0$, and for all s define $y(s)$ so that $h(x(s), y(s), \hat{t}) = h(\tilde{x}, \tilde{y}, \hat{t})$. By assumption, such a function $y(s)$ exists. Because $x'(s) = \lambda$ and h is differentiable with $h_2 \neq 0$, it follows that $y(s)$ is differentiable and

$$
h_2(x(s), y(s), \hat{t}) \frac{dy}{ds} = -h_1(x(s), y(s), \hat{t}) \frac{dx}{ds},
$$

or

$$\frac{dy}{ds} = -\frac{dx}{ds}\frac{h_1(x(s), y(s), \hat{t})}{h_2(x(s), y(s), \hat{t})}.$$

Because $h_2 \neq 0$ and h_2 is continuous, this function has a fixed sign, which we may denote by $\sigma = h_2(\tilde{x}, \tilde{y}, \hat{t})/|h_2(\tilde{x}, \tilde{y}, \hat{t})| = \pm 1$. Then, because $x(\hat{t}) = \hat{x}$ and $x(\tilde{t}) = \tilde{x}$,

$$h(\hat{x}, \hat{y}, t) - h(\tilde{x}, \tilde{y}, t)$$

$$= \int_{\tilde{t}}^{\hat{t}} \frac{d}{ds} h(x(s), y(s), t) ds$$

$$= \int_{\tilde{t}}^{\hat{t}} \left[h_1(x(s), y(s), t)\frac{dx}{ds} + h_2(x(s), y(s), t)\frac{dy}{ds} \right] ds$$

$$= \int_{\tilde{t}}^{\hat{t}} \left[\lambda \frac{h_1(x(s), y(s), t)}{|h_2(x(s), y(s), t)|} + \sigma \frac{dy}{ds} \right] \cdot |h_2(x(s), y(s), t)| \, ds$$

$$\geq \int_{\tilde{t}}^{\hat{t}} \left[\lambda \frac{h_1(x(s), y(s), \hat{t})}{|h_2(x(s), y(s), \hat{t})|} + \sigma \frac{dy}{ds} \right] \cdot |h_2(x(s), y(s), t)| \, ds$$

$$= 0. \tag{4.2}$$

Inasmuch as $dx/ds > 0$, the inequality in (4.2) follows from (1) (because the integrand is everywhere larger with functions evaluated at t). The final equality follows because, by construction, the integrand is everywhere zero.

We now show g^f has the smooth single crossing differences property. Suppose that f is differentiable and $dh(x, f(x), t)/dx = 0$. Suppose $h_2 > 0$ everywhere and consider any $\hat{t}$. Then $dh(x, f(x), \hat{t})/dx = h_1(x, f(x), \hat{t}) + h_2(x, f(x), \hat{t}) f'(x)$, which has the same sign as $h_1(x, f(x), \hat{t})/h_2(x, f(x), \hat{t}) + f'(x)$, which is greater or less than $h_1(x, f(x), t)/h_2(x, f(x), t) + f'(x) = 0$ as $\hat{t}$ is greater or less than t. Accordingly, g^f has the smooth single crossing property when $h_2 > 0$, and a similar argument holds when $h_2 < 0$. ∎

Condition (ii) of the theorem asserts that the second good is sufficiently important that it can be used to compensate for any change in quantity of the first good. This condition is satisfies in all existing auction models and in any model where ordinal preferences are quasi-linear. For quasi-linear models, the Mirrlees–Spence condition takes a particularly simple form.

Theorem 4.5. The function $h(x, y, t) = y + g(x, t)$ satisfies the Mirrlees–Spence condition if and only if $\partial g(x, t)/\partial x$ is increasing in t.

The condition that $\partial g(x, t)/\partial x$ is increasing in t is a differentiable version of the condition known as *increasing differences* or *isotone differences*. The function g has increasing differences when for all $x' > x$ and $t' > t$,

$$g(x', t') - g(x, t') > g(x', t) - g(x, t). \tag{4.3}$$

This condition is stronger than single crossing differences in that the latter requires only that the left-hand side of (4.3) must be positive whenever the right-hand side is. The increasing differences condition is useful both in our analysis and in comparative statics generally.

4.2 Deriving and Verifying Equilibrium Strategies

In this section, we use the preceding theorems to derive the equilibrium strategies for a class of auctions in which the highest bidder wins.[5] In the first few games that we study, a bidder who bids b gets an expected payoff of

$$X^i(b)v^i(t^i) - p^i(b), \tag{4.4}$$

where $v^i(t^i)$ is i's value and $X^i(b)$ and $p^i(b)$ are, respectively, the bidder's probability of winning and the expected payment when he makes a bid of b. If v^i is differentiable and $\beta^i(t^i)$ is the bid that maximizes (4.4), then we may define $x^i(t^i) = X^i(\beta^i(t^i))$. Suppressing the bidder superscript i, the envelope integral formula implies that the payoff of a bidder of type t satisfies

$$V(t) = V(0) + \int_0^t v'(s)x(s)\,ds. \tag{4.5}$$

We may assume without loss of generality that $v(\cdot)$ is nondecreasing,[6] which implies that the payoff (4.4) has single crossing differences. If $v(\cdot)$ is increasing, then the payoff has the strict single crossing differences property, so the bidder's probability of winning is necessarily nondecreasing in his type. If a bidder can win only by making the

---

[5] Klemperer (2002) suggests a similar procedure for deriving equilibria in certain games related to auction games.

[6] If v were not nondecreasing, we could re-label the types to make it so.

highest bid, then by the monotonic selection theorem, any bidder's optimal bid function must be nondecreasing.

The first few examples all employ the auction model that has been most intensively studied and most often incorporated into other analyses – the *symmetric, risk neutral independent private values model*, which we will sometimes call the *benchmark* or standard model. In this model, there are N bidders, indexed by n, and a single item for sale.[7] The types are assumed to be statistically independent and identically distributed according to some continuous density. A bidder who acquires nothing but pays a price p has payoff $-p$; a bidder of type t who acquires the good enjoys a payoff of $v(t) - p$. Bidders are risk neutral.

The above formulation is redundant. We can specify a completely general model by setting $v(t) = t$ and eliminating v from the model. Alternatively, without loss of generality, we can specify that each type is uniformly distributed on $[0, 1]$ and impose any increasing distribution F of bidder values by setting $v = F^{-1}(t)$. The first approach is more common in the literature. The second approach using *distributional strategies* has two advantages: (1) it easily generates predictions about bid distributions for use in empirical work, and (2) it unifies analysis of models with discrete or continuous value distributions.[8] In this chapter, we maintain flexibility by allowing the types to have any distribution F on $[0, 1]$ with a corresponding density f, and each bidder's value to be any differentiable, nondecreasing function of the bidder's type.

4.2.1 The Second-Price Auction with a Reserve Price

A useful standard with which to compare other auctions in this section is a variation of Vickrey's second-price auction in which the seller sets a minimum acceptable bid, or *reserve price*, of r. The auction then determines the allocation just as if the seller had bid r. If no other bid exceeds r, the item remains with the seller; otherwise, the highest bidder acquires the item for a price equal to the second highest actual bid, or for the price of r if it exceeds the second highest bid.

As in chapter 2, bidders in this model have dominant strategies: each bidder always finds it best to bid his value for the item. If $t^{(1)}$ and $t^{(2)}$ denote the highest and second highest types, then the dominant strategy

---

[7] The following analysis generalizes to cases with multiple items for sale provided that each bidder is limited to winning at most a single item.

[8] For more about this approach, see Milgrom and Weber (1985).

leads to a price of $\max[v(t^{(2)}), r]$ if $v(t^{(1)}) > r$, and otherwise to no sale. These strategies constitute a Bayes–Nash equilibrium for any distribution of types.

In the Vickrey auction, neither the seller's nor the bidders' equilibrium payoffs depend on the tie-breaking rule. Nevertheless, because ties are possible if v is not strictly increasing, it will prove convenient to compute payoffs in the event of ties as if the winner were the bidder with the highest type.

4.2.2 The Sealed Tender, or First-Price, Auction

Following Vickrey's introduction of the second-price sealed-bid auction, it became common for economists to refer to standard sealed-bid auctions as "first-price" auctions. These are simply sealed-bid auctions in which the highest bid wins and the highest bidder pays a price equal to his bid. Alternatively, if the bidders are sellers, a standard sealed-bid auction is one in which the low bidder wins and receives the corresponding price.[9] For simplicity, we assume that if two or more bidders make the same highest bid, then the item is awarded to one of the high bidder at random. In addition, we introduce a reserve r so that no award is made unless some bid exceeds r.

We look for a symmetric equilibrium in this auction, that is, a strategy $\beta : [0, 1] \rightarrow \{0\} \cup (r, \infty)$ such that the symmetric strategy profile $(\beta, \ldots, \beta)$ is a Nash equilibrium. A bidder who does not meet the reserve price is said to bid zero. Let us assume that there is some $\hat{t} \in (0, 1)$ such that $v(\hat{t}) = r$, that is, the reserve is more than some possible types would be willing to pay but less than others would be willing to pay.

A preliminary analysis sharply limits the set of potential equilibrium strategies.[10] Observe, first, that it is a dominant strategy for a bidder with value $v(t) < r$ to bid 0. For bidders with $v(t) > r$, it is a dominated strategy to bid less than r or more than $v(t)$. Moreover, there are no *symmetric* equilibria in which players make dominated bids with positive probability. For example, if there were an interval of types with $v(t) < r$

---

[9] Mathematically, these two cases are indistinguishable. A bid to sell can be modeled as an exchange at a negative price. In that case, the "high bid" is the one closest to zero, so the same theory applies. In some actual auctions of packages of contract obligations, it is unclear whether the package has positive or negative value, so any practical distinction between buying and selling blurs as well.

[10] Griesmer, Levitan, and Shubik (1967) pioneered preliminary analysis of this sort, restricting the range of functions that can be equilibrium bidding functions.

that bid r or more, then the event that every bidder's type lies in that interval would have positive probability. But then, types in this interval would have negative expected payoffs (negative payoffs in the identified event and zero payoffs in the complementary event). Negative expected payoffs are inconsistent with equilibrium, for every bidder can earn zero simply by bidding zero.

In a symmetric equilibrium, higher bids necessarily entail a strictly higher probability of winning. If v is increasing, then the payoff function satisfies the strict single crossing differences property, so the monotonic selection theorem implies that any symmetric equilibrium strategy β is nondecreasing.

More strongly, any symmetric equilibrium bid function β must be strictly increasing on the subdomain of types for which $v(t) > r$. If it were not, then the auction would end in a tie with probability $\varepsilon > 0$, with several bidders bidding the same amount $b > r$ and each strictly preferring to win at price b. In that case, a bidder planning to bid b could increase his expected payoff by bidding slightly more, say $b' > b$. This change would increase his probability of winning by ε at a cost of at most $b' - b$, which can be chosen to be arbitrarily small, proving that the original candidate strategy is not an equilibrium.

With an increasing symmetric equilibrium strategy, the bidder with the highest type wins, provided his value for the good exceeds r. Consequently, the decision performance of this auction is the same as that of the Vickrey auction with a reserve price r. Because both auctions also produce an equilibrium payoff of zero to a bidder of type 0, Myerson's lemma implies that the expected payoffs of all types must be identical in the two auctions. Thus, the only possible symmetric equilibrium strategy is the one that makes the expected payments in the two auctions the same for all types $t > \hat{t}$. We analyze the case of bidder 1 of type $t^1 = t > \hat{t}$, introducing the notation $T = \max(t^2, \ldots, t^N)$. If all bidders adopt the increasing equilibrium strategy, β, then bidder 1's expected payment must satisfy

$$\beta(t) F^{N-1}(t) = E[\max(r, v(T)) 1_{\{T < t\}}]$$
$$= r \cdot F^{N-1}(\hat{t}) + \int_{\hat{t}}^{t} v(s) \, dF^{N-1}(s)$$
$$= v(\hat{t}) F^{N-1}(\hat{t}) + \int_{\hat{t}}^{t} v(s)(N-1) f(s) F^{N-2}(s) \, ds. \quad (4.6)$$

In the first line of (4.6), the expression on the left-hand side is the expected payment by bidder 1 in the first-price auction: it pays $\beta(t)$ when it wins and 0 otherwise, and it wins when the $N - 1$ types $t^2, \ldots, t^N$ are all less than bidder 1's realized type, which occurs with probability $F^{N-1}(t)$. The expression on the right-hand side is the corresponding expected payment in a Vickrey auction: the bidder in such an auction wins when $T < t$ and pays $\max(r, v(T))$.

Provided that v is increasing, equation (4.6) identifies the unique candidate for the equilibrium strategy. By Theorem 4.6, the strategy is a symmetric equilibrium strategy.

Theorem 4.6. In the *benchmark* model (with symmetric, risk neutral bidders with independent private values), the strategy given by $\beta(t) = 0$ for $t < \hat{t}$ and otherwise by

$$\beta(t) = E[\max(r, v(T)) | T < t]$$

$$= v(\hat{t})\frac{F^{N-1}(\hat{t})}{F^{N-1}(t)} + (N - 1)\int_{\hat{t}}^{t} v(s)\frac{f(s)F^{N-2}(s)}{F^{N-1}(t)}\, ds$$

is a symmetric equilibrium strategy. If v is increasing, it is the unique symmetric equilibrium strategy.

Remarks. This theorem applies whether values are discretely or continuously distributed. Suppose bidders have values of 5 or 10, each with probability $\frac{1}{2}$. To model this case, let v be any smooth, nondecreasing function with $v(t) = 5$ for $t \in (\frac{1}{4}, \frac{1}{2})$ and $v(t) = 10$ for $t \in (\frac{3}{4}, 1)$ and let F be the uniform distribution on $(\frac{1}{4}, \frac{1}{2}) \cup (\frac{3}{4}, 1)$. One can model any discrete distribution of values in a similar manner. These constructions meet the requirements that F have a corresponding density f and that v be nondecreasing and differentiable.

When v is not strictly increasing, the distribution of values may have an atom. Despite the possibility of an atom in the distribution of values, *the distribution of bids is still atomless and still has a density*. Effectively, β then describes a mixed strategy, incorporating instructions for how a bidder should randomize. If for types t and t', $v(t) = v(t')$, then the bidder is indifferent between bidding $\beta(t)$ and bidding $\beta(t')$ in each case, so the best replies and equilibrium are not unique. But when the distribution of values has an atom, distinct equilibrium bidding strategies differ only in the ways they resolve bidders' indifferences.

Proof of Theorem 4.6. By construction of the equilibrium strategies, the corresponding payoffs satisfy the envelope condition, and we have already observed that weak single crossing always applies. Because the identified strategy is nondecreasing, the sufficiency theorem implies that no bidder of any type has a better reply *among bids in the range of the bid function*. Next, we consider bids outside that range.

Because the strategy implied by (4.6) is continuous and increasing on $t \geq \hat{t}$, the range of the bid function is the interval $[r, \beta(1)]$. By definition, the only permissible bid lower than r is 0, so the only permissible bids possibly outside the range of the bid function are bids of zero or $b > \beta(1)$. The first of these is never a profitable deviation, because it earns a payoff of zero. Any bid $b > \beta(1)$ wins with probability one, given that all bidders play their equilibrium strategy, and generates a payoff of $v(t) - b < v(t) - \beta(1)$, so it is less profitable than bidding $\beta(1)$. Hence, $\beta(t)$ is a best reply on the whole set of permitted bids.

If v is increasing, then our previous arguments, together with the monotonic selection theorem, imply that the equilibrium β must be increasing. Then the envelope condition, which is necessary for optimality, can be written in the form (4.6), so any symmetric equilibrium strategy must coincide with the one we have identified. ∎

The proof consists of two parts, both of which are indispensable. One part verifies that there is no profitable deviation in the range of the equilibrium bid function β. The other verifies that bids outside the range of β cannot lead to higher expected payoffs than bids in the range. To see why this latter step is essential, consider the strategy according to which every type of every bidder bids 10. This is a monotonic strategy, and the corresponding payoffs satisfy the envelope condition. Each type of each bidder is maximizing its profits over bids in the range of the bid function, because that range is a singleton. Yet, this is not an equilibrium, because some bidder types would do better to bid more than 10 and others would do better to bid less.

Next we turn to a question about the empirical implications of auction theory. Laffont, Ossard, and Vuong (1995) investigated the consistency of empirical distributions of bids with equilibrium bidding behavior. Given data about the distribution of bids, when can we find a distribution of values (or, equivalently, a function v) that would produce equilibrium bidding consistent with the observed outcome? For this analysis, it is convenient to use the distributional strategy formulation, taking F to be the uniform distribution on $[0, 1]$.

Theorem 4.7. A distribution of bids G with corresponding density $G' > 0$ is consistent with the equilibrium in the benchmark model with $r = 0$ for some increasing value function v and a uniform distribution of types if and only if $b + \frac{1}{N-1}\frac{G(b)}{G'(b)}$ is an increasing function of b for $b \geq 0$. In that case, the value function that is consistent with G is

$$v(t) = \frac{1}{N-1}\frac{t}{G'(G^{-1}(t))} + G^{-1}(t).$$

Proof. Differentiating the equilibrium strategy equation (4.6) with respect to t, we obtain

$$\beta'(t)F^{N-1}(t) + (N-1)\beta(t)F^{N-2}(t)f(t) = v(t)(N-1)F^{N-2}(t)f(t).$$

Using the assumption that types are uniformly distributed on $[0, 1]$, we obtain

$$\beta'(t)t^{N-1} + (N-1)\beta(t)t^{N-2} = v(t)(N-1)t^{N-2},$$

or

$$v(t) = \frac{t\beta'(t)}{N-1} + \beta(t).$$

Substituting $t = G(b)$ and $b = \beta(t)$ leads to

$$v(G(b)) = \frac{1}{N-1}\frac{G(b)}{G'(b)} + b. \tag{4.7}$$

Because v and G are increasing functions, the right-hand side must necessarily be increasing as well.

Conversely, suppose the right-hand side expression in (4.7) is increasing in b. Then one can use (4.7) to calculate

$$v(t) = \frac{1}{N-1} \frac{t}{G'(G^{-1}(t))} + G^{-1}(t),$$

which is increasing in t because $v(G(b))$ is increasing. To recover (4.6), we simply reverse the steps. Substituting $t = G(b)$ and $b = \beta(t)$, we have

$$v(t) = \frac{1}{N-1} \frac{t}{G'(\beta(t))} + \beta(t)$$

$$= \frac{1}{N-1} t\beta'(t) + \beta(t),$$

where we obtain the second equality by differentiating the expression $t = G(\beta(t))$ with respect to t: $1 = G'(\beta(t))\beta'(t)$. It follows that β is the equilibrium bid function corresponding to v when $r = 0$.[11]   ∎

Laffont, Ossard, and Vuong (1995) used the inversion technique above to estimate the distribution of values that is consistent with bids in an oral auction of eggplants in a marketplace in southern France. Much of the structural econometric literature on auctions proceeds in a similar manner. See Laffont (1997) for a survey of this work.

4.2.3 The War of Attrition Auction

The *war of attrition* auction was initially developed as a model of competition between two animals of the same species for food or a mate. The same model has also been used to analyze economic phenomena, such as exit in oligopoly (Fudenberg and Tirole (1986)) and disputes over government budgets (Alesina and Drazen (1991)). See also Milgrom and Weber (1985) and Bulow and Klemperer (1999).

In the biological version of the model, two hungry animals fight over food until one of them gives up and retreats. The battle is costly to both, because it demands energy and imposes a risk of injury. A strategy for each animal specifies how long to fight before giving up, which we may call the animal's *bid*, b. The animal that makes the higher bid, $\max(b_1, b_2)$, wins. The fight lasts until time $\min(b_1, b_2)$, when one animal quits. Both animals pay $\min(b_1, b_2)$, which is the cost of time spent in battle.

Animals differ in how hungry they are, that is, in how much they value winning the contest, so each chooses a bid depending on its type. If

---

[11] One can extend Theorem 4.6 to cover cases in which $r > 0$ and cases in which both $v(\cdot)$ and $b + \frac{1}{N-1} \frac{G(b)}{G'(b)}$ are nondecreasing, rather than strictly increasing.

each animal optimizes against the strategies played by the others in the population, then the population strategy will be a function $\beta : [0, 1] \rightarrow \mathbb{R}$ that is a symmetric equilibrium of the game.

In view of the interpretations, we set the reserve price in the all-pay auction game to zero. Then, arguing as for the first-price auction, the equilibrium strategy β must be an increasing function of the bidder type. A bidder of the lowest type must expect always to lose, so he must bid zero at any equilibrium, for otherwise he could benefit by deviating and changing his bid to zero. Hence, by Myerson's lemma for the case $N = 2$, any pure strategy equilibrium must equate a bidder's expected payment in the both-pay auction with his expected payment in a Vickrey auction with no reserve price:

$$\int_0^t \beta_{WA}(s) f(s) \, ds + (1 - F(t)) \beta_{WA}(t) = \int_0^t v(s) f(s) \, ds. \qquad (4.8)$$

The left-hand side is the bidder's total expected payment in a both-pay auction, which is the sum of his expected payment when he wins and his expected payment when he loses. The right-hand side is his expected payment in a Vickrey auction with zero reserve and $N = 2$. Differentiating both sides of (4.8) with respect to t yields

$$(1 - F(t)) \beta'_{WA}(t) = v(t) f(t).$$

Equation (4.8) always implies that $\beta_{WA}(0) = 0$, so the unique solution is

$$\beta_{WA}(t) = \int_0^t v(s) \frac{f(s)}{1 - F(s)} \, ds. \qquad (4.9)$$

By inspection, β_{WA} is nondecreasing. By construction, if all bidders use this strategy, then their payoffs satisfy the envelope formula. Hence, the sufficiency theorem applies: no bidder can benefit by deviating to another bid in the range of β_{WA}. It is easy to see that no bidder can strictly increase its payoff by bidding outside that range, so Theorem 4.8 follows.

Theorem 4.8. In the benchmark model, the unique symmetric pure strategy equilibrium of the war of attrition auction game is the strategy defined by (4.9).

The preceding reasoning illustrates the use of the sufficiency theorem for verifying equilibrium bidding strategies. Given a proposed equilibrium strategy, one first verifies that it satisfies the envelope equation, which often holds by construction of the strategy. If $\beta(t)$ is increasing and there is no better bid outside the range of $\beta(t)$, then the sufficiency theorem implies that $\beta(t)$ is a best reply for each bidder and therefore an equilibrium strategy.

4.2.4 The All-Pay Auction

Another auction design in which losers pay is the *all-pay auction*, which is sometimes used to model bribery. The party offering the highest bribe receives a contract or some other valuable consideration. Although only the highest bidder receives the prize, every bidder pays an amount equal to his own bid. One can again use Myerson's lemma to establish that with N players, the only possible equilibrium strategy equates the bid (which is also the bidder's expected payment) with a bidder's expected payment in the Vickrey auction with zero reserve. The candidate strategy is therefore

$$\beta_{AP}(t) = \int_0^t v(s)(N-1)F^{N-1}(s)f(s)\,ds. \tag{4.10}$$

The left-hand side is the payment by the briber of type t, whereas the right-hand side is the corresponding expected payment made in a Vickrey auction with N players.

Theorem 4.9. In the benchmark model, the unique symmetric pure strategy equilibrium of the all-pay first-price auction game is the strategy defined by (4.10).

The proof of Theorem 4.9 uses the sufficiency theorem and resembles others in this chapter.

4.3 Revenue Comparisons in the Benchmark Model

In this section, we present five variations of the benchmark auction model in which expected revenues differ systematically and predictably among the standard auction formats. The conditions that invalidate the revenue equivalence theorem in the five variations are (1) bidding costs, (2) risk aversion, (3) budget constraints, (4) post-auction choices of quantity by the auctioneer, and (5) correlation among bidder types. To simplify notation, we assume except where noted that types are independently and uniformly distributed and that values $v(t)$ are a smooth, increasing function of the type.

We study bidding costs and risk aversion in the same section because they occur in models where payoff equivalence for bidders may obtain even though the revenue equivalence theorem does not hold. Bidding costs are modeled as the costs of participating in an auction while the auction is running, so shorter auctions lead to lower costs. What is interesting in the bidding cost model is that the length of the auction is endogenous. For example, bidders may make jump bids to bring the auction to an early completion.

Risk aversion, as we saw in the last chapter, does not necessarily invalidate payoff equivalence, but it increases bids in first-price auctions. The reason is that risk averse bidders trade lower profits for a greater likelihood of winning by increasing their bids. This effect, which is absent in second-price auctions, increases revenue in first-price auctions.

Budget constraints also induce variation in auctions' performance. The constraints are more damaging in second-price auctions than in first-price auctions, because the equilibrium bids are higher in (unconstrained) second price auctions.

In some procurement auctions, bidders submit price bids to a buyer, who takes the best bid and then determines what quantity to buy. This quantity decision systematically affects the comparison among auctions. If the buyer tends to buy a larger quantity at lower prices, then the bidder in a first-price auction bids less than he otherwise would, because the larger quantity he sells partly offsets his reduced markup. There is no similar effect in the second-price auction, so prices tend to be lower in the first-price auction.

Positive correlation among bidder types is yet another source of systematic variation, operating through what Milgrom and Weber (1982) called the *linkage principle*. Surprisingly, a bidder with a high type cannot avoid paying a higher average price in a second-price auction by bidding as if his type were lower. Because the second highest bid is positively correlated with his own type, the expected price he pays for any given bid is an increasing function of his type. This direct linkage of the price to the bidder's type raises the prices that higher types pay and reduces their profits in the second-price auction, but not in the first-price auction. Because this linkage effect does not affect the efficiency of the outcome, it raises the average revenue in the second-price auction above that in the first-price auction.

In a later chapter, we illustrate other applications of this principle. We will find, for example, that if the seller has verifiable private information correlated with the bidder's information, then revealing it links the bids to the information revealed, which can also increase prices.[12]

4.3.1 Payoff Equivalence without Revenue Equivalence

Risk Averse Sellers

In the symmetric independent private-values model, although the *expected* payoffs are the same for the first- and second-price auctions, the variability of payoffs differs. In a first-price auction, losers always earn zero and a bidder of type t who wins receives payoff $v(t) - b$. In contrast, in a second-price auction, a bidder of type t who is informed that he has won still faces additional uncertainty: he still does not know what price he will pay.

Two propositions below explore the consequences of the additional risk associated with second-price auctions. We find, first, that the extra risk facing a winning bidder in a second-price auction induces more randomness in the seller's payoff as well. So, if the bidders are risk neutral but the seller is risk averse, then the seller should prefer the first-price auction. Theorem 4.10 below formalizes this intuition.

Let $t^{(1)}$ and $t^{(2)}$ denote the first and second order statistics among $(t^1, \ldots, t^N)$. Then the seller's realized equilibrium revenue is $\beta_{\mathrm{FP}}(t^{(1)}) 1_{\{v(t^{(1)}) \geq r\}}$ in the first-price auction and $\max(r, v(t^{(2)})) 1_{\{v(t^{(1)}) \geq r\}}$ in the second-price auction.

Theorem 4.10. In the benchmark model, for any strictly concave utility function function U,

$$E\big[U\big(\beta_{\mathrm{FP}}\big(t^{(1)}\big) 1_{\{v(t^{(1)}) \geq r\}}\big)\big] \geq E\big[U\big(\max\big(r, v\big(t^{(2)}\big)\big) 1_{\{v(t^{(1)}) \geq r\}}\big)\big].$$

That is, the seller's expected utility is higher in the first-price auction than in the second-price auction.

---

[12] When revealing information affects the allocation of the good(s), then doing so need not benefit the auctioneer. See Perry and Reny (1999) for an example.

Proof. Without loss of generality, we may normalize so that $U(0) = 0$. Then

$$
\begin{aligned}
E\big[U\big(\max(r, v(t^{(2)}))\big)1_{\{v(t^{(1)})\geq r\}}\big] &= E\big[E\big[U\big(\max\big(r, v(t^{(2)})\big)\big)1_{\{v(t^{(1)})\geq r\}}|t^{(1)}\big]\big] \\
&= E\big[E\big[U\big(\max\big(r, v(t^{(2)})\big)\big)|t^{(1)}\big]1_{\{v(t^{(1)})\geq r\}}\big] \\
&\leq E\big[U\big[E\big(\max\big(r, v(t^{(2)})\big)|t^{(1)}\big)\big]1_{\{v(t^{(1)})\geq r\}}\big] \\
&= E\big[U\big(\beta_{\mathrm{FP}}\big(t^{(1)}\big)\big)1_{\{v(t^{(1)})\geq r\}}\big].
\end{aligned}
$$

The first step uses the law of iterated expectations; the second follows because the indicator function is measurable with respect to $t^{(1)}$; the third uses Jensen's inequality[13]; and the last follows from our earlier characterization of the equilibrium bidding strategy (namely, when $v(t^{(1)}) > r$, $\beta_{\mathrm{FP}}(s) = E[\max(r, v(t^{(2)})) \mid t^{(1)} = s]$). ∎

The heart of the proof is the observation that, given $t^{(1)}$, the price in the second-price auction is a random variable with mean $\beta_{\mathrm{FP}}(t^{(1)})$. Consequently, the seller's revenues in a second-price auction have the same mean and greater "riskiness" than in a first-price auction. Accordingly a risk averse seller prefers the first-price auction in the benchmark model.

Risk Averse Bidders

In chapter 3, we found (using a particular symmetric model) that when bidders have constant absolute risk aversion, the first- and second-price auctions generate the same expected payoffs. Conditional on his type (but not on the amounts of the other bids), a winning bidder in a second-price auction faces a price risk. If the bidder is risk averse, his expected utility is therefore less than his value minus the expected price. The payoff equivalence theorem therefore implies that the average price must be less in the second-price auction than in the first-price auction.

This conclusion also holds in models more general than the benchmark. A bidder's risk aversion does not change her dominant strategy in a second-price auction, but it increases her equilibrium bid in a first-price auction. Bidders' risk aversion increases bids in a first-price auction, because raising one's bid slightly in a first-price auction is analogous to buying partial insurance: it reduces the probability of a zero payoff and increases the probability of winning, although with a lower profit

---

[13] Recall that Jensen's inequality states that for any convex function f, $E[f(x)] \geq f(E[x])$.

margin. Risk averse bidders value fairly priced insurance, so they bid more than they would if they were risk neutral.

To compare revenues when bidders are risk averse, we must first characterize the equilibrium bidding strategy β_{FP}^U used by an expected-utility-maximizing bidder in the first-price auction. Once again, the constraint simplification theorem is crucial. Throughout our analysis, we make the normalization that $U(0) = 0$. Then, if the greatest opposing bid has distribution H, a bidder of type t who bids b receives an expected payoff of

$$\Pi(b) = U(v(t) - b)H(b). \tag{4.11}$$

A bidder of type t can plainly restrict attention to bids $b \leq v(t)$ and can equivalently maximize the logarithm of his objective function: $\ln \Pi(b) = \ln(U(v(t) - b)) + \ln H(b)$. Because v is increasing, if $\ln U(\cdot)$ is concave, then Theorem 4.5 implies that $\ln \Pi(b)$ satisfies single crossing differences. Then, the bidder's best reply strategy β to any competing strategies must be a nondecreasing function. By arguments like those in section 4.2.2, the equilibrium bid function must actually be increasing. If the bid function is differentiable and the bids satisfy the first-order optimality conditions, then the envelope condition is necessarily satisfied.[14] So an increasing function satisfying the first-order conditions is indeed an equilibrium.

Theorem 4.11.[15] Suppose $\ln U(\cdot)$ is concave and differentiable and define t^* by $v(t^*) = r$. Then the unique symmetric equilibrium strategy β_{FP}^U of the first-price auction is the solution to the following differential equation with boundary condition $\beta_{FP}^U(t^*) = r$:

$$\frac{N-1}{t\beta_{FP}^{U\prime}(t)} = \frac{U'\left(v(t) - \beta_{FP}^U(t)\right)}{U\left(v(t) - \beta_{FP}^U(t)\right)}. \tag{4.12}$$

Proof. The bidder's problem is to maximize

$$\ln \Pi(b) = \ln(U(v(t) - b)) + \ln H(b).$$

---

[14] To see this, suppose that $f_1(b(t), t) = 0$ and that b is differentiable. Then $\frac{d}{dt} f(b(t), t) = f_1(b(t), t)b'(t) + f_2(b(t), t) = f_2(b(t), t)$, and the integral formula follows by the fundamental theorem of calculus.

[15] Charles Holt, Jr., first proved this result.

The first-order condition is

$$-\frac{U'(v(t) - b)}{U(v(t) - b)} + \frac{1}{H(b)} \cdot \frac{dH(b)}{db} = 0.$$

Suppressing the super- and subscripts of β_{FP}^U and using $H(b) = (\beta^{-1}(b))^{N-1}$, we have

$$\frac{1}{H(b)} \cdot \frac{dH(b)}{db} = \frac{N-1}{t\beta'(t)},$$

so

$$-\frac{U'(v(t) - b)}{U(v(t) - b)} + \frac{N-1}{t\beta'(t)} = 0.$$

By inspection, because U, $U' > 0$ for positive arguments, the solution to (4.12) has a non-negative derivative $\beta_{\mathrm{FP}}^U{}'(t)$ everywhere, so the function β_{FP}^U is increasing. Because we obtained the solution from the first-order condition, the corresponding expected payoffs satisfy the envelope formula. Hence, by the constraint simplification theorem, the solution function β_{FP}^U is a best reply to itself. ∎

The next theorem asserts that in a first-price auction, the equilibrium bid function is higher when bidders are risk averse than when they are risk-neutral. Intuitively, this is a plausible conclusion, because when facing the same distribution of opposing bids, a risk averse bidder always bids more than a risk neutral bidder, and in fact the more risk averse the bidder, the higher the optimal bid. Still, the proof is not immediate, because there are equilibrium effects. Once one bidder adjusts his bids to account for risk aversion, the other bidders' problems change, and all effects need to be traced through to equilibrium. There is a simple technique that we will use repeatedly to show that certain rankings of bids, payoffs or distributions that we find out-of-equilibrium are preserved in equilibrium. To highlight our method, we give the basic tool a name: the *ranking lemma*.

Ranking lemma. Suppose $f : \mathbb{R} \to \mathbb{R}$ is a continuously differentiable function such that $f(\underline{t}) \geq 0$. If (i) for all $t \geq \underline{t}$, $f(t) \leq 0 \Rightarrow f'(t) \geq 0$, then (ii) forall $t \geq \underline{t}$, $f(t) \geq 0$. Similarly, if (i') for all $t \geq \underline{t}$, $f(t) = 0 \Rightarrow f'(t) > 0$, then (ii') for all $t > \underline{t}$, $f(t) > 0$.

Proof. Suppose to the contrary that (i) holds, but for some $t > \underline{t}$ we have $f(t) < 0$. Let $\tilde{t} = \sup\{s \in [\underline{t}, t] | f(s) \geq 0\}$. Then, for all $s \in (\tilde{t}, t]$, $f(s) < 0$ and $f(\tilde{t}) = 0$. By the mean value theorem, there exists $\hat{t} \in (\tilde{t}, t]$ such that $f'(\hat{t}) = f(t)/(t - \hat{t}) < 0$, contrary to condition (ii) of the lemma. So no such t exists. The second conclusion is proved similarly. ∎

Armed with this lemma, we show that, at equilibrium in a first-price auction, risk averse bidders bid more than risk neutral bidders.

Theorem 4.12. Let β_{FP} be the symmetric equilibrium strategy in a first-price auction with reserve r for risk neutral bidders, and let β_{FP}^U be the symmetric equilibrium strategy with a differentiable, strictly concave utility function U. Then for all types $t > t^*$, $\beta_{FP}(t) < \beta_{FP}^U(t)$.

Proof. The boundary condition is $\beta_{FP}(t^*) = \beta_{FP}^U(t^*)$. Because for all $t > t^*$ we have

$$\frac{N-1}{t\beta_{FP}^U(t)} = \frac{U'\left(v(t) - \beta_{FP}^U(t)\right)}{U\left(v(t) - \beta_{FP}^U(t)\right)}$$

and

$$\frac{N-1}{t\beta_{FP}'(t)} = \frac{1}{v(t) - \beta_{FP}(t)},$$

it follows that

$$\frac{\beta_{FP}'(t)}{v(t) - \beta_{FP}(t)} = \frac{N-1}{t} = \frac{\beta_{FP}^U(t) \cdot U'\left(v(t) - \beta_{FP}^U(t)\right)}{U\left(v(t) - \beta_{FP}^U(t)\right)}. \tag{4.13}$$

Because U is strictly concave and $U(0) = 0$, it follows for $x > 0$ that $xU'(x) < U(x)$. Combining that inequality with $x = v(t) - \beta_{FP}^U(t)$ and using (4.13) and $\beta_{FP}^U(t) > 0$, we have

$$\frac{\beta_{FP}'(t)}{v(t) - \beta_{FP}(t)} = \beta_{FP}^U(t) \frac{U'\left(v(t) - \beta_{FP}^U(t)\right)}{U\left(v(t) - \beta_{FP}^U(t)\right)} < \frac{\beta_{FP}^U(t)}{v(t) - \beta_{FP}^U(t)}.$$

Hence, for all $t > 0$, $\beta_{FP}(t) > \beta_{FP}^U(t) \Rightarrow \beta_{FP}'(t) < \beta_{FP}^{U'}(t)$, and applying the ranking lemma to the function $\beta_{FP}^U(t) - \beta_{FP}(t)$, we conclude that $\beta_{FP}(t) < \beta_{FP}^U(t)$ for all $t > t^*$. ∎

Jump Bids in Auctions with Costly Bidding

We next study a model in which each bidder's cost of participating in an auction includes the cost of his time. This model is a simplified version of one presented by Avery (1998), who argues that time costs are plausibly important in many kinds of ascending auctions.

To allow for time costs, we expand our description of the outcome of an auction to include the identity of the winner, the price, and the amount of time that each bidder is active. Although the second-price and ascending auctions are strategically equivalent in models where only the winner's identity and the price matter, they are not strategically equivalent here, because the payoffs differ: the ascending auction requires bidders to spend a positive amount of time bidding, whereas the second-price auction has zero duration.

Suppose the auctioneer raises the bids continuously in time. Bidders can drop out of the auction at any time, but that decision is irreversible. Suppose that bidders receive no information about others' bids before the end of the auction. Then one can describe a strategy by a number, or bid, designating the highest price at which the bidder will remain active. As in the second-price auction, the highest bid determines the winner, and the second highest bid determines the price. We select units so that prices rise by one money unit per unit of time. Bidders incur a cost of c per unit of time while they are active.

The point of our model will be to explore the tactic of *jump bidding* to intimidate other bidders. A bidder may open with a high bid to make competitors think: "That guy is determined to bid high. There is no point wasting valuable time participating in this auction, for I'll likely lose. I'll drop out now."

In the equilibrium studied below a high opening bid of B will indeed intimidate certain bidders who would otherwise have bid more than B. Moreover, in equilibrium, bidders who make jump bids benefit both by shortening the auction and, sometimes, by getting a lower price. Jump bidding increases a bidder's payoff in relation to its payoff if it does not jump, but it doesn't follow that allowing jump bidding benefits bidders at the expense of the seller. We will find that, to the contrary, *the seller benefits on average from the jump bids* – obtaining higher expected equilibrium revenues.

Payoff equivalence provides valuable intuition about the effect of jump bidding on revenues. In this model, the highest type bidder still wins. So, applying the envelope theorem, the level of bidding costs c

does not affect the equilibrium expected profits of any type of bidder, regardless of whether there is jump bidding. In equilibrium, the jumps reduce the average duration of the auction, so the total expected surplus is higher. Because the seller's revenue is equal to that total surplus minus bidder profits, it is the seller who benefits on average from jump bidding.

Consider a bidder of type t who chooses a strategy (or "bid") b that wins with probability $p(b)$, results in expected participation time of $\tau(b)$ as an active bidder, and generates an expected payment of $\pi(b)$. Note well that the "bid" in this formula is not a number, but a plan for bidding in the auction. Then, the auction yields an expected profit of $v(t)p(b) - c\tau(b) - \pi(b)$, so if the optimal strategy is b^*, then the envelope formula asserts that $V(t) - V(0) = \int_0^t p(b^*(s))v'(s)\,ds$. In this formula, expected profits depend in the usual way on the probability of winning, but they do not depend on the time cost c. If the highest type bidder always wins, then the envelope formula prescribes that the equilibrium profits are independent of the bidding costs c and the same as in a second-price auction (for which time costs are zero). This observation enables us to guess the equilibrium strategy.

We first analyze an ascending auction in which jump bidding is not permitted. Suppose the game has a strictly increasing symmetric equilibrium bid function β_c. Then, by direct calculation, the expected payoff of a bidder of type t must be

$$V(t) = v(t)t^{N-1} - c\left(\int_0^t \beta_c(s)\,ds^{N-1} + \beta_c(t)(1 - t^{N-1})\right)$$
$$- \int_0^t \beta_c(s)\,ds^{N-1}. \tag{4.14}$$

This formula expresses the bidder's maximal payoff as the expected value received minus the time costs incurred (whether the bidder wins or loses) and minus the expected payments made. As argued above, this payoff must be the same as the expected payoff in a second-price auction without any time cost, which is

$$V(t) = \int_0^t v'(s)s^{N-1}\,ds = v(t)t^{N-1} - \int_0^t v(s)\,ds^{N-1}. \tag{4.15}$$

Equating the right-hand sides of (4.14) and (4.15) and differentiating with respect to t leads to the differential equation $v(t) - \beta_c(t) =$

$\frac{1}{N-1} c t^{2-N}(1 - t^{N-1}) \beta_c'(t)$. We solve this differential equation to identify the equilibrium.

Theorem 4.13. Suppose that $0 < v(0)$ and $0 < v'(0)$. In the symmetric ascending auction model with no jump bidding allowed and a zero reserve price, there is a symmetric equilibrium strategy satisfying

$$\beta_c(0) = 0 \quad \text{and} \quad \beta_c'(t) = (N - 1) \frac{v(t) - \beta_c(t)}{c} \frac{t^{N-2}}{1 - t^{N-1}}. \tag{4.16}$$

Proof. Because p is increasing in b, the expected payoff function $v(t) p(b) - c\tau(b) - \pi(b)$ has increasing differences as a function of (b, t). The solution has $\beta_c'(t) > 0$, so the proposed strategy is increasing. By construction, the solution satisfies the first-order condition, and so it satisfies the envelope formula. Hence, by the sufficiency theorem, there are no profitable deviations from this strategy to bids in the range of β_c. No bids below the range of the equilibrium strategy are possible, and bids above the range lead to the same payoff as $\beta_c(1)$. ∎

Equation (4.16) implies that if $v(0) > 0$, then $\beta_c(t) < v(t)$ for all $t < 1$. Without time costs, bidders would bid up to $v(t)$. So, at equilibrium, bidders bid uniformly less in the ascending auction with time costs than in the corresponding auction without them. Consequently, revenues are uniformly lower than in the sealed-bid second-price auction. Although we used the *payoff* equivalence relationship to guess the equilibrium strategy, the *revenue* equivalence theorem does not apply.

According to (4.16), $\beta_c(0) = 0$, and if $N > 2$ then $\beta_c'(0) = 0$ as well, even though $v(0) > 0$. Thus, low type bidders bid much less than their values. This contrasts sharply with the equilibrium bidding strategies for the benchmark case with $c = 0$, for in that case even low type bidders bid all the way up to their values. Intuitively, when $c > 0$ and $N > 2$, bidders with very low types find the probability of winning to be so small that any substantially positive bid earns negative expected profits. As costs go from zero to something positive, the equilibrium strategies change discontinuously.

If bidders can make jump bids, the equilibrium analysis changes. In addition to intimidating other bidders, bidders can avoid some time costs by jump bidding. Against these advantages, bidders must weigh the disadvantage that a jump bid can jump over the maximum price anyone else would have been willing to pay, leading the bidder to pay too much for the item.

What might an equilibrium with jump bidding look like? In our simple model, we allow bidders at the opening of the auction to jump to some specified number B. The auctioneer tells everyone when someone has jumped to B, but provides no further information.

Under these assumptions, each bidder must make four decisions. First, will this bidder jump at the opening bid? Second, if the bidder does jump, how high (b_1) should he continue to bid after the jump before dropping out? Third, if nobody jumps, how high (b_2) should the bidder continue before dropping out? Fourth, if the bidder does not jump but the auctioneer announces that someone has jumped, how high (b_3) should he continue before dropping out? A bidder's plans for situations that will not arise under its planned strategy are irrelevant. So, limiting attention to *reduced strategies*, we may specify that if the bidder plans not to jump, then $b_1 = 0$, and otherwise $b_2 = b_3 = 0$. Let us say that a *bid* for any given type in this game is the triple $b = (b_1, b_2, b_3)$, and a strategy is a triple $\beta = (\beta_1, \beta_2, \beta_3)$ mapping types into bids.

The symmetric equilibrium strategy is characterized in Theorem 4.14 below. We derive it here using the envelope formula and an analysis of boundary conditions. We look for a symmetric equilibrium in which (i) bidders jump exactly when their types exceed some cutoff $\hat{t}$ and (ii) the winner is always the bidder with the highest type.

We begin by examining equilibrium bidding for $t < \hat{t}$. At equilibrium, bidder payoffs for types in this range must satisfy the following equation:

$$V(t) = v(t)t^{N-1} - c\left(\int_0^t \beta_2(s)\,ds^{N-1} + \beta_2(t)(\hat{t}^{N-1} - t^{N-1})\right)$$
$$-\int_0^t \beta_2(s)\,ds^{N-1}. \tag{4.17}$$

Equation (4.17) is similar to (4.14). The difference reflects the fact that in a model with jump bidding, if some bidder has a type greater than $\hat{t}$, then that bidder jumps at the outset of the auction and bidders with types less than $\hat{t}$ drop out and do avoid any bidding costs.

We can characterize the bidding strategy for types $t < \hat{t}$ by equating the envelope expression for $V(t)$ in (4.15) with the expression in (4.17) and differentiating with respect to t. This leads to a differential equation, which we report as (4.19) in the theorem.

For bidders with $t > \hat{t}$, we use a similar method. The relevant payoff formula is

$$V(t) = v(t)t^{N-1} - c\left(\int_{\hat{t}}^{t} (\beta_1(s) - B) \, ds^{N-1} + (\beta_1(t) - B)(1 - t^{N-1})\right)$$

$$-B\hat{t}^{N-1} - \int_{\hat{t}}^{t} \beta_1(s) \, ds^{N-1}. \tag{4.18}$$

The first term in (4.18) is the value of the item when the bidder wins. The second is the time cost incurred. After a jump to B, bidders incur time costs to the extent they bid above B. The last two terms correspond to cash payments. The winning bidder after a jump pays B if nobody else jumps, and otherwise pays the second highest bid.

We can characterize the bidding strategy for types $t > \hat{t}$ by equating expressions (4.15) and (4.18) and differentiating with respect to t. This again leads to the differential equation, which we report as (4.20) in the theorem below.

The last piece is to determine the smallest type $\hat{t}$ that jumps. At equilibrium, if bidders jump exactly when their types are above $\hat{t}$, then a bidder of type $\hat{t}$ who does not jump expects to win when no competitor jumps, and his expected payment is the amount expressed on the right-hand side of (4.21). Thus, condition (4.21) requires that any bidder's expected payment be exactly the same whether he bids up to $\beta_2(\hat{t})$ without jumping or jumps but drops out immediately in case someone else jumps as well.

Theorem 4.14. In the symmetric ascending auction model with jump bidding to B allowed and a zero reserve price, there is a symmetric equilibrium strategy β. At this equilibrium, there is a type $\hat{t}$ such that all types $t \le \hat{t}$ refrain from jumping, and they drop out if anyone else jumps ($\beta_1(t) = \beta_3(t) = 0$). At equilibrium, $\beta_2(t)$ satisfies

$$\beta_2(0) = 0 \quad \text{and} \quad \beta_2'(t) = (N-1)\frac{v(t) - \beta_2(t)}{c}\frac{t^{N-2}}{\hat{t}^{N-1} - t^{N-1}}. \tag{4.19}$$

Types $t > \hat{t}$ do jump (hence $\beta_2(t) = \beta_3(t) = 0$), and β_1 satisfies

$$\beta_1(\hat{t}) = B \quad \text{and} \quad \beta_1'(t) = (N-1)\frac{v(t) - \beta_1(t)}{c}\frac{t^{N-2}}{1 - t^{N-1}}. \tag{4.20}$$

The type $\hat{t}$ satisfies

$$B\hat{t}^{N-1} = (1+c)\int_0^{\hat{t}} \beta_2(s)\, ds^{N-1}. \tag{4.21}$$

At equilibrium,

$$\beta_2(\hat{t}) = v(\hat{t}) > B. \tag{4.22}$$

Remarks. Jump bidding successfully intimidates bidders in the identified equilibrium; that is, competitors who do not jump themselves all drop out immediately after a jump. According to (4.22), the intimidated bidder types include ones that, but for the jump, would have been prepared to bid strictly more than B.

Proof. By construction, the strategies satisfy the envelope derivative formula for all types except possibly $\hat{t}$, and by (4.21) the payoff function is continuous at $\hat{t}$. Hence, the envelope integral formula holds everywhere. Also by construction, higher types win with higher probabilities, and the payoffs satisfy the increasing differences property. So, by the sufficiency theorem, there is no profitable deviation within the range of the equilibrium strategy. By inspection, there is also no profitable deviation for any type outside the range of the proposed strategy, so the strategy is an equilibrium strategy.

For all $\tilde{t} \in [0, \hat{t}]$, we have

$$\beta_2(\hat{t}) - \beta_2(\tilde{t}) = \int_{\tilde{t}}^{\hat{t}} \beta_2'(s)\, ds$$

$$\geq \frac{N-1}{c} \min_{t\in[\tilde{t},\hat{t}]} [v(t) - \beta_2(t)] \int_{\tilde{t}}^{\hat{t}} \frac{s^{N-2}}{\hat{t}^{N-1} - s^{N-1}}\, ds$$

$$= \frac{N-1}{c} \min_{t\in[\tilde{t},\hat{t}]} [v(t) - \beta_2(t)] \cdot \infty.$$

This implies that for all $\tilde{t}$, the minimum term is zero. Hence, by continuity, $v(\hat{t}) - \beta_2(\hat{t}) = 0$.

By the envelope formula, the expected profit of type $\hat{t}$ is positive, so $B < v(\hat{t})$. ∎

Theorem 4.15. In the equilibrium with jump bidding determined by (4.19)–(4.21), every type of every bidder earns the same profit as in the equilibrium without jump bidding determined by (4.16), and bidders with types less than $\hat{t}$ incur lower time costs in the auction with jump bidding.

Proof. By Myerson's lemma, because $V(0) = 0$ in both auctions and the decision performance is the same, the expected payoff of each bidder type is identical for the two auctions.

For $t \leq \hat{t}$, comparing (4.16) and (4.19), either $\beta_2(t) > \beta_c(t)$ or $\beta_2'(t) > \beta_c'(t)$. Because $\beta_c(0) = \beta_2(0) = 0$, applying the ranking lemma to the function $\beta_2(t) - \beta_c(t)$, it follows that $\beta_2(t) > \beta_c(t)$ for all types $t \in (0, \hat{t}]$. Because the sum of expected payments and time costs of the bidders is the same in the two auctions but the bidders expect to pay more in the auction with jump bidding when $t \leq \hat{t}$, their expected time costs must be less in that auction than in the auction without jump bidding. ∎

Curiously, although bidders with types greater than $\hat{t}$ may save significant amounts of time by jump bidding, no general theorem proves that, in equilibrium, they always save time in this way.

4.3.2 Budget Constraints

Following Che and Gale (1998), we modify the benchmark model by assuming that each bidder has a limited budget and can never pay more than a fixed sum B. To simplify the exposition, we assume that v is strictly increasing and that there exist types t_r and t_B such that $v(t_r) = r$ and $v(t_B) = B$. This change hardly affects our analysis of bidding in the Vickrey auction. Bidders still have a dominant strategy, which is to bid $\min(B, v(t))$ – the lesser of the actual value and the available budget. The argument is similar to the one for a model without budget constraints.

We previously argued that in a first-price auction, ties cannot occur at equilibrium between bidders with values above r, because each bidder would have an incentive to increase his bid very slightly. In that way, he would incur an arbitrarily small cost while discretely increasing his chances of winning profitably, and such a possible deviation is inconsistent with Nash equilibrium. The same argument still holds for prices below the budget limit B. However, ties can occur at B, because increases in bids above B are infeasible. We infer that the symmetric equilibrium bid function, if one exists, must be strictly increasing on the domain of types for which $v(t) > r$ up to the lowest type t_F that bids B.

Applying the envelope formula as before, we conclude that the equilibrium payoffs for types less than t_F must coincide with their payoffs in the unconstrained first-price auction, so the bid functions must coincide as well. Because all higher types will bid B, such a bid must occur with positive probability. Therefore, the equilibrium bid function must jump at the argument t_F; otherwise any bidder with a slightly lower type than t_F would bid B instead, because doing so wins the auction with a discretely higher probability but incurs only a slightly higher cost.

We can identify the lowest type t_F that bids B by equating its expected profit from bidding B to that specified by the envelope formula. As previously noted, there is no loss of generality in assuming that F is the uniform distribution on $[0, 1]$, so $F^{N-1}(s) = s^{N-1}$. We maintain that assumption in these calculations:

$$\int_{t_r}^{t_F} s^{N-1} v'(s)\, ds = (v(t_F) - B)\, P(t_F), \tag{4.23}$$

where

$$P(t_F) = \sum_{k=0}^{N-1} C(N-1, k) t_F^{N-1-k} (1 - t_F)^k (1 + k)^{-1}. \tag{4.24}$$

The left-hand side of (4.23) is the bidder's expected profit according to the envelope theorem. The right-hand side is the expected profit from bidding B, obtained by multiplying the winner's profit $v(t_F) - B$ by the probability of winning $P(t_F)$, as given by (4.24).

To derive (4.24), note first that when the bidder ties with k other bidders, he wins with probability $(1 + k)^{-1}$. Hence, the probability $P(t_F)$ is equal to the sum over k of the probability of a tie involving k other bidders at bid B times $(1 + k)^{-1}$. In expression (4.24) $C(N, k)$ denotes $N!/(k!(N-k)!)$.

Theorem 4.16. There is at most a single solution t_F to (4.23). When a solution exists, it corresponds to the unique budget-constrained symmetric equilibrium of the auction, which is given by

$$\beta_{FB}(t) = \begin{cases} \beta_{FP}(t) & \text{if } t \le t_F, \\ B & \text{if } t > t_F. \end{cases} \tag{4.25}$$

Proof. Observe that the derivative of the left-hand side of (4.23) with respect to t_F is $t_F^{N-1}v'(t_F)$, and that of the right-hand side is $P(t_F)v'(t_F) + (v(t_F) - B)\, P'(t_F)$. The first term of the derivative of the right-hand side is larger than the derivative of the left-hand side,[16] and the second term of the derivative of the right-hand side is positive. Hence, viewing the left- and right-hand sides of (4.23) as functions of t_F, the slope of the left-hand side is always less than that of the right-hand side. So there is at most one solution to (4.23). By the arguments in the text preceding the theorem, if a symmetric equilibrium strategy exists, it must satisfy (4.25).

By the constraint simplification theorem, no type can strictly profit by deviating to any bid in the range of β_{FB}. The only feasible bids not in that range are the bids $b \in (\beta_{FP}(t_F), B)$. Given the equilibrium hypothesis that the other players adopt the strategy β_{FB}, bidding $\beta_{FP}(t_F)$ wins against precisely the same type vectors as any such bid b and reduces the bidder's price conditional on winning, so no such bid can be a strict improvement. Hence, the strategy β_{FB} is a symmetric equilibrium strategy. ∎

The theorem covers the case in which a solution to (4.23) exists. It can fail to exist in two ways. One possibility is that the left-hand side of (4.23) is larger than the right-hand side for all values of t_F. In that case, one can identify the equilibrium by setting $t_F = 1$ in (4.25): the budget constraint does not bind. The second possibility is that left-hand side is smaller than the right for all values of t_F. In that case, one can identify the equilibrium by setting $t_F = 0$ in (4.25): all bids are B, and the auction allocation is entirely random.

The next theorem compares the effects of the budget constraint on the performance of the two kinds of auctions.

Theorem 4.17. The expected revenue from the first-price auction with reserve r and budget constraint B is greater than that of the corresponding Vickrey auction. The first-price auction yields the same decision performance and expected revenue as a Vickrey auction with reserve r and budget $v(t_F) > B$.

Proof. By the preceding theorem, the first-price auction with budget constraint B and where t_F is the lowest type that bids B generates the

---

[16] $P(t_F)$ is a sum of positive terms, including the term t_F^{N-1}.

following allocation performance: (i) no award if the highest type has $v(t^{(1)}) < r$, (ii) type $t^{(1)}$ wins if $t^{(1)} \le t_F$ and $v(t^{(1)}) > r$, (iii) a random award among bidders of types greater than t_F if $t^{(1)} > t_F$. This performance is precisely the same as in the Vickrey auction with budget constraint $v(t_F) > v(t_B) = B$. Therefore, Myerson's lemma implies that the two auctions have the same expected payments. The allocation performance differs from that of the Vickrey auction with budget constraint B, where the lowest type to bid B is $t_B < t_F$. Clearly, a Vickrey auction with a lower budget constraint produces lower expected revenue. ∎

The intuition behind the proof is that the likelihood of high payments varies among auction designs, so the designs vary in how much budgets constrain bidders. The highest payment made by any type in the first-price auction is less than that in the second-price auction, because high-value bidders always pay less than their values in a first-price auction. This suggests that budget constraints are less likely to bind in a first-price auction. The theorem proves a stronger statement – that the first-price auction duplicates the allocation of a second-price auction with a higher budget limit. Therefore, in particular, it generates more revenue than a second-price auction with the same budget limit.

4.3.3 Endogenous Quantities

When buyers conduct auctions, the quantities they buy often depend on the price they pay. For example, consider a large company trying to procure hotel rooms for its traveling management team in a particular city. Each hotel offers a price per room to the large company in a competitive auction. Once the company receives the bids, individual travelers decide how frequently to travel and whether to use the company travel service to reserve rooms. Thus, the number of hotel-room–nights sold will depend both on the winning bidder and on the winning bid. Hansen (1988) has shown that this endogenous quantity choice has effects on bidding incentives similar to those of risk aversion. That is, endogeneity of the quantity traded reduces bids in a first-price auction without changing incentives in the second-price auction.

To facilitate comparisons with earlier results, we continue to assume that bidders are buyers, but now we assume that buyers have a per unit value $v(t)$ and are happy to buy multiple units, while the seller supplies a number of units, $S(p)$, that increases with its price p. Clearly, in this case, the incentives in a second-price auction are just the same as when $S \equiv 1$.

Arguments that by now are familiar imply that in analyzing the first-price auction we can restrict attention to strictly increasing bid functions. The equilibrium bidding function $\beta = \beta_{FP}^{ES}$ must solve

$$\beta(t) \in \arg\max_{b}(v(t) - b)(\beta^{-1}(b))^{N-1}S(b), \qquad (4.26)$$

where $v(t) - b$ is the "profit" margin on each unit, $(\beta^{-1}(b))^{N-1}$ is the probability of winning, and $S(b)$ is the *supply* function stipulating the quantity supplied by the seller given bid b.

Theorem 4.18. Suppose S is increasing and differentiable, log $S(b)$ is concave, and $v'(0) > 0$. Define t^* by $v(t^*) = r$. Then, the unique symmetric equilibrium strategy $\beta = \beta_{FP}^{ES}$ of the first price auction with endogenous supply function S solves the following differential equation with boundary condition $\beta(t^*) = r$:

$$\frac{N-1}{t\beta'(t)} = \frac{1}{v(t) - \beta(t)} - \frac{S'(\beta(t))}{S(\beta(t))}. \qquad (4.27)$$

Proof. Taking the logarithm of the objective (4.26) and then evaluating the first-order optimality condition at $b = \beta(t)$ leads to (4.27). Using (4.27), $\beta(t^*) = r$, and the concavity of log $S(b)$, the bid function $\beta(t)$ is nondecreasing.[17] By the usual argument, $\beta(t)$ is the unique candidate for a symmetric equilibrium. Furthermore, by construction, the equilibrium bid satisfies the first-order conditions and hence the envelope integral formula. By the constraint simplification theorem, β is a symmetric equilibrium strategy. ∎

---

[17] By inspection, $\beta'(t^*) = 0$. We show that there can be no interval $(\underline{t}, \overline{t}) \subset [t^*, 1]$ such that $\beta'(\underline{t}) = 0$ and for all $t' \in (\underline{t}, \overline{t})$, $\beta'(t') < 0$. If there were such an interval, then $\beta'(t) = \int_{\underline{t}}^{t} \beta''(s) \, ds < 0$ for all $t \in (\underline{t}, \overline{t})$. Then, setting $\hat{S} = \log S$, differentiating both sides of (4.27) and multiplying by -1, we would have

$$\frac{(N-1)(\beta'(t) + t\beta''(t))}{(t\beta'(t))^2} = \frac{v'(t) - \beta'(t)}{(v(t) - \beta(t))^2} + \beta'(t)\hat{S}''(\beta(t)).$$

Because $\beta'(t) < 0$ and $\hat{S}$ is concave, the right-hand side of this equation is positive. For the left-hand-side to be also positive, we must have $\beta''(t) > 0$ for all $t \in (\underline{t}, \overline{t})$, which contradicts $\beta'(t) = \int_{\underline{t}}^{t} \beta''(s) \, ds < 0$.

Theorem 4.19. Suppose S is increasing and differentiable, log $S(b)$ is concave, and $v'(0) > 0$. Define t^* by $v(t^*) = r$. Let β_{FP} and β_{FP}^{ES} be the equilibrium bid functions in a first-price auction with reserve r for exogenous supply ($S' = 0$) and endogenous supply $S'_{ES} > 0$ respectively. Then, for all types $t > t^*$, $\beta_{FP}(t) < \beta_{FP}^{ES}(t)$. In other words, bidders bid more when supply is responsive to the price.

Proof. By (4.27), if $\beta_{FP}(t) > \beta_{FP}^{ES}(t)$ then $\beta'_{FP}(t) < \beta_{FP}^{ES'}(t)$. Given the boundary condition $\beta_{FP}(t^*) = \beta_{FP}^{ES}(t^*)$, the conclusion follows from the ranking lemma, applied to the function $\beta_{FP}^{ES}(t) - \beta_{FP}(t)$. ∎

In this model, because equilibrium for the second-price auction does not depend on the supply function, the expected price for the second-price auction is $\beta_{FP}(t)$ when the winner's type is t. Hence, with endogenous supply, first-price auctions lead to higher average prices.

4.3.4 Correlated Types

When real bidders participate in an auction, they sometimes use their own values as initial estimates of other bidders' values. For this procedure to make sense, types must enjoy a positive statistical association rather than being independent as we have previously assumed. Here, we treat the model of correlated types introduced by Milgrom and Weber (1982).

When types are correlated, the problem of choosing an expected-profit-maximizing bid (ignoring ties) becomes

$$\max_b (v^i(t^i) - b) F_B(b|t^i), \tag{4.28}$$

in which F_B is the conditional probability distribution of the highest opposing bid given the bidder's type.

The bidder's problem in this model differs from that of other models in that the probability that a bid b wins depends jointly on the bid and the bidder's type rather than on the bid alone. We may limit attention to bids $b < v^i(t^i)$, as higher bids would be unprofitable. Taking logarithms, the problem becomes

$$\max_b [\ln(v^i(t^i) - b) + \ln F_B(b|t^i)]. \tag{4.29}$$

If v^i is increasing, the first term satisfies the condition of increasing differences and therefore smooth single crossing differences. If the bid induces a positive value of F_B and if the second term also has increasing differences, then the entire objective has the strict single crossing differences property.

In a symmetric two-bidder model, if there is a symmetric, increasing equilibrium strategy β, then $\ln F_B(\beta(t^j)|t^i) = \ln F(t^j|t^i)$, where the unsubscripted F denotes the joint distribution of the bidders' types. It follows by a routine calculation that if $\ln F(t^j|t^i)$ has increasing differences, then so does $\ln F_B(b|t^i)$.

Theorem 4.20. In the two-bidder symmetric model with dependent types, suppose that $\ln F(t^j|t^i)$ is continuously differentiable and has increasing differences and $v'(0) > 0$. Then the unique symmetric increasing equilibrium bid function β_{FP} satisfies $\beta_{FP}(0) = v(0)$ and

$$\frac{1}{\beta'_{FP}(t)} \frac{f(t|t)}{F(t|t)} = \frac{1}{v(t) - \beta_{FP}(t)}. \tag{4.30}$$

Proof. The bidder's optimization problem is

$$\max_b [\ln(v(t) - b) + \ln F(\beta^{-1}(b)|t)],$$

which yields the first-order condition

$$\frac{-1}{v(t) - b} + \frac{f(\beta^{-1}(b)|t)}{F(\beta^{-1}(b)|t)} \cdot \frac{d}{db}\beta^{-1}(b) = 0$$

and therefore (4.30), because $\beta^{-1}(b) = t$. As $\beta_{FP}(t)$ satisfies the first-order optimality condition, it must satisfy the envelope condition. Both $f(t|t)$ and $F(t|t)$ are positive by assumption, and at any solution to (4.30) we have $v(t) - \beta_{FP}(t) > 0$ for all $t > 0$. Then, by inspection of (4.30), $\beta'_{FP}(t) > 0$ for $t > 0$. Hence, by the constraint simplification theorem, β_{FP} is a best reply, and therefore a Nash equilibrium. Note, trivially, that no bids outside the range of $\beta_{FP}(t)$ can pay more for any types than some bid in the range.

Moreover, every Nash equilibrium bidding strategy must, for the usual reasons (see Section 4.2.2), be continuous, increasing, and differentiable, so it must satisfy (4.30) by the definition of best response and $\beta(0) = v(0)$. The bid function is unique, for no ties are allowed and no other boundary conditions are possible. ∎

Next, we compare the expected profits and revenues for the first- and second-price auctions. The key to our analysis is that the expected price paid by the winning bidder in the second-price auction increases in the bidder's type, even holding his bid fixed. This happens in our model because of the assumed positive correlation between bidder types.[18] Because there is no such effect in the first-price auction, bidder profits increase faster as a function of type in that auction, generating different payoffs in the two auctions.

We begin by proving that a bidder's expected payment in the second-price auction increases in his type, even holding his bid fixed.

Lemma. Suppose $\ln F$ has increasing differences. Then (1) $F(s|t)$ is nonincreasing in its second argument and (2) the function $\bar{p}(s|t) = E[v(t^j)|t^j < s, t^i = t]$ is nondecreasing in its second argument.

Proof. Because $\ln F$ has increasing differences, for any $t > \hat{t}$ we have $-\ln F(s|\hat{t}) = \ln F(1|\hat{t}) - \ln F(s|\hat{t}) \leq \ln F(1|t) - \ln F(s|t) = -\ln F(s|t)$. Hence, $F(s|t) \leq F(s|\hat{t})$. Because s is arbitrary, the distribution $F(\cdot|t)$ first-order stochastically dominates $F(\cdot|\hat{t})$, that is, for all s, $F(s|t) \leq F(s|\hat{t})$, which proves (1). Therefore, because v is increasing, $\bar{p}$ is increasing in its second argument. ∎

Theorem 4.21. In the two-bidder symmetric model with dependent types, suppose that $\ln F(t^j|t^i)$ is continuously differentiable and has increasing differences, that is, $\partial^2 \ln F(x|y)/\partial x\, \partial y \geq 0$. Then the expected payoff for each type of bidder is less in a second-price auction than in the first-price auction.

Proof. A bidder's expected payoff in the second-price auction when it bids $v(s)$ is $(v(t) - \bar{p}(s|t)) F(s|t)$, which is its value $v(t)$ minus the price it expects to pay $\bar{p}(s|t)$, conditional on bidding $v(s)$ when its type is t, times the conditional probability $F(s|t)$ that the opposing type is less than s. Let us imagine that the bidder optimizes by choosing s, and set $V_{SP}(t) = \max_s (v(t) - \bar{p}(s|t)) F(s|t)$; this is the bidder's equilibrium payoff. The maximum occurs at $s = t$. Therefore, by the envelope theorem, $V'_{SP}(t) = (v'(t) - \bar{p}_2(t|t))F(t|t) + (v(t) - \bar{p}(t|t))F_2(t|t)$. Substituting $\bar{p}(t|t) = v(t) - V_{SP}(t)/F(t|t)$ leads to

$$V'_{SP}(t) = \left(v'(t) - \bar{p}_2(t|t)\right) F(t|t) + \frac{V_{SP}(t)}{F(t|t)} F_2(t|t). \tag{4.31}$$

---

[18] More precisely, types must be positively correlated conditional on lying in any product set. This *affiliation* condition is explored and exploited in chapter 5.

Arguing similarly for the first-price auction using $V_{FP}(t) = \max_s (v(t) - \beta(s)) F(s|t)$ leads to

$$V'_{FP}(t) = v'(t) F(t|t) + \frac{V_{FP}(t)}{F(t|t)} F_2(t|t). \tag{4.32}$$

Also, $V_{FP}(0) = V_{SP}(0) = 0$. Note that $F_2(t|t) \leq 0$, by the lemma. Hence, from (4.31) and (4.32), at every point t, if $V_{FP}(t) < V_{SP}(t)$ then $V'_{FP}(t) \geq V'_{SP}(t)$. It then follows from the ranking lemma applied to $V_{FP}(t) - V_{SP}(t)$ that $V_{FP}(t) \geq V_{SP}(t)$ for all $t \geq 0$. ∎

When there are more than two bidders, a similar analysis is possible. In that analysis, we replace the requirement that $\ln F(t^j|t^i)$ have increasing differences with a similar condition on the joint cumulative distribution $\bar{F}$ of i's type and the highest type among the $N - 1$ other bidders. See chapter 5 for a more complete development.

4.4 Expected-Revenue-Maximizing Auctions

Among the most famous results in auction theory is the Myerson's theorem about auctions that maximize the seller's expected revenues. Although the original analyses assumed bidders' types were their valuations, we can present the results more intuitively using the distributional strategies discussed in section 4.2.

We assume that each bidder's type t^i is uniformly distributed on $[0, 1]$ and that the value of an item to bidder i is an increasing, differentiable function $v^i(t^i)$. Using formula (4.5), bidder i's *ex ante* expected payoff from the auction is therefore

$$E[V^i(t^i)] = V^i(0) + \int_0^1 \int_0^t \frac{d}{ds} v^i(s) x^i(s) \, ds \, dt$$

$$= V^i(0) + \int_0^1 \int_s^1 dt \frac{d}{ds} v^i(s) x^i(s) \, ds$$

$$= V^i(0) + \int_0^1 (1 - s) \frac{d}{ds} v^i(s) x^i(s) \, ds. \tag{4.33}$$

Before formulating the seller's problem, we first consider the constraints, that is, what decision performance is feasible in this setting. We then derive a formula for the seller's payoff and conveniently express it in terms of mechanism performance. To determine what performance we can implement, we revert to mechanism design notation similar to that in chapter 2, writing i's payoff function as u^i, the performance function (combining allocations and transfers) as z, and the type space as Θ^i instead of $[0, 1]$.

Definition. The performance function z is (*Bayesian*) *incentive-compatible* if and only if for all $\hat{t}^i \in \Theta^i$,

$$E[u^i(z(t^i, t^{-i}), t^i)|t^i] \geq E[u^i(z(\hat{t}^i, t^{-i}), t^i)|t^i].$$

The definition states that a performance function is incentive-compatible if, when participant i's type is t^i, the participant never strictly prefers that the mechanism choose an outcome as if i's type were actually $\hat{t}^i$. The significance of incentive compatibility lies in the *revelation principle*.

Revelation Principle for Bayes–Nash Equilibrium. The Bayes–Nash equilibrium σ of an augmented mechanism (S, ω, σ) achieves performance z if and only if the performance function is incentive-compatible.

Proof. If z is not incentive-compatible, then for some $t^i, \hat{t}^i$,

$$E[u^i(\omega(\sigma^i(t^i), \sigma^{-i}(t^{-i})), t^i)|t^i] = E[u^i(z(t^i, t^{-i}), t^i)|t^i]$$
$$< E[u^i(z(\hat{t}^i, t^{-i}), t^i)|t^i] = E[u^i(\omega(\sigma^i(\hat{t}^i), \sigma^{-i}(t^{-i})), t^i)|t^i],$$

so the player of type t^i strictly prefers to deviate from $\sigma^i(t^i)$ to $\sigma^i(\hat{t}^i)$, contradicting the assumption that σ is a Bayes–Nash equilibrium. In other words, given the players' true types, performance z can be achieved if and only if the performance function is incentive-compatible so all players report their types truthfully.

Conversely, if z is incentive-compatible, then, by inspection, the strategies $\sigma^i(t^i) = t^i$ constitute a Bayes–Nash equilibrium of the direct mechanism. ∎

We now formulate the seller's revenue maximization problem. Notice first that the total *ex ante* joint payoff to buyer i and the seller from sales to buyer i is

$$TV^i = \int_0^1 v^i(t) x^i(t) \, dt, \tag{4.34}$$

so the seller's expected revenue from such sales is

$$E[p^i(t^i)] = TV^i - E[V^i(t^i)]$$

$$= \int_0^1 v^i(t)x^i(t)\,dt - V^i(0) - \int_0^1 (1-s)\frac{dv^i}{ds}x^i(s)\,ds$$

$$= -V^i(0) + \int_0^1 \left(v^i(s) - (1-s)\frac{dv^i}{ds}\right)x^i(s)\,ds. \qquad (4.35)$$

The seller's problem is therefore

$$\max_{x,p} E\left[\sum_{i=1}^N p^i(t^i)\right]$$

subject to

(PC) $V^i(t^i) \geq 0$ for all $i, t^i,$

(IC) $v^i(t^i)E[x^i(t^i, t^{-i})|t^i] - p^i(t^i)$ \hfill (4.36)

$\qquad \geq v^i(t^i)E[x^i(\hat{t}^i, t^{-i})|t^i] - p^i(\hat{t}^i)$ for all $i, t^i, \hat{t}^i$

where (PC) designates the (voluntary) *participation constraint* and (IC) the *incentive constraint*. The participation constraint requires that the bidder always do at least as well by participating in the mechanism as by refusing to do so. The incentive constraint requires the mechanism to be incentive-compatible.

The problem (4.36) can be simplified in several ways. First, using the constraint simplification theorem, the incentive-constraint can be replaced by

(IC′) $\begin{cases} x^i \text{ nondecreasing for } i = 1, \ldots, N, \\ V^i(t) = v^i(t)x^i(t) - p^i(t) = V^i(0) + \int_0^t v^{i\prime}(s)x^i(s)\,ds \\ \text{for } i = 1, \ldots, N, t \in [0, 1], \end{cases}$

where the second expression is from the envelope theorem. We may rewrite bidder i's expected payment as

$$p^i(t) = v^i(t)x^i(t) - \int_0^t \frac{dv^i}{ds}x^i(s)\,ds - V^i(0).$$

Second, because the envelope formula implies that V^i is nondecreasing, the participation constraint reduces to

(PC′) $V^i(0) \geq 0$ for $i = 1, \ldots, N.$

Bulow and Roberts (1989) have suggested an analogy between the optimal auction problem and the standard monopoly pricing problem.

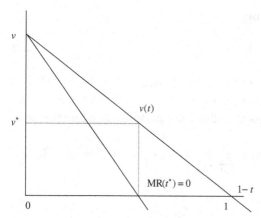

Figure 5. The valuation function v plays a role in the theory of revenue-maximizing auctions similar to that of the inverse demand function in monopoly theory. Notice that the quantity shown on the horizontal axis is $1 - t$.

If one sets the price so as to sell a unit to the bidder if its type is t or greater, then the probability of a sale will be $1 - t$. This probability is the expected quantity sold, so the function $P(1 - t) = v^i(t)$ is interpretable as the inverse demand function. Selling an expected quantity of $1 - t$ at price $v^i(t)$ generates expected *total revenues* of $TR^i(t) = v^i(t)(1 - t)$ (see Figure 5). The corresponding *marginal revenue* is

$$MR^i(t) = \frac{d((1 - t)v^i(t))}{d(1 - t)} = -\frac{d((1 - t)v^i(t))}{dt} = v^i(t) - (1 - t)\frac{dv^i}{dt}.$$

$$(4.37)$$

The optimal auction maximizes expected profits by selling to buyers whose types t satisfy $MR(t) > 0$. The expression $(1 - t)\,dv^i/dt$ is the inverse hazard rate associated with the distribution F^i. To see this recall that the inverse hazard rate is $1/h^i(t) = (1 - F^i)/f^i$, and because $v^i = (F^i)^{-1}$, we know that $F^i(v^i) = t^i$, so $[dF^i(v^i)/dv^i]dv^i/dt^i = 1$. Therefore,

$$\frac{dv^i}{dt^i} = \frac{1}{f^i}, \quad \text{or} \quad (1 - t^i)\frac{dv^i}{dt^i} = \frac{1 - F^i}{f^i}.$$

Using equation (4.37) to define MR^i, we may rewrite (4.35) more compactly and intuitively as

$$E[p^i(t^i)] = -V^i(0) + \int_0^1 MR^i(s^i)x^i(s^i)\,ds^i.$$

$$(4.38)$$

The two uses are related by[19]

$$x^i(t^i) = \int \cdots \int x^i(t^i, t^{-i}) \, dt^{-i}. \tag{4.39}$$

Because the $x^i(\cdot)$ are probabilities, they must satisfy $x^i(t^1, \ldots, t^N) \geq 0$ and $\sum_{i=1}^N x^i(\vec{t}) \leq 1$ for all type vectors $\vec{t} = (t^1, \ldots, t^N)$. The seller's total expected revenue, in terms of the allocation performance function x, is

$$\sum_{i=1}^N E[p^i(t^i)] = -\sum_{i=1}^N V^i(0) + \sum_{i=1}^N \int_0^1 \mathrm{MR}^i(s^i) \int \cdots \int x^i(s^i, s^{-i}) \, ds^{-i} ds^i$$

$$= -\sum_{i=1}^N V^i(0)$$

$$+ \int \cdots \int \left(\sum_{i=1}^N \mathrm{MR}^i(s^i) x^i(s^i, s^{-i}) \right) ds^1 \cdots ds^N. \tag{4.40}$$

Using (4.40), we can rewrite the problem of maximizing expected revenues as

$$\max_{x, p} - \sum_{i=1}^N V^i(0) + \int \cdots \int \left(\sum_{i=1}^N \mathrm{MR}^i(s^i) x^i(s^i, s^{-i}) \right) ds^1 \cdots ds^N,$$

$$(\mathrm{IC}') \begin{cases} \int x^i(t^i, s^{-i}) \, ds^{-i} \text{ is nondecreasing in } t^i \text{ for } i = 1, \ldots, N, \\ p^i(t) = v^i(t) x^i(t) - V^i(0) - \int_0^t v^{i\prime}(s) x^i(s) \, ds \text{ for all } i, t \in [0, 1], \end{cases}$$

$(\mathrm{PC}') \quad V^i(0) \geq 0 \quad \text{for} \quad i = 1, \ldots, N,$

$$(\mathrm{Prob}) \begin{cases} x^i(s^i, s^{-i}) \geq 0 \text{ for } i = 1, \ldots, N, \ (s^i, s^{-i}) \in [0, 1]^N, \\ \sum_{i=1}^N x^i(s^i, s^{-i}) \leq 1 \text{ for } (s^i, s^{-i}) \in [0, 1]^N. \end{cases}$$

$$\tag{4.41}$$

The first condition of (IC') follows from the fact that $x^i(\cdot)$ is nondecreasing, and the (Prob) constraints reflect the facts that x^i is a probability and that the seller owns only one unit.

4.4.1 Myerson's Theorem
As for other monopoly pricing problems, the solution here is easiest to characterize when the marginal revenue functions are decreasing in quantities (here denoted by $1 - s^i$). With this assumption (which implies

---

[19] The notation x^i does double duty here, for a function of either the real variable t^i or the vector variable $\vec{t}$.

that each MR^i function is increasing in the bidder's type), verifying the solution to (4.41) is straightforward.

Theorem 4.22. If each of the functions MR^i is increasing, then an optimal solution to (4.41) is given by

$$x^i(\vec{t}) = \begin{cases} 1 \text{ if } MR^i(t^i) = \max\{0, MR^1(t^1), \ldots, MR^N(t^N)\} \\ \qquad\qquad\qquad\qquad \text{for } i = 1, \ldots, N, \quad \vec{t} \in [0, 1]^N, \\ 0 \text{ otherwise,} \end{cases}$$

$$V^i(0) = 0,$$

$$p^i(t) = V^i(t)x^i(t) - \int_0^t v^{i\prime}(s)x^i(s)\, ds \quad \text{for} \quad i = 1, \ldots, N, t \in [0, 1].$$

$$(4.42)$$

The corresponding maximal revenue is

$$E[\max\{0, MR^1(t^1), \ldots, MR^N(t^N)\}].$$

Remark. In the event of a tie for the highest MR^i, the allocation rule may randomize among the tie bids.

Proof. Consider the relaxed problem in which we omit the constraint that $x(\cdot)$ is nondecreasing. The proposed solution described by (4.42) maximizes the integrand in the objective in problem (4.41) subject only to the constraints (PC′) and (Prob) for each realization of types. Consequently, it maximizes expected revenue if the proposed solution is feasible. To check feasibility, we only need to check that (IC′) is satisfied.

The expected payment condition (which is the integral form envelope condition in this problem) is implied by the assumption imposed on the value function. The monotonicity condition holds because the assumption (in the statement of the theorem) that $MR^i(\cdot)$ is increasing implies that $x^i(t^i, t^{-i})$ is nondecreasing in t^i. ∎

Examples

According to the theorem, the expected-revenue-maximizing auction is any auction that allocates the good according to (4.42) and charges the corresponding expected price, with each $V^i(0) = 0$. Two groups of examples illustrate the application of the theorem.

The first group consists of symmetric examples in which $v^i = v$ for all i. Define t^* to be the solution to $MR(t^*) = 0$, or if MR is everywhere positive, let $t^* = 0$. In the symmetric case, the Vickrey auction with reserve $r^* = v(t^*)$ allocates the good to the bidder with the highest type whenever his value exceeds r^*. Given the assumption that MR is increasing, this performance is precisely what the first equation of (4.42) requires. Because $V(0) = V(t^*) = 0$ for the Vickrey auction with this reserve, we conclude that the auction maximizes the seller's expected revenue over all possible mechanisms.

The Vickrey auction, however, is not the only expected-revenue-maximizing auction. In the first-price auction with reserve r^*, the lowest type to participate is again t^*. Again, $V(0) = V(t^*) = 0$, and a bidder wins if and only if his type is highest and exceeds t^*. Hence, the first-price auction with reserve r^* is another expected-revenue-maximizing auction.

There are still more expected-revenue-maximizing auctions. In the first- and second-price all-pay auctions, if the reserve is set to $(t^*)^{N-1} r^*$, then a bidder makes a positive bid if and only if his type exceeds t^* and wins when that condition holds and, in addition, his type is highest. Again, $V(0) = V(t^*) = 0$, so these auctions, too, are expected-revenue-maximizing auctions in the benchmark model.

Our second group of examples uses an asymmetric model to explore the differences between allocations that maximize revenues and the ones that are most efficient. Toward that end, suppose that types are equal to values ($v(t) = t$) but the distribution of types differ among bidders. Let $\{F_\gamma(t)\}$ denote a family of value distributions on an interval $[\alpha, \beta]$ with corresponding densities $\{f_\gamma(t)\}$. Let us assume that $\ln(1 - F_\gamma(t))$ is a submodular function of t, γ or, equivalently, that $f_\gamma(t)/(1 - F_\gamma(t))$ is decreasing in γ. This is a strong condition that implies the weaker condition that an increase in γ shifts the distribution of values in terms of first-order stochastic dominance.[20] By the theorem, if two competing bidders with different values of γ report the same value, then the optimal auction awards the item to the bidder with the lower value of γ. This identifies a particular sense in which the optimal auction favors the "weaker" bidder.

---

[20] For $\gamma' < \gamma$, submodularity implies that for all $t \in (\alpha, \beta)$, $\ln(1 - F(t|\gamma)) = \ln(1 - F(t|\gamma)) - \ln(1 - F(y|\gamma)) \leq \ln(1 - F(t|\gamma')) - \ln(1 - F(y|\gamma')) = \ln(1 - F(t|\gamma'))$, so $F(t|\gamma) \leq F(t|\gamma')$.

For a more specific example, suppose that G is a distribution function with density g and such that $\ln(1 - G)$ is concave or, equivalently, $(1 - G(t))/g(t)$ is increasing. Letting $F_\gamma(t) = G(t - \gamma)$, we obtain a family of distributions that satisfies our assumptions. This family includes the commonly studied case of uniform distributions. In all these cases, the allocation in the revenue-maximizing auction is biased relative to the efficient allocation by favoring bidders with lower values of γ.

Bulow and Roberts used the marginal revenue concept to highlight the connection between the theory of expected-revenue-maximizing auctions and the theory of monopoly pricing. The simplest case arises when $N = 1$. In that case, we may drop the superscripts identifying the bidder and fix $V(0) = 0$ and again let the bidder's type be uniformly distributed on $[0, 1]$. The monopolist's problem is to determine a price that maximizes its total expected revenue. To sell a total expected quantity $1 - s$, it must set a price of $v(s)$, for if v is increasing, all types greater than s will buy one unit, and all lower types will buy nothing. We again limit attention to the case in which the monopolist's marginal revenue declines continuously in total expected sales $1 - s$, that is, in which the function $MR(s)$ is continuous and increasing. In that case, the expected-revenue-maximizing policy is to set the price equal to $r^* = v(t^*)$, where t^* is determined as before by $MR(t^*) = 0$. Such a price yields the following allocation performance:

$$
x(t) = \begin{cases} 1 & \text{if } MR(t) \geq 0, \\ 0 & \text{otherwise.} \end{cases} \tag{4.43}
$$

By inspection, this solution is a special case of the solution in Theorem 4.22.

Next, let us take account of all N bidders. Imagine that a seller has to decide to which of N separated markets to allocate a marginal unit that has just become available. The type vector $\vec{t} = (t^1, \ldots, t^N)$ describes current conditions in the markets. The seller maximizes his expected total revenue by allocating that unit to the market in which marginal revenue is highest and by withholding the unit altogether if the highest marginal revenue is negative. That is precisely the rule prescribed by (4.42).

4.4.2 Bulow–Klemperer Theorem

A result of Jeremy Bulow and Paul Klemperer offers another illustration of the power of the theory of optimal auctions. Bulow and Klemperer (1996) compared the gains from setting a reserve price optimally against the gains to adding one more bidder to the auction. For simplicity, we assume that $v(0) = 0$. This assumption would seem to make it especially important to set a suitable reserve price, for otherwise the auction revenue could be very low. In a second-price auction, the revenue could be close to zero even if some bidder were willing to pay a high price.

The formal analysis, however, delivers a subtly different conclusion.

Theorem 4.23. The expected revenue from an auction with $N + 1$ bidders and no reserve is at least as high as the revenue from the corresponding auction with N bidders using the revenue-maximizing reserve price $v(\mathrm{MR}^{-1}(0))$.

Proof. Theorem 4.22. gives the revenue in the second case. In the first case, the expected revenue is $E[\max\{\mathrm{MR}^1(t^1), \ldots, \mathrm{MR}^{N+1}(t^{N+1})\}]$. The definition of MR^i implies that $E[\mathrm{MR}^i(t^i)] = \int_0^1 \mathrm{MR}^i(s)\, ds = -(1-t)v(t)|_{t=0}^1 = 0$. Jensen's inequality implies that for any random variable z and constant A, we have $E[\max(A, z)] \geq \max(A, E[z])$. Taking $z = \mathrm{MR}^{N+1}(t^{N+1})$, we have

$E[\text{auction revenue}, N + 1 \text{ bidders and no reserve}]$

$\quad = E[\max\{\mathrm{MR}^1(t^1), \ldots, \mathrm{MR}^{N+1}(t^{N+1})\}]$

$\quad = E[E[\max\{\mathrm{MR}^1(t^1), \ldots, \mathrm{MR}^{N+1}(t^{N+1})\}|t^1, \ldots, t^N]]$

$\quad \geq E[\max\{\mathrm{MR}^1(t^1), \ldots, \mathrm{MR}^N(t^N), 0\}]$

$\quad = E[\text{auction revenue}, N \text{ bidders and optimal reserve}], \qquad (4.44)$

which proves the theorem.   ∎

4.4.3 The Irregular Case

So far, we have limited attention to the case where MR^i is increasing. The problem in the general case is that the performance function x^i prescribed by the theorem will fail to be nondecreasing when MR^i is not nondecreasing, so the incentive compatibility constraint in (4.41) will not be satisfied.

In monopoly pricing, the corresponding problem is that the marginal revenue function may be increasing over some intervals. In that case, the total revenue function TR will not be concave, so for a given expected quantity, a randomized output sometimes leads to higher total expected revenues than a deterministic output. For example, by randomizing $\frac{1}{2}-\frac{1}{2}$ between quantities q and q', the seller can earn a total expected revenue of $\frac{1}{2}\mathrm{TR}(q) + \frac{1}{2}\mathrm{TR}(q')$. As a function of *expected* output, the seller's maximum total revenue is the *concave hull* of the total revenue function, that is, the smallest concave function $\widehat{\mathrm{TR}}(q)$ that satisfies $\widehat{\mathrm{TR}}(q) \geq \mathrm{TR}(q)$ for all q.

The auction problem has an analogous structure. Define $\mathrm{TR}^i(t) = \int_t^1 \mathrm{MR}^i(s)\,ds$; this is the total expected revenue enjoyed by the seller if it sets the price $v(t)$ and sells with probability $1 - t$. Let $\overline{\mathrm{TR}}^j$ be the concave hull of TR^j; this is the revenue the seller can achieve by randomizing its price. Let $\overline{\mathrm{MR}}^i = -d\overline{\mathrm{TR}}^i(t)/dt$ be the corresponding marginal revenue function. Then the expected-revenue-maximizing allocation rule assigns the item to the bidder with the highest marginal revenue $\overline{\mathrm{MR}}^i(t^i)$, provided that is positive. In the event of a tie, it randomizes the allocation:

$$x^i(t^1,\ldots,t^N) = \begin{cases} 0 & \text{if } \overline{\mathrm{MR}}^i(t^i) \neq \max(0, \overline{\mathrm{MR}}^1(t^1),\ldots,\overline{\mathrm{MR}}^N(t^N)), \\ 1/N & \text{otherwise,} \end{cases}$$

(4.45)

where $N = \#\{i : \overline{\mathrm{MR}}^i(t^i) = \max(0, \overline{\mathrm{MR}}^1(t^1),\ldots,\overline{\mathrm{MR}}^N(t^N))\}$ is the number of tying bidders. In contrast to the allocation performance specified in the theorem, the function x^i is guaranteed to be nondecreasing everywhere. The reason is that $\overline{\mathrm{MR}}^i$ is nondecreasing everywhere, because $\overline{\mathrm{TR}}^i$ is concave. We omit the formal proofs.

4.5 Auctions with Weak and Strong Bidders[21]

The analyses of the preceding sections are mostly limited to cases in which the bidders' values are symmetrically distributed. The first issue for asymmetric auctions is how to characterize equilibrium. We focus on the case of two bidders with types uniformly distributed on [0,1], increasing and differentiable value functions v^1 and v^2 with the reserve r in the range of both, and strategies β^1 and β^2. In such a model, one

---

[21] For simplicity, the theory in this section is developed for auctions with just two bidders, but the theory can be extended to auctions with two categories of bidders, weak and strong.

necessary condition for equilibrium is that the bid functions be continuous and increasing. Another is that bidders with value r bid r, that is, $\beta^1((v^1)^{-1}(r)) = \beta^2((v^2)^{-1}(r)) = r$. A third is that the range of the bid functions are the same, so $\beta^1(1) = \beta^2(1)$.

It is convenient to introduce the matching function m as follows:

$$m(t) = (\beta^2)^{-1}(\beta^1(t)). \tag{4.46}$$

This function identifies for each type of bidder 1 the corresponding type of bidder 2 that makes the same bid. Using that notation, the problem facing bidder 1 of type t at equilibrium is to choose a bid b or, equivalently, a type s and its corresponding bid $b = \beta^2(s)$, to maximize $s(v^1(t) - \beta^2(s))$. The first-order condition must be satisfied at equilibrium when $s = m(t)$ or, equivalently, when $t = m^{-1}(s)$. Using the latter, the condition is:

$$0 = v^1(m^{-1}(s)) - \beta^2(s) - s(\beta^2)'(s) \tag{4.47}$$

and the corresponding first-order condition for bidder 2 leads to:

$$0 = v^2(m(t)) - \beta^1(t) - t(\beta^1)'(t). \tag{4.48}$$

We may apply the familiar arguments to conclude that any increasing solution of the first-order conditions identifies best-replies for both bidders, when bidders are restricted to bids in the range of the equilibrium bid function. It is clear that bidders of value less than r cannot increase their profits by making qualified bids. For bidders with values greater than r, if the ranges of the two bid functions coincide and include the reserve r, then any bid outside the range of the bid functions, that is, any bid less than r or greater than $\bar{b} = \beta^1(1) = \beta^2(1)$, is by inspection less profitable than a bid of r or $\bar{b}$, respectively. Hence, any solution satisfying the identified necessary conditions is an equilibrium.

Theorem 4.24. (Maskin and Riley (2000a)).[22] There exists a unique increasing solution to the differential equation system (4.46)-(4.48) satisfying $\beta^1((v^1)^{-1}(r)) = \beta^2((v^2)^{-1}(r)) = r$ and $\beta^1(1) = \beta^2(1)$. This solution is an equilibrium of the asymmetric first-price auction.

---

[22] Maskin and Riley prove this theorem by proving the existence of a solution to the system of differential equation satisfying the stated boundary conditions.

A basic result about equilibrium is that if one player's values are distributed higher than the other's in the sense of first-order stochastic dominance, then that player's bids are distributed higher in the same sense. Since the value functions v^1 and v^2 are also inverse distribution functions for the values, then strict stochastic dominance condition is the condition that for all $t \in (0, 1)$, $v^1(t) > v^2(t)$.

Theorem 4.25. Suppose that for all $t \in (0, 1)$, $v^1(t) > v^2(t)$. Then, for all $t \in (0, 1)$, the equilibrium strategies have $\beta^1(t) > \beta^2(t)$.

Proof. At any point where $\beta^1(t) = \beta^2(t)$, we have $m(t) = t = m^{-1}(t)$. So, by (4.47)-(4.48), $(\beta^1)'(t) < (\beta^2)'(t)$. Also, $\beta^1(1) = \beta^2(1)$. It follows by the ranking lemma applied to the function $f(1 - t) = \beta^1(t) - \beta^2(t)$ that $\beta^1(t) > \beta^2(t)$ for all $t \in (0, 1)$. ∎

In the remainder of this section, we are primarily concerned with auctions in which one bidder is "stronger" than the others. We explore the intuitive idea that when a bidder is stronger, its competitors bid more aggressively. For this exploration, it is most convenient to identify types with values and therefore to fix bid functions so that bids are a function of value.

To see how the strength of a bidder affects its competitor's bids, consider bidder 1's problem when its value is v. Suppose bidder 2's values are drawn from some distribution in the family $\{F(t|s)\}$, where s will parameterize the bidder's strength. For any continuous increasing strategy β that bidder 2 may adopt that specifies bids as a function of its value, bidder 1 chooses a bid b in the range of β to maximize $(v - b)F(\beta^{-1}(b)|s)$ or, equivalently, to maximize $\ln(v - b) + \ln F(\beta^{-1}(b)|s)$. The solution to this problem is nondecreasing in s for every increasing function β if and only if $\ln F(t|s)$ is supermodular. The sufficiency of supermodularity follows from the monotonicity theorem; necessity follows from a theorem of Milgrom (1994). Below, we shall say that s parameterizes strength if $\ln F(t|s)$ is supermodular.

The condition that $\ln F(t|s)$ is supermodular is related to, but different from, the condition that $\ln(1 - F(t|s))$ is submodular, which we used in studying revenue-maximizing auctions. The second condition implied that the revenue-maximizing auction favored the bidder with low values of s whenever both have the same value. We have already shown that the second condition implies that $F(t|s)$ is decreasing in s; a similar argument implies that the first condition implies that as well.

Intuitively, the preceding conclusion that a bidder bids more when its competitor is stronger suggests that, at equilibrium, a weaker bidder would be inclined to bid more than a stronger bidder with the same values. However, the conclusion is not immediate, because the argument supporting that conclusion is not an equilibrium argument. At equilibrium, both bidders' strategies will depend upon both bidders' strengths. The next theorem shows that the expected ranking of strategies does indeed hold at equilibrium.

Theorem 4.26 (Maskin and Riley (2000b)). Consider an auction with two bidders whose values are drawn from distributions $\{F(t|s)\}$ on $[\underline{v}, \bar{v}]$ with corresponding densities $\{f(t|s)\}$, where $\ln F(t|s)$ is supermodular and where the bidder strengths are $s = 0$ and $s = 1$, respectively. Let β_s be the equilibrium strategies, mapping values to bids. Then, the strong bidder bids less for each possible value than does the weak bidder: for all $t \in (\underline{v}, \bar{v})$, $\beta_1(t) < \beta_0(t)$.

Proof. At equilibrium, the range of the equilibrium bidding functions must be the same, so $\beta_0(\bar{v}) = \beta_1(\bar{v})$. For any value v at which $\beta_0(v) = \beta_1(v) < v$, the first-order conditions for the optimal bids are:

$$0 = -1 + (v - \beta_1(v))\frac{f(v|0)}{F(v|0)}/\beta_0'(v)$$

$$= -1 + (v - \beta_0(v))\frac{f(v|1)}{F(v|1)}/\beta_1'(v).$$

(4.49)

Since $f(v|0)/F(v|0) < f(v|1)/F(v|1)$ and $v - \beta_0(v) = v - \beta_1(v)$, it follows that $\beta_1'(v) > \beta_0'(v)$. Hence, applying the ranking lemma to the function $h(\bar{v} - t) = \beta_0(t) - \beta_1(t)$, it follows that for all $t \in (\underline{v}, \bar{v})$, $\beta_1(t) < \beta_0(t)$. ∎

Combining the last two results, we see that a stronger bidder has a higher equilibrium distribution of bids, but that its strategy calls for it to bid less than the weaker bidder for any particular realization of its value. As a result of the bidders' strategies, the strong bidder sometimes loses the auction even when it has the higher value. Indeed, a strong bidder with value v is the high bidder in a first-price auction if and only if the weak bidder has value less than $m(v) \equiv \beta_0^{-1}(\beta_1(v)) < v$. In contrast, in a second-price auction, the strong bidder wins when its value is highest, and that happens strictly more often. Applying the envelope formula, that comparison of frequencies leads to the following result.

Theorem 4.27 (Maskin and Riley (2000b)). The equilibrium expected profit of a strong bidder with any value v is higher in the second-price auction than in the first-price auction. Reversely, the equilibrium expected profit of a weak bidder with any value v is higher in the first-price auction than in the second-price auction.

Proof. For a strong bidder with value v, by the envelope theorem, expected profits are $\int_{\underline{v}}^{v} F(m(r)|0)\, dr$ in the first-price auction and $\int_{\underline{v}}^{v} F(r|0)\, dr$ in the second-price auction. Since $m(r) < r$, the second integral is larger.

For a weak bidder with value v, by the envelope theorem, the expected profits are $\int_{\underline{v}}^{v} F(m^{-1}(r)|1)\, dr$ for the first-price auction and $\int_{\underline{v}}^{v} F(r|1)\, dr$ for the second-price auction. Since $m^{-1}(r) > r$, the first integral is larger. ∎

What general conclusions might we draw from the preceding analysis about when the first-price auction leads to higher revenues on average than the second-price auction? Vickrey's original analysis of auctions includes examples to establish that no completely general ranking on the basis of expected revenues is possible. He gave examples of asymmetric auction models in which the average revenue from the first-price auction is sometimes greater and sometimes less than the average revenue from the second-price auction.

Despite Vickrey's examples, the preceding results and numerical simulations suggest that in asymmetric auction models with one strong bidder, the first-price auction may often lead to higher average revenues than the second-price auction. Intuitively, the reason is that such an auction introduces the right kind of "bias."[23] At equilibrium, since $m(t) < t$, the weak bidder wins more often at equilibrium in the first-price auction than in second-price auction. A similar bias in favor of weaker bidders was found in revenue maximizing auctions, provided that $\ln(1 - F(t|s))$ is submodular.

[23] See Maskin and Riley (2000b) for examples and sufficient conditions for this result.

4.6 Conclusion

This chapter introduced the various single crossing conditions, including the Milgrom–Shannon single-crossing differences condition, the smooth single crossing differences condition, and the Mirrlees–Spence condition, and their various implications, especially the constraint simplification theorem. These provide a compact way to verify equilibrium in a large set of auction models and set the stage for the celebrated optimal auction theory. We used these methods to identify and verify equilibrium strategies in sealed-bid auctions with reserve prices, the war of attrition and the all-pay auction.

The next group of analyses looked beyond the payoff and revenue equivalence results to analyze situations in which auction revenues can be compared. The main tool for this comparison is the *ranking lemma*, which provides a method for showing that certain direct effects on bidding are preserved in the equilibrium analysis. We used this method to establish that bidders increase their equilibrium bids in the first-price auction as they become more risk averse, that bidders bid lower in a first-price procurement auctions (but not in second-price procurement auctions) when the quantity purchased by the bid-taker is a decreasing function of the price, and that correlation among bidder types raises equilibrium revenues from the second-price auction compared to the first-price auction.

In addition to these studies, we investigated the effects of budget constraints and studied how bidding costs can contribute to jump bidding. We also developed the famous "optimal auctions" analysis, which identifies the auctions that maximize the seller's revenue. One conclusion of that theory is that, under certain conditions, revenue-maximizing auctions discriminate against "strong" bidders whose values are expected to be high.

A final section is devoted to the study of auctions in which there is competition between a weak bidder, with a low distribution of values, and a strong bidder, with a higher distribution of values. The characterization of weak and strong bidders in this theory differs from that of the revenue-maximizing auctions theory. The ranking lemma allows us to compare the equilibrium bids of the weak and strong bidders. Among the main findings are that at the equilibrium of the first-price auction, strong bidders bid higher than weak bidders in terms of their distribution of bids, but that they bid less than weak bidders for any particular realization of the bidder's value. This is qualitatively similar to the bias required by revenue-maximizing auctions, and often these auctions lead to higher revenues than do second-price auctions.

The next two chapters develop more lessons of traditional auction theory for evaluating some common auction practices.

REFERENCES

Alesina, Alberto and Allan Drazen (1991). "Why Are Stabilizations Delayed?" *American Economic Review* **81**(5): 1170–1188.

Avery, Christopher (1998). "Strategic Jump Bidding in English Auctions." *Review of Economic Studies* **65**(2, No. 223): 185–210.

Bulow, Jeremy and Paul Klemperer (1996). "Auctions versus Negotiations." *American Economic Review* **86**(1): 180–194.

Bulow, Jeremy and Paul Klemperer (1999). "The Generalized War of Attrition." *American Economic Review* **89**(1): 175–189.

Bulow, Jeremy and John Roberts (1989). "The Simple Economics of Optimal Auctions." *Journal of Political Economy* **97**(5): 1060–1090.

Che, Yeon-Koo and Ian Gale (1998). "Standard Auctions with Financially Constrained Bidders." *Review of Economic Studies* **65**(1, No. 222): 1–21.

Edlin, Aaron and Chris Shannon (1998a). "Strict Monotonicity in Comparative Statics." *Journal of Economic Theory* **81**: 201–219.

Edlin, Aaron and Chris Shannon (1998b). "Strict Single Crossing and the Strict Spence–Mirrlees Condition: A Comment on Monotone Comparative Statics." *Econometrica* **60**(6): 1417–1425.

Fudenberg, Drew and Jean Tirole (1986). "Theory of Exit in Duopoly." *Econometrica* **54**(4): 943–960.

Griesmer, Levitan and Shubik (1967). "Toward a Study of Bidding Processes, Part IV: Games with Unknown Costs." *Naval Research Logistics Quarterly* **14**(4): 415–443.

Hansen, Robert G. (1988). "Auctions with Endogenous Quantity." *Rand Journal of Economics* **19**(1): 44–58.

Klemperer, Paul (2002b). "Why Every Economist Should Learn Some Auction Theory." http://www.paulklemperer.org/.

Laffont, Jean-Jacques (1997). "Game Theory and Empirical Economics: The Case of Auction Data." *European Economic Review* **41**: 1–35.

Laffont, Jean-Jacques, Herve Ossard, and Quang Vuong (1995). "Econometrics of First-Price Auctions." *Econometrica* **63**(4): 953–980.

Maskin, Eric and John Riley (2000a). "Equilibrium in Sealed High Bid Auctions." *Review of Economic Studies* **67**(3): 439–454.

Maskin, Eric and John Riley (2000b). "Asymmetric Auctions," *Review of Economics Studies* **67**(3): 413–438.

Milgrom, Paul and Chris Shannon (1994). "Monotone Comparative Statics." *Econometrica* **62**: 157–180.

Milgrom, Paul and Robert Weber (1985). "Distributional Strategies for Games with Incomplete Information." *Mathematics of Operations Research* **10**: 619–632.

Milgrom, Paul and Robert J. Weber (1982). "A Theory of Auctions and Competitive Bidding." *Econometrica* **50**: 463–483.

Mirrlees, James (1971). "An Exploration in the Theory of Optimal Taxation." *Review of Economic Studies* **38**: 175–208.

Perry, Motty and Philip Reny (1999). "On the Failure of the Linkage Principle." *Econometrica* **67**(4): 895–900.

Spence, A Michael (1973). "Job Market Signaling." *Quarterly Journal of Economics* **87**(3): 355–374.

CHAPTER FIVE

Interdependence of Types and Values

Most of the models in chapters 2–4 are independent private-values models. Values are *private* if each player's value for any outcome depends only on his own type, and *independent* if types are statistically independent. The only exceptions so far are the Jehiel–Moldovanu model of chapter 3, which discards the private-values assumption, and the correlated-types example of chapter 4, which relaxes the independence assumption.

Relaxing the private-values and independence assumptions raises a host of new issues. When bidders do not know their own values, the connection between bids and values is naturally weaker and the bidder with the highest value may win less often. Bidders' ignorance of their values leads us to study what information bidders are likely to acquire, whether they will share this information or keep it secret, and whether the auctioneer can improve the outcome by gathering and disseminating information on its own. The independence assumption is an essential premise of Myerson's lemma and the revenue equivalence theorems. Relaxing this assumption forces us to reevaluate the most basic results of auction theory.

In this chapter, we study issues raised by the two possible kinds of interdependence. Section 5.1 investigates the kinds of simplifying assumptions that are "reasonable" and "useful" in auction models. Section 5.2 explores the consequences of statistically interdependent types in an optimal auction model. Section 5.3 studies the empirically successful *drainage tract model*, which treats bidding for oil on tracts adjacent to a previously developed tract. Section 5.4 introduces a model that relaxes both the private-values and statistical independence assumptions.

5.1 Which Models and Assumptions are "Useful"?

Students sometimes ask their teachers whether a particular assumption is "reasonable" in a particular auction model. The answer is to be found only by restating the question: what is a useful assumption?

Real auctions occur in many different situations. There is no reason to expect that any single set of tractable simplifying assumptions will describe all the situations well – or will even describe any of them well. The test of the suitability of assumptions is whether they are simple enough to make the analysis tractable while still capturing enough essential features of the situation to be useful for the intended purpose, which may be to make quantitative predictions or to lend qualitative insights into some issue.

Model builders can sometimes profit by using theoretical analyses to evaluate simplifying assumptions, exploring consequences of the assumptions within the model, or developing implications of the same assumptions in a wider model. In this section, we use theory in these ways to investigate some common assumptions used in auction models.

5.1.1 Payoffs Depend Only on Bids and Types

In the preceding chapters and throughout mechanism design theory, it is usually assumed that a participant's payoff depends *only* on the outcome x and the vector $\vec{t}$ of participants' types $[u^j(x,\vec{t})]$, but that does not always describe the reality accurately. For example, consider an auction for the right to extract minerals from a certain piece of property, when no one can determine in advance the quantity of minerals in the ground or the cost of extraction. The winning bidder's ultimate payoff will depend on the resolution of these uncertainties. Given this situation, some theorists have written the bidder's payoff as a function of the outcome x and some vector y of random variables, $\hat{u}^j(x, y)$, where y may include both the type profile and unobserved variables.

What are the consequences of these alternative formulations? We show in this subsection that for the limited purpose of characterizing equilibrium bidding strategies as functions of the bidders' types, one can assume without loss of generality that payoffs depend only on the auction outcome and bidder types. For suppose that the actual payoffs $\hat{u}^j(x, y)$ depend on the outcome and a vector y of observed and unobserved quantities. Then the expected payoff to any strategy profile in this model is exactly the same as in a model with the payoffs given by $u^j(x, \vec{t}) = E[\hat{u}^j(x, y)|\vec{t}]$.

To verify this claim, observe that the expected payoff to bidder j in the original game, given strategy profile σ and j's type, is

$$E[\hat{u}^j(x(\sigma(\vec{t})), y)|t^j] = E[E[\hat{u}^j(x(\sigma(\vec{t})), y)|\vec{t}]|t^j]$$
$$= E[u^j(x(\sigma(\vec{t})), \vec{t})|t^j].$$

The left-hand side is the expected payoff in the game with payoff function $\hat{u}^j$, and the right-hand side is the expected payoff in a game with payoff function u^j. Because the two expected payoffs are identical, the equilibrium behavior is identical as well. One might say that the vector y of random variables can always be "integrated out" from the original payoff function to leave a payoff function that depends only on the type profile.

The significance of this finding is that, when types are exogenous, the equilibrium strategies depend only on the information in the reduced form payoff $u^j(x, \vec{t})$. Still, when we want our model to relate equilibrium payoffs to bidders' information, it can be helpful to work with a more detailed payoff function. For example, suppose that we wish to investigate whether the degree of uncertainty about the volume of recoverable hydrocarbons increases profits in an auction of oil leases. Even though bidder information is unobservable so the equilibrium theory cannot be directly tested, if there are usable instruments for the degree of uncertainty and if profits are observable, then the more detailed model can generate testable predictions. Similarly, one may be able to test how improvements in bidders' ability to estimate recoverable oil affect the bidders' strategies, profits, and entry decisions as well as the auction revenues and the efficiency of the auction outcome.

If bidders choose what information to collect or if the seller chooses what information to disseminate, then the types are not exogenous and equilibrium analysis may require more than a reduced form model. Equilibrium analysis requires that the model include all potentially observable information. A model with potentially unobserved information allows us to analyze bidders' choices about what information to gather and the seller's choice about what information to disseminate.

5.1.2 Types Are One-Dimensional and Values Are Private

Here, we evaluate the twin assumptions that a bidder's type is one-dimensional – a real number – and that bidders have private values.

If bidders have private values, then no bidder has information that another bidder might find useful for estimating his value. One might ask: Is that reasonable? Would bidders not want to learn something about one another's values? To answer these questions, we need to distinguish different kinds of information that a bidder may acquire.

We adopt a model similar to that of the Jehiel–Moldovanu theorem in chapter 3, with a single item for sale. Bidder j's information is a vector $t^j = (t_1^j, \ldots, t_N^j)$, in which only the component t_i^j is directly relevant to bidder i's payoff. We allow that i's payoff when he wins the item may depend on information of the other bidders; it is $v^i(t_i^1, \ldots, t_i^N)$ minus the amount he pays. We also assume for now that the types are statistically independent across bidders, and we denote other bidders' strategies by σ^{-j}. From statistical independence, it follows that the probability that j wins with any given bid b is independent of j's type, so

$$E\big[v^j(\vec{t})1_{\{b \text{ wins}\}}|t^j = \tau^j\big] = \Pr\{b \text{ wins}\}E\big[v^j(\tau_j^j, t_j^{-j})|t^j = \tau^j\big]$$
$$= \Pr\{b \text{ wins}\}E\big[v^j(\tau_j^j, t_j^{-j})\big] = f(b, \tau_j^j).$$

Given the mechanism, bidder j's expected payoff when he bids b with type t^j is

$$f(b, t_j^j) - E[\text{Payment}(b, \sigma^{-j}(t^{-j}))] = f(b, t_j^j) - g(b). \tag{5.1}$$

It follows that j's expected-payoff-maximizing bid given his type t^j depends only on t_j^j and not on t_{-j}^j, so the value for j of the information t_{-j}^j is *zero*.

This conclusion is significant if we suppose that there is some positive cost to collecting and evaluating the information t_{-j}^j. In that case, because bidder j's value of that information is zero, he will not collect it at equilibrium. On one hand, this conclusion extends the Jehiel–Moldovanu result, which says that even if such information were available for free, the auctioneer could not take advantage of it. We add here that, subject to our assumption that gathering information is costly, the bidder would not bother to gather such information in the first place.

This argument establishes that, under the other specified assumptions, bidder types are endogenously one-dimensional, and that dimension includes only the information that is directly relevant to bidder j's own payoff.

Even if bidders only gather one-dimensional information about their own values, that still does not establish the appropriateness of the private-values assumption. For example, suppose there are just two bidders and the bidders' types, $t^1 = (t_1^1, t_2^1)$ and $t^2 = (t_1^2, t_2^2)$, are independent. Further suppose that bidder 1 observes only the one component, t_1^1, of its type that affects its value, and similarly that bidder 2 observes only t_2^2. What can we say about bidder 1's expected value conditional on the observed components of the type profile, that is, about $\hat{v}^1(t_1^1, t_2^2) = E[v^1(t_1^1, t_2^1)|t_1^1, t_2^2]$? Does it follow that $\hat{v}^1(t_1^1, t_2^2)$ depends only on its first argument?

The answer is no, because t_1^2 may be correlated with t_2^2. For example, suppose bidder 2 is assessing his value for an oil field. That value will depend on variables particular to bidder 2, but it will depend mostly on the volume of hydrocarbons in the field, which also affects the value of the field to bidder 1. For this reason, t_1^2 and t_2^2 will tend to be high or low together. Consequently, a high value of t_2^2 will be significant to bidder 1, because it suggests bidder 1's value is also high. $\hat{v}^1$ may therefore increase in both arguments if t_1^2 and t_2^2 are correlated.

Notice that even the conclusion that types are effectively one-dimensional rests upon the assumption that different players' types are statistically independent. Without that assumption, a bidder's observations could affect not only its values but also its beliefs about others' values, about their beliefs, and so on, *ad infinitum*. Such beliefs cannot generally be summarized by a one-dimensional type, and bidders could have an incentive to learn about one another's types in order to forecast the competing bids.

5.1.3 Types Are Statistically Independent

Statistical independence is a special, knife-edge assumption, whose role in the analysis of auctions has long been questioned. In auctions of assets, bidders often estimate the net revenue the asset can generate, which is sensitive to demand and technology. To the extent that bidders are estimating the same underlying variables, their estimates will often be positively correlated.

To illustrate this tendency, consider an auction for oil-drilling rights in which each bidder's type is her estimate of the amount of oil in the ground. Suppose that the actual value of the oil is a non-degenerate random variable y with mean μ and that bidder j's estimate is $t^j = y + \varepsilon^j$, where ε^1, ε^2, and y are mutually independent. Then $\text{Cov}(t^1, t^2) = \text{Var}(y) > 0$. So independent errors induce positively correlated types.

This source of correlation is especially important in some of the most empirically successful auction models, which use the polar opposite of the private-values assumption – the *common value* assumption.[1] In auctions for oil and gas drilling rights (and other mineral rights), the value of the rights to the bidders depends mainly on how much oil and gas is in the ground and how easily it can be extracted. Common value models assume that this is the only kind of information bidders have. Most often, the models assume that the good has exactly the same value to each bidder. Under this assumption, because the allocation of the good has no impact on efficiency, analyses of efficiency focus on the resources used by the auctioneer and bidders in the auction. Most published analyses of common value auctions focus on the revenues associated with alternative auction procedures.

5.2 Statistical Dependence and Revenue-Maximizing Auctions

Statistical dependence among types in the optimal auction model fundamentally changes the solution to the optimal auction problem. Indeed, the solution changes *discontinuously* when we move from statistically dependent to statistically independent types. Cremer and McLean (1985) showed that with even a small amount of statistical dependence, an expected-revenue-maximizing auction for the seller always produces efficient outcomes and always reduces all bidders' profits to zero, so that the seller's expected revenue equals the value of the item to the bidder who values it most.

We review Cremer and McLean's analysis in more detail below. First, however, let us recall why the seller in a model with independent types cannot reduce bidders' profits to zero while still selling the item with a positive probability. We saw in chapter 3 that in the independent private-values model, each bidder's expected profit is completely determined by the function $x^j(t^j)$, which specifies the probability that a bidder of type t^j wins the good. Applying the envelope theorem, the bidder's expected payoff is $V^j(\tau) = V^j(0) + \int_0^\tau x^j(s)[dv^j(s)/ds]\,ds$. In the auction designs we have studied, it is always true that $V^j(0) = 0$, but the portion of the

---

[1] Wilson (1967), Ortega-Reichert (1968), and Wilson (1969) analyzed the first common value models.

bidder's profits due to the second term of the sum – sometimes called an *information rent* – is positive if the good is sold at all, and values are an increasing function of the bidder's type.

The key to constructing a revenue-maximizing auction with statistical dependence among types is to link a first-price auction with certain side bets. Suppose that the rules require a bidder who bids b for the item in the first-price auction to enter a bet that depends on b. The bet is designed to have an expected payoff of zero to the bidder if the bidder's value is b, and otherwise to have an expected payoff that is quite negative. These side bets lead bidders to bid truthfully, leave the bidders with expected profits of zero, and allow the auction to assign the item to the bidder with the highest value for a price equal to that value.

The side bets are easiest to construct when the number of types is finite; we limit attention here to this case.[2] Suppose that there are N bidders and the possible types of bidder j are the elements of a finite set $\{1, \ldots, M^j\}$. The private value of the good to bidder j is $v^j(t^j)$, where v^j is invertible.

Let $P^j(t^{-j}|t^j)$ denote the conditional probability function for bidder j. The values of the function can be tabulated in a matrix P^j with M^j rows (indexed by t^j and denoted by $P^j(t^j)$) and $\times_{i \neq j} M^i$ columns (indexed by t^{-j}), with the k–l element of the matrix given by $P^j_{kl} = P^j(t^{-j} = \tau_l^{-j}|t^j = \tau_k^j)$, where τ_k^j is the kth possible type of bidder j, and τ_l^{-j} is the lth possible type profile for the remaining bidders. For example, suppose there are three bidders and the sets of possible types are $\{1, \ldots, 4\}$, $\{1, \ldots, 8\}$, and $\{1, \ldots, 5\}$. Then P^2 is an 8×20 matrix. The key assumption is the following one, which states that no type's beliefs can be expressed as a convex combination of the beliefs of other types.

(A) *Non-degenerate Statistical Dependence.* For each bidder j, the matrix P^j described above has full row rank.

Consider a modified first-price auction in which: (1) bidder j is permitted to bid only amounts in the set $\{v^j(1), \ldots, v^j(M^j)\}$; (2) the usual rules of a first-price auction determine the winner and payment; and (3) if bidder j bids $v^j(t^j)$ and the opposing bidders bid amounts $v^{-j}(t^{-j})$, then the seller pays bidder j the amount $B^j(t^j, t^{-j})$. We call such an auction the *first-price auction with side bets B*.

---

[2] McAfee and Reny (1982) extend the result to certain models with infinite type spaces.

Theorem 5.2.1. Suppose that the distribution of types satisfies assumption (A) (*non-degenerate statistical dependence*). Then there exists a system of side bets B such that the first-price auction with side bets B has these properties:

1. it is incentive-compatible,
2. it yields zero expected profit for each type of each bidder, and
3. conditional on the realized type profile $\vec{t}$, the expected revenues are equal to $\max(v^1(t^1), \ldots, v^N(t^N))$.

Proof. As a result of non-degenerate statistical dependence, each belief $P^j(t^j)$ lies outside the convex hull $\mathrm{Conv}\{P^j(\hat{t}^j) | \hat{t}^j \neq t^j\}$. By the separating hyperplane theorem,[3] there exists a vector $h^j(t^j)$ with $\times_{i \neq j} M^i$ elements such that for all $\hat{t}^j \neq t^j$ one has $h^j(t^j) \cdot (P^j(t^j) - P^j(\hat{t}^j)) > 0$. Moreover, because each belief vector is a probability vector, we can choose $h^j(t^j)$ so that $h^j(t^j) \cdot P^j(t^j) = 0$ and $h^j(t^j) \cdot P^j(\hat{t}^j) \leq -1$ for all $t^j \neq \hat{t}^j$.[4]

Let $\bar{B} = \max_{j, t^j} v^j(t^j)$ and $B^j(t^j) = \bar{B} h^j(t^j)$. By the construction of the mechanism, the expected profit of a bidder j of type t^j who bids $v^j(t^j)$ is zero (that is, he pays his value when he wins and makes additional payments that, by construction, have expected value zero). However, the expected profit of a bidder j of type t^j who bids $v^j(\hat{t}^j)$ ($\hat{t}^j \neq t^j$) is bounded above by

$$v^j(t^j) - v^j(\hat{t}^j) + P^j(t^j) \cdot B^j(\hat{t}^j) = v^j(t^j) - v^j(\hat{t}^j) + P^j(t^j) \cdot \bar{B} \cdot h^j(\hat{t}^j)$$
$$\leq v^j(t^j) - v^j(\hat{t}^j) - \bar{B} \leq 0.$$

We obtain the equality by substituting for $B^j(\hat{t}^j)$; the first inequality uses $P^j(t^j) \cdot h^j(\hat{t}^j) \leq -1$, and the second inequality uses $\bar{B} = \max_{j, t^j} v^j(t^j) \geq v^j(t^j)$. Note that $v^j(t^j) - v^j(\hat{t}^j)$ is the bidder's profit from the auction when the bidder is of type t^j and reports type $\hat{t}^j$ and wins, and $-P^j(t^j) \cdot B^j(\hat{t}^j)$ is the expected loss from the side bet. Since all non-truthful bids make losses, we have established incentive compatibility.

Because all bidders bid their values, the bidder with the highest value receives the item for a price equal to that value, and the expected value of the side bets is zero. Thus claim (3) about expected revenue holds. ∎

---

[3] See, for example, Royden (1968).

[4] Suppose h^j satisfies $h^j(t^j) \cdot P^j(t^j) = \alpha \neq 0$. Let $\lambda(t^j) = \alpha - \max_{\hat{t}^j} h^j(t^j) \cdot P^j(\hat{t}^j) > 0$. Then let $(\hat{h}^j(t^j))_i = [(h^j(t^j))_i - \alpha]/\lambda(t^j)$ for all i. Hence, $\hat{h}^j(t^j) \cdot P^j(t^j) = (\alpha - \alpha)/\lambda(t^j) = 0$ and $\hat{h}^j(t^j) \cdot P^j(\hat{t}^j) \leq -\lambda(t^j)/\lambda(t^j) = -1$ for $\hat{t}^j \neq t^j$.

Theorem 5.2.1 is provocative; it is an extreme implication of the theory of optimal auctions. The proof relies on condition (A), which asserts that no type's beliefs are a probability mixture of the beliefs of other types. In that case, we can find bets that break even for only one type and that lead to huge expected losses for all other types of the same bidder. By bundling the bet with a bid, incentives for truthful bidding are ensured.

The theorem describes nothing that is found in practice and reminds us of how important it is to check the practical reasonableness of solutions suggested by a model before implementing any practical policy based on the model. The theorem also suggests a long list of questions a careful designer should ask about any mechanism. We consider some of these below.

Is the mechanism of Theorem 5.2.1 unrealistically sensitive to the theorem's assumptions about the distribution of types? In the present model, solutions require increasingly large side bets as the beliefs of different types become close. However, when beliefs do not depend on the types – i.e. when types are independent – the revenue-maximizing mechanism does not use side bets at all. The sensitivity of the conclusions to the assumptions is disturbing.

Does the mechanism designer have the information necessary to implement a mechanism like that of Theorem 5.2.1? This question relates to the first one. The sensitivity of the solution to the designer's assumptions means that the designer needs very accurate information to get good results. Robert Wilson (1987), in what has come to be known as the "Wilson doctrine," has argued that useful auction designs must be independent of the fine details of unknowable bidder valuations and beliefs.

Does the model capture the situation in a way that is useful for making predictions, or does it simplify reality excessively for reasons of tractability? The Cremer–McLean mechanism exploits bidders' beliefs to induce truthful bidding. Neeman (2001) argues that the model is unrealistic in assuming that one can infer a bidder's value from his beliefs about other bidders' types. If we drop that assumption and formulate a model where beliefs and values can vary separately, then Cremer and McLean's conclusion must change. To see why, suppose a bidder has a two-dimensional type (t_1, t_2) in which his value is $v(t_1)$ and his probability of winning with a bid of b is $p(b|t_2)$. Then his payoff is $V(t_1, t_2) = \max_b v(t_1) p(b|t_2) - X(b|t_2)$, where $X(b|t_2)$ is his expected payment when he bids b. If his optimal bid in any mechanism is $\beta(t_1, t_2)$, then, by the envelope theorem,

$\partial V(t_1, t_2)/\partial t_1 = v'(t_1) p(\beta(t_1, t_2)|t_2)$. This implies that a bidder's expected profits are increasing in t_1 on the domain of types that sometimes win at auction, so bidder profits cannot always be zero. Nevertheless, the optimal mechanism still generally involves side bets that allow the seller to exploit the correlation between values and beliefs.

Could the mechanism designer really implement this mechanism if he wanted? Risk averse bidders would certainly be deterred by this mechanism, because the side bets impose costly risks on the bidders and the expected profits are zero. More generally, in real auctions, bidders frequently refuse to participate if the proposed mechanism seems strange or unfair. Many might apply those adjectives to a mechanism that links bids to side bets. Precedent and familiarity often limit the set of practically feasible designs.

5.3 Wilson's Drainage Tract Model

Wilson (1969) developed the drainage tract model to describe bidding in the first-price auctions for rights to extract oil from tracts on the US outer continental shelf. A *drainage tract* is a tract adjacent to one already being developed by some oil company – the *neighbor* – whose activities give it particularly good information about the geology of the drainage tract. For example, the neighbor may have found bountiful oil near the boundary that separates its tract from the drainage tract, or it may have found only dry holes without recoverable oil. To model the neighbor's superior information, Wilson assumed that the neighbor knows the value V. In this model, the competitor's value is also V, but the competitor has only public information to use in estimating that value.

The drainage tract model has subsequently received plentiful attention from both theoretical and empirical researchers. In a series of subsections, we will characterize the equilibrium of the model, the expected profits enjoyed by the neighbor and the corresponding revenues for the seller, and how those profits and revenues are affected by research by the neighbor and non-neighbor and by whether the seller collects and reveals information. We will also study second-tier effects, concerning whether a neighbor or non-neighbor who gathers information wants its competitors to know that. Among our findings is that the neighbor wants it to be known that it is well informed, because the better informed it is believed to be, the more timidly its competitors are inclined to bid. Reversely, the poorly informed non-neighbors prefer that the neighbor believe they are poorly informed, because it will bid less aggressively under those circumstances.

It is convenient to assume that the neighbor – bidder 1 – observes a type t^1, and that the value of the lease is $V = v(t^1)$ to all bidders, where v is nondecreasing. The non-neighbors have uninformative types $t^2, \ldots, t^N$, which can serve only to guide the randomization of bids. By the monotonic selection theorem, we lose no generality in assuming that all bidders use nondecreasing bid functions $\beta^j : [0, 1) \to \mathbb{R}_+$.

5.3.1 Equilibrium[5]

We first state the equilibrium for the case of two bidders. The model is one of a first-price auction.

Theorem 5.3.1. Suppose that v is continuously differentiable, is nondecreasing, and has positive right-hand derivative at zero. Then the two-bidder drainage tract auction model has a unique Nash equilibrium. At equilibrium, the neighbor and non-neighbor bidders both bid $\beta(s) = \frac{1}{s} \int_0^s v(r)\, dr$. The non-neighbor receives an expected profit of zero, conditional on winning: $E[v(t^1)|\beta(t^1) < x] - x = 0$ for all x in the range of β.

Remark. The equilibrium strategy prescribes that each bidder of type s bid $E[v(t^1)|t^1 < s]$. Although the setting is very different from the two-person independent private-values model, the equilibrium bid functions in the two models are identical. At equilibrium in the drainage tract model, the non-neighbor randomizes: Its type bears no relation to the value of the tract or his rival's type, but it uses it to select a bid randomly. To provide the neighbor with appropriate incentives, the non-neighbor must randomize in a way that reproduces the bid distribution it would have generated in the two-person independent private-values model, in which its value is $v(t^2)$ instead of $v(t^1)$. The non-neighbor is willing to randomize because, given the bidding strategy of the neighbor, all bids in the range of the bid function have the same expected payoff of zero. The neighbor is willing to play the same equilibrium strategy as in

---

[5] The equilibrium characterizations in this subsection are based primarily on Engelbrecht-Wiggans, Milgrom, and Weber (1983) and the extensions developed by Hendricks, Porter, and Wilson (1994). Weverbergh (1979) was the first to identify a Nash equilibrium in a version of the drainage tract model.

the independent private-values model because, given the strategy of the non-neighbor, it faces the same decision problem in both games.

Proof. We begin by verifying that the proposed strategies constitute an equilibrium. The payoff maximization problem for bidder 1 is

$$\max_{x} (v(s) - x)\beta^{-1}(x).$$

The first-order condition is $0 = -\beta^{-1}(x) + (v(s) - x)\frac{d}{dx}\beta^{-1}(x)$. Recall that by the inverse function theorem $\frac{d}{dx}\beta^{-1}(x)|_{x=\beta(s)} = 1/\beta'(s)$. Also, if β is an equilibrium strategy, then $x = \beta(s)$ maximizes bidder 1's payoff. Substituting $x = \beta(s)$, $s = \beta^{-1}(x)$, $\frac{d}{dx}\beta^{-1}(x)|_{x=\beta(s)} = 1/\beta'(s)$ into the first-order condition leads to $0 = -s\beta'(s) + v(s) - \beta(s)$. We can rewrite this equation as $\frac{d}{ds}[s\beta(s)] = v(s)$. Integrating both sides, we obtain $\beta(s) = \frac{1}{s}\int_0^s v(r)\,dr$.

By construction, $\beta(s)$ satisfies the first-order condition for all s, so it must satisfy the envelope formula. Because $v(s) - \beta(s) \geq 0$, we see from the first-order condition that β is also increasing.[6] Bidder 1 has no more profitable bid outside the range of β: bidding $\beta(1)$ dominates any bid higher than $\beta(1)$, and any bid lower than $\beta(0)$ does no better than bidding $\beta(0)$. By the constraint simplification theorem, if bidder 2 plays the strategy β, then bidder 1's best reply is to play β.

When bidder 2's type is s, his expected payoff from making any bid $\beta(s)$ in the range of β is

$$\int_0^s (v(\tau) - \beta(s))\,d\tau = s(E[v(t^1)|t^1 < s] - \beta(s)) = 0.$$

By inspection, bidder 2 cannot earn a higher expected payoff by bidding outside the range of β, so the prescribed bid of $\beta(s)$ is a best reply. Therefore, the proposed strategies constitute an equilibrium.

Note that the preceding equation also establishes the last statement of the theorem: for x in the range of β, say $x = \beta(s)$,

$$E[v(t^1)|\beta(t^1) < x] - x = E[v(t^1)|t^1 < s] - \beta(s) = 0.$$

Next, we show that the equilibrium is unique. We begin with the familiar arguments of chapter 4, which impose necessary conditions for any equilibrium. First, the range of the bid functions β^1 and β^2 must be the same and must be a convex set, for otherwise some type could profitably

---

[6] This conclusion also uses our assumption that $v'_+(0) > 0$.

reduce its bid without reducing its probability of winning. Second, because bidder 2 randomizes, the bids in the support of the randomization must have equal expected profits. Third, bidder 2's lowest equilibrium bid $\beta^2(0)$ never wins, so bidder 2 must earn a zero expected profit from all his bids, and we must have $\beta^1(0) = \beta^2(0) = v(0)$. Fourth, player 1 makes only profitable bids: $\beta^1(s) \le v(s)$. Fifth, bidder 2's bid distribution must be atomless, except possibly at $v(0)$, for otherwise bidder 1 could profit by increasing his bid slightly when the bid falls just below the atom. Given the identical ranges of the bid function, bidder 1's bid distribution must be atomless everywhere, for otherwise 2 would have a strictly profitable bid. Last, bidder 1's strategy must be nondecreasing, and, because it is atomless, it must be strictly increasing.

If bidder 1 uses the increasing strategy $\beta^1 = \beta$ and bidder 2 bids x, then bidder 2 wins when $\beta(t^1) < x$ and earns a payoff of $v(t^1) - x$, so his expected payoff from a bid of $x > \beta(0)$ is

$$\int_0^{\beta^{-1}(x)} (v(s) - x)\, ds = 0.$$

Substituting $x = \beta(r)$, bidder 1's equilibrium strategy must satisfy

$$\int_0^r (v(s) - \beta(r))\, ds = 0.$$

Therefore,

$$\beta(r) = \frac{1}{r} \int_0^r v(s)\, ds.$$

The preceding argument establishes that bidder 1 has a unique equilibrium strategy $\beta^1 = \beta$.

Now suppose that player 2 bids according to the increasing strategy β^2. Then its bid distribution F is the inverse, that is, $F(\beta^2(s)) = s$. Then, when bidder 1's type is s, bidder 1's payoff maximization problem is $\max_x (v(s) - x)F(x)$. The first-order condition for bidder 1's problem evaluated at his equilibrium bid $x = \beta(s)$ is $-F(x) + (v(\beta^{-1}(x)) - x)f(x) = 0$. We rewrite this equation as a differential equation: $\frac{d}{dx} \ln F(x) = 1/(v(\beta^{-1}(x)) - x)$. The rewritten equation is valid for $x > v(0) = \beta(0)$, because $v(s) > \beta(s)$ for $s > 0$.

Because the supports of the bid distributions for the two bidders are identical, they must make the same highest bid: $\beta^2(1) = \beta^1(1)$. Recalling that $\beta^2 = F^{-1}$, we have $1 = F(\beta^2(1)) = F(\beta^1(1))$. Thus, the differential equation $\frac{d}{dx} \ln F(x) = 1/(v(\beta^{-1}(x)) - x)$ and boundary condition

$1 = F(\beta^1(1))$ completely determine F, so bidder 2's equilibrium strategy is also unique. ∎

The equilibrium has a feature that is common in game theoretic models but nevertheless puzzling: bidder 2 is indifferent among his various bids, and his strategy fixes probabilities to make bidder 1's optimization problem have the prescribed solution. The puzzle is how such a pattern of behavior might arise in reality, i.e., how the bidders might learn to bid in this fashion. This puzzle is beyond the scope of this book, so we leave to others the problem of explaining how this "equilibrium" could arise over time.

When there is one neighbor, but multiple non-neighbors participate in the auction, then there are many equilibria, but all are closely related to the equilibrium identified in theorem 5.3.1.

Theorem 5.3.2. Suppose there are one neighbor ($j = 1$) and $N - 1$ non-neighbors ($j = 2, \ldots, N$), where $N \geq 2$. Suppose the value function v is continuously differentiable with $v'(0) > 0$. Let $\beta^1 = \beta$ denote an increasing strategy for the neighbor, and ($\beta^2, \ldots, \beta^N$) denote increasing strategies for the non-neighbors. Let $F^j = (\beta^j)^{-1}$, $j = 1, \ldots, N$, denote the corresponding bid distributions (with $F = F^1$). Then the strategy profile ($\beta, \beta^2, \ldots, \beta^N$) constitutes a Nash equilibrium if $\beta(s) = E[v(t^1)|t^1 \leq s]$ and for all x in the range of β we have $F(x) = F^2(x) \cdots F^N(x)$. Each non-neighbor's expected profit is zero conditional on his equilibrium bid and the event that his bid wins.

Proof. Note that when a non-neighbor, say bidder 2, wins with a bid of x, its expected profit is $E[v(t^1)|\beta^j(t^j) < x, j \neq 2] - x = E[v(t^1)|\beta^1(t^1) < x] - x = 0$. The first equality follows because types are independent; the second follows from theorem 5.3.1. Therefore, the prescribed strategies for the non-neighbors are best replies to the strategies of the other bidders.

When $t^1 = s$, the neighbor solves $\max_x (v(s) - x)F^2(x) \cdots F^N(x) = \max_x (v(s) - x)F(x)$. This payoff function is identical to the one studied in theorem 5.3.1, so bidding $\beta(s)$ is a best reply for bidder 1 of type s. Hence, the strategies form a Nash equilibrium. ∎

Theorem 5.3.2 derives two more surprising conclusions from the model, namely, that the neighbor's *bidding behavior* is independent of the number of opposing bidders and that its *expected payoff* is similarly independent. Because the non-neighbors are indifferent about their bids, any bid distribution with the same support as the neighbor's bid distribution is a best reply. The condition that the non-neighbors' bids all earn zero expected profit determines the neighbor's bids, and the condition that the neighbor's strategy is a best reply determines the distribution of the non-neighbors' maximum bid.

Hendricks, Porter, and Wilson (1994) tested the conclusions of the model about bidding and profits using data on oil leases on drainage tracts on the outer continental shelf. They found fewer relatively low bids among non-neighbors than the model predicted, but were otherwise unable to reject even the most striking of the model's predictions. They estimated that non-neighbors earned zero profits and that neighbors earned positive profits. The bid distribution of the neighbor and the bid distribution of the highest bid among the non-neighbors are the same, and they do not vary with the number of non-neighbors. The diagram in Figure 1, drawn from their paper, plots the bid distributions.

As the plot shows, high non-neighbor bids were comparatively scarce in the range between about $60,000 and $1 million, but matched the bid distribution of the high neighbor bid in the higher range of bids. To account for this pattern of bidding, the authors suggested modifying the preceding model by allowing the seller to set a random reserve price that

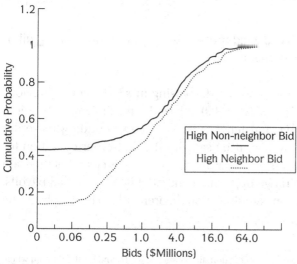

All bids are represented in 1972 dollars.

Figure 1. Distribution of bids.

may be correlated with the value. Because we introduce the methods required to analyze correlated bids later in the book, we restrict attention here to a variation of their model in which the reserve price is not correlated with the value.

Theorem 5.3.3. Suppose there are one neighbor ($j = 1$) and $N - 1$ non-neighbors ($j = 2, \ldots, N$), where $N \geq 2$. Suppose the value function v is continuously differentiable and $v'(0) > 0$. Let G denote the distribution of the random reserve price r set by the seller, and assume that G is continuously differentiable. Let $\beta(s) = E[v(t^1)|t^1 \leq s]$. Assume that there is some reserve price r such that:

1. $\forall x < r$, $d \ln G(x)/d \ln x \geq d \ln \beta^{-1}(x)/d \ln x$, and
2. $\forall x > r$, $G(x) > \beta^{-1}(x)$.

Given a profile of increasing strategies ($\beta^1, \ldots, \beta^N$), let $F^j = (\beta^j)^{-1}$ be the corresponding bid distributions. Then ($\beta^1, \ldots, \beta^N$) is a Nash equilibrium if the following two conditions hold:

$$
G(x)F^2(x) \cdots F^N(x) = \begin{cases} G(x) & \text{for } x \leq r, \\ \beta^{-1}(x) & \text{for } x \geq r \end{cases} \tag{5.2}
$$

and

$$
\beta^1(s) = \begin{cases} \arg\max_{x \leq r} (v(s) - x)\, G(x) & \text{for } s \leq \beta^{-1}(r), \\ \beta(s) & \text{for } s \geq \beta^{-1}(r). \end{cases} \tag{5.3}
$$

Each non-neighbor's expected profit is zero, conditional on its equilibrium bid and the event that its bid wins.

Proof. By construction β^1 is nondecreasing in s.[7] Using our previous analysis, for $s \geq \beta^{-1}(r)$, $\beta^1(s) = \beta(s)$ solves the maximization problem $\max_{x \geq r} (v(s) - x)\beta^{-1}(x)$ and hence satisfies the corresponding first-order condition. By construction, $\beta^1(s)$ satisfies the first-order condition for the problem $\max_{x \leq r} (v(s) - x)G(x)$ for $s \leq \beta^{-1}(r)$. It is clear that there are no bids outside the range of β^1 that generate higher expected payoffs. Hence, by the constraint simplification theorem, β^1 is a best reply for the neighbor (bidder 1).

---

[7] By inspection, β^1 is increasing on the domain where $s < \beta^{-1}(r)$ and on the domain where $s > \beta^{-1}(r)$, and β^1 is continuous at $s = \beta^{-1}(r)$.

Consider the family of maximization problems $\max_{x \leq r} \ln (v(s) - x) + H(x, \lambda)$, where $H(x, \lambda) = \lambda \ln G(x) + (1 - \lambda) \ln \beta^{-1}(x)$. By the assumption that $d \ln G(x)/d \ln x \geq d \ln b^{-1}(x)/d \ln x$, $H(x, \lambda)$ is supermodular.[8] From theorem 5.3.2, we know that $\beta(s)$ solves the problem for $\lambda = 0$, and by construction we know that $\beta^1(s)$ solves it for $\lambda = 1$. Because $H(x, \lambda)$ is supermodular and hence has single-crossing differences, the monotonic selection theorem implies that $\beta^1(s) \geq \beta(s)$. It follows that if a non-neighbor bids any amount $x \leq r$, then his expected profit, conditional on winning, is $E[v(t^1)|x \geq \beta^1(t^1)] - x \leq E[v(t^1)|x \geq \beta(t^1)] - x = 0$, where the equality follows from theorem 5.3.2. So, for a non-neighbor, any bid less than r earns a non-positive payoff. By construction, bids above r in the range of β lead to zero profits, by theorem 5.3.2. Any bid $x > \beta(1) = E[v(t^1)]$ always wins but earns negative expected profits ($E[v(t^1)] - x < 0$), and any bid $x < \beta(0)$ always loses. So each non-neighbor's strategy is a best reply as well. ∎

At any equilibrium, introducing a reserve cannot reduce the neighbor's bid. If the probability that the seller's reserve is greater than some number x is low, then the equilibrium is supported by having the non-neighbors bid above that level sufficiently often to make the probabilities match those of theorem 5.3.2. That is consistent with equilibrium for the non-neighbors, because they are indifferent about their bids. It is also consistent with equilibrium for the neighbor, because his problem is the same as in the preceding analysis. If the probability that the seller's reserve exceeds some number x is high, then the neighbor's bids are adjusted to be a best reply to those bids, and the non-neighbors do not place bids in that range.

5.3.2 Profits and Revenues[9]

The theorems presented thus far in this section conclude that non-neighbors always earn zero profits, but what of the neighbor? Here we derive a formula for the neighbor's profits when there is no reserve price or, more generally, when $G(x) \geq \beta^{-1}(x)$ for all x, i.e. when the seller's reserve does not crowd out non-neighbor bids at any level. In such cases,

---

[8] Observe that $\partial H/\partial \lambda = \ln[G(x)/\beta^{-1}(x)]$. Condition (1) of the theorem holds that this expression increases in x, so $H(x, \lambda)$ is supermodular.

[9] The results of the next three sections are due to Milgrom and Weber (1982b).

the probability that a neighbor of type s wins is just s, so by the envelope theorem, the maximum expected profit of a neighbor of type t is

$$\Pi(t) = V(0) + \int_0^t sv'(s)\,ds = \int_0^t sv'(s)\,ds. \tag{5.4}$$

The corresponding *ex ante* expected profit of the neighbor is therefore

$$\int_0^1 \Pi(t)\,dt = \int_0^1 \int_0^t sv'(s)\,ds\,dt = \int_0^1 \int_s^1 dt\,sv'(s)\,ds$$

$$= \int_0^1 (1-s)sv'(s)\,ds. \tag{5.5}$$

In the applications to follow, it will be important to keep track of the information on which bids are based. In the next theorem, we use the subscript V to mean that the neighbor observes the value or value estimate V. Later, we will replace that subscript with whatever information the neighbor is supposed to have observed.

Theorem 5.3.4. Suppose that v is nondecreasing and continuously differentiable, and define $H_V(x) = \Pr\{v(t^1) \le x\}$.[10] Then, conditional on $v(t) = w$, the neighbor's expected profit is

$$\Pi_V(w) = \int_0^w H_V(z)\,dz, \tag{5.6}$$

the neighbor's *ex ante* expected profit is

$$\bar{\pi}_V = \int_0^\infty H_V(z)(1 - H_V(z))\,dz, \tag{5.7}$$

and the seller's expected revenue is $E[v(t^1)] - \bar{\pi}_V$.

Proof. Perform the change of variables $z = v(s)$ and $s = H_V(z)$ wherever $v'(s) > 0$. Then, using (5.4) with $v(t) = w$, we have $\Pi_V(w) = \Pi(t) = \int_0^t sv'(s)\,ds = \int_0^w H_V(z)\,dz$. Similarly,

$$\bar{\pi}_V = \int_0^\infty \Pi_V(w)\,dH_V(w) = \int_0^\infty \int_0^w H_V(y)\,dy\,dH_V(w)$$

$$= \int_0^\infty \int_y^\infty dH_V(w)\,H_V(y)\,dy = \int_0^\infty (1 - H_V(y))H_V(y)\,dy. \qquad \blacksquare$$

---

[10] If v is invertible, then H_v is the inverse of v.

Theorem 5.3.4 puts the profit and revenue expressions into a form that is handy for further analysis.

5.3.3 Bidder Information Policy

Information is valuable for decision making when it makes better decisions possible. In classical decision theory, the value of information cannot be negative. Relevant information allows more accurate decisions, and irrelevant information can just be ignored.

In game theoretic models, a similar claim holds when the information gathering process is unobserved: the decision maker can simply use the information to make better decisions. But information in games can also have a second effect: it can alter the way others behave, even if they do not learn the information. For example, in the drainage tract model, the (uninformed) non-neighbor's strategy depends on what the (informed) neighbor knows. In general games, information can either help or harm the informed party. These effects create incentives for the party to reveal or conceal the extent of its information.

In this subsection, we explore how each bidder's information affects others' bids by asking the following questions. Does improving the neighbor's information make the non-neighbor bid more timidly or more aggressively? If the neighbor acquires additional information, would it prefer that the non-neighbors know it has acquired it? Or would it prefer to conceal its access to the extra information? If the non-neighbor gains access to information, would it prefer to reveal or conceal that access?

We begin by evaluating the value of information to the neighbor. Suppose that the full information value of the tract is V and that the neighbor observes a random variable X that provides information relevant to V. If the neighbor could also observe a random variable Y that provides additional information about V, would it prefer to observe Y even if the non-neighbors were aware of its observing Y? If it observed Y, would it *want* the non-neighbors to be aware it had obtained this additional information? Are these incentives uniform, or do the answers to the preceding questions depend on the realizations of X and Y?

As we have seen, the neighbor's profits do not depend on the number of non-neighbors, so we simplify the discussion by focusing on the case of just two bidders. We begin by studying the neighbor's profits in two auction games, distinguished by whether the neighbor observes (and is believed to have observed) just X or both X and Y. Let $V_X = E[V|X]$

and $V_{XY} = E[V|X, Y]$, and let H_X and H_{XY} be the respective distributions of these two random variables. Let F_X and F_{XY} be the equilibrium bid distributions for the non-neighbor in the two games, and let

$$\Pi_X(w) = \max_x(w - x)F_X(x) \quad \text{and} \quad \Pi_{XY}(w) = \max_x(w - x)F_{XY}(x)$$

(5.8)

be the neighbor's expected profit in the events that $V_X = w$ or $V_{XY} = w$, respectively. With these definitions, we can state the main result:

Theorem 5.3.5. For every possible realization of X and Y, one has $\Pi_X(w) \le \Pi_{XY}(w)$. (That is, the neighbor's expected payoff is higher if the non-neighbor believes it has observed both X and Y.)

Proof. In view of theorem 5.3.4 (particularly (5.6)), we have

$$\Pi_X(w) = \int_0^w H_X(z)\, dz \quad \text{and} \quad \Pi_{XY}(w) = \int_0^w H_{XY}(z)\, dz.$$

(5.9)

By the law of iterated expectations, $E[V_{XY}|X] = E[E[V|X, Y]|X] = E[V|X] = V_X$. So V_{XY} is a *mean-preserving spread* of V_X, and hence, for every number w, $\int_0^w H_X(z)\, dz \le \int_0^w H_{XY}(z)\, dz$. ∎

The neighbor's expected profit, given its value estimate, depends on how the non-neighbor bids, which depends, in turn, on what the non-neighbor believes. According to theorem 5.3.5, the non-neighbor bids "more timidly" when it believes the neighbor is better informed; that is, the maximum expected profit that the neighbor can earn is uniformly higher in that case.

One way to proceed would be to create a model in which it is uncertain whether the neighbor observes just X or both X and Y. If the neighbor can either make unverifiable announcements or offer proof it has observed Y, what information will it provide in equilibrium? In equilibrium, the neighbor will offer proof whenever it observes both variables; it will never conceal its information gathering. The non-neighbor will base its strategy on proven statements but will ignore the neighbor's unproven announcements, which might include false claims about the information the neighbor has observed. The analysis would follow in the path of Grossman (1981) and Milgrom (1981a).

Rather than developing that model, we focus on the stark contrast between the neighbor's and non-neighbor's incentives to reveal or conceal information gathering capabilities. Suppose it is common knowledge that the neighbor observes X and Y and everyone anticipates that the non-neighbor will observe nothing. Suppose that, contrary to expectation, the non-neighbor manages to observe Y. Would it, like the neighbor, wish to publicize that fact? Or, if it could, would it prefer to convince the neighbor by its silence that it has not observed anything?

If the non-neighbor reveals publicly that it has observed Y, then the only private information in the model will be the neighbor's observation X. We have already seen that, in such cases, the non-neighbor earns an expected profit of zero. In contrast, if the neighbor believes that the non-neighbor is uninformed, the non-neighbor's expected profits are generally positive. Given those beliefs and any realization of X and Y, the neighbor never bids more than $E[V]$.[11] Hence, whenever $E[V|Y] > E[V]$, the non-neighbor can earn an expected profit of $E[V|Y] - E[V] > 0$ simply by bidding $E[V]$. Consequently, the non-neighbor's optimal disclosure policy is strikingly different from the neighbor's:

Theorem 5.3.6. Suppose it is common knowledge that the neighbor observes X and Y. Then, for every realization of Y, if the non-neighbor learns Y, his expected profit is at least as high if the neighbor believes it has not learned Y.

We observed above that we could embed the neighbor's decision to reveal its acquisition of information in a larger game in which it only observes Y with some probability, and obviously we could do the same for the non-neighbor. Theorem 5.3.6 suggests that there is no equilibrium of the larger game in which the non-neighbor always reveals the fact that it has observed Y.

5.3.4 Seller Information Policy
The seller cares as much as the bidders about who knows what, because the distribution of information can affect the expected sale price or the efficiency of the allocation (although the second effect is obviously absent from common value models like the drainage tract model).

---

[11] The neighbor bids $E[V_{XY}|V_{XY} < w]$, so he never bids more than $E[V_{XY}|V_{XY} < \infty] = E[V_{XY}] = E[V]$.

In managing leases of oil rights on federal lands, the US Department of the Interior requires the company developing a tract to make periodic reports, which the Department uses in determining royalty payments. Before drainage tract auctions, the government could reveal some of the information in those reports to other bidders. The government also could itself conduct research, such as seismic studies, to reveal information about the value of various government-owned properties. In this section, we investigate the effects of policies like these on seller revenues.

We first model the policy of revealing bidder-generated information. Suppose the neighbor observes the pair (X, Y) and reports Y to the government (the seller). If the seller does not make Y public, then, in analogy to (5.7), the neighbor's *ex ante* expected payoff is

$$\bar{\pi}_{XY} = \int_0^\infty H_{XY}(z)(1 - H_{XY}(z))\, dz,$$

where $H_{XY}(z) = \Pr\{V_{XY} \le z\}$. If the seller publicly announces Y, the non-neighbor's beliefs about the neighbor's estimate are $H_{XY}(z|Y) = \Pr\{V_{XY} \le z|Y\}$. The neighbor's expected profit conditional on Y is therefore

$$\pi(Y) = \int_0^\infty H_{XY}(z|Y)(1 - H_{XY}(z|Y))\, dz.$$

Theorem 5.3.7. When the seller makes the bidder's report Y public, the neighbor's expected profit falls:

$$E\left[\pi(Y)\right] \le \bar{\pi}_{XY}, \tag{5.10}$$

and the seller's expected revenue rises.

Proof. When the seller discloses Y, the neighbor's expected payoff is

$$
\begin{aligned}
E[\pi(Y)] &= E\left[\int_0^\infty H_{XY}(z|Y)\,(1 - H_{XY}(z|Y))\, dz\right] \\
&= \int_0^\infty E\left[H_{XY}(z|Y)\,(1 - H_{XY}(z|Y))\right] dz \\
&\le \int_0^\infty E\left[H_{XY}(z|Y)\right](1 - E\left[H_{XY}(z|Y)\right])\, dz \\
&= \int_0^\infty H_{XY}(z)\,(1 - H_{XY}(z))\, dz = \bar{\pi}_{XY},
\end{aligned}
$$

where the inequality follows from Jensen's inequality and the last step holds by the law of iterated expectations, because

$$H_{XY}(z) = E[1_{\{V_{XY} \le z\}}] = E[E[1_{\{V_{XY} \le z\}}|Y]] = E[H_{XY}(z|Y)].$$

Because the non-neighbor's expected profit is zero in both cases, the seller's expected revenue rises from $E[V] - \bar{\pi}_{XY}$ to $E[V] - E[\pi(Y)]$. ∎

Now we examine the seller's decision to generate its own information. Intuitively, this kind of information can have two effects. First, as when the seller reveals the neighbor's information, the seller's disclosure tells the non-neighbor something about the value of the drainage tract and thus makes the neighbor's information less private. Intuition suggests, and the following analysis confirms, that this effect always reduces the neighbor's expected profit and increases the seller's expected revenue. However, there is a second effect, which can either increase or decrease the bidder's expected profits, depending on whether the seller's information is a substitute or a complement to the neighbor's information for the purpose of estimating the value of the drainage tract.

We now formalize these two effects. Suppose that the neighbor observes X and the seller observes Y, where both are real-valued random variables. Denote the respective conditional expectations by $\bar{v}(x) = E[V|X = x]$ and $\hat{v}(x, y) = E[V|X = x, Y = y]$. Assume that both $\bar{v}$ and $\hat{v}$ are continuously differentiable and increasing in x, with $\bar{v}'(x) > 0$ and $\hat{v}_1(x, y) = \partial \hat{v}(x, y)/\partial x > 0$. Let G_X be the distribution function for X. Then, using expression (5.5) and substituting $s = G_X(x)$ and so $v(s) = \bar{v}(x)$, we obtain the neighbor's *ex ante* expected profit when Y is not revealed:

$$\int_0^1 s(1 - s)v'(s)\, ds = \int_0^\infty G_X(x)(1 - G_X(x))\bar{v}'(x)\, dx.$$

Similarly, when Y is revealed, the neighbor's *ex ante* expected profit is

$$E\left[\int_0^\infty (1 - G_X(x|Y))G_X(x|Y)\hat{v}_1(x, Y)\, dx\right].$$

So the change in the neighbor's expected profit when the seller reveals Y is

$$\Delta = E\left[\int_0^\infty (1 - G_X(x|Y))G_X(x|Y)\hat{v}_1(x, Y)\, dx\right]$$
$$- \int_0^\infty (1 - G_X(x))G_X(x)\bar{v}'(x)\, dx. \qquad (5.11)$$

Our objective is to analyze this change Δ.

Theorem 5.3.8. The change in the neighbor's expected profits when the seller reveals its own private information Y is Δ and the change in the seller's expected revenue is $-\Delta$, where $\Delta = P + W$,

$$P = \int_0^\infty \{E[(1 - G_X(x|Y))G_X(x|Y)] - (1 - G_X(x))G_X(x)\}\bar{v}'(x)\, dx,$$
$$\qquad (5.12)$$

and

$$W = E\left\{\int_0^\infty (1 - G_X(x|Y))G_X(x|Y)[\hat{v}_1(x, Y) - \bar{v}'(x)]\, dx\right\}. \qquad (5.13)$$

For all X and Y, $P \leq 0$.

Proof. Compute $\Delta = P + W$ by adding (5.12) and (5.13) to get (5.11). As the non-neighbor's expected profit is zero, the seller's expected revenue is the expected value of the tract minus the neighbor's expected revenue, so the change in the seller's expected revenue is $-\Delta$. Using $E[(1 - G_X(x|Y))G_X(x|Y)] \leq (1 - E[G_X(x|Y)])E[G_X(x|Y)] = (1 - G_X(x))G_X(x)$ (by Jensen's inequality and the law of iterated expectations), multiply both sides by $\bar{v}'(x) > 0$, and integrate to establish that $P \leq 0.\blacksquare$

Theorem 5.3.8 decomposes the total effect on revenue of the seller's announcement into the sum of two terms. The *publicity effect* P shows how the neighbor's expected profit would change if the information Y contributed nothing to the neighbor's value estimate, that is, if $\bar{v} = \hat{v}$. In that case, the only effect of revealing Y would be to give the non-neighbor some information about the neighbor's estimate. The theorem's assertion that $P \leq 0$ emphasizes that this effect always reduces the neighbor's expected profit.

The *weighting effect* W depends on the difference $\hat{v}_1(x, Y) - \bar{v}'(x)$, which shows how the observation of Y amplifies or reduces the impact of the observation X on the neighbor's estimate of the value. If the term $\hat{v}_1(x, Y) - \bar{v}'(x)$ is everywhere negative, then $W < 0$; we call this the case of *informational substitutes*. To illustrate this case, suppose that $\hat{v}(x, y) = b_0 + b_x x + b_y y$ with $b_x, b_y > 0$. Then $\bar{v}(x) = \hat{v}(x, E[Y|X = x]) = b_0 + b_x x + b_y E[Y|X = x]$. So, if $E[Y|X = x]$ is increasing, then $\hat{v}_1(x, Y) - \bar{v}'(x) < 0$. When the observations are informational substitutes, revealing Y further reduces the neighbor's profits.

Corollary 5.3.1. If X and Y are informational substitutes, then $\Delta < 0$.[12]

The weighting effect is zero when the seller's information is poorer than the neighbor's, that is, when $Y = X + \varepsilon$ for some error term ε that is independent of the other random variables in the model. In that case, learning Y has no effect on the neighbor's estimate.

It is also possible that X and Y are *informational complements* ($W > 0$), that is, that revealing Y increases the usefulness of the neighbor's private information X. For example, suppose that $X = V + \varepsilon_X$, where ε_X is an independent error term, and suppose $\bar{v}(x) = a + bx$. Naturally, $b < 1$. Suppose that $Y = \varepsilon_X$. Then, revealing information results in $\hat{v}(x, y) = x - y$, so revealing Y increases the weight assigned to X in estimating V. In this case, $W > 0$: the weighting effect benefits the neighbor when the information Y is revealed. Moreover, in this specification, X and Y are independent, so $G_X(x) \equiv G_X(x|Y)$ and hence $P = 0$. In this example, the seller does strictly worse by revealing its information Y.

5.4 Correlated Types and Interdependent Values

Several of the results in this section use the notion of affiliation, which Milgrom and Weber (1982a) introduced into the auction literature. Affiliation captures the idea that higher values of one variable make higher values of the others more likely. We begin this section by presenting important results about affiliation we will use. In the subsections to follow, we study two models of ascending auctions that differ in how much bidders can infer from earlier bids, characterizing the equilibrium in each case. We study the efficiency and revenues of these ascending auctions and compare them with first-price auctions. We also study how

---

[12] Milgrom and Weber (1982b) show that a sufficient condition for X and Y to be informational substitutes is that (X, Y, V) is affiliated. Section 5.4 defines affiliation and explores some of its consequences.

the seller's policy about revealing or concealing information affects the auction outcomes.

5.4.1 Affiliation

The definition of affiliation uses concepts from lattice theory. Recall that given two points $x, y \in \mathbb{R}^N$, we write $x \geq y$ to mean that $x_1 \geq y_1, \ldots, x_N \geq y_N$, and $x > y$ to mean that $x \geq y$ and $x \neq y$. The *meet* is defined by $x \wedge y = (\min(x_1, y_1), \ldots, \min(x_N, y_N))$, and the *join* by $x \vee y = (\max(x_1, y_1), \ldots, \max(x_N, y_N))$. A function $f : \mathbb{R}^N \to \mathbb{R}^M$ is *isotone* if $x \geq y \Rightarrow f(x) \geq f(y)$. A particularly important condition for this chapter is *affiliation*, which we now define.

Definition. Suppose the random variables $X_1, \ldots, X_N$ have joint density f.[13] Then the random variables are *affiliated* if and only if $f(x) f(y) \leq f(x \wedge y) f(x \vee y) \, \forall x, y \in \mathbb{R}^N$.

To see how the definition captures our intuitive description of affiliation, let $N = 2$, and consider $x_1 > y_1$ and $x_2 < y_2$. Then we can rewrite the affiliation condition, which is $f(x_1, x_2) f(y_1, y_2) \leq f(x_1, y_2) f(y_1, x_2)$, as $f(x_1, x_2)/f(y_1, x_2) \leq f(x_1, y_2)/f(y_1, y_2)$. Dividing both the numerator and denominator on the left-hand side by the marginal density $f_2(x_2)$ and on the right-hand side by $f_2(y_2)$ leads to $f(x_1|x_2)/f(y_1|x_2) \leq f(x_1|y_2)/f(y_1|y_2)$. Thus, the original condition is equivalent to the intuitive statement that a higher value of X_2 makes higher values of X_1 relatively more likely.

Notice that (letting $\log 0 = -\infty$) the affiliation inequality is equivalent to the statement that the logarithm of the joint density function f is supermodular:

$$\log f(x) + \log f(y) \leq \log f(x \wedge y) + \log f(x \vee y).$$

We say that a function f satisfying the above condition exhibits *log-supermodularity* and call the corresponding inequality the *affiliation inequality*. When the random variables $X_1, \ldots, X_N$ are statistically

---

[13] Milgrom and Weber (1982a) give a general definition that applies even when the random variables have no densities. They establish that it is equivalent to the definition above for random variables that do have a joint density. Athey (2001) analyzes the existence of monotonic equilibrium using log-supermodularity and related conditions. See also Athey (2002).

independent, they are trivially affiliated; the affiliation inequality holds with equality.

The observation that affiliation is log-supermodular reminds us that order-preserving transformations of the underlying variables do not affect the property. This fact is important for our theory, because when bidders' strategies $\beta^i : [0, 1) \to \mathbb{R}$ are increasing, the vector of bids is an order-preserving transformation of the unobserved vector of types.

To illustrate the principle in the context of auctions, let f_t and f_b denote the joint densities of the bidders' types and bids respectively. For convenience, assume for now that these densities exist and are positive and that the equilibrium bid function is differentiable. Fix two type profiles $\hat{t}$ and $\bar{t}$ and corresponding bid profiles $\hat{b} = (\beta^1(\hat{t}^1), \ldots, \beta^N(\hat{t}^N))$ and $\bar{b} = (\beta^1(\bar{t}^1), \ldots, \beta^N(\bar{t}^N))$, which we write compactly as $\hat{b} = \beta(\hat{t})$ and $\bar{b} = \beta(\bar{t})$.[14] Because bidder strategies are increasing in type, the cumulative density of types must equal the cumulative density of bids: $F_t(\hat{t}) = F_b(\hat{b}) = F_b(\beta(\hat{t}))$. One derives the relation between the corresponding densities by differentiating N times, as follows. First, $\partial F_t/\partial t^1 = (\partial F_b/\partial b^1) \cdot \beta^{1'}(t^1)$; next, $\partial^2 F_t/\partial t^1 \partial t^2 = (\partial^2 F_b/\partial b^1 \partial b^2) \cdot \beta^{1'}(t^1) \cdot \beta^{2'}(t^2)$; and so on, until we reach the following:

$$f_t(\hat{t}) = f_b(\hat{b})\beta^{1'}(\hat{t}^1) \cdots \beta^{N'}(\hat{t}^N),$$
$$f_t(\bar{t}) = f_b(\bar{b})\beta^{1'}(\bar{t}^1) \cdots \beta^{N'}(\bar{t}^N),$$
$$f_t(\hat{t} \vee \bar{t}) = f_b(\hat{b} \vee \bar{b})\beta^{1'}(\hat{t}^1 \vee \bar{t}^1) \cdots \beta^{N'}(\hat{t}^N \vee \bar{t}^N),$$
$$f_t(\hat{t} \wedge \bar{t}) = f_b(\hat{b} \wedge \bar{b})\beta^{1'}(\hat{t}^1 \wedge \bar{t}^1) \cdots \beta^{N'}(\hat{t}^N \wedge \bar{t}^N). \tag{5.14}$$

For each i, the set $\{\hat{t}^i, \bar{t}^i\} = \{\hat{t}^i \wedge \bar{t}^i, \hat{t}^i \vee \bar{t}^i\}$, so $\beta^{j'}(\hat{t}^j) \cdot \beta^{j'}(\bar{t}^j) = \beta^{j'}(\hat{t}^i \wedge \bar{t}^i) \cdot \beta^{j'}(\hat{t}^i \vee \bar{t}^i)$. Hence, combining the four equations of (5.14) and simplifying, we obtain

$$\frac{f_t(\hat{t} \wedge \bar{t}) f_t(\hat{t} \vee \bar{t})}{f_t(\hat{t}) f_t(\bar{t})} = \frac{f_b(\hat{b} \vee \bar{b}) f_b(\hat{b} \wedge \bar{b})}{f_b(\hat{b}) f_b(\bar{b})}.$$

Affiliation is the requirement that the ratios in the preceding equation exceed one, so the bids are affiliated if and only if the types are affiliated.

The next several results facilitate application of the theory of affiliated random variables to auctions. The first states that affiliation of every pair of variables in a set implies affiliation of the set and that, if the density

---

[14] Here, as above, we read the notation to respect the structure of the game, in which each bidder's bid depends just on his own type. Thus, $\hat{b}^j = \beta^j(\hat{t}^j)$ and $\bar{b}^j = \beta^j(\bar{t}^j)$.

function is smooth, one can check affiliation using a simple derivative formula.

Theorem 5.4.1. The function f is log-supermodular if and only if for every $i \neq j$, x_{-ij}, $x_i > \hat{x}_i$, and $x_j > \hat{x}_j$, one has

$$f(x_i, \hat{x}_j, x_{-ij}) f(\hat{x}_i, x_j, x_{-ij}) \leq f(x_i, x_j, x_{-ij}) f(\hat{x}_i, \hat{x}_j, x_{-ij}).$$

If f is positive and twice continuously differentiable, then f is log-supermodular if and only if $\partial^2 \log(f(x))/\partial x_i \partial x_j \geq 0$.

One can restate both parts of this theorem simply as theorems about supermodular functions. Proofs can be found in Topkis (1978) or Topkis (1998).

Theorem 5.4.2. If $f : \mathbb{R}_+^2 \to \mathbb{R}$ is log-supermodular, then $g(x_1, x_2) = \int_0^{x_1} f(s, x_2)\, ds$ is log-supermodular.

Proof. Let $x_1 > \hat{x}_1$ and $x_2 > \hat{x}_2$. Then

$$\frac{g(x_1, x_2)}{g(\hat{x}_1, x_2)} = \frac{\int_0^{x_1} f(s, x_2)\, ds}{\int_0^{\hat{x}_1} f(s, x_2)\, ds} = 1 + \frac{\int_{\hat{x}_1}^{x_1} \dfrac{f(s, x_2)}{f(\hat{x}_1, x_2)}\, ds}{\int_0^{\hat{x}_1} \dfrac{f(s, x_2)}{f(\hat{x}_1, x_2)}\, ds}$$

$$\geq 1 + \frac{\int_{\hat{x}_1}^{x_1} \dfrac{f(s, \hat{x}_2)}{f(\hat{x}_1, \hat{x}_2)}\, ds}{\int_0^{\hat{x}_1} \dfrac{f(s, \hat{x}_2)}{f(\hat{x}_1, \hat{x}_2)}\, ds} = \frac{g(x_1, \hat{x}_2)}{g(\hat{x}_1, \hat{x}_2)}.$$

The inequality follows because $f(s, x_{-1})/f(\hat{x}_1, x_{-1})$ is increasing in x_{-1} for $s > \hat{x}_1$ and decreasing in x_{-1} for $s < \hat{x}_1$. ∎

Theorem 5.4.3. If $f(x_1, x_2)$ is a log-supermodular probability density on $\mathbb{R}_+^2$, then

(1) the conditional density $f(x_1|x_2)$ is log-supermodular,
(2) the conditional cumulative distribution function $F(x_1|x_2)$ is log-supermodular, and
(3) the conditional cumulative distribution function $F(x_1|x_2)$ is non-increasing in x_2.

Proof. To show (1), note that the conditional density is $f(x_1|x_2) = f(x_1, x_2)/f_2(x_2)$, so $\ln f(x_1|x_2) = \ln f(x_1, x_2) - \ln f_2(x_2)$. It follows that $f(x_1|x_2)$ is log-supermodular if (and only if) $f(x_1, x_2)$ is log-supermodular.

To show (2), note that $F(x_1|x_2) = \int_0^{x_1} f(s|x_2)\, ds$, and apply theorem 5.4.2.

To show (3), fix x_1 and let $x_2 > \hat{x}_2$. By (2), $F(x_1|\hat{x}_2)/F(x_1|x_2) \geq \lim_{x\to\infty} F(x|\hat{x}_2)/F(x|x_2) = 1$, so $F(x_1|\hat{x}_2) \geq F(x_1|x_2)$. ∎

Notice that according to part (3), affiliation implies that certain conditional distributions are ordered by first-order stochastic dominance. The following result demonstrates another important property of affiliation: if a set of variables is affiliated, then any subset of the variables is also affiliated.

Theorem 5.4.4. If $f(x_1, \ldots, x_n)$ is a log-supermodular probability density, then $g(x_1, \ldots, x_{n-1}) = \int f(x_1, \ldots, x_{n-1}, s)\, ds$ is also a log-supermodular probability density.

Proof. It is trivial that g is a probability density, and the log-supermodularity result is trivial for the case $n = 2$. Accordingly, suppose that $n \geq 3$. It suffices to prove the result for any pair of variables x_i, x_j where $1 \leq i, j \leq n - 1$, so we focus on the case $i = 1, j = 2$. Fix $y = (x_3, \ldots, x_{n-1})$ (y is null if $n = 3$) and let $x_1 > \hat{x}_1$ and $x_2 > \hat{x}_2$. Because $f(s|\hat{x}_1, \hat{x}_2, y) = f(\hat{x}_1, \hat{x}_2, y, s)/\int f(\hat{x}_1, \hat{x}_2, y, t)\, dt$, it follows that

$$
\begin{aligned}
\frac{g(\hat{x}_1, x_2, y)}{g(\hat{x}_1, \hat{x}_2, y)} &= \frac{\int f(\hat{x}_1, x_2, y, s)\, ds}{\int f(\hat{x}_1, \hat{x}_2, y, s)\, ds} \\
&= \int \frac{f(\hat{x}_1, x_2, y, s)}{f(\hat{x}_1, \hat{x}_2, y, s)}\, f(s|\hat{x}_1, \hat{x}_2, y)\, ds \\
&\leq \int \frac{f(x_1, x_2, y, s)}{f(x_1, \hat{x}_2, y, s)}\, f(s|\hat{x}_1, \hat{x}_2, y)\, ds \\
&\leq \int \frac{f(x_1, x_2, y, s)}{f(x_1, \hat{x}_2, y, s)}\, f(s|x_1, \hat{x}_2, y)\, ds \\
&= \frac{\int f(x_1, x_2, y, s)\, ds}{\int f(x_1, \hat{x}_2, y, s)\, ds} = \frac{g(x_1, x_2, y)}{g(x_1, \hat{x}_2, y)}.
\end{aligned}
$$

The first inequality follows because, by log-supermodularity, the integrand is everywhere larger. Two observations imply the second inequality. First, by part (3) of theorem 5.4.3, the distribution $F(s|x_1, \hat{x}_2, y) \leq F(s|\hat{x}_1, \hat{x}_2, y)$ for all s. The conditional distribution given $x_1, \hat{x}_2, y$ is thus higher in the sense of first-order stochastic dominance than the conditional distribution given $\hat{x}_1, \hat{x}_2, y$.[15] Second, the ratio $f(x_1, x_2, y, s)/f(x_1, \hat{x}_2, y, s)$ is nondecreasing in s (by log-supermodularity of f). The inequality then follows from the definition of first-order stochastic dominance. ∎

Theorem 5.4.5. Suppose the random variables $X_1, \ldots, X_N$ are affiliated. Then, for every bounded isotone function $g : \mathbb{R}^N \to \mathbb{R}$, the function $h(x) = E[g(X_1, \ldots, X_N)|X_1 = x]$ is isotone.

Proof. The theorem is obvious in case $N = 1$. For $N = 2$, let $x_1 > \hat{x}_1$. Then $h(\hat{x}_1) = E[g(\hat{x}_1, X_2)|X_1 = \hat{x}_1] \leq E[g(x_1, X_2)|X_1 = \hat{x}_1] \leq E[g(x_1, X_2)|X_1 = x_1] = h(x_1)$. The first inequality follows from the isotonicity of g. Stochastic dominance implies the second; observe that $g(x_1, \cdot) : \mathbb{R} \to \mathbb{R}$ is nondecreasing and (by theorem 5.4.3, part (3)) that $F(x_2|x_1) \leq F(x_2|\hat{x}_1)$.

Next, consider $N \geq 3$, and suppose the theorem holds for all $m \leq N - 1$. Let $\hat{g}(x, y) = E[g(X_1, \ldots, X_N)|X_1 = x, X_2 = y]$. Holding $X_1 = x$, the right-hand side integrates a function of $N - 1$ variables, namely, $g(x, \cdot) : \mathbb{R}^{N-1} \to \mathbb{R}$. So, by the inductive hypothesis, $\hat{g}$ is nondecreasing in y. By a similar argument, it is also nondecreasing in x. Hence, $\hat{g}$ is isotone.

So $h(x) = E[g(X_1, \ldots, X_N)|X_1 = x] = E[E[g(X_1, \ldots, X_N)|X_1, X_2]|X_1 = x] = E[\hat{g}(X_1, X_2)|X_1 = x]$. Applying the inductive hypothesis again establishes that this last expression is nondecreasing in x. ∎

Theorem 5.4.6 (Milgrom and Weber). Suppose that the random variables $(X_1, X_2, \ldots, X_N, Y)$ have a joint density f that is symmetric in the components of X. Then $(X_1, X_2, \ldots, X_N, Y)$ is affiliated if and only if $(X^{(1)}, \ldots, X^{(N)}, Y)$ is affiliated.

Proof. The density of $(X^{(1)}, \ldots, X^{(N)}, Y)$ is $N! f(x, y) 1_{\{x_1 > \cdots > x_N\}}$, for there are $N!$ ways to arrange the components of X, and the indicator yields the value of the density only when these components are ordered. This density satisfies the affiliation inequality if and only if f does. ∎

---

[15] For the definition of first-order stochastic dominance, see, for example, definition 6.D.1 in Mas Colell, Whinston, and Green (1995). That reference also includes the characterization of stochastic dominance used here.

5.4.2 The Milgrom–Weber Ascending Auction Models

Ascending auctions follow a variety of formats. Oral outcry versions are the most commonly used. In these auctions, bidders call out bids until the auctioneer determines that bidding has stopped, and she then sells the lot or item at the highest bid price. In auctions for fish or livestock, a system of hand signals is often used to convey bids. The auctioneer can also control the progression of prices called out. For example, in the so-called Japanese auctions, the auctioneer raises the price until only one bidder is still willing to bid.

Vickrey introduced the second-price auction as a model of the English ascending auction. His now familiar idea was that each bidder's optimal strategy would be to bid until the bidding reaches his own predetermined reservation price, at which point the bidder would withdraw. The winning bidder would then be the one with the highest reservation price, and the winning bid would be approximately the second highest reservation price.

Vickrey's model omits the possibility that bidders learn something during the course of the auction that might cause them to change their reservation prices. If bidders can learn during the auction, then we need to pay close attention to auction rules influencing what bidders observe during the bidding process. For example, suppose that the auctioneer continuously raises the required bid and each bidder makes only one decision: when to quit bidding. We can think of the bidder as bidding by holding down a button and quitting by releasing the button (alternatively, quitting by pressing a button). Quitting in this way is assumed to be irreversible. In the version of this model that provides the least information to bidders, the auction mechanism provides no feedback to the bidder about the number of active bidders or their identities during this process. In this model, one can describe any pure strategy with a single reservation price,[16] so the Vickrey model incorporates any learning

---

[16] This reasoning is slightly informal, conflating *strategies* with *reduced strategies*. A *strategy* in a game specifies what a player does at every information set where he must act. So, formally, a bidder's strategy in this game must specify what he would do if he were still active when the required bid rose to x, even if the strategy also specifies that the bidder will withdraw when the required bid is $x - 1$. The actual outcomes in the auction game described here are completely determined by the *lowest* bid at which each bidder drops out, and two strategies that have the same lowest bid always lead to the same outcome. In game theory, a reduced strategy is a class of equivalent strategies in which each element always leads to the same outcome. So, in this auction game, it is the reduced strategy that specifies only the lowest price at which the bidder will drop out.

opportunities that bidders may have. That is, the ascending auction without feedback about active bidders is *strategically equivalent* to the Vickrey second-price auction model. We say that an ascending auction mechanism that offers bidders no information about the numbers or identities of active bidders provides *minimal information* in the class of ascending auction mechanisms.

In real English auctions, bidders usually observe additional information. We discuss one model of such a situation below, in which bidders observe the number of other bidders who are still active at every moment during the auction. We limit attention, however, to *button auction* models, in which a bidder's only decision is when to withdraw irreversibly from the bidding.[17] This model, due to Milgrom and Weber (1982a), is the first model of a button auction as well as the first model with general interdependent values and correlated types.

Throughout many of the models analyzed below, the *winner's curse* is a key feature. The winner's curse is a form of adverse selection. A bidder who wins in competition against well-informed bidders must be cognizant that the others' unwillingness to bid higher is unfavorable information about the value of the item. In the drainage tract model, we calculated the non-neighbor's profits in just that way: a non-neighbor wins with a bid of b exactly when the neighbor bids less than b, which is informative about the neighbor's estimate of the value. When more than one bidder has relevant information, each bidder needs to be aware of the information content of others' bids when making his own bidding decision. There can also be an important *loser's curse* in multi-object auctions.[18]

5.4.2.1 The (Second-Price) Button Auction with Minimal Information

Assume the payoff to each bidder is the value received minus the amount paid. For losing bidders, the value received is zero. The winning bidder, i, receives value $v^i = v^i(t^i, t^0, t^{-i})$, where t^0 is a variable that may not be observed by the bidders, such as the seller's information. We assume that v^i is nondecreasing.

---

[17] In doing so, we omit models in which bidders may "jump" to communicate information to other bidders. Jump bidding involves significantly (and asynchronously) increasing the current high bid. See Avery (1998).

[18] The loser's curse was first introduced by Pesendorfer and Swinkels (1997). The possibility of a loser's curse has important implications for bidders' incentives to gather information. A first attempt to study those is found in Hernando-Veciana (2003).

We begin with the symmetric case, which imposes three restrictions. First, all bidders have the same valuation function v, so $v^i = v(t^i, t^0, t^{-i})$. Second, the valuation function is symmetric in the other players' types, that is, $v^1 = v(t^1, t^0, t^{-1}) = v(t^1, t^0, t^{(1)}, \ldots, t^{(N-1)})$, where $t^{(1)}, \ldots, t^{(N-1)}$ denote the order statistics (in order from highest to lowest) of $t^2, \ldots, t^N$. Third, the distribution of types is symmetric in the same way as the valuation function.

Consider the button auction with minimal information, which we have seen is strategically equivalent to the second-price auction model. Define $\hat{v}(r, s) = E[v^1 | t^1 = r, t^{(1)} = s]$. If the types are affiliated and symmetrically distributed, then by theorems 5.4.5 and 5.4.6, the function $\hat{v}$ is *isotone*, that is, nondecreasing in each argument. For comparing the following results, it will be convenient to treat $\hat{v}$ as primitive and assume that it is isotone and strictly so in its first argument.

Theorem 5.4.7 (Milgrom (1981b)). Suppose that the function $\hat{v}$ is isotone and increasing in its first argument. Then the strategy $\beta(s) = \hat{v}(s, s)$ is a symmetric equilibrium strategy of the second-price auction. The equilibrium has the property that if any bidder learned the highest opposing type and this type's bid, the bidder could not gain by changing his bid.

Proof. Suppose players other than bidder 1 play the symmetric equilibrium strategy. After learning $t^{(1)}$ and the corresponding bid $\beta(t^{(1)}) = \hat{v}(t^{(1)}, t^{(1)})$, bidder 1's problem is $\max_b (\hat{v}(t^1, t^{(1)}) - \hat{v}(t^{(1)}, t^{(1)})) 1_{b > \beta(t^{(1)})}$. If $t^1 > t^{(1)}$, then any bid $b > \beta(t^{(1)})$ maximizes the bidder's payoff, including the bid $\beta(t^1)$. If $t^1 < t^{(1)}$, then any bid $b < \beta(t^{(1)})$ maximizes the objective, including the bid $\beta(t^1)$. Because $\beta(t^1)$ is a best reply conditional on every realization of $t^{(1)}$, it is an unconditional best reply. ∎

An equilibrium in which the players can never gain by changing their strategies even if they learn the other players' types and actions is called an *ex post* equilibrium. According to theorem 5.4.7, the identified equilibrium of the second-price auction is an *ex post* equilibrium if there are just two bidders. Recent papers on auction theory have given renewed emphasis to *ex post* equilibria.

Ex post equilibria in ascending auctions have two attractive features. First, each bidder's *ex post* equilibrium strategy depends only on the bidder's own type, so the bidder can implement the strategy with that information alone. Second, each strategy is a best reply to the strategy of the other players even when the bidder knows all types and bids. The strategy is a best reply for any intermediate information structure, so it remains a best reply for a wide range of assumptions about bidders' knowledge.

In an *ex post* equilibrium, no player has any incentive to expend effort gathering information about other players' types or actions, because his optimal action does not depend on that information. Therefore, by theorem 5.4.7, bidders in a second-price auction have no incentive to expend effort gathering such information. In contrast, bidders do generally have such an incentive in first-price auctions; in particular, they could use information about others' bids to good advantage in choosing their own bids. Consequently, the second-price auction can reduce some kinds of bidder costs. The costs of participating in an auction are a serious concern for practical auction design, so this advantage is significant.

Several variations of the model used for theorem 5.4.7 have also proved tractable. We consider next a pure common value model with two players. There are a multitude of *ex post* equilibria in this case.

Theorem 5.4.8 (Milgrom (1981b)). Consider a two-player version of the preceding model in which v is symmetric, that is, $v^1 = v(t^1, t^2) = v(t^2, t^1) = v^2$. Then for every increasing, continuous function $f : \mathbb{R} \to \mathbb{R}$, the strategy profile $\beta^1(s) = v(s, f^{-1}(s))$ and $\beta^2(s) = v(f(s), s)$ is an *ex post* equilibrium.

Proof. Consider bidder 1's *ex post* problem. After learning t^1 as well as t^2 and the corresponding bid $\beta^2(t^2)$, bidder 1 solves $\max_b (v(t^1, t^2) - \beta^2(t^2)) 1_{b > \beta^2(t^2)}$. So $\beta^1(t^1)$ is a best reply for all t^1 if $\beta^1(t^1) > \beta^2(t^2) \Leftrightarrow v(t^1, t^2) > \beta^2(t^2)$.

By construction, if $t^1 = f(t^2)$, then $\beta^1(t^1) = v(t^1, f^{-1}(t^1)) = v(f(t^2), t^2) = \beta^2(t^2)$. Because v is increasing, $\beta^1(t^1) > \beta^2(t^2) \Leftrightarrow t^1 > f(t^2)$. By construction, $t^1 > f(t^2) \Leftrightarrow \beta^2(t^2) = v(f(t^2), t^2) < v(t^1, t^2)$, so $\beta^1(t^1) > \beta^2(t^2) \Leftrightarrow \beta^2(t^2) < v(t^1, t^2)$, as required.

An analogous argument shows bidder 2's strategy is also a best reply. ∎

Theorem 5.4.8 allows for some extreme equilibria in which the seller's revenues can be very low. For example, let us apply the theorem using the function $f(s) = s^\alpha$ where α is a large positive number. Recalling that the type spaces are $[0, 1]$, when bidder 2's type is $s \in (0, 1)$, his equilibrium bid is $\beta^2(s) = v(s^\alpha, s) \approx v(0, s)$. Bidder 1's equilibrium bid when $s \in (0, 1)$

is $\beta^1(s) = v(s, s^{1/\alpha}) \approx v(s, 1)$. Using these approximations, bidder 2's bids are all less than $v(0, 1)$, and bidder 1's bids are all larger than the same amount. Consequently, bidder 1 wins nearly all the time and pays a price of approximately $v(0, t^2)$. Extending the example, suppose that $v(r, s) = rs$. Then the price will always be approximately $v(0, t^2) = 0$. Of course, if this equilibrium were anticipated, bidder 2 might be so discouraged that he would not enter at all, particularly if the entry costs were significant.

Are such extreme equilibria plausible? Klemperer (1998) has argued that in situations with "almost common values," extreme equilibria like these may be the only "reasonable" equilibria. Klemperer illustrates his point with the wallet game, in which two bidders each bid for the sum of the (privately known) contents of the bidders' wallets. Here, the value function $v(r, s) = r + s$ is symmetric and isotone, so according to theorem 5.4.8, there are many equilibria corresponding to different values of f. What happens when one player has an advantage, even an arbitrarily small one, over the other? The next theorem shows that extreme equilibria are commonplace and the disadvantaged bidder has no chance of winning in any equilibrium in undominated, continuous strategies.

Theorem 5.4.9. Suppose that bidder values are given by $v^1(t^1, t^2)$ and $v^2(t^2, t^1)$, where each function is continuous, isotone, and strictly increasing in its first argument. Suppose that for every possible realization of t^1 and t^2, $v^1(t^1, t^2) > v^2(t^2, t^1)$. Then the following bid functions yield an *ex post* equilibrium in undominated, increasing, continuous strategies: $\beta^1(t^1) = v^1(t^1, 1)$ and $\beta^2(t^2) = v^2(t^2, 0)$. In this equilibrium, bidder 1 always wins. Moreover, in any Nash equilibrium in undominated, continuous strategies, bidder 1 wins with probability one.

Proof. First, we verify that the proposed strategies form an *ex post* equilibrium. Because v^1 and v^2 are isotone, for all t^1 and t^2 we have $\beta^1(t^1) = v^1(t^1, 1) \geq v^1(t^1, t^2) > v^2(t^2, t^1) \geq v^2(t^2, 0) = \beta^2(t^2)$. Because $\beta^1(t^1) > \beta^2(t^2)$, bidder 1 always wins. Bidder 1 solves $\max_b(v^1(t^1, t^2) - \beta^2(t^2))1_{b>\beta^2(t^2)}$, and, by inspection, any bid that always wins is optimal. Bidder 2 solves $\max_b(v^2(t^2, t^1) - \beta^1(t^1))1_{b>\beta^1(t^1)}$, and, by inspection, any bid that always loses is optimal. So the proposed strategies are mutual best replies and hence form an equilibrium.

At any Nash equilibrium in undominated strategies, bidder 2 of type $t^2 = 0$ bids no more than $v^2(0, 1)$, and bidder 1 of type $t^1 = 1$ bids no less than $v^1(1, 0) > v^2(0, 1)$. So there is no equilibrium in undominated strategies at which bidder 2 always wins. Hence, if bidder 2 wins with positive probability, then because the bid functions are continuous, there exists an open interval of bids that is in the range of both bid functions. Let b be a bid in that interval, and suppose t^1 and t^2 are types such that $b = \beta^1(t^1) = \beta^2(t^2)$. If $v^1(t^1, t^2) > b$, then this cannot be an equilibrium outcome, because bidder 1 would benefit by increasing his bid slightly, winning more often when winning is profitable. Similarly, if $v^1(t^1, t^2) < b$, then bidder 1 would do better to reduce this bid. So, at equilibrium for any bid in that interval, it must be true that $b = v^1(t^1, t^2)$ and similarly that $b = v^2(t^2, t^1)$. That contradicts our hypothesis that $v^1(t^1, t^2) > v^2(t^2, t^1)$ for all type pairs. Hence, all types of bidder 2 win with probability zero and all types of bidder 1 win with probability one.   ■

According to theorem 5.4.9, a small asymmetry can make a huge difference in the equilibrium strategies and revenues in the pure common value auction. To illustrate the logic of this conclusion, consider a variant of the wallet game in which one participant receives an extra dollar whenever he wins. Suppose the wallets are known to contain between $0 and $100. Then, according to the theorem, the advantaged bidder bids the amount in his own wallet plus $101 in a second-price auction, while the other bidder timidly bids just the contents of his own wallet. The reason that there is no equilibrium at which bidder 2 ever wins is this: Suppose that at some other equilibrium, there is some price p at which bidder 2 wins if bidder 1's value is low enough, say less than $15. Then, bidder 2 should bid up to p exactly when his wallet contains at least $p - 15$. But then, if bidder 1's wallet contains $v \in (14, 15)$ and he bids up to p and wins at that price, the value to him is no less than the amount in his own wallet, plus $1, plus the amount in bidder 2's wallet, which is at least $p - 15$, so his total net winnings are $(v + 1 + p - 15) - p > 0$, and the original strategies could not be an equilibrium.

In this example, the average winning bid is just the average amount in the timid bidder's wallet. As the theorem suggests, there are other plausible equilibria in this case, but they differ little from the equilibrium just described. For example, the timid bidder may bid $1 more than the contents of his wallet. Still, in equilibrium, the advantaged bidder always wins and the average price does not exceed the average content of the loser's wallet plus $1. The winning bidder's profit is high, and the seller's revenue is correspondingly low.

Bulow, Huang, and Klemperer (1999) used a common value model to study takeover battles, treating these contests as auctions. They show that when a bidder has a small toehold in a takeover battle, owning some shares of the target's stock before the battle begins, then equilibrium theory predicts that the bidder can win the takeover battle at an alarmingly low price. This application reinforces the lesson that a common value environment greatly magnifies small asymmetries.[19]

So far, we have emphasized revenue comparisons in button auctions, but traditional economic theory often focuses on efficiency. Maskin (1992) investigated the existence of efficient equilibrium in an asymmetric version of the two-player button auction above. Again, we treat $v^1(t^1, t^2)$ and $v^2(t^2, t^1)$ as primitive functions. The following condition proves important.

Definition. Values display *(strict) single crossing interpersonal differences* (SCID) for bidder i if for all $j \neq i$ and all t^{-i}, the quantity $\Delta^{ij}(t^i|t^{-i}) = v^i(t^i, t^{-i}) - v^j(t^j, t^i, t^{-ij})$ – regarded as a function of t^i – has the (strict) single crossing property. That is, SCID holds if $(t^i > \bar{t}^i, \Delta^{ij}(\bar{t}^i|t^{-i}) \geq 0) \Rightarrow \Delta^{ij}(t^i|t^{-i}) \geq 0$ and $\Delta^{ij}(\bar{t}^i|t^{-i}) > 0 \Rightarrow \Delta^{ij}(t^i|t^{-i}) > 0$; and strict SCID holds if $(t^i > \bar{t}^i, \Delta^{ij}(\bar{t}^i|t^{-i}) \geq 0) \Rightarrow \Delta^{ij}(t^i|t^{-i}) > 0$.

In words, the SCID property means that if i's value exceeds j's value for some profile of types, then increasing i's type cannot reverse that relationship. Intuitively, if such a reversal were possible, it would mean that j's value was more sensitive to i's information than was i's own value.

The SCID condition ensures a kind of alignment between a bidder's incentives and the efficiency criterion. In general, a higher type for bidder j suggests he has a higher value and so is willing to pay more to win. When SCID holds, a higher type for j also suggests bidder j is more likely the efficient winner. According to theorem 5.10 below, this alignment is sufficient for the ascending auction to have an *ex post* equilibrium with efficient outcomes. According to theorem 5.4.11, a refinement of the SCID condition is also necessary.

Theorem 5.4.10 (Maskin). Suppose that each v^i is continuous and increasing, that $v^1(0, 0) = v^2(0, 0)$, and that players are labeled to satisfy

---

[19] Bulow and Klemperer (2002) report additional results in the same vein.

$v^1(1, 1) \geq v^2(1, 1)$. If the values display strict SCID for both bidders, then there is an increasing function f such that the strategies (β^1, β^2) constitute an *ex post* equilibrium of the second-price auction game, where $\beta^1(s) = v^1(s, f^{-1}(s))$ and $\beta^2(s) = v^2(s, f(s))$. Furthermore, equilibrium outcomes are efficient.

Proof. Suppose $t^2 \in (0, 1)$. By strict SCID for bidder 2, because $v^1(1, 1) - v^2(1, 1) \geq 0$, it follows that $v^1(1, t^2) - v^2(t^2, 1) > 0$. Also, because $v^1(0, 0) - v^2(0, 0) = 0$, strict SCID for bidder 2 implies that $0 > v^1(0, t^2) - v^2(t^2, 0)$. Hence, by continuity of the values, there exists a type $t^1 = f(t^2)$ such that $v^1(f(t^2), t^2) = v^2(t^2, f(t^2))$. By strict SCID for bidder 1, the $f(t^2)$ that satisfies this equation is unique. By strict SCID for both bidders, $f(\cdot)$ is increasing.

Suppose that the bidders adopt the strategies $\beta^1(s) = v^1(s, f^{-1}(s))$ and $\beta^2(s) = v^2(s, f(s))$. By construction, both strategies are increasing. After bidder 1 learns bidder 2's type t^2 and bid $\beta^2(t^2)$, bidder 1's problem becomes

$$\max_b (v^1(t^1, t^2) - v^2(t^2, f(t^2))) \cdot 1_{b > \beta^2(t^2)}.$$

Because $\beta^1(t^1) = \beta^2(t^2) \Leftrightarrow t^1 = f(t^2)$ and both the bid functions and f are increasing, it follows that $\beta^1(t^1) > \beta^2(t^2) \Leftrightarrow t^1 > f(t^2)$. Thus, if bidders play according to these strategies, then 1 wins exactly when $t^1 > f(t^2)$, that is, when $v^1(t^1, t^2) > v^2(t^2, t^1)$. Thus, the outcome when bidders use these strategies is always efficient.

Next, $t^1 > f(t^2) \Leftrightarrow v^1(t^1, f^{-1}(t^1)) > v^1(f(t^2), t^2) = v^2(t^2, f(t^2))$. Hence, $\beta^1(t^1) > \beta^2(t^2) \Leftrightarrow v^1(t^1, f^{-1}(t^1)) > v^2(t^2, f(t^2)) = \beta^2(t^2)$.

The inequality $v^1(t^1, f^{-1}(t^1)) > \beta^2(t^2)$ determines when a bid $b > \beta^2(t^2)$ is *ex post* optimal for bidder 1. The conclusion that the inequality holds if and only if $\beta^1(t^1) > \beta^2(t^2)$ means that bidder 1 is playing an *ex post* best reply. A similar analysis applies to bidder 2, verifying that the strategies form an *ex post* equilibrium.   ∎

The next theorem states a partial converse of the efficiency result in Theorem 5.4.10: we cannot achieve efficient outcomes without at least the weak form of SCID.

Theorem 5.4.11 (Maskin). Suppose that v^1 is continuous and increasing and there exist types such that SCID for bidder 1 is violated, that is,

$\exists t^1 > \hat{t}^1$ and t^2 such that $v^1(\hat{t}^1, t^2) - v^2(t^2, \hat{t}^1) > 0 > v^1(t^1, t^2) - v^2(t^2, t^1)$. Then there is no *ex post* equilibrium at which outcomes are always efficient.

Proof. Because v^1 is increasing, by the monotonic selection theorem the bid must be increasing in type, so bidder 1 must be weakly more likely to acquire the item when his type is t^1 than when his type is $\hat{t}^1$ when 2's type is t^2. In particular, 1 must sometimes acquire the item when the type profile is (t^1, t^2). However, this outcome is inconsistent with efficiency, because $0 > v^1(t^1, t^2) - v^2(t^2, t^1)$. ∎

5.4.2.2 The Button Auction with Maximal Information

The symmetric model studied above assumes bidders receive minimal information about the numbers and identities of active bidders. In this model, bidders either know nothing about others' bids or cannot draw inferences from them. We now model the opposite extreme. Suppose all bidders learn whenever any bidder drops out. Moreover, the bidders use this information to make inferences about the dropout's type. Of course, with just two bidders, the button auctions with minimal and maximal information are equivalent, because in neither auction does any bidder learn another's dropout price before the end of the auction. With more than two bidders, however, we can conceive of the auction as taking place in two stages. During the first stage, $N - 2$ bidders drop out and their decisions provide information to the last two active bidders. When the kth bidder drops out at price p_k, each remaining bidder figures that the dropout's type is the $(N - k)$th highest among his competitors, estimates that type to be some number $\hat{t}^{(N-k)}$, updates his estimates, and continues accordingly. When only two bidders remain, those two effectively bid in a second-price auction.

In the formal analysis below, we use $t^{(n)}$ to denote the nth highest type *among the competitors* of some bidder.

Because we assume the game to be symmetric, it is convenient to treat bidder 1 as the typical bidder and focus on his bidding problem. A (reduced) strategy for this game specifies whether bidder 1 drops out when the price reaches some level, given the observed history up to that time. Let $\beta_n(s, p_1, \ldots, p_n)$ describe the lowest price at which the bidder of type s will drop out when n bidders have already dropped out at prices $p_1 \leq \cdots \leq p_n$. Clearly, $\beta_n(s, p_1, \ldots, p_n) \geq p_n$.

To facilitate study of variations in bidder information, let v be a primitive value function whose arguments include the type profile and the seller's information t^0, and let $\bar{v}(t^1, \ldots, t^N) = E[v(t^1, t^0, t^2, \ldots, t^N)|t^1, \ldots, t^N]$ be the reduced-form value function when the seller reveals no information about her type.

Theorem 5.4.12. Suppose that $\bar{v}$ is continuous, isotone, and strictly increasing in its first argument. Then the following strategy, defined inductively, is a symmetric *ex post* equilibrium strategy of the ascending auction:

$$\beta_0(s) = \bar{v}(s, \ldots, s),$$
$$\beta_n(s, p_1, \ldots, p_n) = \bar{v}\left(s, \ldots, s, \hat{t}^{(N-n)}, \ldots, \hat{t}^{(N-1)}\right), \tag{5.15}$$

where $\hat{t}^{(N-k)}$ solves

$$p_k = \beta_{k-1}\left(\hat{t}^{(N-k)}, p_1, \ldots, p_{k-1}\right)$$
$$= \bar{v}\left(\hat{t}^{(N-k)}, \ldots, \hat{t}^{(N-k)}, \hat{t}^{(N-(k-1))}, \ldots, \hat{t}^{(N-1)}\right) \tag{5.16}$$

and $\hat{t}^{(N-k)} = 0$ if $p_k \leq \bar{v}(0, \ldots, 0)$.

Proof. Because $\bar{v}$ is continuous and strictly increasing in its first argument, $\beta_k(\cdot, p_1, \ldots, p_k)$ is continuous and increasing as well. Hence, there is a unique solution $\hat{t}^{(N-k)}$ to $p_k = \beta_{k-1}(\hat{t}^{(N-k)}, p_1, \ldots, p_{k-1})$ on the relevant domain. By construction, if the bidders besides bidder 1 adopt the equilibrium strategy, then when bidder 1 wins, regardless of his strategy, he pays $\bar{v}(t^{(1)}, t^{(1)}, t^{(2)}, \ldots, t^{(N-1)})$ to acquire the good. This price is less than bidder 1's value $\bar{v}(t^1, t^{(1)}, t^{(2)}, \ldots, t^{(N-1)})$ precisely when $t^1 > t^{(1)}$. Also, because the symmetric equilibrium bid function is increasing, bidder 1 wins using the function only when $t^1 > t^{(1)}$. Hence, the *ex post* best-reply property is satisfied. ∎

Each of the component strategies β_n reflects a sort of myopic bidding behavior. The bidder asks himself: "If everyone else were to drop out right now, before I have a chance to react, would I be happy to be declared the winner?" He remains active in the auction just as long as the answer to that question is yes.

To understand the equilibrium strategies better, suppose no bidder has yet dropped out ($n = 0$). Suppose the price reaches the level $\beta_0(\hat{t})$ when bidder 1's type is t^1. Bidder 1 infers from the bidding that the others' types are all at least $\hat{t}$. If bidders $2, \ldots, n$ were to quit instantly, then bidder 1 could infer that their types were exactly $\hat{t}$. In that case, bidder 1 would want to acquire the item at price $\beta_0(\hat{t})$ exactly when $\bar{v}(t^1, \hat{t}, \ldots, \hat{t}) \geq \beta_0(\hat{t}) = \bar{v}(\hat{t}, \hat{t}, \ldots, \hat{t})$, which holds when $t^1 > \hat{t}$.

The analysis is similar when $k > 0$ bidders have dropped out. If all play the equilibrium bidding strategy, then one can invert the bid function to determine the types of the early dropouts. At equilibrium, the remaining bidders incorporate that information into their values and the auction proceeds as an $N - k$ bidder auction. The formula for the strategy in (5.15) then takes the same form as when no bidders had dropped out; each bidder assesses what her value would be if every other bidder dropped out immediately at the current price. The only difference is that bidder 1's conjectures about the first k bidders no longer change as the bid increases.

Bikchandani, Haile and Riley (2002) have pointed out other equilibria in this auction with different strategies but the same outcome. With at least $N \geq 3$ bidders, one alternative equilibrium $\tilde{\beta}$ specifies that the first $N - 2$ bidders drop out at bids a fraction $\alpha \in (0, 1)$ of the bids at which they dropped out under strategy β, and the last two bidders bid as before:

$$\tilde{\beta}_0(s) = \alpha \bar{v}(s, \ldots, s),$$

$$\tilde{\beta}_n(s, p_1, \ldots, p_n) = \begin{cases} \alpha \bar{v}\left(s, \ldots, s, \hat{t}^{(N-n)}, \ldots, \hat{t}^{(N-1)}\right) & \text{for } n < N - 1, \\ \bar{v}\left(s, \ldots, s, \hat{t}^{(N-n)}, \ldots, \hat{t}^{(N-1)}\right) & \text{for } n = N - 1, \end{cases}$$

with the inferences $\hat{t}^{(k)}$ adjusted accordingly. It is routine to verify that this strategy combination is an *ex post* equilibrium, because dropout levels besides the last one have no effect of the outcome of the auction.

The multiplicity of equilibria indicates the weak incentives losing bidders have to use any particular bidding strategy. Those weak incentives may make inferences about the losing bids unreliable and suggest that this model may not capture the essence of the real-world inference problem, where signaling and jump bidding may play a prominent role. As in our discussion of the Cremer–McLean theory, this multiplicity objection reminds us that the real-world applicability of equilibrium models cannot be taken for granted, and that considerations omitted by the logic of equilibrium can be important in practice.

In the symmetric equilibrium above, the highest type always wins the auction. When does the highest type also have the highest value? We can derive an analog to SCID for this model by observing that if $t^1 = t^2 = s'$, then $v^1 = v^2 = \bar{v}(s', s', t^{-12})$. Thus, a suitable version of SCID must imply that increasing bidder 1's type makes his value higher than bidder 2's value: for $s > s'$, we have $\bar{v}(s, s', t^{-12}) > \bar{v}(s', s, t^{-12})$. This inequality implies that the highest type in the model has a higher value than any other bidder, so we have the following:

Theorem 5.4.13. Suppose that $\bar{v}$ has the property that for $s > s'$ one has $\bar{v}(s, s', t^{-12}) > \bar{v}(s', s, t^{-12})$. Then, in the equilibrium of theorem 5.4.12, the outcome is efficient.

5.4.2.3 Some Revenue Comparisons
We next examine the effect of auction design on revenue in ascending auctions. Does the theory predict any systematic differences between the button auctions with minimal and maximal information? How does revealing seller information influence expected revenues?

For the remainder of this chapter, it will be important to keep track of the difference between the primitive form of the value function and its various reduced forms. We denote value estimates based on all information by $v(t^i, t^{-i}, t^0)$. The expected value given the bidders' types but not the seller's information is $\bar{v}(t^i, t^{-i}) = E[v(t^i, t^{-i}, t^0)|t^i, t^{-i}]$. Finally, the expected value given just bidder 1's type and the highest opposing type is $\hat{v}(t^1, t^{(1)}) = E[\bar{v}(t^1, t^{-1})|t^1, t^{(1)}] = E[v(t^1, t^{-1}, t^0)|t^1, t^{(1)}]$. We also write $\hat{v}(t^1, t^{(1)}, t^0) = E[v(t^1, t^{-1}, t^0)|t^1, t^{(1)}, t^0]$.

Theorem 5.4.14. Suppose $\bar{v}(t^1, \ldots, t^N)$ is increasing and types are affiliated, and consider the equilibria identified in theorem 5.4.12. Then

$$\hat{v}(t^{(1)}, t^{(1)}) \leq E[\bar{v}(t^{(1)}, t^{(1)}, t^{(2)}, \ldots, t^{(N-1)}|t^1, t^{(1)}]. \tag{5.17}$$

That is, the price paid by each type of bidder 1 when he wins in the second-price auction is no higher than the conditional expected price he pays given his type t^1 and the highest opposing type $t^{(1)}$ in the button auction with maximal information.

Proof. The price paid by winning bidder 1 of type s in the second-price auction when the second highest type is r is $\hat{v}(r, r)$. But

$$\hat{v}(r, r) = E[\bar{v}(r, r, t^{(2)}, \ldots, t^{(N-1)})|t^1 = r, t^{(1)} = r]$$
$$\leq E[\bar{v}(r, r, t^{(2)}, \ldots, t^{(N-1)})|t^1 = s, t^{(1)} = r],$$

by theorems 5.4.6 and 5.4.5, because the density of types is affiliated and v is isotone. The right-hand side is the expected revenue in the ascending auction with maximal information. ∎

The theorem implies that every type of every bidder expects to pay a higher price on average in the button auction with maximal information than in the auction with minimal information. By (5.17) and the law of iterated expectations, $E[\hat{v}(t^{(1)}, t^{(1)})|t^1] \leq E[\bar{v}(t^{(1)}, t^{(1)}, t^{(2)}, \ldots, t^{(N-1)}|t^1]$, so the expected price with maximal information is higher.

We now consider how a seller's decision to reveal information affects the efficiency and revenues of an auction. The two effects can have opposite signs. For example, suppose that there are two bidders with values 1 and 3, but only the seller knows which bidder has which value. If the seller reveals that information, then a second-price auction between the two parties will lead to the bidder with the higher value winning and paying a price of 1. If the seller does not reveal that information and positions are *ex ante* symmetric, then each bidder will bid as if his value were 2. The seller's revenue will be 2 and, on average, the value to the winner will be 2 as well.

To focus on other effects, we abstract from such possibilities, turning to a symmetric model in which the seller's information is irrelevant to efficient allocation. For example, the seller may have information about the distribution from which types are drawn – information that, given the bidders' realized types, does not bear on any bidder's value.

Theorem 5.4.15. Suppose $v(t^1, \ldots, t^N, t^0)$ is increasing and the types are affiliated. Then, in both forms of the ascending auction, a policy of always revealing t^0 cannot reduce the expected price paid by any type of winning bidder.[20] That is, for $s > r$,

$$\hat{v}(r, r) \leq E\big[\hat{v}(r, r, t^0)|t^1 = s, t^{(1)} = r\big] \tag{5.18}$$

and

$$\bar{v}\big(r, r, t^{(2)}, \ldots, t^{(N-1)}\big)$$
$$\leq E\big[v\big(r, r, t^{(2)}, \ldots, t^{(N-1)}, t^0\big)|t^1 = s, t^{(1)} = r, t^{(2)}, \ldots, t^{(N-1)}\big]. \tag{5.19}$$

---

[20] When bidders are risk averse, revealing information may reduce the risk premium assessed by bidders and therefore increase their bids. Milgrom and Weber (1982a) analyze this effect.

Proof. For the auction with minimal information, we argue as follows:

$$\hat{v}(r, r) = E\big[\hat{v}(r, r, t^0)|t^1 = r, t^{(1)} = r\big]$$
$$\leq E\big[\hat{v}(r, r, t^0)|t^1 = s, t^{(1)} = r\big].$$

The inequality follows from theorems 5.4.5 and 5.4.6, using $s > r$.

The argument is similar for the auction with maximal information:

$$\bar{v}\big(r, r, t^{(2)}, \ldots, t^{(N-1)}\big)$$
$$= E\big[v\big(r, r, t^{(2)}, \ldots, t^{(N-1)}, t^0\big)|t^1 = r, t^{(1)} = r, t^{(2)}, \ldots, t^{(N-1)}\big]$$
$$\leq E\big[v\big(r, r, t^{(2)}, \ldots, t^{(N-1)}, t^0\big)|t^1 = s, t^{(1)} = r, t^{(2)}, \ldots, t^{(N-1)}\big].$$

The inequality again follows from theorems 5.4.5 and 5.4.6, using $s > r$. ∎

To use a term we introduced in discussing the drainage tract model, the preceding theorem identifies a *weighting effect*. Observe that in the maximum information model, if v does not depend on t^0, then the price effect of revealing that information is zero. In contrast, in the first-price version of the drainage tract model, revealing information could also have the *publicity effect* of making the bidders' types more predictable, thereby encouraging more intense competition from the losing bidders. No such effect appears in the auctions above.

5.4.3 First-Price Auctions

Next, we turn to another very common auction form: the standard sealed-bid auction, also known as the first-price auction. As in the preceding section, the types $t = (t^0, t^1, \ldots, t^N)$ are affiliated and have a density $f(t^0, t^1, \ldots, t^N)$ that is symmetric in the bidder types, but not necessarily in the seller type. We denote by $f(t^{(1)}|t^1)$ the conditional density of the order statistic $t^{(1)}$ and by $F(t^{(1)}|t^1)$ the corresponding cumulative distribution function.

Again, we focus our attention on bidder 1's optimization problem. Given a type $t^1 = s$, bidder 1 chooses a bid x to solve

$$\max_x E\big[(\bar{v}(s, t^{-1}) - x)1_{\{x > \beta(t^{(1)})\}}|t^1 = s\big]$$
$$= \max_x E\big[E\big[(\bar{v}(s, t^{-1}) - x)1_{\{x > \beta(t^{(1)})\}}|t^1, t^{(1)}\big]|t^1 = s\big]$$
$$= \max_x E\big[E\big[(\bar{v}(s, t^{-1}) - x)|t^1, t^{(1)}\big]1_{\{x > \beta(t^{(1)})\}}|t^1 = s\big]$$

$$= \max_x E\left[(\hat{v}(s, t^{(1)}) - x)1_{\{x > \beta(t^{(1)})\}}|t^1 = s\right]$$

$$= \max_x \int_0^{\beta^{-1}(x)} (\hat{v}(s, \tau) - x) f(\tau|s)\, d\tau.$$

The first equality follows from the law of iterated expectations; the second, from the fact that the indicator is a function of $t^{(1)}$; and the remaining ones, from the definitions.

Theorem 5.4.16. The following is a symmetric equilibrium strategy for the first-price auction:

$$\beta(s) = \hat{v}(0, 0) + \int_0^s \hat{v}(\alpha, \alpha)\, dL(\alpha|s),$$

where $\quad L(\alpha|s) = \exp\left(-\int_\alpha^s \frac{f(z|s)}{F(z|s)}\, dz\right).$ (5.20)

Proof. Define $U(x, y, s) = \int_0^y (\hat{v}(s, \tau) - x) f(\tau|s)\, d\tau$. Using numbered subscripts of U to denote partial derivatives with respect to the first and second arguments, we have $U_1(x, y, s) = -F(y|s)$ and $U_2(x, y, s) = (\hat{v}(s, y) - x) f(y|s)$.

By theorem 5.4.3, $F(y|s)$ is log-supermodular, so $\frac{\partial^2}{\partial s \partial y} \log F(y|s) = \frac{\partial}{\partial s} \frac{f(y|s)}{F(y|s)} \geq 0$. Hence, $U(x, y, s)$ satisfies the Mirrlees–Spence condition on $x \leq \hat{v}(s, y)$, because

$$\frac{U_1(x, y, s)}{|U_2(x, y, s)|} = \frac{-F(y|s)}{(\hat{v}(s, y) - x) \cdot f(y|s)}$$

is nondecreasing in s (because it is negative and its absolute value is decreasing). Therefore, by theorem 4.4, the objective has single crossing differences. Hence, we may use the constraint simplification theorem to establish that the proposed strategy is optimal for a bidder. We must show that b is increasing and solves the first-order condition (and hence the envelope condition).

Using (5.20), one can verify that β satisfies the differential equation

$$\beta'(s) = \left[\hat{v}(s, s) - \beta(s)\right] \cdot \frac{f(s|s)}{F(s|s)}.$$ (5.21)

Because $\beta(0) = \hat{v}(0, 0)$ and $\hat{v}$ is isotone and strictly increasing in its first argument, it follows that the solution of the differential equation (5.21) must satisfy $\hat{v}(s, s) > \beta(s)$, so $\beta'(s) > 0$ and the bid function is increasing.

Suppose the bidders besides bidder 1 use the strategy β specified in (5.20). Because β is increasing, then for all s, $\beta(s)$ is a best reply for 1 if it solves $\max_x U(x, \beta^{-1}(x), s)$. The bid then satisfies the first-order condition at $x = \beta(s)$ if

$$\begin{aligned}
0 &= U_1(\beta(s), s, s) + U_2(\beta(s), s, s)/\beta'(s) \\
&= -F(s|s) + (\hat{v}(s, s) - \beta(s)) f(s|s)/\beta'(s).
\end{aligned} \tag{5.22}$$

Because β satisfies the differential equation (5.21), it satisfies the equivalent expression (5.22).

Thus, the bid is increasing and satisfies the envelope formula. By the constraint simplification theorem, bidder 1 has no better reply in the range of the bid function and satisfying the constraint $x \leq \hat{v}(s, y)$. By inspection, any bid x that violates the constraint leads to a lower expected payoff than the bid $x = \hat{v}(s, y)$, and any bid above or below the range of the bid function produces a lower expected payoff than $\beta(0)$ or $\beta(1)$, respectively. Hence, β is a best reply for bidder 1. ∎

The derivation of the equilibrium strategy is quite straightforward. Starting from the description of the game and assuming that there is a symmetric, increasing equilibrium, one can derive the first-order condition (5.22) and restate it as the differential equation (5.21). The boundary condition for this equation comes from the zero-profit condition for the lowest type of bidder, who must be just indifferent about winning at his optimal bid. Thus, $\beta(0) = \hat{v}(0, 0)$. Solving the differential equation with that boundary condition leads to (5.20).

The next theorem restates the result of chapter 4 holding that the second-price auction generates more revenue for each type of winning bidder than the first-price auction.

Theorem 5.4.17. For each type of bidder, the conditional expected price in the second-price auction, given that the type wins, is higher than the corresponding bid in the first-price auction; that is, for all $s \in [0, 1)$, $E[\hat{v}(s, t^{(1)})|t^{(1)} < s] \geq \beta(s)$.

Proof. In this proof, we denote the equilibrium strategy in the first-price auction by β^F, and we let $\beta^S(s, t) = E[\hat{v}(t^{(1)}, t^{(1)})|t^1 = s, t^{(1)} < t]$. (Observe that $\beta^S(s, t)$ is the price that bidder 1 of type s expects to pay if he bids as if his type were t and his bid wins.) We must show that $\beta^F(s) \leq \beta^S(s, s)$.

Suppose bidder 1 of type s bids as if he were of type t, and let $\tilde{v}(s, t) = E[\hat{v}(s, t^{(1)})|t^1 = s, t^{(1)} < t]$. Then the bidder's maximum value in the first-price auction is $V^F(s) = \max_t (\tilde{v}(s, t) - \beta^F(t))F(t|s)$. Similarly, for the second-price auction, $V^S(s) = \max_t (\tilde{v}(s, t) - \beta^S(s, t))F(t|s)$. At equilibrium, a bidder of type s optimally bids as his own type $t = s$, so $V^F(s) = (\tilde{v}(s, s) - \beta^F(s))F(s|s)$ and $V^S(s) = (\tilde{v}(s, s) - \beta^S(s, s))F(s|s)$. Hence, $V^F(s) \geq V^S(s)$ if and only if $\beta^F(s) \leq \beta^S(s, s)$.

By the envelope theorem, $V^{F'}(s) = F_2(s|s)(\tilde{v}(s, s) - \beta^F(s)) + F(s|s)\tilde{v}_1$ (s, s) and $V^{S'}(s) = F_2(s|s)(\tilde{v}(s, s) - \beta^S(s, s)) + F(s|s)\tilde{v}_1(s, s) - F(s|s)\beta^S_1$ (s, s). Using theorem 5.4.3, part (3), $F_2(s|s) \leq 0$. So, if there is any $s > 0$ at which $V^F(s) < V^S(s)$, then $\beta^F(s) > \beta^S(s, s)$ and hence $V^{F'}(s) \geq V^{S'}(s)$. However, we have already established that, at equilibrium, $V^F(0) = V^S(0)$, so applying the ranking lemma to the function $V^F(s) - V^S(s)$, we conclude that $V^F(S) \geq V^S(S)$ and hence $\beta^F(s) \leq \beta^S(s, s)$ everywhere. ∎

The last theorem in this section establishes that revealing information increases expected prices in the first-price auction, just as we have already established for the second-price auction. As in the drainage tract model, and unlike in our model of the second-price auction, there are again two effects at work: a *publicity effect* and a *weighting effect*. Both effects tend to reduce the winning bidder's profits.

Theorem 5.4.18. For each type of bidder, the conditional expected payment in the first-price auction when the seller reveals t^0, given that the type wins, is higher than the bid made by the same type when the seller reveals nothing: $E[\beta(s, t^0)|t^{(1)} < s] \geq \beta(s)$.

Proof. To emphasize the unity of ideas, we present this proof using virtually the same words as the proof of 5.4.17 and only slightly vary the notation.

Let $B(s, t) = E[\beta(t, t^0)|t^1 = s, t^{(1)} < t]$. (Observe that $B(s, t)$ is the price that bidder 1 of type s expects to pay if he always bids as if his type were t and his bid wins.) We must show that $\beta(s) \leq B(s, s)$.

Suppose bidder 1 of type s bids as if he were of type t, and let $\tilde{v}(s, t) = E[\hat{v}(s, t^{(1)})|t^1 = s, t^{(1)} < t]$. Then the bidder's maximum value in the auction in which the seller reveals no information must satisfy $V^N(s) = \max_t (\tilde{v}(s, t) - \beta(t))F(t|s)$. Similarly, when the seller reveals his information, the bidder's maximum value is $V^I(s) = \max_t (\tilde{v}(s, t) - B(s, t))F(t|s)$. In equilibrium, a bidder of type s optimally bids as his own type $t = s$, so $V^N(s) = (\tilde{v}(s, s) - \beta(s))F(s|s)$ and $V^I(s) = (\tilde{v}(s, s) - B(s, s))F(s|s)$. Hence, $V^N(s) \geq V^I(s)$ if and only if $\beta(s) \leq B(s, s)$.

By the envelope theorem, $V^{N'}(s) = F_2(s|s)(\tilde{v}(s, s) - \beta(s)) + F(s|s)\tilde{v}_1(s, s)$ and $V^{I'}(s) = F_2(s|s)(\tilde{v}(s, s) - B(s, s)) + F(s|s)\tilde{v}_1(s, s) - F(s|s)B_1(s, s)$. Using theorem 5.4.3, part (3), $F_2(s|s) \leq 0$. So, if there is any $s > 0$ at which $V^N(s) < V^I(s)$, then $\beta(s) > B(s, s)$ and hence $V^{N'}(s) \geq V^{I'}(s)$. However, we have already established that, in equilibrium, $V^N(0) = V^I(0)$, so applying the ranking lemma to the function $V^N(s) - V^I(s)$, we conclude that for all s, $V^N(s) \geq V^I(s)$ and hence $\beta(s) \leq B(s, s)$. ∎

5.5 Conclusion

In this chapter, we have relaxed the assumptions of previous chapters that types are statistically independent and that a bidder's value depends only on his own type. These changes raise many new questions and highlight important qualifications to the conclusions of the simpler models.

This chapter first investigated what kinds of information bidders might gather when information is costly and types are independent. We found that information about other bidders' values, as opposed to information about what they know, is of no value to a bidder in choosing his optimal bid. When types are independent and evaluations are costly, that analysis offers a rationale for assuming that bidder types are one-dimensional. We showed, however, that this argument loses force when bidder values may be interdependent.

Next, we studied the drainage tract model, which has been empirically successful in organizing facts about bidding for offshore oil in certain circumstances. The equilibrium in these models has the surprising (and empirically verified) property that the distribution of bids for the better-informed bidder (the *neighbor*) should be just the same as for the worse-informed bidder (the *non-neighbor*). The model also generates results about revenues and profits. Neighbor profits are positive and increasing in the quality of the neighbor's information. Moreover, they are also increasing in the non-neighbor's perception of the quality of the neighbor's information, so bidders have an incentive to convince others that they are well informed. The perceived quality of the neighbor's information may matter, because well-informed bidders exacerbate the winner's curse suffered by non-neighbors, so that, in equilibrium, the non-neighbors bid more timidly, allowing the neighbor higher profits.

The seller can reduce the value of bidders' private information by gathering and disseminating information. Such a policy can help in two ways. To the extent the seller's information makes the neighbor's information less private, this *publicity effect* reduces the neighbor's profit to the seller's benefit. In addition, revealing information changes the weight bidders place on the neighbor's information in estimating value. When the seller's information is a substitute for the neighbor's information, this *weighting effect* reinforces the publicity effect and further increases the seller's revenue. However, it is also logically possible that the seller's information complements the neighbor's information so that the weighting effect is negative. It is even possible that this effect is large enough to overwhelm the publicity effect, lowering seller revenues.

After the drainage tract model, we turned attention to symmetric models with correlated types and interdependent values. We found that the two models of the ascending auction then have *ex post* equilibria – equilibria in which no bidder would want to change his bid after learning the others' bids and types. Such equilibria discourage bidders from gathering information about others' types, for those do not affect the optimal bid. This feature of the ascending auction helps economize on transaction costs.

We also investigated the efficiency of *ex post* equilibrium outcomes in a model of any asymmetric ascending auction. The equilibrium is efficient if a certain interpersonal single crossing condition holds that aligns the bidder's incentives with those of the auctioneer.

We also investigated the impact on revenue of the seller's disclosures of his information. Generally, the seller's disclosures reduce bidders' equilibrium profits and increase equilibrium revenues in the ascending auction models through a *weighting effect*. Revealing information also reduces bidders' equilibrium profits and increases equilibrium revenues in the first-price auction through a *publicity effect*, which the literature has previously called the "linkage principle." Theory also predicts that because of a publicity effect, ascending auctions will generate greater revenue than the first-price sealed-bid auction.

REFERENCES

Athey, Susan (2001). "Single Crossing Properties and the Existence of Pure Strategy Equilibria in Games of Incomplete Information." *Econometrica* **69**(4): 861–890.

Athey, Susan (2002). "Monotone Comparative Statics under Uncertainty." *Quarterly Journal of Economics* **117**(1): 187–223.

Avery, Christopher (1998). "Strategic Jump Bidding in English Auctions." *Review of Economic Studies* **65**(2, No. 223): 185–210.

Bikchandani, Sushil, Philip Haile, and John G. Riley (2002). "Symmetric Separating Equilibria in English Auctions." *Games and Economic Behavior* **38**: 19–27.

Bulow, Jeremy, Ming Huang, and Paul Klemperer (1999). "Toeholds and Takeovers." *Journal of Political Economy* **107**(3): 427–454.

Bulow, Jeremy and Paul Klemperer (2002). "Prices and the Winner's Curse." *Rand Journal of Economics* **33**(1): 1–21.

Cremer, Jacques and Richard P. McLean (1985). "Optimal Selling Strategies under Uncertainty for a Discriminating Monopolist When Demands Are Independent." *Econometrica* **53**(2): 345–361.

Engelbrecht-Wiggans, Richard, Paul Milgrom, and Robert Weber (1983). "Competitive Bidding with Proprietary Information." *Journal of Mathematical Economics* **11**: 161–169.

Grossman, Sanford (1981). "The Informational Role of Warranties and Private Disclosure about Product Quality." *Journal of Law and Economics* **24**(3): 461–483.

Hendricks, Kenneth, Robert Porter, and Charles Wilson (1994). "Auctions for Oil and Gas Leases with an Informed Bidder and a Random Reservation Price." *Econometrica* **63**(1): 1–27.

Hernando-Veciana, Angel (2003). "Successful Uninformed Bidding." *Games and Economic Behavior* (forthcoming).

Klemperer, Paul (1998). "Auctions with Almost Common Values: The Wallet Game and Its Applications." *European Economic Review* **42**: 757–769.

Mas Colell, Andreu, Michael Whinston, and Jerry Green (1995). *Microeconomic Theory*. New York: Oxford University Press.

Maskin, Eric (1992). Auctions and Privatisation. *Privatisation*. H. Siebert. 115–136.

McAfee, R. Preston and Philip Reny (1982). "Correlated Information and Mechanism Design." *Econometrica* **60**(2): 395–421.

Milgrom, Paul (1981a). "Good News and Bad News: Representation Theorems and Applications." *Bell Journal of Economics* **12**: 380–391.

Milgrom, Paul R. (1981b). "Rational Expectations, Information Acquisition, and Competitive Bidding." *Econometrica* **49**(4): 921–943.

Milgrom, Paul and Robert J. Weber (1982a). "A Theory of Auctions and Competitive Bidding." *Econometrica* **50**: 463–483.

Milgrom, Paul and Robert J. Weber (1982b). "The Value of Information in a Sealed-Bid Auction." *Journal of Mathematical Economics* **10**(1): 105–114.

Neeman, Zvika (2001). "The Relevance of Private Information in Mechanism Design." Boston University Working Paper.

Ortega-Reichert, Armando (1968). "Models for Competitive Bidding under Uncertainty." Stanford, CA: Department of Operations Research, Stanford University.

Pesendorfer, Wolfgang and Jeroen Swinkels (1997). "The Loser's Curse and Information Aggregation in Common Value Auctions." *Econometrica* **65**: 1247–1281.

Royden, H.L. (1968). *Real Analysis.* New York: Macmillan.

Topkis, Donald (1978). "Minimizing a Submodular Function on a Lattice." *Operations Research* **26**: 305–321.

Topkis, Donald (1998). *Supermodularity and Complementarity.* Princeton University Press.

Weverbergh, Marcel (1979). "Competitive Bidding with Asymmetric Information Reanalyzed." *Management Science* **25**: 291–294.

Wilson, Robert (1967). "Competitive Bidding with Asymmetric Information." *Management Science* **13**: 816–820.

Wilson, Robert (1969). "Competitive Bidding with Disparate Information." *Management Science* **15**(7): 446–448.

Wilson, Robert (1987). Bidding. *The New Palgrave: A Dictionary of Economics.* J. Eatwell, M. Milgate, and P. Newman. London: MacMillan Press. Volume 1, 238–242.

CHAPTER SIX

Auctions in Context

Chapters 2–5 focus on strategies played *in the auction* and their consequences for economic performance. The auction itself, however, is just one part of a transaction, the success of which depends even more on what happens before and after the auction. Understanding the transaction as a whole requires one to ask who participates and what guarantees quality, delivery, and payment. One must also ask why participants use an auction at all rather than another method of transacting.

To illustrate the challenges of designing procedures for trade, we now discuss two idealized transactions – the sale of an asset and the choice of a supplier.

When an owner sells assets, he must consider what to sell and who might want to buy the assets. If the asset is a commodity frequently traded at an auction site – for example, a major brand of laptop computer sold online at eBay – then the simplest approach may be to list the item for sale at that site. A public auction of this sort reduces the seller's costs of marketing, because the auctioneer supplies most of the required marketing, and maintains a physical or online catalog to help buyers find products they want. The auctioneer's reputation for selling this type of asset helps attract buyers. The availability of similar products at the auction site makes it hard for the seller to get a higher price by conducting his own private auction.

For specialized assets, however, the situation is quite different. Specialized assets are ones with few close substitutes, and few potential bidders are likely to value them highly. To obtain a high price, the seller must identify and attract the most likely purchasers, so independent marketing to seek out such bidders can be especially valuable.

In practice, auctions for valuable yet highly specialized assets often fail because of insufficient interest by bidders. The European auctions for radio spectrum for use with third-generation mobile telephones presents several useful case studies;[1] sale prices per capita for the spectrum licenses varied enormously across these auctions. In 2000, after auctions in England and Germany had generated tens of billions of euros for government treasuries, the Swiss sold licenses at close to the reserve price after only four bidders showed up to bid for the four available licenses. In per capita terms, the difference in prices was about 30 to 1. Though the Swiss example is an extreme one, it is not atypical. Spectrum auctions with few participants and low sale prices have also occurred in Austria, Israel, and Italy.

A combination of factors likely contributed to the disappointing outcome of the Swiss auction. The rules created an all-or-nothing contest, so that only participants who expected to win a large license would be willing even to participate. Buyers are naturally reluctant to begin an expensive, time-consuming evaluation of an asset when they believe they are unlikely to win at a favorable price. High spectrum prices in Germany and England likely dissuaded some bidders from participating in the Swiss auction and encouraged some to merge to reduce competition in the auction. Despite these problems, the Swiss authorities could have achieved a higher price if they had wished. The auction rules could have provided that if few bidders entered the auction, the government would sell the spectrum in the form of three licenses, rather than four, to create meaningful competition.

Events like the Swiss spectrum auction of 2000 highlight the important roles of planning and marketing for asset auctions. The seller or seller's agent needs to approach the right buyers, make sure that there is demand for the assets, package the assets appropriately, and convince buyers to participate. A seller who neglects these considerations may encounter low participation by bidders and low revenue.[2]

Marketing performs valuable economic functions by providing information to buyers and adapting the terms of sale to their needs. To

---

[1] See Klemperer (2002).

[2] Paul Klemperer, who helped design the British spectrum auction, has advocated the use of an "Anglo-Dutch" auction explicitly designed to have some inefficiency to encourage participation by bidders who do not expect to have the highest values for the items being offered.

illustrate the second function, consider the sale of a factory by auction. The potential buyers and seller may decide together what commitments to make to existing workers or what contractual commitments to transfer with the factory. Potential buyers may have different regulatory concerns. For example, if one buyer is a major supplier in Europe, it may need European Commission approval to make the purchase, while another buyer requires no such approval. Sellers must anticipate and accommodate such concerns to attract a sufficient number of high-value buyers to the auction.

An auction's timing can also significantly influence its attractiveness to bidders. For example, in the United States, the most lucrative spectrum auction took place under a shadow of litigation. After Nextwave defaulted on obligations to pay for spectrum licenses won at an earlier auction, the FCC ordered Nextwave to return the licenses. The FCC then scheduled another auction for these same licenses. That auction appeared to have raised $17 billion for the Treasury,[3] until the bankruptcy judge in the Nextwave case ordered the FCC to delay reassigning the licenses. This action left the licenses in limbo; neither the bidders nor the FCC knew whether the new buyers of Nextwave's licenses would eventually receive them. These uncertainties cast a shadow over all future spectrum auctions, as potential buyers were unsure about what licenses they could keep and what sums they were obligated to pay.

In a typical auction for a company or a large factory, sellers give bidders access to a *data room* containing confidential details about the asset. Bidders' access to confidential information provides another reason to select participants in the auction carefully. Otherwise, some participants with little serious interest in buying the factory might pose as bidders to acquire information they could use to compete more effectively with the seller in product or labor markets. The investment bankers who manage these sales usually restrict access to the information and, for additional security, may prohibit bidders without a bona fide business plan from viewing the confidential information in the data room.

Whereas the seller markets his assets to encourage competition, bidders sometimes adopt countervailing strategies. One such countervailing strategy arose in a 1994 US spectrum auction,[4] in which a single license covering all of southern California was among those offered.

---

[3] The auction described is FCC auction #35.
[4] This was auction #4, for the A and B blocks of PCS spectrum.

California's regional telephone company, Pacific Bell, publicly committed to winning this license[5] and began an investment program to demonstrate that commitment. The investments included large expenditures to buy or lease cell sites, which are physical locations in each geographic unit, or *cell*, of the cellular phone system where equipment is placed to transmit and receive radio signals.

These actions persuaded other companies hoping to operate in southern California of Pacific Bell's commitment to win the license. To ensure their own access to the southern California market, they acquired spectrum outside the auction, swapping spectrum and buying spectrum rights from smaller cellular operators. The FCC rules limited the amount of spectrum companies could control in any market, so bidders who acquired spectrum outside the auction became ineligible to bid on the southern California area license. Consequently, Pacific Bell faced only one, marginal competitor for the valuable southern California license and acquired the license for a bargain price.

Sellers who are wary of possibilities like this can sometimes adopt their own counter-strategies. A striking example is the 1989 sale of LIN Communications, which was faced with a hostile takeover bid from Mc-Caw Cellular. LIN's management wanted a friendlier bidder, or at least some other bidder, but realized none would be forthcoming against Mc-Caw, because the costs of bidding are so high and the chances of success so low. To attract BellSouth to participate, LIN promised to pay its expenses ($15 million) plus a consolation fee in case it lost the bidding ($54 million). The competition forced McCaw to raise its offer from $110 per share (about $5.36 billion) to a range between $124–138 per share, roughly a $1 billion increase. LIN's increased price added about $100 million to the value of LIN's executives' stock options, eliminating the resistance by LIN's executives.

Like asset sales, procurement auctions range from the straightforward to the very complex. Although price alone is the basis of choice for a few standardized items, most large business purchases weigh price

---

[5] The author, then a consultant to Pacific Bell, appeared on the CNN nightly news the evening before the auction affirming that competitors would learn "just how determined we are" at Pacific Bell to win the license. In the event, McCaw Cellular, whose owner was a personal rival of the Pacific Bell CEO, decided not to allow Pacific Bell to win the license too cheaply. McCaw became Pacific Bell's only real competitor for the southern California license, forcing the price hundreds of millions of dollars higher than it might otherwise have been. Even so, the eventual price paid per unit of population was low compared to the prices in other market areas containing such a large urban center.

along with a variety of other attributes. These include *product attributes* such as quality and style of the product or service and delivery arrangements, *contract attributes* such as the length of the contract and terms of payment, and *supplier attributes* such as reliability, capacity, and compatibility of order-processing and tracking systems.

Procurement decisions based on price alone may endanger other important attributes such as quality and service. Buyers mitigate this risk in a number of ways. In the United States, where law requires governments to make procurement decisions according to objective criteria, the purchasing agency develops detailed non-price specifications and rejects all bids or contracts that do not comply with the exact specifications. Although this practice may appear fair, it sometimes forces suppliers to adapt their goods for government use, adding fixed costs, reducing scale economies, and increasing prices.

In the private sector, buyers often develop lists of qualified suppliers and leave suppliers on the list only so long as their performance is satisfactory in all respects. Buyers can use this pre-qualification process to favor suppliers they believe to have greater capacity to meet the buyers' future needs – for example, those expected to improve the quality of their products and services, to reduce future prices, to expand capacity if needed, to customize inputs, and so on.[6]

If auctions are used at all in a purchase of complex goods, they are typically just one part of a larger process. A major purchase might start with a *request for information* (RFI) that asks potential suppliers to indicate their ability to provide the goods or services in question and suggest specifications for the goods or services. A *request for proposals* (RFP) meeting the buyer's specifications might follow the RFI. A proposal might specify products and services, payments, and how to handle contingencies. Sometimes a *request for quotes* (RFQ) follows or replaces the RFP. The RFQ asks suppliers to name a firm price for a particular package or initiates an auction among the suppliers.

Additional negotiations may follow receipt of the bids or proposals. Particularly if the final proposals differ in several dimensions, the buyer

---

[6] The discussion in the text treats the buyer as a single entity that can set standards, make forecasts, and evaluate alternatives in a coherent way. Complications arise when the buyer is a firm having several units with independent budget authority. These units typically need to purchase collectively to take advantage of the firm's size in negotiating a low price. Managers must agree on the timing of purchases as well as standards and minimum quantities to be purchased from selected suppliers. If each department's commitment reduces prices for all, free rider problems can interfere with efficient buying arrangements.

may simply use the auction outcome as a starting point from which to bargain. Experienced sellers build some margin into their bids in anticipation of the negotiations. This multistage process can be so costly relative to any anticipated profit margin for the winner that some sellers will decline to participate.

In this chapter, we will treat auctions as mechanisms having precise rules to determine the *best bid* so no negotiations need follow the conclusion of the auction. Although more research is needed to understand interactions between the bidding and bargaining stages, understanding auctions in simple settings is an important precursor to the analysis of more complicated settings.

To distinguish auctions from negotiations, we define auctions to include mechanisms that allow explicit and objective comparison of two or more competing offers that are open at the same time. We define bargaining to include mechanisms in which offers are short-lived and evaluated one at a time. This dichotomy leaves out situations in which multiple offers are available but the comparisons are not objective. Economists have not extensively studied mechanisms of this sort, so it is not yet clear whether it is most helpful to classify them as auctions or negotiations.

Bargaining anticipated to occur after the parties sign a contract may influence transactional design as strongly as the bargaining that precedes the contract. Bargaining may occur during performance of the contract when parties want changes to accommodate events the contract did not anticipate. If the parties expect extensive revision of whatever contract they sign, then they could benefit from using a cost-plus contract, that is, a contract in which the buyer pays the supplier its actual accounting cost plus a mark-up. Cost-plus contracts make it easier to negotiate changes, because they fix in advance the compensation for any agreed changes. However, cost-plus contracts make auctions less useful, because the initial bids play a smaller role in determining the eventual cost to the buyer. On the other hand, fixed price contracts, which establish a firm price for the contract and provide for negotiations to determine the price for any changes, are especially useful when the parties expect few changes.

According to Bajari and Tadelis (2001), these generalities characterize the actual pattern of contracting in the US construction industry. They observe that the party purchasing construction services can reduce the need for changes with thorough planning. Prolonged planning, however, delays completion of the project. When speed is essential or substantial changes are unavoidable, buyers eschew auctions in favor of finding a reliable builder and using a cost-plus contract.

The main focus on this chapter is bidder participation decisions and how those interact with auction design. Most of the existing theory about auctions with entry uses a symmetric model in which there are no *ex ante* differences among potential bidders. The theory for that case is well developed, and this chapter discusses it in considerable detail.

In both asset sales and procurement contexts, businesspeople are often concerned about whether and how to run auctions when some bidders are more qualified than others. Should the auctioneer encourage participation by less qualified bidders in order to increase competition in the auction? Can it be worthwhile to favor new suppliers to increase competition, even if those new suppliers are expected to supply poorer quality? The theory of auctions with *asymmetric* potential bidders is much less developed than the theory of symmetric auctions, so we explore it in less detail, using a series of examples.

6.1 The Profit and Surplus Contribution of an Entrant

We begin by studying a set of models with endogenous entry. Entry is endogenous when bidders themselves decide whether to participate in a particular auction. Will bidders, acting in their own interests, decide efficiently? Or are they likely to be too reluctant or too eager, relative to the efficient standard?

In our model, the entrant to the auction directly bears the costs of entry, so the question boils down to what share of the benefits of entry accrue to the individual entrant. Increased entry clearly affects the payoffs of the other participants: it benefits the seller by raising the sale price, and it harms other bidders both by raising the prices that they pay when they win and by reducing their chance of winning. What is the net effect of these apparent externalities? One might guess that if it is positive, there will be too little entry; if negative, too much.

Our analysis begins with two results. First, in certain private-values models, we find, surprisingly, that the net external effect of entry is zero: an entrant's expected profit in a second-price auction precisely equals his expected incremental contribution to total surplus. In these models, the marginal bidder's entry decision is just what a social planner would want it to be.

The second result is that, in symmetric models, the total value enjoyed by the bidders and the auctioneer is a concave function of the number of bidders or, more precisely (inasmuch as the number of bidders must be an integer), that the expected contribution to welfare of the last entrant in a second-price auction declines in the number of entrants. This concavity finding will have several important uses below.

To prove the first result, suppose a potential bidder is considering entry into a second-price auction. Suppose that entry costs the bidder an amount c, that the highest value among the n other bidders is x, and that a bidder enters with value y. If $y < x$, the bidder will lose the auction and make a net loss of c. If $y > x$, he will win the auction and enjoy net earnings of $y - x - c$. In general, the bidder's net profit will be $(y - x)^+ - c$, where the notation z^+ means $\max(0, z)$. Notice that regardless of whether the bidder wins or loses, his payoff exactly equals his incremental contribution to total surplus. This result is our first theorem.

Theorem 6.1. Suppose entry costs are c, the maximum value among existing bidders is x, and the last entrant's value is y. Then, if the entrant decides to enter a second-price auction, its net profit and its incremental contribution to total surplus both equal $(y - x)^+ - c$.

Theorem 6.1 establishes that in a second-price auction, the marginal bidder's entry decision aligns perfectly with the objective of maximizing social surplus. If the bidder knows x, y, and c at the time of entry, then he finds entry profitable if and only if his entry increases the total surplus. Even if the bidder does not know some of the relevant information and bases his entry decision on *expected* profits, the conclusion is similar: he enters if and only if his entry increases the expected total surplus.

The theorem shows that changing the entry decision of a single potential bidder cannot increase the surplus, but it does not establish that entry decisions are efficient. For example, consider an asymmetric model with a single good for sale and two buyers with values 8 and 10. Suppose the cost of entry is 5. If the first buyer enters but the second does not, neither buyer can do better by changing his decision unilaterally. In that event, the total surplus will be 3, which is less than the maximum total surplus of 5 that could be achieved if the entry decisions were reversed and only the second bidder entered.

The preceding example indicates the value of examining the efficiency of entry decisions in more detail. Thus, suppose there are many potential bidders who have values of $v^1, v^2, \ldots$ and who decide in sequence whether to enter a second-price auction. If the first n potential bidders have already entered the auction, then the highest value among them is $\max(v^1, \ldots, v^n)$.[7] Consider the entry decision of the $n + 1$st potential entrant. Let $I(n, y, v) = (y - \max(v^1, \ldots, v^n))^+ - c$; this is the entrant's contribution to surplus and net profit from entry when $v^{n+1} = y$. By inspection, the difference $I(n, y, v) - I(n + 1, y, v) = (y - \max(v^1, \ldots, v^n))^+ - (y - \max(v^1, \ldots, v^{n+1}))^+$ is always nonnegative, and is positive exactly when $v^{n+1} > y > \max(v^1, \ldots, v^n)$. Thus, the entrant's contribution is (weakly) declining in n, and his conditional expected contribution $E[I(n, y, v)]$, given any realization $v^{n+1} = y$, is a nonincreasing function of n and is strictly decreasing if $\Pr\{v^{n+1} > y > \max(v^1, \ldots, v^n)\} > 0$.

These preliminary conclusions are particularly handy for analyzing symmetric models or models in which the order of potential entry is determined in advance, for example, by the auctioneer. In both cases, $E[I(n, y, v)]$ is a nonincreasing function of n.

6.2 Symmetric Models with Costly Entry

Let us apply the preceding insights to our benchmark model: the symmetric independent private-values model with a single good for sale. In that model, $\Pr\{v^{n+1} > v^{n+2} > \max(v^1, \ldots, v^n)\} = [(n + 1)(n + 2)]^{-1} > 0$.[8] Because this probability is strictly positive, the expected profit of an entrant is strictly decreasing in n, the number of bidders who have already entered the auction.

In real auctions, as in the models studied in this chapter, participation is costly. For example, before bidding for an asset, each bidder needs to study it carefully and plan how he would use it in his business. Identifying the bidder's value for the asset is the first step in preparing a bid. In our models, the bidder decides whether to participate and incur this cost before knowing his value.

There are three groups of models in this chapter. In the first group, the seller designs the rules of bidding but exercises no direct control over who enters the auction. The interesting issues in this case arise

---

[7] By convention, the maximum value and maximum type are taken to be zero when $n = 0$.

[8] By symmetry, the probability that v^{n+1} is the largest value among the $n + 2$ values is $1/(n + 2)$. Conditional on that fact, again by symmetry, the probability that v^{n+2} is the largest of the remaining values is $1/(n + 1)$. Multiplying these ratios gives the expression in the text.

when entry costs are *moderate*. If the entry cost is low enough that all potential bidders will find it profitable to participate, then the analysis merges into the analysis of the preceding chapters with a fixed number of bidders, N. If the entry costs are so high that no bidder can profitably participate, the analysis is trivial. When entry costs are moderate, the equilibrium will, with positive probability, involve entry by some, but not all, potential bidders.

We begin by studying a symmetric model in which each bidder's decision about whether to enter is randomized. A bidder who randomizes at equilibrium must be indifferent between entering and not entering. Accordingly, entrants must earn zero expected profits, so the *entire* net surplus created by the auction accrues to the seller. This observation has important consequences for auction design; for example, it implies that an auction maximizes the seller's payoff if and only if it maximizes total net surplus. In expectation, the seller bears the burden of all participation costs incurred by bidders, so the seller takes full account of those costs in designing the optimal auction.

In a second group of models, the seller exercises tighter control over entry. The seller can economize on participation costs by coordinating entry into the auction. We will find that screening bidders results in less waste, a more predictable number of bidders, and higher average revenues for the seller than a process with unrestricted bidder entry. This conclusion is particularly striking in the symmetric model, because it holds even when the screening process cannot select among bidders according to any actual differences between them. Even so, limiting bidder entry can increase the seller's expected revenues. In other models, screening can identify the bidders who are most likely to have high values, producing still greater improvements in performance. We assess how much sellers can increase revenue with a procedure in which bidders share information with the seller before the auction about the extent of their interest in the asset being sold.

A third kind of model pits an auction mechanism against a negotiation mechanism or a hybrid of the two. For our purposes, the distinction between auctions and negotiations is that auctions involve a simultaneous comparison of offers whereas negotiations take place sequentially. The advantage of auctions lies in their use of explicit competition to determine prices. In our model, the advantage of negotiations is that they economize on participation costs although, in practice, a more important advantage is the ability to tailor the deal to the particular buyer and seller. Bargaining achieves economies in our model because it sometimes allows a sale to one of the first entrants, if that entrant's value is sufficiently high, rendering unnecessary the costs of additional entry.

Hybrid mechanisms that combine the advantages of auctions and bargaining are important in practice. In this chapter, we analyze a simple one – auctions with a *buy price*. In these auctions, the seller announces that if any buyer offers a certain price, then the auction will end immediately and the seller will transact with that buyer at that price. This hybrid mechanism combines some of the advantages of auctions (if no bidder is willing to offer the buy price) and bargaining (if some bidder accepts the buy price). We present a symmetric auction model in which the seller always prefers to use a buy price rather than use a simple auction.

6.2.1 Symmetric Bidders and Uncoordinated Entry

This section presents a model first studied by Levin and Smith (1994). There are N potential bidders, each with no initial information. Bidder i incurs a cost $c > 0$ to enter and learn his type t^i. In a symmetric equilibrium, each bidder randomizes, entering with probability p. If a bidder enters, he bids according to a function β that depends on the rules of the auction. We use the distributional strategy formulation in which bidder i's value is $v(t^i)$, where v is increasing[9] and differentiable, and in which types are distributed independently and uniformly on $[0, 1]$.

6.2.1.1 Equilibrium in Entry and Bidding Decisions

First suppose the auction is a first-price auction with reserve price r. Let ρ be the type with value equal to the reserve: $r = v(\rho)$. We will consider both the possibility that the bidder learns the number of entrants, n, before he bids, and the alternative sealed-bid auction in which the seller conceals the number of bidders who participate.

Chapter 4 characterizes the symmetric equilibrium strategy $\beta(\cdot, n)$ for the case when everyone knows the number of bidders, n. When the

---

[9] All the results reported here extend to the case where v is merely nondecreasing, provided we appropriately resolve ties and indifferences. Chapter 3 describes the relevant method. Here, we take v to be increasing in order to limit the amount of text devoted to indifferences and ties.

bidder learns his type t^i but has not yet learned n, he bids differently. First, the bidder makes a bid exceeding the reserve r only if his value is at least r (that is, if $t^i \geq \rho$). In that event, he expects to outbid any particular potential bidder if that bidder does not enter (which occurs with probability $1 - p$) or enters but has a lower type (which occurs with probability pt^i). Dropping superscripts, the total probability that an entrant of type $t \geq \rho$ bids more than any other particular bidder is $1 - p + pt$, so the probability that he is the highest bidder in an auction with $N - 1$ other potential bidders is $x(t) = (1 - p + pt)^{N-1}$. Using the envelope theorem, the bidder's expected net profit when he first learns his type is

$$V(t; p, N, \rho) = -c + \int_{\rho}^{t} (1 - p(1 - s))^{N-1} v'(s) \, ds. \tag{6.1}$$

This value is decreasing in p and N.

It is convenient to define

$$\hat{V}(p, N, \rho) \equiv E[V(t^i; p, N, \rho)]. \tag{6.2}$$

As discussed above, we focus on the case of moderate participation costs. This condition rules out the two extreme cases in which either $\hat{V}(1, N, \rho) > 0$, meaning that entry is always profitable even if all bidders choose to participate, or $\hat{V}(0, N, \rho) < 0$, so that entry is unprofitable regardless of the entry decisions of the other bidders.

Our analysis focuses on the remaining case in which a bidder's optimal entry decision depends on what the other bidders do. Define

$$\hat{t}(n) = \max(t^1, \ldots, t^n). \tag{6.3}$$

Let $n(p)$ be a random variable that has the binomial distribution with parameters N and p.

Theorem 6.2 Suppose that the entry cost c is moderate, as defined above. Then there is a unique solution $p = p^*(N, \rho)$ to $\hat{V}(p, N, \rho) = 0$, and the solution lies in $(0, 1)$. Further suppose that the auction used is a first-price auction with reserve $r = v(\rho)$ and that the auctioneer reveals the number of entrants before bids are placed. Then there is a unique symmetric equilibrium of the model. In equilibrium, each bidder enters with probability $p^*(N, \rho)$, and an entrant uses the following bid function, conditional on its type t and the number of bidders, n:

$$\beta_{FK}(t, n, \rho) = \begin{cases} 0 & \text{if } t < \rho, \\ E[\max(r, v(\hat{t}(n-1)))|\hat{t}(n-1) < t] & \text{otherwise.} \end{cases} \quad (6.4)$$

Writing n^* for $n(p^*(N, \rho))$, the seller's *ex ante* expected revenue is

$$\begin{aligned} R_{FK}(N, \rho) &= E[\beta_{FK}(\hat{t}(n^*), n^*, \rho)] \\ &= E[v(\hat{t}(n^*))1_{\{\hat{t}(n^*)\geq\rho\}} - cn^*]. \end{aligned} \quad (6.5)$$

Remark. The subscript *FK* on the bid and revenue functions indicates that the model involves a *first*-price auction and that each bidder *knows* how many bidders are present when he decides how much to bid. The first expression for $R_{FK}(N, \rho)$ above is the expected winning bid. The second is the expected *net* surplus, that is, the expected value of the item to the entrant with the highest value (provided that value exceeds the reserve) minus the total expected entry costs.

Proof. Bidding proceeds as it would without the explicit model of entry, so formula (6.4) follows from the analyses of chapter 4.

In the entry stage, any mixed strategy solution entails a probability of entry that solves $\hat{V}(p, N, \rho) = 0$. (If instead $\hat{V}(p, N, \rho) > 0$, any individual bidder could gain by switching to the strategy of entering with probability one. Similarly, if $\hat{V}(p, N, \rho) < 0$, then any individual bidder could gain by switching to the strategy of entering with probability zero.) Conversely, if all bidders randomize in this way, then bidders are indifferent between entering and not, so each bidder finds randomizing between the two to be a best reply.

Because costs are moderate, $\hat{V}(0, N, \rho) > 0$ and $\hat{V}(1, N, \rho) < 0$. Then, because $\hat{V}$ is continuous and decreasing in p, there is a unique solution $p^*(N, \rho)$ to $\hat{V}(p, N, \rho) = 0$.

The first line of (6.5) is merely the definition of expected revenue. The second line follows the observation that for every realization of n^*, the net payoff to the bidder with the highest type is $(v(\hat{t}(n^*)) - \beta_{FK}(\hat{t}(n^*), n^*, \rho))1_{\{\hat{t}(n^*)\geq\rho\}} - c$. The net payoffs of the $n^* - 1$ other bidders are all $-c$, and the seller's payoff is $\beta_{FK}(\hat{t}(n^*), n^*, \rho)1_{\{\hat{t}(n^*)\geq\rho\}}$. Hence, the total net payoff is the argument of the expectation in the second line of (6.5). Because the bidders' expected net payoffs are all zero in equilibrium, the expected seller payoff equals the total net payoff. ∎

Theorem 6.2 describes equilibrium when all bidders know how many rivals participate. We now examine the case where the seller can conceal the total number of bidders. In this case, bidders perceive the number of bidders to be random. Nonetheless, we can still write a bidder's expected payoff as $u(x, t) = v(t)x(b) - P(b)$, where $x(b) = \Pr\{\text{bid } b \text{ wins}\}$ and $P(b) = bx(b)$ is the bidder's expected payment. By inspection, $u(x, t)$ has the single crossing differences (SCD) property, so, as argued in chapter 3, any symmetric equilibrium bidding strategy of the first-price auction must be increasing. Consequently, for any probability p of entry, the probability that a bidder of type $t > \rho$ outbids any particular rival is $1 - p + pt$, the sum of the probability that the other bidder does not enter and the probability that he enters but has a type less than t. So the probability that a bidder of type t wins is $x(t) = (1 - p + pt)^{N-1}$. Applying the envelope theorem, because this formula is the same as when the bidder observes n, the expected payoff and expected payment must be the same as well. These observations establish the following result.

Theorem 6.3. Suppose that the entry cost c is moderate, as defined above. Then there is a unique solution $p = p^*(N, \rho)$ to $\hat{V}(p, N, \rho) = 0$, and the solution lies in $(0, 1)$. Further suppose that the auction used is a first-price auction with reserve $r = v(\rho)$ and that the auctioneer conceals the number of entrants before bids are placed. Then there is a unique symmetric equilibrium of the model. In equilibrium, each bidder enters with probability $p^*(N, \rho)$, and an entrant uses the following bid function, conditional on its type t:

$$\beta_{FN}(t, \rho) = \begin{cases} 0 & \text{if } t < \rho, \\ E\left[\beta_{FK}(t, n^*, \rho)\right] & \text{otherwise.} \end{cases} \tag{6.6}$$

Writing n^* for $n(p^*(N, \rho))$, the seller's *ex ante* expected revenue is $R_{FN}(N, \rho) = R_{FK}(N, \rho)$.

Remark. The subscript *FN* indicates that the model involves a *first*-price auction and that *no* bidder knows how many other bidders have entered when he chooses his bid.

The first two theorems analyze first-price auctions. If instead the seller uses a second-price auction, then the dominant bidding strategy does not depend on the number of competitors, so the analysis does not depend on whether the seller announces the number of entrants.

Theorem 6.4. Suppose that the entry cost c is moderate, as defined above. Then the second-price auction with reserve $r = v(\rho)$ has a unique, symmetric equilibrium. At equilibrium, each bidder enters with probability $p^*(N, \rho)$; an entrant bids zero if $v(t^i) < r$ and otherwise bids $\beta_S(t, \rho) = v(t)$. The seller's *ex ante* expected revenue is $R_S(N, \rho) = R_{FK}(N, \rho)$.

In summary, the payoff and revenue equivalence results developed in the preceding chapters assuming exogenous entry also hold when entry is endogenous and bidders randomize entry decisions. Because expected payoffs are the same across auctions, incentives to enter and therefore entry decisions are also the same.

6.2.1.2 Setting the Reserve Price

In the benchmark symmetric model with a fixed number of bidders n, if the seller sets a reserve price of r, then the expected proceeds of the sale are $E\left[\max\left(r, v(t^{(2)})\right)1_{\{v(t^{(1)})>r\}}\right] = \Pr\{v(t^{(1)}) > r\}E\left[\max(r, v(t^{(2)}))|v(t^{(1)}) > r\right]$, where, as usual, $t^{(1)}$ and $t^{(2)}$ are the highest and second highest types. The formula expresses the trade-off involved in setting the reserve in the benchmark model: increasing the reserve reduces the probability that any transaction takes place, but raises the average price conditional on any transaction occurring. The optimal reserve in the benchmark model attracts participation by all types whose *marginal revenue* is positive. That is, $r^* = v(t^*)$, where t^* solves $0 = MR(t^*)$ and where $MR(t) \equiv v(t) - (1 - t)v'(t)$.

When entry is endogenous, the analysis changes drastically. The key observation for understanding reserve prices in a symmetric model with moderate entry costs is that the bidders' expected profits are zero. The reason is that bidders in the equilibria described above randomize their entry decisions, so they must be indifferent between entering and not entering, and not entering entails a payoff of zero.

Because bidders earn zero equilibrium payoff regardless of the reserve, the seller cannot squeeze buyer profits by raising the reserve.

Increasing the reserve above the seller's actual value blocks efficient trades and discourages efficient entry, reducing the total payoff to be shared. Because the seller captures the entire expected net payoff in this case, he can never gain by raising the reserve above his own value. Thus, the reserve price that maximizes expected revenue is the seller's value, which is zero in our model.

Because we have assumed that the minimum possible bidder value $v(0)$ is non-negative, any reserve price in the interval $[0, v(0)]$ yields the same equilibrium bids and entry decisions, and hence the same expected revenue. Consequently, the theorems below identify *an* optimal auction rather than *the* unique optimal auction.

Theorem 6.5. Suppose that the entry cost c is moderate, as defined above. Then the reserve price $r = v(0)$ maximizes expected revenue in each of the three auctions studied above:

$$(0, p^*(N, 0)) \in \arg \max_{\rho, p} E[v(\hat{f}(n(p)))1_{\{\hat{f}(n(p)) \geq \rho\}} - cn(p)]$$

$$\text{subject to } p = p^*(N, \rho). \quad (6.7)$$

Proof. Because the conclusion about expected revenues does not depend on the seller's value, we may assume without loss of generality that the seller's value is zero. With that assumption, the objective in (6.7) equals the total expected surplus generated by the auction. Because the entrants have expected total profits of zero in equilibrium, the objective equals the seller's expected revenues.

Consider the relaxed problem in which we replace the constraint $p = p^*(N, \rho)$ with the less restrictive constraint $p \in [0, 1]$. We solve this problem in two steps. First, we fix p and maximize revenue with respect to ρ, showing that the optimum occurs at $\rho = 0$. We use this solution to characterize the maximal profits $G(p)$ in the relaxed problem. Then, we choose p to maximize $G(p)$, showing that the maximum occurs at $p = p^*(N, 0)$. Finally, we observe that this solution of the relaxed problem is feasible for the original problem, so it is an optimum of the original problem.

The first step is simple. By inspection of (6.7), for all fixed values of p, $\rho = 0$ maximizes expected revenue. Substituting $\rho = 0$ into (6.7), we denote the resulting objective by $G(p) = E[v(\hat{f}(n(p))) - cn(p)]$.

Next, we evaluate the derivative of G:

$$\frac{1}{N}G'(p) = \frac{1}{N}\frac{d}{dp}E[v(\hat{f}(n(p))) - cn(p)]$$

$$= \frac{1}{N}\frac{d}{dp}\sum_{n=1}^{N}E[v(\hat{f}(n)) - cn]\binom{N}{n}p^n(1-p)^{N-n}$$

$$= \sum_{n=1}^{N}E[v(\hat{f}(n)) - cn]\binom{N-1}{n-1}p^{n-1}(1-p)^{N-n}$$

$$\quad - \sum_{m=0}^{N-1}E[v(\hat{f}(m)) - cm]\binom{N-1}{m}p^{m-1}(1-p)^{N-m}$$

$$= \sum_{m=0}^{N-1}E[v(\hat{f}(m+1)) - v(\hat{f}(m)) - c]\binom{N-1}{m}p^m(1-p)^{N-m-1}$$

$$= \hat{V}(p, N, 0). \qquad (6.8)$$

The second equality follows from the facts that the distribution of $n(p)$ is a binomial with parameters N and p and that, when $n = 0$, the value of the expectation is zero (because, by the convention adopted above, $v(\hat{f}(0)) = 0$). The third equality uses the product rule for derivatives, and the fourth combines the sums using the substitution $n = m + 1$. By inspection, the next to last expression is the bidder's expected contribution to surplus upon entry when the other $N - 1$ bidders enter with probability p. By Theorem 6.1, for any entry decisions by the first $N - 1$ bidders, any realization of the values, and any entry costs, bidder N's contribution to surplus in a second-price auction equals his realized profit upon entry. The next to last line of (6.8) thus equals $\hat{V}(p, N, 0)$, bidder N's expected profit from entry.

As previously shown, $\hat{V}(p, N, 0)$ is continuous and decreasing in p. Because costs are moderate, the range of the function includes both positive and negative values. Therefore, there is a unique solution $p = p^*(N, 0)$ to $\hat{V}(p, N, 0) = 0$. Also, because $\hat{V}(p, N, 0)$ is decreasing in p, $G'(p) = N\hat{V}(p, N, 0)$ is decreasing in p. Hence, G is concave and achieves its maximum where its derivative is zero, which occurs at $p = p^*(N, 0)$.

Because the optimal solution to the relaxed problem is feasible in the original problem (6.7), it solves the original problem as well. ∎

Theorem 6.5 asserts that in the auctions studied above, the optimal reserve does not exclude any valuable trade. In the model, that means the seller chooses a reserve of $v(0)$ or less. In general, the optimal reserve excludes only inefficient trades, so the optimal reserve is equal to the seller's value of the good. Any higher reserve reduces the expected total surplus and the seller's expected total value. It does so by blocking some efficient trades and by reducing entry below its efficient level.

It is crucially important for the preceding analysis that the seller commits to the reserve before the bidders make their entry decisions. If potential bidders do not know the reserve, then changing it cannot affect their entry decisions. The seller will then be tempted to set a positive reserve and even to set the *ex post* optimal reserve $r^* = v(t^*)$, where $MR(t^*) = 0$. If the bidders anticipate such behavior, the equilibrium probability of entry will fall, to the seller's net disadvantage.

The seller may also want to choose a reserve above her valuation if she uses a non-public auction, in which only invited bidders may participate. We discuss this rationale for limiting trade next.

6.2.2 Coordinating Entry among Symmetric Competitors

Why would a profit-maximizing seller ever want to limit participation in an auction? In the model of the previous section, independent, uncoordinated entry decisions by potential bidders induced a random number of bidders to enter. The entry probability was optimal, but only given the constraint that all bidders must make independent entry decisions. In the unconstrained problem, the expected total surplus is maximized by some deterministic number of bidders, and the seller can maximize her revenues by inviting exactly that number of bidders to the auction. This is *strictly* better than randomizing, because the net surplus is a strictly concave function of the number of bidders.

The next theorem formalizes this argument. To state the theorem, we adopt the notation $\lfloor z \rfloor = \sup\{m \in \mathbb{Z} | m \le z\}$; this is the *integer part* of z. We also define $\lceil z \rceil = \inf\{m \in \mathbb{Z} | m > z\} = \lfloor z \rfloor + 1$; this is the smallest integer greater than z. Let $H(n) = E[v(\hat{t}(n))] - nc$ denote the expected net revenue from the auction when exactly n bidders participate and the reserve price is no more than $v(0)$.

Theorem 6.6. Let $\tilde{n}$ be the random number of bidders in some auction, and suppose that the support of $\tilde{n}$ includes at least three points. Suppose bidders are symmetric and have independent private values. Assume the entry cost c is moderate. Then there is an auction with a deterministic number of bidders and a greater expected net surplus, involving approximately the same expected number of bidders: $E[H(\tilde{n})] < \max(H(\lfloor E[\tilde{n}] \rfloor), H(\lceil E[\tilde{n}] \rceil)$.

Proof. As we have seen, if the seller's value is zero, then for any positive integer n, $H(n)$ is the expected surplus from the auction, so $H(n + 1) - H(n)$ is the expected contribution of the marginal entrant: $H(n + 1) - H(n) = E[I(n, v^{n+1}, v)] = E[I(n, v^N, v)]$. By the analysis at the beginning of section 6.1, the last expression is decreasing in n. Because the support of $\tilde{n}$ includes at least three points, H is not linear over the support of $\tilde{n}$. To extend the domain of H to $\mathbb{R}_+$ let $H(x) = (x - \lfloor x \rfloor)H(\lceil x \rceil) + (\lceil x \rceil - x)H(\lfloor x \rfloor)$; this *linear interpolation* is a concave function.

Let $q = E[\tilde{n}] - \lfloor E[\tilde{n}] \rfloor$ be the fractional part of $E[\tilde{n}]$. By Jensen's inequality,

$$
\begin{aligned}
E[H(\tilde{n})] &< H(E[\tilde{n}]) \\
&= qH(\lceil E[\tilde{n}] \rceil) + (1 - q)H(\lfloor E[\tilde{n}] \rfloor) \\
&\leq \max(H(\lfloor E[\tilde{n}] \rfloor), H(\lceil E[\tilde{n}] \rceil)).
\end{aligned}
\tag{6.9}
$$

The first inequality is strict, because H is concave and not linear on the support of $\tilde{n}$. The equality simply uses the linear interpolation above. The final inequality follows because $q \in [0, 1]$. ∎

Theorem 6.6 suggests a reason why the seller might want to control entry into his auction. It asserts that even if pre-qualification of bidders identifies a purely random selection of bidders rather than identifying ones likely to have high values, a pre-qualification process could still be worthwhile simply as a tool to reduce randomness in the number of entrants.

When the number of entrants is deterministic, the zero-expected-profit condition of the random entry model does not apply. One might wonder whether a reserve is useful in such a context. The next result, due to McAfee and McMillan (1987), shows that if it is also possible to charge an entry fee, then an auction with a positive reserve price never maximizes expected revenue.

Theorem 6.7. In the symmetric independent private-values model with moderate entry cost c, suppose the seller can choose the number n of entrants, the reserve r, and an entry fee e for use with a second-price auction, subject to the (*participation*) constraint that each bidder's expected net profit must be non-negative. Then the seller can maximize expected revenue by choosing $n = \max\{m|\, E[v(\hat{t}(m)) - v(\hat{t}(m-1))] > c\}$, $r = v(0)$, and $e = E[v(\hat{t}(n)) - v(\hat{t}(n-1))] - c$.

Proof. Suppose the seller's value is zero. For any given number n of entrants and a reserve price $v(\rho)$, the expected total surplus is $H_\rho(n) = E[v(\hat{t}(n))1_{\{\hat{t}(n) > \rho\}}] - nc$. By inspection, setting $\rho = 0$, which is the same as setting the reserve to $r = v(0)$, maximizes total surplus.

As argued earlier, an entrant's incremental contribution to surplus, $H_\rho(n) - H_\rho(n-1)$, declines with increasing n. Hence, total surplus is maximized by the largest integer n such that $H_\rho(n) - H_\rho(n+1) > 0$ or, equivalently, the largest n such that $E[v(\hat{t}(n)) - v(\hat{t}(n-1))] - c > 0$.

As the entrant's expected profits must be non-negative, the seller's maximum expected revenue cannot exceed the maximum expected total surplus. With the specified entry fee, the expected net profit of each bidder is zero, and the seller's expected revenue is then equal to the maximized expected net surplus. ∎

6.2.2.1 Pre-qualifying Bidders
The practice of pre-qualifying bidders puzzles some observers. It would seem that limited competition can only harm the seller and reduce efficiency, so why would a seller wish to do that?

There are several possible answers. The one explored in the preceding section is that inviting just a few bidders can motivate each to participate, reducing the randomness in participation and increasing the efficiency of the outcome. A second answer is that pre-qualification before a bidder gets access to the data room can improve the security of confidential business information. A third is that that even when participation is not random, it is possible that the bidders who choose to participate are ones with relatively low values and that their participation deters higher-value bidders. We illustrated that possibility by example earlier in this chapter.

In this sub-subsection, we delve into the last of these answers. We model pre-qualification for the sale of a valuable asset by adding a preliminary reporting stage to the benchmark model. In actuality, a potential buyer's report may be as complicated as a business plan establishing the bidder's genuine interest in the asset, or it may be a *preliminary bid* or *indication of interest* that estimates how much the bidder might bid if he were invited to participate in the actual auction. The auctioneer or investment banker who receives the report serves as confidential intermediary and uses the reports along with other information to choose which bidders to invite. In a billion dollar asset sale, the auctioneer might invite five to ten bidders to make binding bids, basing his choice on the indicative bids, bidder financial statements, and other information.

Advocates of the two-stage process say that, in practice, bidders are highly motivated to make their indicative bids honestly. They claim that bidders have no motive to exaggerate their interest, because, given the substantial cost of bidding, they do not want to be invited to make a bid if their chances of winning are slight. Bidders also have no motive to understate their interest, because they want to avoid being excluded when their actual values are high.[10]

Ye (2002) has subjected these claims about incentives to formal analysis. In his model, there are N potential bidders, each with a rough estimate of his own value. These initial values are distributed independently and identically. A bidder can acquire more information to refine his estimate by incurring cost c. This models the possibilities that the bidder might gather information about the condition of the asset, which affects the values of all bidders similarly, or about how the bidder could best use the asset. The model treats a situation in which the auctioneer asks bidders to make preliminary bids based on their rough estimates. These bids are non-binding and do not affect the transaction price, but, Ye assumes, the seller invites the n highest bidders from the first round to make binding bids in a second round. The invited bidders then incur a cost c before preparing a final, binding bid.

Does this procedure screen bidders effectively, selecting those with the highest value estimates to bid in the second round auction? If so, then there must exist an increasing equilibrium bid function β that maps the bidders' initial types into their indicative bids, so that the highest bidders have the highest value estimates. Ye finds that, to the contrary, there cannot be any strictly increasing bidding equilibrium, so the bidders

---

[10] In addition, the bidders value their relationships with investment bankers and want to avoid acquiring a reputation for dishonesty or unfair dealing. We do not analyze that incentive here.

selected by this procedure will not generally be those with the highest values.

Ye's conclusion does not imply that there are no gains to the two-stage procedure. The characterization of optimal procedures in the environment that Ye analyzes is a currently unsolved problem.

We present a simplified version of Ye's model, in which we assume that the potential bidders' information at the first stage is perfect, so bidders acquire no new information if invited to the second round. One might imagine bidders incur cost c to verify the information underlying their indicative bids before making a firm offer.

Each bidder makes an indicative bid, and the seller invites the highest n bidders to make final bids in a second-price auction. To focus analysis on the indicative bidding problem, we assume that bidders play their dominant strategies at the second stage, so the payoffs in the second stage are the Vickrey payoffs minus the entry cost c. Let $\bar{b}^i$ denote the nth highest bid in the indicative bidding stage among bidder i's competitors, and let $\bar{t}^i = \max\{t^j \mid j \neq i, b^j \geq \bar{b}^i\}$; $\bar{t}^i$ is the type of the competitor i must beat to win the final auction. Then bidder i's payoff is

$$\Pi^i(b^i, \bar{b}^i, t^i) = \begin{cases} 0 & \text{if } b^i \leq \bar{b}^i, \\ -c & \text{if } b^i > \bar{b}^i \text{ and } t^i < \bar{t}^i, \\ -c + v(t^i) - v(\bar{t}^i) & \text{otherwise.} \end{cases} \qquad (6.10)$$

In words, i's payoff is zero if he is not among the highest n bidders in the indicative stage; it is $-c$ if he is among the highest n bidders but loses the final auction; and it is $-c + v(t^i) - v(\bar{t}^i)$ if he is selected to make a bid and wins the final auction.

Theorem 6.8. The reduced form indicative bidding game has no increasing, symmetric equilibrium strategy.

Proof. Let $\beta : [0, 1] \to \mathbb{R}$ be any increasing function representing an indicative bidding strategy adopted by all potential bidders. We show that β is not an equilibrium strategy by demonstrating a profitable deviation. Indeed, we claim that any bidder i of any type $t^i \in (0, 1)$ can earn a higher expected payoff by reducing his bid to $\beta(s) < \beta(t^i)$ for any s satisfying $0 < v(t^i) - v(s) < c$. The increase in i's payoff on account of the proposed deviation is

$$\Pi^i(\beta(s), \bar{b}^i, t^i) - \Pi^i(\beta(t^i), \bar{b}^i, t^i)$$

$$= \begin{cases} 0 & \text{if } \beta(t^i) \leq \bar{b}^i \text{ or } \beta(s) > \bar{b}^i. \\ c & \text{if } \beta(t^i) > \bar{b}^i > \beta(s) \text{ and } t^i < \bar{t}^i. \\ c - v(t^i) + v(\bar{t}^i) & \text{otherwise.} \end{cases} \qquad (6.11)$$

According to the first line of (6.11), the deviant bid has no effect on i's payoff if neither bids results in an invitation or if both do. According to the second line, it increases the deviant's payoff by $c > 0$ if the higher bid would result in entry and losing the auction but the lower bid would result in no entry. Finally, if the higher bid would result in entry and winning the auction, but the lower bid would result in no entry, then $t^i > \bar{t}^i > s$, so it increases the deviant's payoff by $c - v(t^i) + v(\bar{t}^i) \geq c - v(t^i) + v(s) > 0$.

Because all the lines in (6.11) are non-negative and some are positive, $\beta(s)$ has a higher expected payoff than $\beta(t^i)$, so strategy β is not a best reply to itself. ∎

Although the proof applies only to the particular model of indicative bidding specified here, the conclusion of the theorem holds in a much wider class of models.

6.2.2.2 Auctions, Negotiations, and Posted Prices

When participation costs are high and bidder values do not vary widely, an auction with multiple participants may incur unnecessary costs. One might expect that the seller could save on costs by negotiating with a single buyer and capture part of that saving in the form of a higher price. If the initial negotiation failed, the seller could still approach other buyers and negotiate with them. Alternatively, the seller might just post a price and wait for a buyer to appear who is willing to pay that price. Before comparing auctions, negotiations, and posted prices, it is helpful first to review some results of the theory of sequential search.

Consider the following model of search by a single agent, which might represent a buyer's search for a valuable good, a seller's search for a high-price buyer, and so on. The searcher anticipates encountering a series of alternatives. He incurs costs of c to examine each item and receives a take-it-or-leave-it offer each time he does so. Once he accepts an offer, his search ends, and his payoff is the value of the item minus the total search costs incurred.

Suppose the searcher can examine a potentially infinite number of items and, after examining the ith item, can take the item and enjoy a value $v(t^i)$ or reject it irretrievably and continue to search. Let R be the searcher's payoff from an optimal search strategy. Because the problem is stationary, after any rejection, the searcher's maximal payoff from continuing to search is R. The optimal strategy is therefore to accept the item if $v(t^i) > R$ and otherwise to continue to search. Also because the problem is stationary, Bellman's equation takes a particularly simple form: $R = E[\max(R, v(t^i))] - c$. It is not difficult to show that there is a unique R that solves this equation and that it represents the value of the search problem.

If we imagine that there is a seller searching for a buyer, we obtain a model that is analogous to the preceding one, but with the costs, which are the buyers' costs of evaluating the good, incurred by the buyers. More precisely, suppose that each buyer must incur a cost of c to determine his value for the good. The seller then designs a selling mechanism subject to the constraint that each buyer's expected profit upon entering and evaluating the good must be non-negative. The following result, adapted from Riley and Zeckhauser (1983), establishes that the resulting problem is very much like the optimal search problem.

Theorem 6.9. The seller maximizes expected revenue in the model described above by a posted price mechanism, in which the seller invites buyers one at a time to buy or not at a fixed price R that solves $R = E[\max(R, v(t^i))] - c$. At equilibrium, each buyer enters successively. Bidder i accepts the offer if and only if $v(t^i) \geq R$. Each buyer's expected profit is zero, and the seller's expected revenue is R.

Proof. We begin by studying the performance of the proposed posted price mechanism. Assume first that each buyer enters and buys exactly when its value exceeds R. Then the sequence of buyers' purchase decisions is the same as the searcher's sequence of decisions in the corresponding search problem, so the expected total surplus of R is also the same. By inspection, the seller's expected total revenue is R. Because the problem is stationary, it follows that each buyer's expected payoff must be zero. Hence, entering is a best reply for each buyer, so the specified behavior is consistent with equilibrium.

Because each buyer must earn a non-negative expected profit at equilibrium, the seller's expected payoff in any equilibrium is bounded above by R. Because the proposed mechanism achieves that bound, it is an expected-revenue-maximizing mechanism.   ■

6.2.2.3 Buy Prices

Advertisements for used cars in newspapers and on bulletin boards sometimes include a line like "Will sell for $12,000 or best offer." Such a statement indicates that the seller is ready to negotiate, but wants to collect several offers before deciding if the best offer is less than $12,000. Interpreting such a sale as an auction, the $12,000 offer that would end the bidding is sometimes called a *buy price*. A similar device is found at some on-line electronic auctions, where the seller may post a price at which a bidder can "buy now!"

The use of a buy price creates a selling mechanism that mixes the characteristics of an auction with those of serial negotiations. We showed that in our model of serial negotiations, the seller's optimal strategy is to specify a buy price and never accept any lower bid. This conclusion depends on three important assumptions: (1) the seller knows the distribution of bidders; (2) the stream of potential buyers is infinite; and (3) the seller does not care how long it takes to complete the sale.

Changing any of these three assumptions would make the model non-stationary, which might lead the seller to hold offers that are below his buy price and eventually accept the best such offer – that is, to run an auction. In this section, we approach the question from the opposite angle, asking why a seller would ever want to hold an auction *without* a buy price.

Bidding costs lie at the heart of the analysis. On one hand, there may be cost economies in bringing all buyers together at one time. For example, a major auction of similar goods allows the auctioneer to bring many interested buyers and sellers together at once. The costs of participation are mostly fixed; a buyer waiting to bid on his most preferred item may be able to evaluate and bid on substitutes at negligible incremental cost. Such a cost structure would obviate the advantages of serial negotiation. On the other hand, if the goods being sold are costly to evaluate – one must drive the used car or study the condition of the asset – then either serial negotiations or the use of a buy price might economize on such costs.

To model the latter possibility, suppose that there are N periods, N potential bidders, and a moderate entry cost c. Our model is a symmetric one in which the seller is allowed to specify a buy price b. In each period, a potential bidder arrives without knowing his place in the queue. He considers every possible position in the queue equally likely. If the auction is in progress when a new bidder arrives, the bidder can choose to incur the cost c to learn his type. He may then pay the buy price b to acquire the item and end the auction, or he may instead place a bid less than b. If no bidder takes the buy price, then a second-price auction determines the outcome.

By the monotonic selection theorem of chapter 4, when bidders optimize, each bidder's probability of acquiring the item is a nondecreasing function of his value and type. Because paying the buy price wins with strictly higher probability than bidding less, it follows that types of bidders exceeding some threshold type $\bar{t}(b)$ find it optimal to pay the buy price. Accordingly, bidders with types less than $\bar{t}(b)$ win precisely when all competing types are lower. Because the valuation function v is continuous, if $\bar{t}(b) \in (0, 1)$, a bidder of that type will be just indifferent between taking the buy price or bidding some lower amount. We use this observation below to derive a formula to compute $\bar{t}(b)$.

Suppose that our model has a symmetric equilibrium. Recall that for any integer n, type $\hat{t}(n - 1) = \max(t^1, \ldots, t^{n-1})$ is the highest type among the first $n - 1$ bidders. If bidder n is of type $\bar{t}$ and takes the buy price, then he wins when $\hat{t}(n - 1) < \bar{t}$ and earns $v(\bar{t}) - b$. Given our assumption that the bidder's position in the queue is equally likely to be any element of $\{1, \ldots, N\}$, if the bidder plans to take the buy price, then his expected profit is $(v(\bar{t}) - b) \frac{1}{N} \sum_{n=1}^{N} \Pr\{\hat{t}(n - 1) < \bar{t}\}$. If, instead, the bidder plans *not* to take the buy price, then he will acquire the good exactly when all other types are less than $\bar{t}$. Because the bidder of type $\bar{t} = \bar{t}(b)$ must be indifferent between the two options, $\bar{t}$ must solve

$$E[(v(\bar{t}) - v(\hat{t}(N - 1)))1_{\{\hat{t}(N-1)<\bar{t}\}}] = (v(\bar{t}) - b)\frac{1}{N}\sum_{n=1}^{N}\Pr\{\hat{t}(n - 1) < \bar{t}\}.$$

(6.12)

Turning the problem around, any $\bar{t} \in (0, 1)$ corresponds to some buy price. Indeed, solving (6.12) for b, the buy price that implements $\bar{t}$ is

$$b(\bar{t}) = \frac{v(\bar{t})\sum_{n=1}^{N}\Pr\{\hat{t}(n - 1) < \bar{t}\} - NE[(v(\bar{t}) - v(\hat{t}(N - 1)))1_{\{\hat{t}(N-1)<\bar{t}\}}]}{\sum_{n=1}^{N}\Pr\{\hat{t}(n - 1) < \bar{t}\}}.$$

(6.13)

We represent the situation in which the seller sets no buy price by the choice $b \geq E[v(\hat{t}(N-1))]$ or, equivalently, $\bar{t} = 1$. According to the next theorem, in this model it is always optimal to set $\bar{t} < 1$.

Theorem 6.10. Assume the entry cost c is moderate and the seller sets the reserve r and the buy price b. Then any auction that maximizes expected revenue has (i) $\rho = 0$ (so that $r \leq v(0)$) and (ii) $b < E[v(\hat{t}(N-1))]$ (so that $\bar{t} < 1$).

Proof. With moderate costs, it is optimal to set the parameters so that bidders enter with positive probability and randomize their entry decisions. In that case, the bidders' expected profits are zero and the expected revenue equals the expected total surplus.

The proof of theorem 6.5 establishes that at the optimum, $\rho = 0$. In view of (6.13), we can use the buy price to select any $\bar{t}$, so the problem reduces to choosing $\bar{t}$ to maximize total surplus.

Consider any selection of $\bar{t}$ satisfying $v(1) > v(\bar{t}) > v(1) - c$ and compare it to the choice $\bar{t} = 1$. The resulting allocation differs for these two choices if and only if some entering bidder other than the last has a type exceeding $\bar{t}$. In all such cases, the lower buy price saves entry costs of at least c and reduces the value of the allocation by at most $v(1) - v(\bar{t}) < c$, so the total surplus in every realization is at least as high. Hence, $\bar{t} < 1$ rather than $\bar{t} = 1$ is optimal. ∎

6.3 Asymmetric Models: Devices to Promote Competition

In major asset sales and large procurements, it is typically very costly to prepare bids. When the likely winner of the auction is not in much doubt, the prospect of incurring unrecoverable costs can depress entry. Spectrum auctions in Germany, Italy, Israel, and Switzerland have all suffered from insufficient entry. Concerns about low participation also help explain second-supplier policies in business procurement: to negotiate lower prices, businesses must avoid excessive dependence on any single supplier, so they encourage multiple suppliers to bid in their procurement auctions.

In this section, we show how a seller can structure an auction to encourage entry, increase competition, and promote higher prices. The same considerations apply to procurement auctions as well. The ideas presented here resemble ones in the industrial organization literature about price discrimination – a group of practices that often increases revenues and sometimes also increases efficiency.

We present several related tactics for increasing participation. The first tactic is the use of *bidding credits* and *set-asides*, as studied by Ayres and Cramton (1996). In the United States, the FCC endeavored to promote the interests of small businesses and minority-owned companies using two techniques. It (1) set aside some licenses for which only the favored businesses could bid and (2) allowed favored bidders who outbid non-favored bidders to pay only a fraction of their winning bids. In various auctions, these fractions ranged from 65% to 85%. Another tactic to encourage entry is to allow losing bidders to earn some profits when the number of bidders is small. One auction design that uses this tactic is the so-called *premium auction*, in which the highest losing bidder receives a premium proportional to the excess of his bid over the next highest bid.[11] With a small number of bidders, this procedure encourages both entry and aggressive bidding by bidders with relatively low values. Another example is the *Anglo-Dutch* design proposed by Klemperer (1998), in which an ascending auction eliminates all but two bidders, who then compete with sealed bids. This design may allow a low-value bidder a real chance to win. We present each of these ideas using a simple example.

6.3.1 Example of Set-asides

Suppose there are two licenses for sale and no bidder is eligible to win more than one license. Two large bidders have the highest values for the licenses; their values are distributed uniformly on $(\underline{v}, \bar{v})$. In addition, two smaller bidders have values distributed uniformly on $(0, \underline{v})$. All values are independently distributed, and there is an entry cost of $c > 0$. The auction rules dictate that the highest two bids win licenses and winning bidders pay the third highest bid. (These are simple rules designed to approximate the outcome of rules similar to those of the FCC.) In this situation, if the two large bidders enter, they are certain to win items.

When bidders decide whether to enter, they anticipate all entrants will play their dominant strategies in the subsequent auction. If c is not too large, then the entry game has a unique Nash equilibrium in which only the two large bidders enter. As a result, the auction price for each license

---

[11] See Goeree and Offerman (2002).

is the reserve, which we take to be zero. This simple model describes an auction with disastrously insufficient competition.

Can set-asides help? In the same model, suppose that the seller sets aside one of the licenses so only small bidders can bid for it. Consider a baseline situation in which one large bidder and one small bidder have already committed to enter the auction. If there are no additional entrants, the expected total surplus from the set-aside license is the expected value $\frac{1}{2}\underline{v}$ of the small bidder. If a second small bidder enters, then the expected value of the set-aside license is $\frac{2}{3}\underline{v} = \int_0^{\underline{v}} x \cdot 2x \cdot \underline{v}^{-2}\, dx$. So the expected addition to surplus from entry by a second small bidder is $\frac{2}{3}\underline{v} - \frac{1}{2}\underline{v} = \frac{1}{6}\underline{v}$.

Similar calculations apply to the large bidders. Entry by a second large bidder adds $\frac{1}{6}(\bar{v} - \underline{v})$ to the expected surplus. Recall that these marginal contributions are also the entrants' expected profits from the auction.

Suppose first that $6c < \min(\underline{v}, \bar{v} - \underline{v})$. This assumption implies that even after one large and one small bidder commit to enter the auction, costs are still low enough for a second large bidder and a second small bidder to enter profitably as well. If all bidders enter, the outcome is the same as if a separate auction were conducted for each license. The expected price in the auction for small bidders is the corresponding expected total surplus minus the expected total profits of the two bidders: $\frac{2}{3}\underline{v} - 2 \cdot \frac{1}{6}\underline{v} = \frac{1}{3}\underline{v}$. Similarly, the expected price in the auction for the large bidders is $\underline{v} + \frac{1}{3}(\bar{v} - \underline{v})$. So the total expected price from the two combined auctions is $\underline{v} + \frac{1}{3}\bar{v}$. This is much higher than the revenues of the unified auction.

Set-asides in this example are really a form of price discrimination. A price-discriminating monopolist often finds it profitable to withhold some supply from a high-value market to increase the price there, while supplying a low-value market. The set-aside licenses correspond to goods offered only in the low-value market. Both setting aside licenses and price discrimination require that the seller be able to restrict resale. Otherwise, large bidders might refrain from competing in the auction, hoping instead to acquire a license cheaply from a smaller bidder after the auction.

Using set-asides in an auction with entry costs differs from classic price discrimination in one important respect. In our example, entry costs amplify the risk that revenues may be very low because too few bidders participate. For that reason, a seller can sometimes gain much more by setting aside a license than can a monopolist by dividing a market and setting different prices for each segment.

6.3.2 Example of Bidding Credits

Another device by which the auctioneer can encourage entry by smaller bidders is bidding credits. For example, suppose that the seller does not use set-asides in the preceding model, but that a small bidder must pay only a fraction of his bid if he wins. For example, if the fraction is $\underline{v}/\bar{v}$, then a small bidder with value $\underline{v}$ can profitably outbid a large bidder with any possible value. Again, if c is small, this rule increases entry by smaller bidders and helps the auctioneer get a higher price.

Promoting entry, however, is not the only reason to use bidding credits. Credits can sometimes increase prices even when entry costs are zero, as the following example demonstrates.

Suppose there are only two bidders and their values are distributed uniformly and independently on $(0, 1)$ and $(0, \alpha)$, respectively, where $\alpha < 1$. Then the total expected value of the two bidders is $\frac{1}{2}(1 + \alpha)$. The expectation of the highest value is

$$\int_0^\alpha x \cdot \frac{x}{\alpha} dx + \int_\alpha^1 x \ dx + \int_0^\alpha y^2 \, dy = \frac{1}{2} - \frac{1}{6}\alpha^2 + \frac{1}{3}\alpha^3. \tag{6.14}$$

The three terms on the left-hand side of (6.12) correspond to the three cases, respectively, when (1) the first bidder's value is highest and is less than α, (2) the first bidder's value is greater than α, and (3) the second bidder's value is highest. Because the total expectation of the highest and second highest values is $\frac{1}{2}(1 + \alpha)$, the expectation of the second highest value must be $\alpha(\frac{1}{2} + \frac{1}{6}\alpha - \frac{1}{3}\alpha^2)$. This is the seller's expected revenue in the absence of bidding credits. It converges to zero as α goes to zero.

If the seller offers a bidding credit so that bidder 2 needs to pay only a fraction α of his winning bid, then the winning bid in the auction is just the same as in an auction with two bidders whose values are distributed uniformly on $(0, 1)$. Hence, the expectation of the second highest "value," and therefore of the winning bid, is $\frac{1}{3}$. Half the time, the winning bidder is not entitled to credits, so the seller receives revenue of $\frac{1}{3}$, but half the time a favored bidder wins and the seller gets only $\frac{1}{3}\alpha$. So the expected revenue is $\frac{1}{6}(1 + \alpha)$. Because expected revenue is bounded away from zero for all positive α, it follows that for small enough α, the expected revenues are higher when the seller uses a bidding credit.

6.3.3 Example of Lot Structure and Consolation Prizes

Another way to encourage entry is to ensure that even bidders without the highest value benefit from participating in the auction.[12] In procurement settings, split-award auctions sometimes serve this purpose: providing for more than one winner promotes entry into the auction by more than one bidder. In many of the FCC spectrum auctions, the large numbers of licenses offered have encouraged many small- and medium-size bidders to participate. This increased participation can drive up the prices of all licenses, even those that would not, by themselves, have attracted the participation of the additional bidders.

Splitting items to encourage entry can also be a risky strategy. With a fixed number of bidders, splitting items can often *reduce* competition and prices by encouraging the bidders to accommodate each other.[13] The following example illustrates this point.

Suppose two bidders compete for two identical items. Each bidder is willing to pay 10 for one item and 15 for two. The seller conducts a simultaneous ascending auction, which we model as a sealed-bid auction in which the highest rejected bid sets the price. If the seller offers the two items as a single lot and resale is impossible, then in equilibrium both bidders will bid 15 and the price will be 15. If instead the seller offers the items individually and the bidders bid their actual values, then the price for each item will be 5, producing total revenue of 10. If bidders are strategic, the outcome could be even worse. In the situation described, each bidder would find it in his separate interest to demand one unit at prices less than ten and zero units at higher prices. The prescribed strategies constitute a subgame perfect equilibrium and induce an equilibrium price of zero.[14]

Thus, splitting lots can reduce revenues sharply when the set of participants is fixed, but in other circumstances the same tactic can benefit the seller by attracting entry. For example, consider a spectrum auction in which three units of spectrum are available. Suppose one large bidder has a value of $\bar{v}$ *per unit* for each unit of spectrum, and three smaller bidders each wish to acquire one unit of spectrum. Suppose that the small bidders' possible values are $\frac{1}{4}\bar{v}$, $\frac{1}{2}\bar{v}$, or $\frac{3}{4}\bar{v}$, for the first unit acquired,

---

[12] A related point, about the role of consolation prizes in encouraging entry into monopolized markets, is developed by Gilbert and Klemperer (2002).

[13] Anton and Yao (1992) make a similar point about procurement auctions.

[14] See chapter 7 for additional analysis of this class of multi-unit models.

and zero for any additional units. For simplicity, we assume that exactly one small bidder has each of these three values, but that a bidder can only learn which of the three positions he occupies by incurring a small positive entry cost: $0 < c < \frac{1}{12}\bar{v}$.

In this situation, if the auctioneer sells the three units of spectrum as a single lot or license, then the small bidders will not bid. If a small bidder enters, he incurs the entry cost but cannot win any licenses.

If the seller sells the three units as separate licenses, however, a different outcome arises. Suppose the seller conducts a simultaneous ascending auction, which we again model as a highest-rejected-bid auction in which the highest rejected bid sets the price. It is a dominant strategy for the three small bidders to bid their values in such an auction. Given the specified values, any best reply for the large bidder involves winning two licenses and bidding less than $\frac{1}{2}\bar{v}$ for the third license, in which event the price is $\frac{1}{2}\bar{v}$ per unit of spectrum. Given our assumption that $c < \frac{1}{12}\bar{v}$, it pays each small bidder to enter. Selling licenses individually rather than in a single lot increases the seller's total revenue from zero to $\frac{3}{2}\bar{v}$.

6.3.4 Premium Auctions

Another tactic to attract entry and encourage aggressive bidding is to offer a subsidy to the highest losing bidder that increases with his bid. For example, one kind of premium auction is an ascending auction in which the highest losing bidder receives a fraction, such as 50%, of the difference between his bid and the next highest bid below his. In such an auction, a strategy for each bidder is a single number indicating the level at which to stop bidding. To avoid technical complications, we resolve any ties in favor of the bidder with the higher value and otherwise break ties at random. Roughly, this assumption presumes that in the event of ties, the bidder with the lower value stops bidding an instant earlier than the higher value bidder.[15]

We analyze premium auctions by first studying bidding with a fixed number of bidders and then studying the entry decisions that precede the bidding. For the first step, we use a simple model with complete information, a single indivisible good for sale, and two or three bidders. We assume that the auction is an ascending auction and that resale is impossible.

---

[15] For justification of this procedure, see Simon and Zame (1990).

Suppose there is a single high-value bidder with value 1 and a single low-value bidder with value $v < 1$. Then there is a unique pure strategy equilibrium that does not depend on v. In equilibrium, both bidders bid $\frac{2}{3}$ and the high-value bidder wins at that price. The high-value bidder earns a profit of $\frac{1}{3}$, equal to his value minus the price he pays, while the low-value bidder earns the premium of half the price, which is also $\frac{1}{3}$. Therefore, the seller's net revenue is just $\frac{1}{3}$. In this equilibrium, the low-value bidder pays no attention to his own value and bids just to capture the premium.

Next, we add a second low-value bidder. There is again a unique pure strategy equilibrium. In equilibrium, all three bidders bid 1 and the high value bidder wins at that price. The seller pays no premium, because the second and third highest bids are identical. In this case, the seller's revenue is 1 and all bidders earn zero profits.

Finally, suppose that there is a small positive entry cost c. We look for an equilibrium that is symmetric in the entry decisions of the low-value bidders, that is, one in which both low-value bidders enter with the same probability p and in which the high-value bidder always enters.[16] We suppress the entry cost of the high-value bidder, for the high-value bidder always enters in equilibrium.

By inspection, no equilibrium with a positive entry cost entails $p = 1$, and, with small enough entry costs, none entails $p = 0$. With $0 < p < 1$, the low-value bidder must be indifferent between (1) entering and earning $-c + (1 - p)\frac{1}{3}$ and (2) not entering and earning zero. Consequently, the equilibrium probability of entry must be $p = \max(0, 1 - 3c)$, and the two low-value bidders must earn zero expected profits.

At this equilibrium, the high-value bidder earns positive profits if either low-value entrant fails to enter, so his expected profit (excluding his entry cost) is $(1 - p)^2 \cdot 1 + 2p(1 - p) \cdot \frac{1}{3}$. For $c < \frac{1}{3}$, this profit equals $c(2 + 3c)$. The seller's expected revenue is the expected total surplus $1 - 2pc$ minus the expected profits of the bidders. For $c < \frac{1}{3}$, the expected revenue is $(1 - c)(1 - 3c)$.

According to this model, if entry costs are small and there are enough potential bidders, then a premium auction can encourage entry and aggressive bidding, enabling the seller to extract nearly the full value of the items sold.

---

[16] There can also be an equilibrium in this model in which only the low-value bidders enter.

The analysis above is preliminary and omits some significant features of reality. First, if the seller really has the power to choose any selling mechanism, then with complete information he might just fix a price and make a take-it-or-leave-it offer to the high-value bidder. The simple model above does not adequately address the balance of bargaining power between seller and buyers.[17] Second, if costless bargaining is possible after the auction, then the high-value bidder would be unlikely to accept such a small profit in the auction. He might do much better to bid low in the auction and then bargain with the low-value auction winner. Third, uncertainty about values would discourage low-value bidders from bidding much above their own values, thereby attenuating the premium auction's ability to raise prices. Until all of these complications are addressed, the case for premium auctions remains uncertain.

6.3.5 Dutch vs. English Auctions and the Anglo-Dutch Design

Researchers frequently compare Dutch and English auctions, or first-price and second-price auctions. The English and second-price auctions claim efficiency as an advantage, but that efficiency can sometimes cost sellers a great deal of revenue.

Suppose two bidders bid for a single item. The high-value bidder is known to have value $\bar{v}$ for the item. The other bidder's value is distributed on $(0, \bar{v})$. In an English auction, if both bidders enter, then the low-value bidder is sure to lose. So, if there is an entry cost, this bidder never enters in equilibrium. In any pure strategy equilibrium, the price is zero and the auction fails for lack of participation. It is even possible that there is a pure strategy equilibrium in which only the low-value bidder enters, so the English auction need not always be efficient.

Next, consider the Dutch auction, and suppose that the large bidder is certain to enter. In any equilibrium, the large bidder has equilibrium expected profit $\pi > 0$, so he never bids more than $\bar{v} - \pi$. Consequently, the second bidder earns positive expected profits in equilibrium whenever his value exceeds $\bar{v} - \pi$. Thus, in equilibrium the Dutch auction always has some inefficient outcomes, in which bidders without the highest

---

[17] Bargaining power may be the most important feature of the auction. If a seller cannot commit to keep an item but can commit to sell if the conditions of the auction are met, and if resale cannot be restricted, then auctions are often the most effective means of sale. See Milgrom (1986).

value acquire the item. Consequently, if entry costs are small enough, it pays for the low-value bidder to enter.

If the seller conceals the number of bidders and sets a zero reserve, then even for high entry costs, the low-value bidder enters with positive probability in any equilibrium. The proof is by contradiction. If the low-value bidder never entered, then the high-value bidder would always bid zero. But then, so long as the mean low value was larger than c, entry would be profitable – a contradiction. Thus, the Dutch or sealed-bid design can encourage entry, particularly when the number of participants is kept secret.

To capture advantages of both the English and Dutch auction designs, Klemperer (1998) has advocated a hybrid auction: the *Anglo-Dutch* design. For an auction of several identical items, the Anglo phase of Klemperer's design involves raising the price of the items gradually until the number of remaining bidders is equal to the number of items plus one. After the Anglo phase follows a Dutch phase, in which the bidders who survive the Anglo phase make sealed bids for the items, subject to the constraint that no bid can be less than the current price.

A formal model of the Anglo-Dutch design follows. Bidders for n items in the Anglo-Dutch auction place bids in two rounds. After the first round, the seller identifies the $n+1$ highest bidders (whom we call *survivors*) and announces the $n+2$nd highest bid. That bid becomes the minimum allowed bid r in a second auction in which the $n+1$ survivors participate. The survivor who bids highest wins and pays his bid.

It is evident that if each bidder can acquire only one item, then it is a dominant strategy for bidders in this auction to bid their values at the first round. This feature limits the inefficiency of the auction, for the n items will be assigned to bidders whose values are among the $n+1$ highest values. Nonetheless, low-value bidders need not lose all hope of winning. When $n = 1$, for example, a low-value bidder may enter in hopes of winning the second round auction.

The main advantage of the Anglo-Dutch design may be its ability to attract entry. The examples above confirm that such an auction design can encourage bidder participation. They also illustrate how sensitive auction design must be to details of the environment. The same choices that can help a seller in some situations by attracting entry can hurt him in others by reducing competition among the bidders who are there.

6.4 After the Bidding Ends

For both buyers and sellers, planning for an auction also involves anticipating what will happen after the bids are collected. Several important considerations complicate the process of completing the transaction. In asset auctions, one common task is to evaluate the barriers to closing the sale. Large asset transactions often require approvals by some interested parties, including stockholders, bankers, regulators, employees and their unions, and so on. The seller may choose the winning bidder partly on the basis of his ability to close the deal.

Buyers in procurement settings care about more than just the terms of the winning bid. A supplier's other attributes, such as its ability to expand capacity, upgrade its product, adapt to changes, and so on may also create value after the auction.

Bidders, too, may be concerned about what happens after the auction. In Europe, incumbent wireless telephone companies may have been particularly eager to keep assets out of the hands of new entrants, whose presence in the retail wireless services market would intensify retail competition. A seller interested in maximizing revenues in such a setting can sometimes take advantage of such a buyer's preferences, inducing a buyer to pay both for its use of the asset and for the opportunity to keep it out of the hands of a feared competitor (Jehiel, Moldovanu, and Stacchetti (1996)). On the other hand, governments interested in fostering retail competition for the benefit of consumers have an opposing interest in limiting the ability of incumbents to block entry by hoarding spectrum.

6.4.1 Bankruptcy and Non-performance[18]

One critical concern for sellers is whether the winning bidder will be able to perform under its contract. Although the risk of non-performance may seem most severe in service contracts, it can also be important in asset sales when the seller extends credit, allowing bidders to pay over time. In such cases, pre-qualifying the bidders to ensure they can perform can be critical to the success of the auction.

US spectrum auctions illustrate the consequences of offering generous credit without ensuring bidders' ability to pay. The FCC offered special terms to encourage small businesses to purchase spectrum

---

[18] The model in this section is a simplified version of the one introduced by Zheng (2001). See Board (2002) for additional development of this sort of model.

licenses. The FCC offered reduced down payments and financing at very low interest rates over a period of ten years, and restricted the sales of some licenses so that only small businesses could bid.

The FCC defined small businesses by asset ownership and sales. So, by their very definition, small businesses were not creditworthy for purchasing billions of dollars of spectrum licenses, particularly at the high prices that prevailed during the 1990s technology boom. It is therefore hardly a surprise that several bidders defaulted. The most spectacular default was by Nextwave, which went into bankruptcy holding rights to some $10 billion worth of spectrum licenses. A tension between spectrum policy and bankruptcy law resulted in a struggle for control of these licenses. While the legal disputes dragged on for years, the spectrum lay dormant, wasting a large part of its economic value.

The possibility of default or non-performance can have perverse affects on the bidding in the auction itself. To illustrate the possibilities, suppose that, at the time of the auction, a bidder believes the item for sale has expected value v, but that payment is deferred and certain uncertainties about the value (for example, about technology, demand, or competitors' plans) will be resolved before payment is due. Suppose the bidder enjoys limited liability and owns assets worth B. If the bidder wins the auction at price p, then, after the auction, the bidder will learn the actual value $v + \tilde{\varepsilon}$, where $\tilde{\varepsilon}$ has *ex ante* mean zero. The bidder may then default and forfeit his assets, suffering a loss of B, or he may complete the purchase, enjoying a payoff $v + \tilde{\varepsilon} - p$.

Theorem 6.11. Suppose that the support of $\tilde{\varepsilon}$ is all of $\mathbb{R}$. Then the bidder has a dominant strategy $\hat{p}(B, v)$ in the second-price auction. The strategy $\hat{p}$ is nondecreasing in v and nonincreasing in B. For any given distribution of competing bids, the bidder's maximal expected profit is nonincreasing in B.

Proof. After learning $\tilde{\varepsilon}$, the winning bidder receives a payoff of $\max(-B, v + \tilde{\varepsilon} - p)$. Before learning $\tilde{\varepsilon}$, the winner expects a payoff of $\pi(p, B, v) = E[\max(-B, v + \tilde{\varepsilon} - p)]$. If the bidder bids b and the highest opposing bid is p with distribution F, then the bidder's expected profit is

$$\bar{\pi}(b, v, B) = \int_0^b \pi(p, v, B) \, dF(p). \tag{6.15}$$

By inspection, π is decreasing in p, so $\bar{\pi}$ is concave in b. By inspection of (6.15), $b = 0$ maximizes $\bar{\pi}$ if $\pi(0, B, v) \leq 0$. In that case, we set $\hat{p}(B, v) = 0$. If $\pi(0, B, v) > 0$, then the optimal b solves $\pi(b, B, v) = 0$. A unique solution exists, because $\pi(p, B, v)$ is decreasing and continuous in p and is negative for p sufficiently large. In that case, we set $\hat{p}(B, v)$ equal to the unique solution.

By construction, $\hat{p}(B, v)$ does not depend on F, so it is an always optimal strategy, and the construction itself implies that no other strategy is ever optimal if F has full support. Hence, $\hat{p}(B, v)$ is a dominant strategy.

Because $\pi(p, B, v)$ is increasing in v and decreasing in p and B, $\hat{p}(B, v)$ is nondecreasing in v and nonincreasing in B. Because $\pi(p, B, v)$ is decreasing in B, $\bar{\pi}(b, B, v)$ is nonincreasing in B. (The monotonicity is strict unless $F(b) = 0$.)   ∎

According to theorem 6.11, a bidder with a smaller budget is both more likely to enter the auction and, upon entering, more likely to place the winning bid. In this sense, the auction rules amplify the problem of default by tending to choose as a winning bidder someone who has an unusually high likelihood of default.

It is not immediately clear how the auctioneer should respond to this problem. If there are many bidders with small budgets but few with large budgets, then qualifying only the bidders with large budgets can unduly reduce competition in the auction. Addressing this problem more specifically requires addressing larger questions about how to design an auction when the seller has more information than just the prices bid.

6.4.2 Scoring Rules vs. Price-Only Bids

We now analyze the problem of evaluating multidimensional bids that differ in more than price. Sellers often rank each bid with a *score*; the winning bid is the one with the highest score. The process of scoring is itself costly and may involve not only evaluation of the bid and bidder but also some negotiation between the bidder and the seller to tailor the bid to create value for both sides.

Researchers have not extensively studied scoring rules. Che (1993) and Rezende (2002) have shown that in an auction with an exogenous set of bidders, sellers can sometimes benefit by biasing the scoring rules to increase competition in the auction. This tactic works in much the same way as bidding credits: both can increase the competitiveness of weaker bidders, forcing strong bidders to offer more attractive terms. The same authors also find that the seller fares best when he reveals to the bidders any scoring information that he plans to use. We refer the reader to these papers for more about this interesting, but not yet fully explored, topic.

This section focuses on scoring and entry. For consistency, we continue to focus on auctions run by sellers. In the auction, each bidder i submits a bid that involves a price b^i and also some non-price attributes. The seller assigns a value to the non-price attributes and determines the winning bidder as if bidder i had bid $b^i + \varepsilon^i$. We assume that the ε^i's are non-degenerate, independent, identically distributed random variables with mean zero, and independent of the bidder types.

Suppose there are N potential bidders, whose types are independently and uniformly distributed on $(0, 1)$. Bidder i's value is $v(t^i)$, where the function v is increasing and differentiable.

Suppose the seller conducts an English ascending auction using scores, rather than prices, to determine the winner. If bidder i wins with a bid score of $\bar{b}$, the price he actually pays is $\bar{b} - \varepsilon^i$, so his profit is $v(t^i) + \varepsilon^i - \bar{b}$. With this expression in mind, we define bidder i's *full value* to be $v(t^i) + \varepsilon^i$; this is the total value accruing to the bidder and the seller when bidder i wins the auction.

Let F be the distribution of $v(t^i) + \varepsilon^i$, and suppose it is smooth and strictly increasing, with $w = F^{-1}$. Notice that the expected maximum value among n bidders is $E[\max(v(t^1) + \varepsilon^1, \ldots, v(t^n) + \varepsilon^n)] = n \int_0^1 s^{n-1} w(s)\, ds$ with scoring, and $E[\max(v(t^1), \ldots, v(t^n))] = n \int_0^1 s^{n-1} v(s)\, ds$ without scoring.

Theorem 6.12. For all $n > 1$, $\int_0^1 w(s) s^{n-1}\, ds > \int_0^1 v(s) s^{n-1}\, ds$. Thus, the expected maximum value among n bidders is higher with scoring than without scoring.

Proof. The expected maximum values satisfy:

$$
\begin{aligned}
n \int_0^1 s^{n-1} w(s)\, ds &= E[\max(v(t^1) + \varepsilon^1, \ldots, v(t^n) + \varepsilon^n)] \\
&> E[\max(v(t^1), \ldots, v(t^n))] = n \int_0^1 s^{n-1} v(s)\, ds.
\end{aligned}
$$

The inequality follows because the max operator is convex and its arguments in the first line are a mean-preserving spread of those in the second line. ∎

Theorem 6.13. Given n existing bidders, the expected marginal contribution of an additional entrant without scoring is $\int_0^1 (1 - s)s^n v'(s)\, ds$. With scoring, the corresponding expression is $\int_0^1 (1 - s)s^n w'(s)\, ds$.

Proof. Without scoring, the expected value from the auction with n bidders is the expected maximum value among the bidders, which is $\int_0^1 v(s)\, ds^n$. Integrating by parts, this is also equal to $v(1) - \int_0^1 s^n v'(s)\, ds$. With $n + 1$ bidders, the corresponding value is $v(1) - \int_0^1 s^{n+1} v'(s)\, ds$. The expected marginal contribution is the difference of these two, which is $\int_0^1 (1 - s)s^n v'(s)\, ds$. One can derive the second expression similarly. ∎

The use of scoring causes a mean-preserving spread in bidder valuations, so it is intuitive that the maximum total value is higher on average with scoring. Theorem 6.12 confirms this intuition. In addition, if scoring leads to a fatter right-hand tail of the distribution in the sense that $\int_0^1 (1 - s)s^{n-1} v'(s)\, ds < \int_0^1 (1 - s)s^{n-1} w'(s)\, ds$, then it increases the profitability of entry, encouraging more.

The idea that scoring can increase bidders' profits without reducing the auctioneer's value has been one of the main appeals of multidimensional bidding in procurement. Bidders (sellers) dislike bidding in price-only auctions in which their special advantages and characteristics receive no weight. By encouraging a more complete comparison of the attributes of suppliers and products, scoring may increase bidders' expected profits and encourage participation by more bidders, serving the interests of all parties.

The theory does not give unqualified support to this intuitive argument. The conditions under which scoring benefits bidders and auctioneers alike remain an open question.

6.5 Conclusion

Comparing this chapter with the preceding ones highlights several key facts. First, many of the most important practical issues in auction design concern the interaction of the design and entry decisions.

In the first class of models we studied, with a large number of symmetric potential bidders and moderate entry costs, we found that the conflict between efficiency and revenues disappears. Unlike traditional studies of optimal (revenue-maximizing) auctions with a fixed number of bidders, in which we found it is optimal to set a high reserve that discourages some efficient exchange, that policy is never optimal in the symmetric model with moderate entry costs. We found that the seller can profit by managing the entry process, sometimes excluding bidders to reduce randomness in the process, to protect business secrets, or to encourage entry by the potential buyers with the highest values. Two-stage designs that select bidders on the basis of initial indications of interest have some appeal, but their formal analysis shows that they are unlikely to succeed in selecting the most qualified bidders.

One way to economize on bidders' costs of participation is to bargain with a sequence of agents, rather than run an auction. We showed that if the seller can set a take-it-or-leave-it price, then the optimal auction has the same value to the seller as the related optimal search problem. Seeing buyers in sequence then has the same advantages as sequential search has over searching a batch of items at a time.

Another device that can economize on entry costs is the buy price in an ascending auction. When the auctioneer imposes a buy price, the auction ends if any bidder makes an early bid at the specified level. That early ending saves later bidders from incurring evaluation costs, and those savings ultimately accrue to the seller. In the benchmark model, the seller can always benefit by setting a suitable buy price.

Models with entry and asymmetric bidders have received much less attention than symmetric models, despite the great influence of asymmetries among bidders on entry. A variety of tactics can encourage entry into auctions despite bidders' asymmetries. We have shown that setting aside assets or using bidding credits can encourage entry and ultimately increase the seller's revenues. Sellers' packaging of assets can also affect competition in an auction and potential buyers' decisions to enter the bidding. Variations in auction rules can also affect participation. Premium auctions and the Anglo-Dutch auction are two designs that can sometimes increase participation. Premium auctions, however, can also yield very low revenues when the set of potential bidders is limited.

It can be important to select bidders who can perform after the auction, paying or delivering as promised. We found that weak firms with limited collateral may be more eager than others to make high bids, expecting to default if the asset turns out to have low value. We also found that scoring bids based on all the bid's attributes tends to increase the total value of the allocation chosen by the auction.

The models of this chapter lead to a variety of findings, showing that the same practices that attract entry and benefit the seller in some environments can lead to poor performance in other environments where the number of bidders is exogenously limited. In practice, the design of an effective auction requires a detailed knowledge of the particular circumstances in which the auction is to be run.

REFERENCES

Anton, James J. and Dennis A. Yao (1992). "Coordination in Split Award Auctions." *Quarterly Journal of Economics* **CVII**: 681–707.

Ayres, Ian and Peter Cramton (1996). "Deficit Reduction through Diversity: How Affirmative Action at the FCC Increased Auction Competition." *Stanford Law Review* **48**(4): 761–815.

Bajari, Patrick and Steven Tadelis (2001). "Incentives versus Transactions Costs: A Theory of Procurement Contracts." *Rand Journal of Economics* **32**(3): 387–407.

Board, Simon (2002). "Bidding into the Red." Stanford GSB Working Paper.

Che, Yeon-Koo (1993). "Design Competition through Multidimensional Auctions." *Rand Journal of Economics* **24**(4): 668–680.

Gilbert, Richard and Paul Klemperer (2002). "An Equilibrium Theory of Rationing." *Rand Journal of Economics* **33**(1): 1–21.

Goeree, Jacob and Theo Offerman (2002). "The Amsterdam Auction." http://ideas.repec.org/p/wpa/wuwpmi/0205002.html.

Jehiel, Philippe, Benny Moldovanu, and Ennio Stacchetti (1996). "How (Not) to Sell Nuclear Weapons." *American Economic Review* **86**: 814–829.

Klemperer, Paul (1998). "Auctions with Almost Common Values: The Wallet Game and Its Applications." *European Economic Review* **42**: 757–769.

Klemperer, Paul (2002). "How (Not) to Run Auctions: The European 3G Telecom Auctions." *European Economic Review* **46**(4–5): 829–845.

Levin, Dan and James L. Smith (1994). "Equilibrium in Auctions with Entry." *American Economic Review* **84**(3): 585–599.

McAfee, R. Preston and John McMillan (1987). "Auctions with Entry." *Economics Letters* **23**: 343–348.

Milgrom, Paul (1986). Auction Theory. *Advances in Economic Theory: Fifth World Congress of the Econometric Society*. T. Bewley. London, Cambridge University Press: 1–32.

Rezende, Leonardo (2002). "Biased Procurement." Stanford University Working Paper.

Riley, John G. and Richard Zeckhauser (1983). "Optimal Selling Strategies: When to Haggle, When to Hold Firm." *Quarterly Journal of Economics* **98**: 267–289.

Simon, Leo K. and William R. Zame (1990). "Discontinuous Games and Endogenous Sharing Rules." *Econometrica* **58**: 861–872.

Ye, Lixin (2002). "A Theory of Two-Stage Auctions." Ohio State University Working Paper.

Zheng, Charles (2001). "High Bids and Broke Winners." *Journal of Economic Theory* **100**(1): 129–171.

PART TWO

MULTI-UNIT AUCTIONS

Chapters 3–6 study auctions in which just one kind of item is for sale and each bidder can buy at most a single item. When items are heterogeneous or bidders demand multiple units, new questions arise.

First, even when each bidder wants to buy only one item, if the items are not identical, the mechanism needs to solve the *matching problem*: who gets which items? One can study the matching problem with a fixed set of bidders to learn how efficiently auctions assign items to bidders and how much revenue they generate. In principle, one could combine these results with analysis of entry to determine who participates in the auction and what kinds of pre-auction investments bidders might make. So far, the auction literature contains little analysis of these questions.

Second, when bidders demand multiple units, market power becomes important. Bidders in auctions, like participants in other kinds of markets, can often reduce the prices they pay by buying fewer units than they would want at the final prices. Reducing demand in this manner can be profitable for a single large bidder even if all the other bidders want to buy only a single unit. When several large bidders each seek to buy multiple units, it is also possible that the larger bidders will coordinate strategies, for example by agreeing to reduce demand in concert. The likelihood of bidder cartels and rings[1] depends largely on the setting – the identities of the bidders and the relationships among them – but it can also depend on auction design. When the risk of cartels is significant,

---

[1] *Rings* are organizations of bidders that choose a single member to bid on behalf of all. After the public auction, the ring holds a private auction to allocate the good and divide the profits among its members. See Graham and Marshall (1987).

minimizing opportunities for collusion becomes a primary objective of auction design.[2]

Third, the conception of auctions as mechanisms for finding competitive prices, plausible when each bidder wants just one good, becomes problematic when bidders want multiple units. If goods are not substitutes, market clearing prices generally do not exist,[3] forcing us to conceive of auctions broadly as mechanisms for resource allocation rather than narrowly as mechanisms for price discovery.

This broad view of auctions has led some to recommend wide use of the Vickrey auction. However, in chapter 2 we observed that the performance of Vickrey auctions, too, could depend on whether goods are substitutes. When goods are substitutes, Vickrey auction outcomes are core allocations, shill bidding is unprofitable, losing bidders have no profitable joint deviations, and bidders' profits are decreasing (and the seller's revenues increasing) in the size of the set of bidders. All of these conclusions fail when the set of possible valuations includes valuations for which goods are not substitutes. Designing auctions to work well when goods are not substitutes is a subject that has only recently attracted serious attention.[4] Chapter 8 presents some of the relevant theory.

Fourth, many auction applications involve complicated constraints on the auctioneer. For example, suppose a firm offers its production capacity to produce a set of products. To maximize profits, it will need to take account of its possibly complex operating constraints in deciding which bids to accept. Similarly, an industrial buyer may evaluate suppliers according to multiple criteria, including price, quality, capacity, and delivery schedules. Allowing accurately for such details imposes a burden that has so far proved too heavy for practical auction designs.

Finally, auctions in settings as complex as the ones above pose serious challenges to theories that assume optimal bidding. Planning for

---

[2] Several authors have emphasized the roles of both competition in the auction and competition among the winners when the auction affects the market structure. See Dana and Spier (1994), Milgrom (1997), and Klemperer (2002).

[3] If bidder valuations are a subset of all valuations for which all goods are substitutes, then a competitive equilibrium price vector exists. However, if the set includes any other valuation, then there are preference profiles drawn from the set such that no competitive equilibrium price vector exists. See Milgrom (2000) and Gul and Stacchetti (1999).

[4] Recent design contributions include Parkes and Ungar (2000) and Ausubel and Milgrom (2002).

such auctions is complicated, and experience suggests that many real bidders – even ones with substantial resources to spend on planning – are daunted by the complexity and adopt simple and often sub-optimal strategies. In practice, auction designers place a tremendous value on the simplicity of an auction's design. Their priorities always include ensuring that the mechanics of bidding are easy, that simple strategies are effective for bidders, and that outcomes are acceptable when bidders use simple strategies. Simplicity helps attract participants into the auction, and in practice, hardly anything matters more.

The theory of Part II, which analyzes the problems of multi-object auctions discussed above, is less developed than that of Part I. Chapter 7 examines multi-item auctions in which bids consist either of prices for individual items or of quantities to be supplied or demanded at prices specified by an auctioneer. The chapter emphasizes auctions that encourage arbitrage, so that similar items tend to sell for similar prices. Several widely used auctions are in this class. Chapter 7 studies simultaneous ascending auctions used for spectrum sales, clock auctions used for power sales, and various sealed-bid auctions used for securities sales.

Chapter 8 investigates auctions in which participants may place either bids for *packages* of several items or *contingent bids*. For example, contracts for London bus services are determined by package bidding, in which bus companies quote prices to serve various individual routes and also specify package discounts that apply if they win particular combinations of routes.[5] The auctioneer accepts the combination of bids yielding the lowest total price. Similar auctions have been used for industrial procurement.[6] In addition, there have been proposals to use the related device of contingent bids in spectrum auctions. For example, a bidder in a spectrum auction might bid for licenses to serve the cities of Buffalo and Syracuse in the state of New York with the proviso that it will withdraw the bids if it does not also win a license to serve New York City. The auctioneer would accept the combination of bids that produced the highest total price.

Package bidding and contingent bidding are closely related. In the spectrum auction example, if package bids were allowed, the bidder could achieve the same outcome as with contingent bids. Instead of

---

[5] For a detailed description, see Cantillon and Pesendorfer (2002).
[6] Hohner, Rich, Ng, Reid, Davenport, Kalagnanam, Lee, and An (2001).

bidding for New York City and placing contingent bids for Buffalo and Syracuse, a bidder could accomplish the same thing by placing four bids: one for the NYC license, a second for the package of the NYC and Buffalo licenses, a third for the package of the NYC and Syracuse licenses, and a fourth for the package of all three licenses.

Auctions with package bids or contingent bids are sometimes dubbed *combinatorial auctions*, because running the auction can involve solving a combinatorial optimization problem. It is difficult to compute solutions to these problems – one possible reason why such auctions have only recently attracted attention. There are other reasons, too, including the complexity of the bidder interface required for a combinatorial auction. We return briefly to these issues in chapter 8.

REFERENCES

Ausubel, Lawrence and Paul Milgrom (2002). "Ascending Auctions with Package Bidding." *Frontiers of Theoretical Economics* **1**(1): Article 1.

Cantillon, Estelle and Martin Pesendorfer (2002). "Combination Bidding in Multi-unit Auctions." http://www.people.hbs.edu/ecantillon/combinationJuly2002.pdf.

Dana, James and Kathryn Spier (1994). "Designing a Private Industry." *Journal of Public Economics* **53**: 127–147.

Graham, Daniel and Robert Marshall (1987). "Collusive Bidder Behavior at Single-Object, Second-Price and English Auctions." *Journal of Political Economy* **95**: 1217–1239.

Gul, Faruk and Ennio Stacchetti (1999). "Walrasian Equilibrium with Gross Substitutes." *Journal of Economic Theory* **87**(1): 9–124.

Hohner, Gail, John Rich, Ed Ng, Grant Reid, Andrew J. Davenport, Jayant R. Kalagnanam, Ho Soo Lee, and Chae An (2001). "Combinatorial and Quantity Discount Procurement Auctions with Mutual Benefits at Mars, Incorporated." IBM-Mars Report.

Klemperer, Paul (2002). "What Really Matters in Auction Design." *Journal of Economics Perspectives* **16**(1): 169–190.

Milgrom, Paul (1997). Procuring Universal Service: Putting Auction Theory to Work. *Le Prix Nobel: The Nobel Prizes, 1996.* Stockholm: Nobel Foundation. 382–392.

Milgrom, Paul (2000). "Putting Auctions Theory to Work: The Simultaneous Ascending Auction." *Journal of Political Economy* **108**(2): 245–272.

Parkes, David and Lyle Ungar (2000). "Iterative Combinatorial Auctions: Theory and Practice." *Proceedings of the 17th National Conference on Artificial Intelligence AAAI.* 74–81.

CHAPTER SEVEN

Uniform Price Auctions

The resurgence of interest in auction theory owes much to recent large-scale auctions using designs suggested by economic theorists. From the spectrum auctions of 1994 onward, virtually all of these auctions have been *uniform price auctions*, in which auction rules either mandate equal prices for identical goods or encourage some sort of arbitrage, generating approximately uniform prices.

Many traditional auction designs fail to promote the *law of one price,* according to which identical goods have identical prices. One example is the first spectrum auction – Sotheby's 1981 auction of rights to use seven functionally identical transponders on a single RCA communications satellite. Sotheby's sold these rights using a sequence of seven auctions that produced seven different prices. The first transponder sold for $14.4 million, and the prices of the second through sixth transponders successively declined. The sixth transponder sold for the lowest price, $10.7 million, and the seventh sold for $11.2 million. When an auctioneer sells several identical lots, bidders always have to guess about the prices of future lots, so some price variation is inevitable.

A striking aspect of the RCA transponder auction is the way prices declined from one item to the next. Ashenfelter (1989) has found that a similar pattern is common in auctions of wine and art, and this observation is now known as the *declining price anomaly.*[1] Many have attempted to explain this anomaly. One possible explanation is that this pattern arises from a kind of selection bias akin to a winner's curse. At the RCA auction, bidders for the first transponders had to guess about

---

[1] Subsequent research reaffirms that this phenomenon is widespread. See Ashenfelter and Graddy (2002) and the references therein.

the prices that the later ones would fetch. Even if each individual bidder estimates future prices without bias, the winner of the first transponder will tend to be a bidder whose estimate of future prices is high and who is surprised to see lower prices in later sales.[2] Other explanations run the gamut from psychological models of individual behavior to equilibrium models of the kind studied in this book, in which fully rational actors act on perfect forecasts of competitors' strategies.

Many bidders dislike price variation of the sort described above in sales of homogeneous items. In spectrum auctions like the RCA auction, companies' officers bid on their behalf. The highest bidders are uncomfortable having to explain to their superiors or shareholders why others paid less for an identical transponder or license. Even individual bidders may care more about "paying too much" than about the chance of getting a bargain. An advantage of uniform price auctions is that they insulate bidders and their bosses from price risk of this form.

Uniform price auctions have become more popular because they avoid the price risk that corporate bidders dislike and reduce the transaction costs of bidding repeatedly for identical goods. Uniform price auctions include uniform price sealed-bid auctions and various ascending auctions that either enforce uniformity by rule or promote it by encouraging arbitrage.

We begin by analyzing uniform price sealed-bid auctions and then turn to simultaneous ascending auctions.

---

[2] The *winner's curse* in auction theory traditionally refers to the selection bias that arises because a bidder tends to win more often when his *value* estimate is too high than when it is too low. If we regard the value of the first transponder as a value net of opportunity cost, then the explanation offered here is a variant of the winner's curse. In the equilibrium analyses of the previous chapters, rational bidders allow for the effect of the selection bias by adjusting their bids downward.

In practice, learning about the ordinary winner's curse is probably slow, because the data needed to recognize it, which include data about realized values, are difficult to obtain and sometimes unavailable for years after the sale has closed. Part of what makes the declining price anomaly so striking is that data about declining prices are instantly and publicly available, yet bidders still do not adjust to them.

There is extensive evidence that even experienced bidders in laboratory experiments do not adjust their bids as equilibrium theory suggests to allow for the winner's curse (Kagel and Levin (2002)), despite the quick availability of performance data to experimental subjects. To the extent that bidders in real art and wine auctions have similar difficulty adapting to declining prices, the evidence would be consistent with the explanation of the declining price anomaly offered here.

7.1 Uniform Price Sealed-Bid Auctions

The simplest kind of uniform price auctions are sealed-bid auctions. In this section, we show that when each bidder has demand for multiple units, these auctions inevitably create incentives for bidders to reduce demand to avoid driving up prices and that there exist Nash equilibria of these auctions with very low prices.

In a uniform price auction, a bid is an order to purchase quantity q at any price up to p. A bidder may make several such price–quantity bids. The auctioneer then organizes the bids to create a demand curve, determining for each price p the total quantity demanded at that price. The auctioneer sets the price so that the quantity demanded equals the available supply.

In general, there may be a range of prices at which the quantity demanded is equal to the available supply. For example, if there are N goods for sale and a distinct price is bid for each unit, then supply equals demand at any price between the Nth highest bid (the lowest accepted bid) and $N + 1$st highest bid (the highest rejected bid). For concreteness, we focus on auctions in which the $N + 1$st highest bid (the highest rejected bid) sets the price. Our major conclusions extend qualitatively to all auctions with market clearing prices in this range.

In analyzing the uniform price auction with sealed bids, we assume the bidders have declining marginal values for the goods they acquire. That is, a bidder's value is highest for the first unit, and the same or lower for each successive unit. (Little is known about how this auction performs in general when this value assumption is not satisfied.)

We begin by observing that any bidder whose value for each item after the first is zero has a dominant strategy in the auction. If the value of the first item is v, then the dominant strategy is to place just one bid for a quantity of 1 at a price of v. The argument is much the same as in the standard analysis of the Vickrey auction: a bid in this situation can never affect the price the bidder pays, so the bidder is effectively a price taker and maximizes his payoff by specifying a demand function that corresponds to his actual demand. If every bidder has demand for just a single item (and can only bid for a single unit), then the highest-rejected-bid auction would be a Vickrey auction. The equilibrium price would then equal the opportunity cost of the item, which is its value to the highest rejected bidder.

7.1.1 Demand Reduction

When a bidder wants to buy more than one unit and when the units have declining marginal values, a bidder generally has an incentive to reduce his demand, that is, to bid less than his value for some units. The example below illustrates how strong this incentive can be.[3]

Suppose there are two bidders and two units for sale. Bidder 1 demands only a single unit, and his value, $v(t^1) = t^1$, is uniformly distributed on $(0, 1)$. As we have seen, bidder 1's dominant strategy is to bid an amount equal to his value. Bidder 2 has demand for two units. The first unit is worth v_1 and the second is worth v_2, where $1 > v_1 \geq v_2 > 0$. With two units for sale, bidder 2 is assured of winning one if he places a positive bid. If he bids $x \geq 0$ for the second unit, then he wins two units if $t^1 < x$ and one unit if $t^1 > x$, so his expected payoff is

$$E[(v_1 + v_2 - 2t^1)1_{\{t^1 < x\}} + (v_1 - x)1_{\{t^1 > x\}}]$$

$$= \int_0^x (v_1 + v_2 - 2s)\, ds + (v_1 - x)(1 - x) = v_1 - x(1 - v_2). \quad (7.1)$$

This expression is maximized at $x = 0$, that is, *the optimal bid is zero*.[4] Thus, the second bidder always finds it optimal to bid as if he had demand for only one unit, regardless of his actual values.

Although the example is extreme, the logic of this incentive is familiar to students of economics, because it is almost identical to the textbook logic explaining a monopsonist's withholding of demand. In a classic monopsony, when the buyer demands a quantity q, he understands that his total expenditure will be $\text{TE}(q) = qP(q)$. His *marginal expenditure* is the derivative of total expenditure, $\text{TE}'(q) = P(q) + qP'(q)$. It is the additional expenditure per unit resulting from the last unit purchased. If, as we normally expect, P' is positive, then $\text{TE}'(q) > P(q)$. Buying a larger quantity requires not only paying the price for those units, but

---

[3] We borrow this example and the general conclusions about demand reduction from Ausubel and Cramton (2002). Engelbrecht-Wiggans and Kahn (1998) analyze the conditions under which prices of zero occur. Weber (1997) discusses demand reduction in the FCC spectrum auctions.

[4] A similar effect arises in procurement sales, when bidders offer prices at which they will supply the auctioneer. When a bidder becomes confident that he controls the marginal unit, extreme prices are likely. Experience in the California electricity markets in 2000 and 2001 confirms the extreme vulnerability of uniform price auctions in practice when one supplier can cause a shortage by withholding supply.

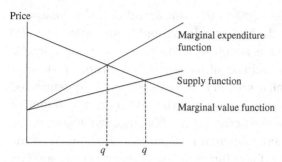

Figure 1.

also paying a higher price for the first q units – the *inframarginal* units. The increase in the price of inframarginal units when the buyer increases his purchases accounts for the second term of the marginal expenditure formula.

The fact that marginal expenditure exceeds price makes it optimal for a buyer to reduce his demand below what it would be if prices did not change with the quantity purchased. If $V(q)$ denotes the value of acquiring q units, then the buyer's objective is to maximize $V(q) - TE(q)$. If the functions are differentiable, then the derivative is $V'(q) - TE'(q) = V'(q) - P(q) - qP'(q)$. At the quantity $q > 0$ at which price equals marginal value, the derivative is $-qP'(q) < 0$, provided P' is positive.

Figure 1 shows this argument in its familiar graphical form. The profit-maximizing quantity q^* is the one at which the marginal value of the unit equals the marginal expenditure needed to acquire it. As we have argued, the marginal expenditure function lies above the supply function, so q^* is less than the quantity q at which the marginal value of an additional item is equal to its price. The profit-maximizing choice involves *demand reduction*.

Demand reduction is not a problem peculiar to the sealed-bid form: a similar effect plagues any market mechanism in which identical goods sell for identical prices. In auction models, *expected quantity* assumes the role played by quantity in classic monopsony theory. For simplicity, we describe the bids not as price–quantity pairs but as individual price bids for each unit demanded. This description entails no loss of generality, because a bid for q units at price p is functionally equivalent to q separate bids for one unit at price p.

The incentive to reduce demand arises because the bids for the second and subsequent units in the highest-rejected-bid auction affect both the expected quantity the bidder acquires and the expected price he pays for each unit he buys, if one of these subsequent bids does not win. Raising the bid for the second unit from p to p' increases the quantity demanded for prices in that range from one unit to two units. If the distribution of opposing bids has a positive derivative on this range (analogous to the positive slope of the supply function in classic monopsony), then the marginal expected expenditure function lies above the corresponding supply function, just as in the Figure 1.

To restate the argument algebraically, suppose some bidder has potential demand for two of the N units offered in an auction. Suppose the first unit is worth v_1 to the bidder and the second is worth $v_2 \leq v_1$. Let X^{N-1} and X^N denote the $N-1$st and Nth order statistics from among the opposing bids. Then the bidder's expected profit from bidding v_1 for one unit and $b \leq v_1$ for the second unit is

$$\pi(b) = E[(v_1 + v_2 - 2X^{N-1})1_{\{b > X^{N-1}\}}$$
$$+(v_1 - \max(b, X^N))^+ 1_{\{X^{N-1} > b\}}]. \tag{7.2}$$

The two terms inside the expectation reflect the possibilities that the second bid b is a winning bid and that it is not. When the bid wins, the buyer acquires two units at a price of X^{N-1} each. When it does not win, then if b is higher than X^N, the bidder acquires one unit at price b; otherwise, provided $v_1 > X^N$, he acquires one unit at price X^N.

If the joint distribution of (X^{N-1}, X^N) has a positive density on the whole set $\{X^N < X^{N-1}\}$, then the derivative of the profit function simplifies to $\pi'(v_2) = -\Pr\{X^{N-1} > v_2 > X^N\} < 0$. Intuitively, increasing the bid in a neighborhood of v_2 causes the price to increase when $X^{N-1} > v_2 > X^N$, and all other effects of the bid increase are of second order.

As in classic monopsony, the ability to reduce the price paid for inframarginal units by reducing marginal bids creates an incentive to reduce demand. In this case, we are evaluating the bid for the second unit, and the first unit is the inframarginal unit. It follows that the optimal bid for the second unit is less than v_2.

Because bidders have incentives to bid full value for the first unit but reduce demand for subsequent units, they use different mark-ups for different items. The equilibrium outcome can therefore be inefficient.

The following proposition summarizes these properties. In the proposition, each bidder draws values for two items.

Theorem 7.1. Consider a sale with N bidders and k items, where $2 \leq k < N$. Suppose that each bidder may buy two items and that the value of the first item is always at least as high as the value of the second item: $v_1^j \geq v_2^j$. In the highest-rejected-bid auction, any strategy for bidder j in which j bids less than v_1^j for the first unit is weakly dominated by a strategy in which j bids v_1^j for the first unit. Moreover, if the bidders' values for the two items are distributed according to any positive joint density on $\{v \in [0, \bar{v}]^{2N} | (\forall j)\ v_1^j \geq v_2^j\}$, then

- there is no equilibrium at which bidders all bid full value for both items, and
- there is no equilibrium in undominated strategies in which the outcomes always maximize total value.

Proof. All claims besides the last one about efficiency follow directly from the discussion preceding the theorem. To prove the last claim, consider any equilibrium in undominated strategies. Because not all bidders bid full value for both items, there is some value profile at which bidder 1 has values $v_1^1 > v_2^1$ for the two items and bids $b < v_2^1$ for the second item. With positive probability, the other bidders have values satisfying $b < \min\{v_1^1, \ldots, v_1^k\}, v_2^1 > \max\{v_1^j | j = k, \ldots, N\}$, and $v_2^1 > \max\{v_2^j | j = 2, \ldots, N\}$.

Because the bidders are assumed to use undominated strategies, the first inequality assures that the bid b is not a winner, so bidder 1 acquires at most one item. The next two inequalities assures that the value v_2^1 is among the highest k values, so that total value maximization requires that bidder 1 acquire two items. When all these inequalities hold, the outcome of the auction fails to maximize total value. By assumption, the probability that this set of inequalities holds is positive. ∎

One can intuitively understand demand reduction either

(A) as reducing the total number of units demanded at or above any price or, equivalently,

(B) as reducing the price bid for each unit after the first.

From perspective (A), the preceding analysis looks very much like the traditional theory of monopsony: the incentive to reduce the quantity demanded depends on the number of units being purchased and the price elasticity of expected supply at that price. Perspective (B) suggests that the expected gain to reducing a price bid increases with the number of inframarginal units and the probability that the price will become the market clearing price.

With respect to two-sided markets in which buyers bid to purchase and sellers offer to sell, theory supports the idea that thick markets eliminate incentives to withhold trade. Perspective (A) suggests that when there are many buyers and sellers whose supplies and demands are small relative to the market, it is a nearly dominant strategy to report those demands and supplies accurately and eschew any attempt to influence prices.[5] Perspective (B) indicates that if all parties' supplies and demands are small portions of the market volume, then all consider it unlikely that their marginal bid will set the price, so the incentive to distort supply or demand is small.[6] In two-sided markets, at least, theory predicts large numbers will eliminate demand reduction and its associated inefficiencies.

7.1.2 Low-Price Equilibria

Theoretical results for one-sided markets are less favorable to the proposition that large markets reduce withholding of demand than their counterparts for two-sided markets. Simple examples demonstrate that even when all bidders are small relative to the market, there can be Nash equilibria of uniform price auctions in which prices remain far below the competitive price.

A variety of examples establish this possibility. The simplest assumes that goods are discrete. Suppose there are N bidders each of whom wants $k > 1$ items and is willing to pay up to \$1 for each item. Suppose that there are exactly N objects for sale and that the highest-rejected-bid rule applies. Then there is a symmetric equilibrium in which each bidder bids \$1 for the first item and \$0 for each additional item. (With more than N objects for sale, similar equilibria support any allocation in which each bidder gets at least one item.)

---

[5] For example, see Postlewaite and Roberts (1976).
[6] See Swinkels (2001).

Similar results arise in examples with infinitely divisible goods. Such examples might model the sale of electrical power or of Treasury bills, for which any indivisibilities are likely unimportant. Suppose there is one unit of a divisible good for sale and that each bidder has a value of $V(q) = q - q^2$ to acquire $q \leq 1$ units of the good. The bidder's inverse demand function is then $P(q) = 1 - 2q$. With N bidders, if all report their demands truthfully, the market clearing price will be $P = 1 - 2/N$ and each bidder will acquire $1/N$ units. The market clearing price converges to 1 as the number of bidders grows large.

The corresponding auction game admits many symmetric equilibria involving severe demand reduction. Thus, suppose that each bidder bids according to the demand schedule $p(q) = a - bq$. This means that the bidder offers to pay the amount $p(q)$ for the qth unit or, equivalently, to buy $q(p) = (a - p)/b$ units at any price $p < a$. Suppose the $N - 1$ other bidders play this strategy, and consider the Nth bidder's choice of bids. If the last bidder acquires q units in the auction, then the other bidders will each acquire $(1 - q)/(N - 1)$ units, so the price will necessarily be $a - b(1 - q)/(N - 1)$, and the last bidder's profit will be $V(q) - q(a - b(1 - q)/(N - 1))$. In a symmetric equilibrium, $q = 1/N$ will maximize the bidder's profit. Hence, in equilibrium, $q = 1/N$ necessarily satisfies the bidder's first-order condition:

$$0 = \frac{d}{dq}\bigg|_{q=1/N} [q - q^2 - q(a - b(1 - q)/(N - 1))]$$

$$= 1 - \frac{2}{N} - a + \frac{b}{N - 1} - \frac{2b}{N(N - 1)} = 1 - a - \frac{2}{N} + b\frac{N - 2}{N(N - 1)}. \quad (7.3)$$

Solving (7.3) for a yields

$$a = 1 - \frac{2}{N} + b\frac{N - 2}{N(N - 1)}. \quad (7.4)$$

The restriction (7.4) allows a continuum of equilibria. In each equilibrium, the price is $p = a - b/N$, so $a = p + b/N$. Substituting this value into (7.4) yields

$$b = \left(1 - p - \frac{2}{N}\right) N(N - 1). \quad (7.5)$$

Using (7.5) and (7.4), one can construct symmetric equilibria with a wide range of prices. For example, to find an equilibrium with price $p = 0$, we substitute $p = 0$ into (7.5) to find $b = (N - 1)(N - 2)$ and $a = b/N = (N - 1)(N - 2)/N$. This describes a symmetric zero-price equilibrium closely analogous to the zero-price equilibrium in the preceding discrete example. This continuous example demonstrates that the problem of low-price equilibrium is not an artifact of the particular numbers of goods and players. There are low-price equilibria regardless of the number of bidders N.

The significance of these low-price equilibria is uncertain. In the zero-price equilibrium, the bidders have many best replies to the other bidders' equilibrium strategies. Perhaps this fact means that the model is not detailed enough to reflect bidders' actual incentives. That suspicion finds further support in the observation that in a discrete model of roughly the same setting, an undominated strategy entails never bidding more than one's actual value and bidding full value for the first unit. The equilibrium above lacks both properties. However, changing the zero-price equilibrium strategy $p(q) = a - bq$ to $p(q) = \min(V(q), a - bq)$ generates another zero-price equilibrium strategy and has the properties of the undominated strategies in the corresponding discrete game.

Some research explores the robustness of the low-price equilibria to uncertainty. Wilson (1979) introduced a version of the model with common value uncertainty. In that model, bidders have unique best replies to their competitors' strategies, but there is still a multiplicity of equilibria, some of which involve prices only a fraction of the value of the goods being sold. Back and Zender (1993) showed that this model has low-price equilibria that earn approximately the reserve price for any arbitrarily low reserve the seller may set.

Later in this chapter, we present a more effective way to identify a unique equilibrium. We model a uniform price ascending auction and employ backward induction arguments to ensure that bidders plan to optimize at all possible prices. We will find that, in those models, low prices are not only possible; the unique equilibrium consistent with backward induction often entails a low price.

Uniform price sealed-bid auctions are important in practice, both for selling relatively homogeneous goods (such as Treasury bills) and buying such goods (electrical power). The issue of extreme price equilibria is plainly of great practical importance, so the topic discussed here is an important one for continuing study.

7.2 Simultaneous Ascending Auctions

Besides the sealed-bid auctions, other important kinds of uniform price auction include the *simultaneous ascending auction* introduced by the Federal Communications Commission (FCC) in 1994 and its *clock auction* variants. The main difference between these is that in the FCC design the bidders call the prices, whereas in a clock auction the auctioneer calls the prices (and posts them on a digital or analog *clock*). Unlike the sequence of ascending auctions that Sotheby's used for the RCA transponder sale described earlier, the simultaneous ascending auction facilitates arbitrage among similar items by allowing bidders to compare prices of different items and to shift their bids to those that are relatively cheap.

Our principal findings are several. First, if goods are substitutes and bidders are non-strategic, then the outcome of the auction is approximately a competitive equilibrium, with the approximation limited only by the size of the bid increment. Despite the discreteness of the goods, a competitive equilibrium exists. Next, like the uniform price sealed-bid auction, these auctions have equilibria with very low prices. Finally, using a model with elastic supply, we find that the lowest equilibrium prices are the Cournot prices. This suggests a reinterpretation of the earlier low-price equilibria as Cournot equilibria of games with inelastic supply.

Table 1 illustrates the uniformity of prices in a simultaneous ascending auction, using data from the first FCC spectrum auction. Each license in the auction packaged rights to use two kinds of spectrum. Notice that, within each group of licenses, prices were approximately uniform.

Moreover, the prices suggest that the auction priced the two kinds of spectrum consistently across groups of licenses. For engineering reasons, the individual licenses in the auction covered two different parts of the spectrum. The FCC reserved one part for transmitting relatively powerful signals from high-powered transmitters at fixed locations to be received by mobile, handheld devices. It reserved the other part for transmitting relatively weak signals from the low-powered mobile devices back to the fixed stations. The two numbers characterizing each license in the table indicate the bandwidth of the license in the two parts of the radio spectrum. If the bidders valued the bandwidth of the first type of spectrum at about \$740,000 per kilohertz and the second type at about \$860,000 per kilohertz, these values would produce market prices of \$80 million for the first type of license, \$47.75 million for the second

Table 1. Winning bids in FCC Auction #1.

License Name	License Bandwidths (kHz)	Winning Bid
N-1	50–50	$80,000,000
N-2	50–50	80,000,000
N-3	50–50	80,000,000
N-4	50–50	80,000,000
N-5	50–50	80,000,000
N-6	50–12.5	47,001,001
N-7	50–12.5	47,505,673
N-8	50–12.5	47,500,000
N-10	50–0	37,000,000
N-11	50–0	38,000,000
Total		$617,006,674

type, and $37 million for the third type, which are quite close to the actual prices. The $38 million winning bid for license N-11, which occurred when a participant made a jump bid early in the auction, appears to be a small jump beyond the market clearing price.

We now discuss the rules of FCC auction #1 that encouraged such effective arbitrage and consistent pricing.

Bids are placed in a series of rounds. Each bid commits the bidder to pay the stated price to buy a spectrum license. At the end of each round n, the auctioneer determines a *standing high bid* for each license, which is the larger of the standing high bid from the previous round and the highest new bid for that license. Until some firm bids for a license, the *standing high bidder* is the seller; afterwards, it is the bidder that placed the standing high bid. (If two or more bidders make the same high bid during a round, the tie may be broken in favor of the bidder that bid first, or it may be broken at random.)

At the end of round n, the auctioneer determines a *minimum bid* for round $n + 1$ by adding an increment to the standing high bid. Increments may vary during the auction. For example, increments in the early rounds may be about 15% of the standing high bid, and those in the late rounds may be about 5%. In the early FCC auctions, bidders could make any bid exceeding the minimum bid. However, because bidders sometimes used the less significant digits of the bids to communicate information,[7] the rules were changed so that bidders had to choose bids from a menu constructed from the standing high bid by adding from 1 to 9 bid increments.

The auction *closing rule* is especially important: the auction ends only after a round in which there are no new bids on any license. Until then, bidders can bid on any license. This ending rule is important for enabling arbitrage among substitutes, because a bidder may become interested in bidding on one license only after the price of another, substitute license has risen sufficiently.

The FCC's *activity rule* prevents bidders from waiting until late in the auction to begin bidding seriously. In its simplest form, the activity rule simply provides that activity can never increase from round to round: a bidder that places eligible bids for n units at round t cannot place bids for more than n units at any subsequent round $t' > t$.[8]

Another feature of most of the FCC auctions has been that, at the end of each round, the bidders and the public learn the identity of and the bids made by all bidders during the just-completed round.

The FCC's rules bear important similarities to some older designs. One of these is the famous *Walrasian tatonnement*, which has been used to study price adjustments in multi-good systems. In that design, an auctioneer calls the prices and adjusts each price up or down over time according to whether the net demand at current prices for the item is positive (demand exceeds supply) or negative (supply exceeds demand). Prices in the *tatonnement* continue to adjust by some rule until supply and demand exactly balance. No actual trades take place at the intermediate prices of this Walrasian auction process; trade takes place only at final market clearing prices. The Walrasian design differs from the FCC design in several respects. In the Walrasian *tatonnement*, the auctioneer calls the prices, bids can be freely withdrawn whenever any price

---

[7] Table 1 hints at this use of the low digits; note, for example, the winning bid of $47,505,673. In the DEF auction, US West made several bids terminating in the digits 378 on licenses where McLeod Wireless had been standing high bidder. These bids appear to have been retaliation for McLeod's bids in license area 378, covering Rochester, Minnesota. One might therefore understand US West's use of trailing digits as an attempt to intimidate McLeod. See Cramton and Schwartz (2001).

[8] The FCC has used several versions of the activity rule. In some, bidders have more freedom to delay adding bids early in the auction. For example, there may be an initial stage consisting of several rounds, at the end of which a bidder can increase its activity by 25%. There can also be *waivers* that allow a bidder to be inactive in a particular round in order to take time for planning.

changes, prices can both rise and fall, and the process is not guaranteed to end in any finite amount of time.

Another similar design that influenced the FCC rules is the *silent auction*, commonly used in charity sales. In these auctions, the auctioneer sets out the items for sale (or descriptions of them) on a series of tables. Next to each item is a piece of paper on which a bidder can write his bid along with his name or identifying number. As bidders wander the room, they can raise the bid on any item they wish. The auction typically ends at a fixed hour, often just before a meal is served.

Silent auctions are simultaneous ascending auctions in much the same sense as the FCC auctions. Goods are for sale simultaneously, and prices can only rise. However, the fixed ending time distinguishes the silent auction from the FCC design.

Careful observers of silent auctions often see the following scene. As the fixed ending hour approaches, some bidder approaches a table. He lifts the pencil and slowly writes his name and bid as the bell rings announcing the end of the auction. Often, this is the only bid the bidder ever makes for this item. He plans to keep the price low and place a bid only when nobody has time left to respond.

The practice of bidding low at the last possible moment – known as *sniping* in on-line auctions – does not do much damage at charity auctions, because most bidders are feeling charitable. They are happy to pay high prices to acquire what they want, knowing that the higher the prices, the more they have contributed to charity.

Bidders at FCC auctions have decidedly different motives from donors at a charity auction, so the FCC auction rules aim to eliminate some of the strategic bidding possible at a silent auction. A pair of distinctive rules eliminates sniping. These are the closing rule, which always allows the bidder an opportunity to respond to late bids, and the activity rule, which prevents bidders from suddenly raising demands near the end of the auction. These rules also help ensure that bidders receive an orderly flow of information during the course of the bidding, so they can plan their bids more effectively.

7.2.1 The Simultaneous Ascending Auction and the Walrasian *Tatonnement*

We analyze the simultaneous ascending auction in two parts. In the first part, we assume bidders adopt certain simple strategies and identify the resulting outcomes. This part of the analysis, like the traditional analysis of the Walrasian *tatonnement,* focuses on the convergence of prices and quantities to a competitive equilibrium. We analyze convergence to competitive equilibrium both for the FCC's simultaneous ascending auction, in which bidders call their own bids, and for a clock auction, in which the auctioneer sets prices to which the bidders respond.

The second part concerns strategic analysis, and it builds upon the first part. We return to the Nash equilibrium analysis in section 7.2.3.

We begin by asking when competitive, market clearing prices exist. Traditional theories of competitive equilibrium assume that preferences are convex and that the goods are divisible, but the model we study here does not satisfy those conditions. Might there be other general conditions under which one can guarantee that competitive equilibrium prices exist? If such prices do exist, is it possible that they will emerge from a monotonic process like the simultaneous ascending auction, in which the standing high bids can never decrease from round to round? The answers to these questions require a careful, formal analysis.

Let N denote the set of bidders, and $L = \{1, \ldots, L\}$ the set of goods for sale, with typical subset S. Equivalently, we may describe any subset S of L by a vector x of 0's and 1's, with $x_l = 1 \Leftrightarrow l \in S$. If bidder j acquires the allocation x and pays m for it, his payoff is $v^j(x) - m$. The demand correspondence for j is $D^j(p) = \arg\max_x \{v^j(x) - p \cdot x\}$. We assume that there is *free disposal,* that is, $x \leq x'$ implies that $v^j(x) \leq v^j(x')$.

Generally, as prices change and demands change with them, there will be some prices at which bidders are just indifferent between two different sets of goods. To make our definition of substitutes similar to the usual one, we limit attention to price vectors p for which the demand set $D^j(p)$ is *single-valued,* that is, for which the optimization problem $\max_x \{v^j(x) - p \cdot x\}$ has a unique solution.

Definition.[9] Goods are *substitutes* for bidder j if on the price domain where D^j is single-valued, for any good l, increasing the prices of the

---

[9] Recent authors, beginning with Kelso and Crawford (1982), offer an equivalent definition and call the corresponding condition "gross substitutes." In standard economic terminology, "gross substitutes" and "gross complements" conditions are conditions based on Marshallian ("uncompensated") demand, as distinguished from the substitutes and complements conditions based on Hicksian ("compensated") demand. In models with quasilinear utility such as the ones studied in the text, there is no difference between Hicksian and Marshallian demand.

other goods does not reduce demand for good l:

$$[\hat{p}_{-l} \geq p_{-l}, \hat{p}_l = p_l] \quad \Rightarrow \quad D_l^j(\hat{p}) \geq D_l^j(p).$$

We assume that the prices that can emerge during the auction include only ones at which demand is single-valued. Because the demand is single-valued for almost all price vectors, this is not a significant restriction.

As new bids occur, the standing high bids and the standing high bidders change. We slightly simplify actual FCC procedures. Let p be the vector of standing high bids after some round. Then we will suppose that the vector of minimum bids for the next round is $(1 + \varepsilon)p$ for some $\varepsilon > 0$, that is, the minimum bid is the standing high bid plus some fixed percentage.[10] We assume that the auction opens with some positive vector of standing high bids $\hat{p}$; we treat the seller as the initial *standing high bidder* for each good. Thus, the vector of initial minimum bids is $\hat{p}(1 + \varepsilon)$.

During a simultaneous ascending auction, the gap between the standing high bid and the minimum bid for the next round implies that different bidders have different opportunities. The standing high bidder with a bid of b on some good could, in principle, acquire the good for a price of b if no more bids are made, but any other bidder would have to pay a minimum price of at least $b(1 + \varepsilon)$ to acquire the same good, regardless of how the others bid.

We will use these minimum prices – which vary by bidder – to organize our analysis, so we need to introduce corresponding notation.

Notation and Definitions

1. S^j is the set of goods on which j is the current standing high bidder.
2. $p^j = (p_{S^j}, (1 + \varepsilon)p_{L-S^j})$ is the vector of *personalized prices* for bidder j.
3. j bids *straightforwardly* if for every possible realization of the auction, the following conditions hold: (1) $S^j \subset D^j(p^j)$, (2) j makes new bids in each round on the set of goods $\hat{S}^j = D^j(p^j) - S^j$, and (3) j's new bid for any good $k \in \hat{S}^j$ is the minimum bid price, p_k^j.

Intuitively, p^j is the vector of minimum prices at which j could acquire the various goods under the rules of the auction. These prices vary among

---

[10] The actual rules for setting the bid increment can be more complicated and can vary from round to round. The rule adopted here simplifies our notation.

bidders, because the standing high bidder on any good could possibly acquire it at a price lower than is available to any other bidder.

In general, under the rules of the simultaneous ascending auction, it may not be *possible* for a bidder to bid straightforwardly, because the condition (1) may not hold. In the Walrasian *tatonnement*, condition (1) poses no problem because a bidder can withdraw bids, but in the simultaneous ascending auction the bidder is committed to his standing high bids. The next theorem identifies exactly how restrictive condition (1) is.

Theorem 7.2. Straightforward bidding is a feasible strategy for bidder j for all initial prices $\hat{p}$, all increments ε, and all feasible price paths if and only if goods are substitutes for bidder j.

Proof. The auction does not restrict the vector x on which bidder j can bid in the first round, so straightforward bidding is feasible for that round. Suppose that straightforward bidding is possible through n rounds and that j's personalized prices after that round are p^j. Straightforward bidding requires that j bid p^j for the items described by vector $D^j(p^j)$. In round $n + 1$, j's personalized prices are $\bar{p}^j \geq p^j$, and j is the standing high bidder on those goods l for which $\bar{p}_l^j = p_l^j$.

If goods are substitutes, $D_l^j(\bar{p}^j) \geq D_l^j(p^j)$, so straightforward bidding calls for j to make the required bid on goods for which he is the standing high bidder. Hence, the strategy satisfies the bidding constraints imposed by the auction, and is therefore a feasible strategy.

Conversely, if goods are not substitutes for bidder j, then there exist two goods k and l and price vectors p and $\bar{p}$ such that $\bar{p}_{-k} = p_{-k}$, $\bar{p}_k/p_k = 1 + \varepsilon > 1$, and $0 = D_l^j(\bar{p}^j) < D_l^j(p^j) = 1$. With an initial vector of minimum bids $\hat{p} = p$ and increment factor ε, suppose j bids straightforwardly at the first round. Then $D_l^j(p^j) = 1$; j demands good l and may become the standing high bidder for it, while another bidder may bid for good k and become standing high bidder on that good. In that case, j's demand in the second round has $D_l^j(\bar{p}) = 0$, so condition (1) of the definition of straightforward bidding is violated. ∎

The impossibility of bidding straightforwardly when goods are not substitutes is very problematic for an auction design. It means that even a small bidder who expects to be unable to exert much influence on prices cannot just respond to prices, because past bids may restrict future ones made at different (higher) prices. This difficulty can drastically increase the costs of bidding.

On the other hand, when goods are substitutes for all bidders, straightforward bidding is not only feasible, it also produces outcomes similar to competitive equilibrium outcomes. The next theorem shows that the simultaneous ascending auction generates prices and allocations that are competitive equilibrium allocations for an economy with nearly the same bidder values. In particular, the auction outcome maximizes the total value over all possible allocations to within a single bid increment.

Theorem 7.3. Assume the goods are substitutes for all bidders and that all bidders bid straightforwardly. Then the auction ends with no new bids after a finite number of rounds. Let $(\bar{p}, \bar{x})$ be the final standing high bids and assignment of goods. Then $(\bar{p}, \bar{x})$ is a competitive equilibrium for an economy with valuation functions $\hat{v}^j(x) = v^j(x) - \varepsilon \bar{p} \cdot (x - \bar{x}^j)^+$ for each bidder j. The final assignment maximizes total value to within a single bid increment:

$$\max_x \sum_j v^j(x^j) \le \sum_j v^j(\bar{x}^j) + \varepsilon \sum_j \bar{p}_j.$$

Proof. Consider bidder j after round n. Because goods are substitutes and j bids straightforwardly, if j's personalized prices at the end of round n are p^j and if j is the standing high bidder on goods z^j, then j demands z^j when prices for those goods are fixed and the prices of the other goods rise to high levels. It follows that j would earn a non-negative profit if the auction ended after any round n. Because that statement holds for all bidders, the maximum total value of the goods is an upper bound for the total price of all goods after any round of the auction. Because the bid increments have positive lower bounds, the auction ends after a finite number of rounds.

Bidder j's final personalized price for any good k satisfies $p_k^j = \bar{p}_k(1 + \varepsilon(1 - \bar{x}_k^j))$. So, when we modify bidder j's valuation as in the statement of the theorem, j's demand at the final price vector $\bar{p}$ solves $\max_x(\hat{v}^j(x) - \bar{p} \cdot x) = \max_x(v^j(x) - \varepsilon \bar{p} \cdot (x - \bar{x}^j)^+ - \bar{p} \cdot x) = \max_x(v^j(x) - p^j \cdot x)$. Comparing the first and last expressions, we have $D^j(p^j) = \hat{D}^j(\bar{p})$.

By the closing rule, we infer that j made no new bids in the final round. So, because j bids straightforwardly, $\bar{x}^j \in D^j(p^j)$. By the previous paragraph, this implies $\bar{x}^j \in \hat{D}^j(\bar{p})$ for all j, so $(\bar{p}, \bar{x})$ is a competitive equilibrium with the modified valuations.

To show the auction maximizes total value to within one bid increment, observe that

$$\max_x \sum_{j=1}^N v^j(x^j) = \max_x \sum_{j=1}^N [\hat{v}^j(x^j) + \varepsilon \bar{p} \cdot (x^j - \bar{x}^j)^+]$$

$$\leq \max_x \sum_{j=1}^N [\hat{v}^j(x^j) + \varepsilon \bar{p} \cdot x^j]$$

$$\leq \max_x \sum_{j=1}^N \hat{v}^j(x^j) + \varepsilon \sum_l \bar{p}_l$$

$$= \sum_{j=1}^N \hat{v}^j(\bar{x}^j) + \varepsilon \sum_l \bar{p}_l$$

$$= \sum_{j=1}^N v^j(\bar{x}^j) + \varepsilon \sum_l \bar{p}_l.$$

The first equality follows from the definition of the modified valuations; the first inequality from the restriction that all prices are non-negative; and the following inequality from the fact any feasible allocation assigns each good at most once. In the fourth step, we use the facts (i) that $(\bar{p}, \bar{x})$ is a competitive equilibrium for the modified valuations, (ii) that competitive equilibria are efficient, and (iii) that when payoffs are quasilinear, efficient allocations maximize total value. Finally, the last equality follows the definition of $\hat{v}^j(\cdot)$, which coincides with $v^j(\cdot)$ when evaluated at $\bar{x}^j$. ∎

In practice, the most relevant bid increment for assessing outcomes in the FCC auctions is the increment that applies when bidders are last eligible to make new bids, which is normally near the end of the auction. We might therefore expect the auction's outcomes to approximate competitive equilibria very closely when bid increments near the end of the auction are very small. The Milgrom–Wilson rules originally adopted in the United States by the FCC followed this intuition in reducing minimum bid increments in the final stages of the auction.[11]

---

[11] The FCC later changed this rule to reduce transaction costs: smaller increments late in the auction produced large numbers of costly rounds with relatively little bidding activity.

The next theorem asserts that if every bidder regards the goods as substitutes, then a competitive equilibrium must exist in this model, despite the indivisibility of the goods. In addition, the theorem asserts that if the bid increments are small, the auction allocation is a competitive equilibrium allocation. Milgrom (2000) derived these results.[12]

Theorem 7.4. Suppose that for every bidder the goods are substitutes and that all goods have strictly positive marginal values. Then the economy with modified valuations as in Theorem 7.3 has a competitive equilibrium, and for initial prices $\hat{p}$ and bid increments $\varepsilon > 0$ sufficiently small, the final assignment $\bar{x}(\varepsilon, \hat{p})$ is the assignment for some competitive equilibrium.

Proof. We fix $\hat{p}$ low enough that each good attracts some bids at the first round. The auction must therefore allocate every good to some bidder. With $\hat{p}$ fixed, we may suppress the corresponding argument of $\bar{x}$.

Consider a sequence of positive numbers $\{\varepsilon_n\} \to 0$, and define $(\bar{x}(\varepsilon_n), \bar{p}(\varepsilon_n))$ to be the corresponding sequence of auction outcomes, and $\hat{v}_n = (\hat{v}_n^j)_{j \in N}$ to be the corresponding sequence of modified valuation functions. Because there are only finitely many possible assignments of goods, there must exist some assignment $\bar{\bar{x}}$ that occurs infinitely often along the sequence.

Because each equilibrium price is non-negative and bounded above by the maximum value of the complete package of all goods, the price vectors all lie in a compact set. Hence, there exists a subsequence $n(k)$ along which $\bar{x}(\varepsilon_{n(k)}) = \bar{\bar{x}}$ and $\bar{p}(\varepsilon_{n(k)})$ converges to some price vector $\bar{\bar{p}}$. By theorem 7.3, for every k, $\bar{\bar{x}} = \bar{x}(\varepsilon_{n(k)}) \in D(\bar{p}(\varepsilon_{n(k)}) | \hat{v}_{n(k)})$. By construction, because $\varepsilon_{n(k)} \to 0$, we have $\hat{v}_{n(k)} \to v$. Because the demand correspondence D has a closed graph in prices and values, we have $\bar{\bar{x}} \in D(\bar{\bar{p}} | v)$, that is, $(\bar{\bar{x}}, \bar{\bar{p}})$ is a competitive equilibrium. ∎

[12] Kelso and Crawford (1982) introduced a closely related model of labor markets in which firms make a sequence of wage offers to workers analogous to the sequence of bids in a simultaneous ascending auction. The Kelso–Crawford auction has the same ending rule as the simultaneous ascending auction and similarly limits bid withdrawals. The main differences between the models are two. First, the Kelso–Crawford model is more general in allowing workers to evaluate offers by considering both the identity of the firm and the wage it offers. Second, it requires only that a firm's bid to a worker beat its own best previous bid to the same worker, rather than the best bid from any firm to that worker.

Theorems 7.2, 7.3, and 7.4 all assume that goods are substitutes. We have noted that spectrum licenses are an important class of assets sold by ascending auction. In practice, whether spectrum licenses are substitutes or complements may often depend on how the licenses are defined. When licenses are large, as in many of the US spectrum auctions, assembling multiple licenses may not produce significant economies of scale and scope, and the licenses may be approximate substitutes. However, when licenses are so small that a bidder must combine several to achieve economies of scale or scope, the licenses are not likely substitutes.

How serious is failure of the assumption that goods are substitutes? Can we extend theorems 7.2, 7.3, and 7.4 to a broader set of valuations, for which goods need not be substitutes? Theorem 7.2 demonstrated that it is not generally possible to bid straightforwardly when the goods are not substitutes. According to the next theorem, due to Milgrom (2000), we cannot even guarantee the existence of competitive equilibrium when the substitutes condition fails.

Theorem 7.5. Suppose that the set of possible individual valuation functions includes all the ones for which goods are substitutes and also includes at least one other valuation function. Then, if there are at least three bidders, there is a profile of possible individual valuations such that no competitive equilibrium exists.[13]

A two-license, two-bidder example, summarized in Table 2, provides intuition for this theorem. The table shows the value to each of two bidders of licenses A and B singly and of the package AB. If $c > 0$, then the two licenses are not substitutes for bidder 1, for at prices up to $a + 0.5c$ and $b + 0.5c + \varepsilon$, the bidder would want to buy both licenses if $\varepsilon < 0$ but neither if $\varepsilon > 0$, so demand for license A falls with an increase in the price of license B. If there is one bidder for whom licenses are not substitutes, then we can find valuations such that licenses will be substitutes for another bidder (here, bidder 2) but no competitive equilibrium exists.

---

[13] Gul and Stacchetti (1999) prove a related theorem. They assume that the set of possible valuations includes all those in which bidders demand only a single item and that the number of bidders is at least as large as the number of goods plus one. They conclude that if the set of possible valuations includes one for which goods are not substitutes, then there is a profile of possible individual valuations such that no competitive equilibrium exists.

Table 2.

Bidder	Value		
	A	B	AB
1	a	b	$a+b+c$
2	$a+0.6c$	$b+0.6c$	$a+b$

If $c > 0$, then the second bidder does find the two goods to be substitutes.

Suppose there is a competitive equilibrium in this example. Then the equilibrium allocation must be efficient, so bidder 1 must acquire both licenses. As bidder 2 does not demand any licenses, the equilibrium prices must satisfy $p_A \geq a + 0.6c$ and $p_B \geq b + 0.6c$. However, these conditions imply that $p_A + p_B \geq a + b + 1.2c$, so bidder 1 does not wish to buy, either. Hence, no competitive equilibrium prices exist.

The third bidder required by the theorem allows us to reduce any auction with multiple items to an equivalent auction with just two items.

Proof of Theorem 7.5. We first outline the proof. We choose a bidder (bidder 1) for whom goods 1 and 2 are not substitutes and then introduce two other bidders with identical linear valuations for goods. We fix their values to ensure that the equilibrium prices of goods other than 1 and 2 are p_{-12}. With those prices fixed, we define the indirect value function of bidder 1 conditional on whether 1 acquires good 1, good 2, both, or neither. We then introduce a fourth bidder who values only goods 1 and 2 to create a non-existence problem like that of the example preceding this theorem. Finally, we observe that removing one of the bidders with identical valuations does not change the conclusion.

Suppose bidder j has a valuation function v^j such that goods are not substitutes. Then there exist a price vector $(p_{-k}, \bar{p}_k)$, a number $\varepsilon \in \mathbb{R}_+$, and a pair of goods, say goods 1 and 2, such that $D_1^j(p_{-1}, \bar{p}_1) = D_2^j(p_{-1}, \bar{p}_1) = 1$ and $D_1^j(p_{-1}, \bar{p}_1 + \varepsilon) = D_2^j(p_{-1}, \bar{p}_1 + \varepsilon) = 0$. We may take $j = 1$.

Introduce bidders 2 and 3, with identical linear valuations for bundles x: $\bar{v}(x) = (0, 0, p_{-12}) \cdot (x_1, x_2, x_{-12})$. Define $\hat{v}(x_1, x_2) = \max_{x_{-12}}$

$v^1(x_1, x_2, x_{-12}) - p_{-12} \cdot x_{-12}$. Let $a = \hat{v}(1, 0) - \hat{v}(0, 0), b = \hat{v}(0, 1) - \hat{v}(0, 0)$, and $c = \hat{v}(0, 0) + \hat{v}(1, 1) - \hat{v}(1, 0) - \hat{v}(0, 1)$. Bidder 1's demand pattern implies that $c > 0$.

Bidder 4 values only goods 1 and 2. Just as in Table 2, he will pay up to $a + 0.6c$ for license 1, up to $b + 0.6c$ for license 2, and up to $a + b$ for the pair.

By construction, in any competitive equilibrium, the prices of goods besides 1 and 2 must be at least p_{-12}. If any competitive equilibrium has higher prices for those goods, then reducing those prices to p_{-12} preserves a demand of 1 for each unit, so there is also an equilibrium with prices of p_{-12} for goods other than 1 and 2. Hence, we may limit attention to such equilibria.

The next part of the proof exactly follows the example. A competitive equilibrium allocation must maximize total value, so it must assign goods 1 and 2 to bidder 1. Because the fourth bidder acquires no licenses, the prices of goods 1 and 2 must be at least $a + 0.6c$ and $b + 0.6c$, respectively, but such prices are inconsistent with bidder 1's purchasing goods 1 and 2.

Finally, remove bidder 3, and suppose that, contrary to the statement of the theorem, this economy has some competitive equilibrium $(\hat{p}, \hat{x})$. For any item $m \neq 1, 2$, if bidder 1 acquires item m, then bidder 2 does not, so $\hat{p}_m \geq p_m$. If bidder 1 does not acquire the item, then bidder 2 does, so $\hat{p}_m \leq p_m$ and there is another equilibrium with $\hat{p}_m = p_m$. Hence, $((\hat{p}_1, \hat{p}_2, \hat{p}_{-12} \vee p_{-12}), \hat{x})$ is a competitive equilibrium with three bidders, and if we reintroduce bidder 3, we may take his demands at those prices to be zero. So the preceding prices and allocation also form a competitive equilibrium of the economy with the four bidders identified above, contrary to our finding that no such equilibrium exists. ∎

The non-existence of competitive equilibrium relates to the *exposure problem* faced by participants in a simultaneous ascending auction. A bidder who starts out by bidding straightforwardly according to his demand schedule exposes himself to the possibility of bidding off his demand schedule in later rounds, winning a collection of goods he does not want at the prices he has bid because complementary goods have become too expensive.

In the example in Table 2, if bidder 2 plays an undominated strategy, then he will not quit until the prices of the two items reach their reservation levels. At those prices, bidder 1 loses money. So, if bidder 1 suspects bidder 2 will bid in this fashion, he will not bid aggressively for the two items, and the outcome of the auction will be inefficient.

One puzzle raised by the preceding analysis is that some spectrum auctions involving complementary licenses appear to have functioned well. In the US regional narrowband auction in 1994, several bidders successfully assembled collections of regional paging licenses in single spectrum bands to create the package needed for a nationwide paging service. In Mexico, the 1997 sale of licenses to manage point-to-point microwave transmissions in various geographic areas exhibited a similar pattern. What appears to be special about these auctions is that licenses that were complementary for bidders planning nationwide paging or microwave transmission networks were not substitutes for any other bidders.

The theorems identify a problem in situations in which licenses that are complements for one bidder are substitutes for another. The Netherlands DCS-1800 auction, which took place in February 1998, illustrates the practical importance of this possibility. In that auction, eighteen lots were offered for sale. Two of the lots were designed to be large enough that a new entrant could use them to establish a new wireless telephone business. The remaining sixteen lots were too small to be valuable singly to new entrants, but could be used to expand the systems of incumbent wireless operators. Alternatively, a new entrant who acquired perhaps four or six small licenses could combine them to support entry at an efficient scale. The smaller licenses would therefore likely be complements for the new entrants, but substitutes for the incumbents. The preceding theorems identify exactly this pattern as problematic.

According to theorem 7.2, the new entrants were certain to find bidding for the smaller licenses difficult. Bidding straightforwardly in every round is *infeasible* under the auction rules. One might hope to use competitive prices to predict bidding, but, according to theorem 7.5, competitive, market clearing prices may not exist. As our numerical example demonstrates, even bidders who are certain that they have the highest values might wisely refrain from bidding aggressively under these circumstances, because there may be no way to win profitably.

The outcome of the Netherlands auction seems to confirm these concerns. The final prices per unit of bandwidth for the two large lots were more than twice as high as for any of the sixteen smaller lots. The entrants, willing to pay high prices for large chunks of spectrum, appear to have been unwilling to risk losses assembling smaller chunks of spectrum.[14]

We return in the next chapter to the problem of bidding for complements.

7.2.2 Clock Auctions

The FCC's implementation of the simultaneous ascending auction has worked reasonably well for spectrum licenses, in which each item sold is arguably unique. One of its main practical disadvantages has been the length of the resulting auctions. In practice, allocations for almost all goods change little after the half-way point of the auction; the second half merely refines the allocation of a few smaller licenses.

To see why the auction runs so slowly and how one might speed it up, consider a simple example. Suppose $n + 1$ bidders compete to buy n identical objects; a bidder can acquire only a single object. Suppose that prices start at zero, that each bidder bids straightforwardly, that the minimum new bid for any object is the standing high bid plus 1, and that each bidder has a value $v > 1$ for any one object. In the first round of the auction and up to $n - 1$ subsequent rounds, all new bids will be at a price of 1 for some object that has not yet received a bid. In each round after this initial stage, n of the bidders will be standing high bidders on some item and will place no new bid, while the remaining bidder will raise the price of some item by 1. Total auction revenue will therefore rise by 1 per round. Hence, the auction will take between $n\lfloor v - 1 \rfloor + 1$ and $n\lfloor v \rfloor$ rounds.[15]

One reason the standard simultaneous ascending auction is so slow is that it fails to take advantage of the homogeneity of the items. For sales of commodities like securities or electrical power, this defect is decisive. Two alternatives to the simultaneous auction design address this defect. The simplest is a kind of sealed-bid auction such as the highest-rejected-bid auction described earlier. If bidders behave straightforwardly, this auction generates a competitive price when there is just one kind of good for sale. Even with straightforward bidding, such an auction is not suitable when there are several imperfectly substitutable goods to be sold.

---

[14] Some of the price difference may also be attributed to other differences in the spectrum offered in the different kinds of license.

[15] The notation $\lfloor v \rfloor$ denotes the largest integer less than or equal to v.

The second alternative is the clock auction, in which the auctioneer posts prices for each kind of good on a digital clock. Intuitively, the clock auction is simple: in each round, the auctioneer increases prices by one increment for goods for which demand exceeds supply. Clock auctions embody many of the same principles as the simultaneous ascending auction, and the design can accommodate both heterogeneous items requiring individual prices and homogeneous items requiring a single price.

Though the clock auction is simple in principle, implementing it poses practical challenges. Because the auctioneer increases bids in discrete increments, prices can overshoot, requiring subtle adjustments to the auction design. For example, in the simple case described above, what should the rules specify if ten units of a good are offered but demand drops from eleven to nine in some round when the price increases?

As discussed below, one theoretical solution to this problem is for the auctioneer to get more information from bidders than just point estimates of their demands at prevailing prices. The auctioneer can use the additional information to decide to whom to assign goods as changing prices change the signs of excess demands. To date, actual clock auctions have also asked bidders for additional information beyond their demands at current prices.

The 2002 New Jersey power purchase, in which electrical utilities bought power for their customers, illustrates some of the difficulties of implementing a clock auction. Suppose bidders demand four kinds of power products, labeled A through D. Suppose that, in some round, products A and B are *oversubscribed* (demand exceeds supply at the current prices) and products C and D are *undersubscribed* (demand is less than supply). Suppose the auctioneer increases prices for products A and B and that after the change, products A and B become undersubscribed and products C and D become oversubscribed. How should the rules respond to this scenario? New Jersey's auction rules asked bidders switching from bidding on A or B to bidding on C or D to attribute their new bids on C and D to *switches* from A and B. A complex set of rules sometimes disallowed switches to avoid creating an undersubscribed product. The rules also provided that if a bidder's switch from A to B were disallowed and the bidder were eventually to win product A, then the bidder's price for A would be no higher than the highest price at which he had voluntarily bid.

Electricité de France (EDF) used a related but distinct clock auction design for its power sales in 2002 and 2003.[16] The EDF sales take place every three months. The products sold are supply contracts of different durations, ranging from 3 months to 36 months. In principle, these multiple durations could create the same kinds of complexities as those caused by multiple products in the New Jersey auction. In practice, those complexities were avoided by the way the sale was structured.

Before each auction, EDF determines the total capacity it wishes to offer, based primarily on the capacity it has available over the first three months of the contract period. Using the prices in other European markets, it determines differences Δ_n and requires that the price per megawatt-hour for a contract of n months must be Δ_n more than the price of the basic three-month contract. The Δ's define a *scoring rule* that allows EDF to run the auction as if it were selling a single homogeneous product, namely, capacity in the first three-month period of the contracts.

The EDF auction uses electronic bidding *agents* to speed the bidding while mimicking what would happen in a clock auction, with continuously increasing prices. The actual auction proceeds in a series of rounds. The rules specify a planned price increase δ for each round. Within the round, only the electronic agents bid, specifying quantities demanded at each price. Prices on each kind of contract increase continuously during the round. The round ends when either (1) prices on contracts of every duration have increased by δ, or (2) total demand decreases below total supply. When the second condition occurs, the auction ends. EDF chooses a δ large enough that the auction will end within about five rounds.

The electronic rounds are essentially instantaneous. Between rounds, there is a long enough pause for bidders instruct their agents how to bid during the next round. The auctioneer provides a form for entering these instructions. Each human bidder gives his agent an initial vector of quantity demands for the round, which (except in the first round) must equal his final demands from the preceding round. In addition, the human bidder may specify any finite number of changes in demand during the round. A typical instruction to an agent to change the bidder's

---

[16] The EDF products were call "virtual power plants" because the buyers had contractual access to the capacity of the plant but EDF continued to operate the physical power plants.

demand specifies that 40% of the way through the round, when all prices have increased by 0.4δ, the electronic agent is to reduce its demand for product 1 by 100 units and increase its demand for product 2 by 50 units. In general, an instruction specifies a percentage and a list of demand changes, subject to the restriction that the total number of units demanded cannot increase as prices rise.

When the auction ends, EDF is committed to a certain supply capacity for the first three months and some lower capacity for each subsequent month. Because EDF's uncommitted capacity is approximately constant, this plan is always technically feasible. The outcome typically leaves uncommitted capacity available for the next auction, which takes place three months later.

EDF conducts its sales as if it faced only one constraint, the availability of capacity in the first three-month period, and the result is a drastically simplified design. The reality of multiple constraints is accommodated by running a series of auctions over time. This sort of design was not feasible for the New Jersey situation, in which multiple kinds of product constraints all applied over the same period and all needed to be resolved together. New Jersey needed an auction that could solve a multi-product matching problem, not merely the problem of setting total overall demand equal to total overall supply.

Demange, Gale, and Sotomayor (1986) devised a theoretically sound way to run clock auctions for situations similar to New Jersey's, but their analysis assumes that each buyer wants just a single item. Gul and Stacchetti (2000) have extended that analysis to the general case of demands for goods that are substitutes for each bidder.

Discrete goods create practical and theoretical problems for clock auctions, because at critical moments during the auction, prices leave bidders exactly indifferent between different bundles of products. To raise prices on the products that are overdemanded, one needs a definition of excess demand when bidders are indifferent among some allocations.

The theoretically correct way to identify overdemanded goods requires that each bidder report the whole set of bundles among which he is indifferent at current prices. To explain the Gul–Stacchetti procedure, we begin by thinking about the simple case in which there are no indifferences. In this case, each bidder demands a particular bundle of products, so one can identify the collection of products for which demand strictly exceeds supply. That set of goods is a *maximally overdemanded set*, that is, a set that maximizes the difference between demand and supply. By construction, it is also the *smallest* such set. In the general case, when indifferences are possible, the auctioneer again must identify the smallest maximally overdemanded set. If this set has positive excess demand, then the auctioneer must increase the prices of exactly this set of goods.

To identify the smallest maximally overdemanded set, we introduce the following notation. For each set of products B and price vector p, let $\#D(B, p)$ denote the number of products demanded from set B. If at least one bidder has more than one payoff-maximizing allocation, then let $\#D(B, p)$ be the minimum total number of products demanded from set B at any profile of optimal choices for the bidders. Let $\#S(A)$ denote the total number of units supplied of all products in set A. Then a set B is *maximally overdemanded* at price vector p if $\#D(B, p) - \#S(B) = \max_A (\#D(A, p) - \#S(A))$. A *smallest maximally overdemanded set* is any maximally overdemanded set B such that no subset is maximally overdemanded.

To illustrate the calculation of a maximally overdemanded set, suppose there are two products and just one bidder, and that the bidder is indifferent between the bundles $(4, 3)$ and $(3, 4)$. In that case, $\#D(\{1\}, p) = 3$, $\#D(\{2\}, p) = 3$, and $\#D(\{1, 2\}, p) = 7$. If the seller has three units of each product available for sale, then the individual products are not overdemanded, because the minimum number of units demanded of each individual product does not exceed the supply. In this example, however, the set $\{1, 2\}$ is overdemanded, because the minimum total number of units demanded from that set is 7, which exceeds the available supply.

The clock auction proceeds by raising the prices on both goods in tandem until the demand set changes. For example, it may happen that as the prices increase, the buyer reaches a point at which, in addition to the bundles $(4, 3)$ and $(3, 4)$, the bundle $(3, 3)$ becomes an optimal choice. At that point, the clock auction will end, with demand equal to supply for each product.

Gul and Stacchetti (2000) study a model of a clock auction, assuming that valuations are integers and that prices increase by a single unit in each round. They apply matroid theory to prove that if goods are substitutes and all bidders report their demands truthfully, then there exists an allocation at the final prices that exactly clears the market.

In other words, if goods are substitutes, prices from the just-described procedure converge to a competitive equilibrium price vector.

From one perspective, this result is intuitive: the clock auction seems to generate prices similar to those of the FCC simultaneous ascending auction with straightforward bidding, and we have already seen how the FCC auction design yields competitive outcomes when goods are substitutes. Research to date, however, is merely suggestive and has not yet unified the two approaches.

7.2.3 Strategic Incentives in Uniform Price Auctions

Next, we return to the issue of incentives for strategic behavior in uniform price auctions. Our earlier analysis focused on sealed-bid auctions and revealed equilibria with prices well below the goods' marginal values. Particularly in continuous models, we showed that such equilibria are common regardless of the number of bidders. We obtained similar results for discrete models with many goods and many bidders.

In each case, we used a full information model, and the equilibrium we identified allowed each bidder an infinite set of best replies. Moreover, one of the models produced a continuum of Nash equilibria – a conclusion that hardly inspires confidence in the model's predictions. One might wonder whether more detailed modeling of the environment, adding uncertainty or dynamics or both, could identify the most plausible equilibria. Earlier, we discussed some attempts to add uncertainty to the model and the mixed results they produced. In this section, we create a dynamic model of a clock auction and demonstrate its strategic equivalence to a certain sealed-bid auction. Then, we use weak dominance and a concept based on backward induction to try to rule out some of the extreme equilibria found in our previous analyses.

7.2.3.1 The Basic Clock Auction Model

We model a clock auction with N bidders in which NS units of a perfectly divisible good are offered for sale. A bidder j who acquires q units at price p earns a payoff of $V^j(q) - pq$. Suppose that V^j is continuous and strictly concave, and let $\hat{q}^j(p) = \arg\max_{x \in \mathbb{R}_+}(V^j(x) - px)$ be the associated demand function.

The clock starts at some reserve price r and increases in small increments from round to round. Each bidder announces the quantity he demands at the current price, and the activity rule prohibits increasing this quantity from round to round. The auction ends as soon as the total quantity demanded by all bidders is less than or equal to the quantity supplied, which is NS units. To ensure that the game is well defined, assume that the auction will terminate for certain if the auction reaches a pre-specified very high price. When the auction terminates, the transaction price is set at the current price showing on the clock, and each bidder receives the quantity he demanded at that price.

To minimize the possibility that bidders might support collusive equilibria by retaliating against one another for deviations, assume that the only information the bidders receive during the auction is the current price. With this assumption, the current price summarizes all public information at any time during the auction, so (reduced) pure strategies specify bids that depend only on the current price.[17] If the set of possible prices is the set of all non-negative numbers, then a strategy is a nonincreasing function $q : \mathbb{R}_+ \to [0, NS]$ mapping possible prices to quantities.

This model highlights the close connections between the clock auction and the sealed-bid uniform price auction. When we model the clock auction as above, both have the same strategy space and payoff mapping. The only differences are that (1) the clock auction allows a dynamic analysis using backward induction and (2) we have so far used a discrete price space in the clock auction and a continuous price space in the sealed-bid auction. Let us now remove that latter difference, so that prices are continuous in both cases. Also, for technical reasons, we restrict attention to continuous strategies.

First, we identify and eliminate some weakly dominated strategies.

---

[17] Recall that a *reduced strategy* is an equivalence class of pure strategies that always induce the same outcome. Our analyses of the Dutch auction and the ascending auction in earlier chapters also used reduced strategies.

In the present case, because bidders know the history of their own past bids in addition to the current price, a pure strategy is formally a map from the current price and the bidder's own past quantities into a current quantity demand. Notice, however, that given any pure strategy Q and any price p, one can identify a unique quantity a bidder will demand if the price reaches p. Thus pure strategy Q implies a map q from prices to quantities. Any two strategies that induce the same map q necessarily generate the same outcomes, so such strategies are equivalent. The nonincreasing function $q(p)$ that maps prices to bid quantities characterizes the equivalence class, so we call this the reduced strategy and use it for our analysis. In the text, we usually call q a "strategy," omitting the adjective "reduced."

Theorem 7.6 Suppose there are $N \geq 2$ bidders. Let $q(p)$ be any strategy for the clock auction game, and let $\bar{q}(p) = \min(q(p), \hat{q}(p))$. If $q \neq \bar{q}$, then $\bar{q}$ weakly dominates q.

Proof. Suppose $q \neq \bar{q}$. Because $N \geq 2$, there exist strategies for the other bidder(s) such that q and $\bar{q}$ lead to different prices at the outcome of the auction. So it suffices to prove that whenever the outcomes corresponding to the two strategies differ, $\bar{q}$ always earns strictly more than q.

For any opposing strategy profile, suppose the outcomes $(p, q(p))$ and $(\bar{p}, \bar{q}(\bar{p}))$ that result from playing q and $\bar{q}$ are unequal. Then because $\bar{q} \leq q$ at every price, we have $\bar{p} < p$. By the definition of $\hat{q}$, the outcome $(p, \hat{q}(p))$ is weakly more profitable for a bidder than $(p, q(p))$. Because $\bar{p}$ is not a market clearing price for the demand function q, it follows that $(\bar{p}, \bar{q}(\bar{p})) = (\bar{p}, \hat{q}(\bar{p}))$. Also, a bidder prefers $(\bar{p}, \hat{q}(\bar{p}))$ to $(p, \hat{q}(p))$, because both are price-taking demands and the latter entails a higher price. So a bidder prefers $(\bar{p}, \bar{q}(\bar{p}))$ to $(p, q(p))$. ∎

Next, we illustrate the use of backward induction using a simple symmetric model. In this model, each bidder has the same strictly increasing, concave, continuously differentiable valuation function $V(q)$ with corresponding demand function $\hat{q}$.

Theorem 7.7. For any reserve price r and any number N of bidders, the strategy $q(p) = \min(S, \hat{q}(p))$ is a symmetric Nash equilibrium of the clock auction game.

Proof. If each bidder adopts the specified strategy, then no bidder demands more than S, so the bidding stops immediately at the reserve price r, and each bidder acquires $\min(S, \hat{q}(r))$ units at price r. By inspection, among all deviations that lead the deviator to acquire a quantity less than S, none earns a higher payoff than the equilibrium strategy, because none produces a lower price than r.

So, if there is any profitable deviation, it must enable the deviator to acquire $\bar{q} > S$ at some price $\bar{p} > r$. Using Theorem 7.6, we may assume without loss of generality that $\bar{q} \leq \hat{q}(\bar{p})$. The preceding two inequalities imply that at price $\bar{p}$, the $N - 1$ bidders who do not deviate each acquire

$\min(S, \hat{q}(\bar{p})) = S$. Hence, the total quantity purchased is $\bar{q} + (N-1)S > NS$, demonstrating the market cannot clear. ∎

Notice that, if $\hat{q}(r) \geq S$, then the value to a bidder from playing the equilibrium strategy is $V(S) - rS$, which is decreasing in r. If $\hat{q}(r) \leq S$, then the corresponding value is $V(\hat{q}(r)) - r\hat{q}(r)$, which is again decreasing in r. Because this value is everywhere decreasing in r, it follows that it is always in a bidder's interest to act to stop the auction immediately. One can formalize this argument to give an alternative proof of Theorem 7.7.

The theorem identifies an equilibrium consistent with backward induction. After any history of bidding, the bidders effectively find themselves in a new game starting at the current price. The theorem asserts that the proposed strategy, restricted to the new game, is a symmetric Nash equilibrium of that game. This backward induction property is similar, but not identical, to the defining property of subgame perfect equilibrium.[18]

Notice that the equilibrium strategy identified by the theorem depends on the per capita supply S but not on the number of bidders, N. Thus, the theory predicts that a proportionate increase in the number of bidders and the total supply does not necessarily increase the effective competition in the auction. We also discover something about the selection of equilibrium: weak dominance and backward induction alone do not eliminate equilibria with very low prices.

7.2.3.2 The Alternating-Move Clock Auction

Ausubel and Schwartz (1999) explore the idea that backward induction may actually select an equilibrium with a low price as the unique equilibrium. To eliminate the multiplicity of equilibria found in other models, Ausubel and Schwartz add two novel assumptions. First, bidders bid in sequence, so moves are not simultaneous as in other models. Second, each bidder observes the previous bids before choosing his own quantity. These changes convert the auction into an extensive form game with perfect information. It is a standard result of game theory that, generically,

---

[18] In a game of perfect recall such as this one, a subgame starts only at a node where no bidder has private information. Bidders in the model treated here are privately informed about their own past quantity choices, so what is called a "new game" in the text is not a subgame according to the standard definition.

finite games with perfect information have unique equilibria consistent with backward induction.[19] Although we cannot apply this result directly to auctions, we will see below that a certain model of a clock auction with alternating moves has a unique equilibrium.[20]

In our model, two bidders have increasing, strictly concave, and continuously differentiable valuation functions $V^1(q)$ and $V^2(q)$, with $V^1(0) = V^2(0) = 0$. There is one divisible good for sale. The auction has a reserve price of r.

The *state* of the auction is a pair (p, q), where p represents the current price on the clock and q represents the number of units currently demanded by all bidders except the current bidder. The initial state of the auction is $p = r$ and $q > 1$.

At any round $n \geq 1$, only one bidder moves.

If n is odd, bidder 1 observes the state variable (p, q) and chooses a quantity q_1. If $q_1 + q \leq 1$, then the auction ends at price p, bidder 1 gets quantity q_1 and bidder 2 gets the quantity q. In this case, we say that 1 *accepts* the state. If 1 does not accept the state, then the round advances. The state variable for the next round becomes $(p + 1, q_1)$. Intuitively, 1 is the standing high bidder at quantity q_1 and price $p + 1$.

If n is even, an analogous process occurs, but it is bidder 2 who moves. Bidder 2 observes the state variable (p, q) and chooses a quantity q_2. If $q + q_2 \leq 1$ (2 accepts), the auction ends at price p, and bidders 1 and 2 get q and q_2 units, respectively. Otherwise, the auction proceeds to the next round with state $(p + 1, q_2)$.

We will see shortly that there is a unique equilibrium of this game consistent with backward induction. For now, let us temporarily assume uniqueness and characterize the equilibrium strategies. Given the state (p, q), j can accept and earn a payoff of

$$\alpha^j(p, q) = \max_{x \in [0, 1-q]} (V^j(x) - px). \tag{7.6}$$

---

[19] This means that if there are N players and K terminal nodes in the extensive form and if we regard the payoffs as an element in $\mathbb{R}^{NK}$, then the set of payoffs for which the game has more than one equilibrium has Lesbesgue measure zero. This fact suggests that failure of uniqueness requires either a rare coincidence or some reason why the terminal nodes have special structure. Auction games have the latter property: several paths through the auction can lead to identical prices and allocations and hence identical payoffs.

[20] The model developed in the text differs slightly from the original Ausubel–Schwartz model. They modeled a simultaneous ascending auction in which prices of different units could vary, whereas the text models a clock auction with a uniform price.

Alternatively, he can reject and make a bid that is acceptable to bidder i:

$$\beta^j(p) = \max_{x \in [0,1]} (V^j(x) - (p+1)x)$$

$$\text{subject to} \quad \alpha^i(p+1, x) \geq \beta^i(p+1). \tag{7.7}$$

Calculating α^1 and α^2 is straightforward. To calculate β^1 and β^2, observe that if the price p is high enough, then $0 \leq \beta^j(p) \leq \max_{x \in [0,1]} (V^j(x) - (p+1)x) = 0$. So one can construct the two functions iteratively, starting with high prices.

Theorem 7.8. The alternating clock auction game described above has a unique equilibrium. At equilibrium, given the state (p, q), the active bidder j accepts if $\alpha^j(p, q) \geq \beta^j(p)$. Otherwise, the active bidder j makes a bid leading to a state that the other bidder will accept. The bid solves (7.7), and j's payoff is $\max(\alpha^j(p, q), \beta^j(p))$.

Proof. We prove uniqueness by induction. By assumption, there is some price at which the optimal demands are zero; for any sufficiently high price, the active bidder always accepts and the auction ends. The active bidder j's payoff is then $\max(\alpha^j(p, q), \beta^j(p))$. We proceed by mathematical induction.

Let $\bar{p}$ be a price for which the theorem predicts a unique equilibrium. At price $\bar{p} - 1$, the active bidder j has three options. His first option is to accept, earning the payoff $\alpha^j(\bar{p} - 1, q)$. His second option is to make an acceptable offer. By the inductive hypothesis, the other bidder will accept such an offer in the next round, so j will earn payoff $\beta^j(\bar{p} - 1)$ and, by (7.7), the other bidder will earn $\alpha^i(\bar{p}, q) = \beta^i(\bar{p})$. His third option is to make an unacceptable offer. In that case, by the inductive hypothesis, the other bidder's payoff is again $\beta^i(\bar{p})$. The total payoff in the continuation game must be lower in this case than if j makes an acceptable offer, because the price increases in the continuation game. Hence, j's payoff in this case is less if he makes an unacceptable offer.

Hence, j's maximal payoff at $\bar{p} - 1$ is $\max(\alpha^j(\bar{p} - 1, q), \beta^j(\bar{p} - 1))$. Hence, the equilibrium characterization applies to any price. ∎

Corollary 7.9. The final price in the unique equilibrium of the alternating clock auction consistent with backward induction is $p = r$ or $p = r + 1$.

Proof. According to theorem 7.8, in the first round, bidder 1 either accepts or makes a bid leading to a state that 2 accepts. In the first case, the price is $p = r$. In the second, the price is $p = r + 1$.   ∎

Thus, the clock auction with alternating bids does restrict the set of equilibria, but not to competitive equilibria. As in bargaining models with alternating offers, a bidder who can foresee he will ultimately win just x units has an incentive to end the auction early, obtaining those units at a low price. The winning bidders therefore bid just enough to win all the items.

7.2.3.3 Strategic Incentives with Elastic Supply[21]

So far, we have restricted attention to models in which the quantity supplied is fixed and tried to rule out low-price equilibria by studying auction designs in detail. Fixed supplies are an important feature of some real environments. For example, in the California electric power markets of 1999–2000, consumers of power paid a regulated price and an auction market determined supply to meet the fixed demand. Would much be gained if both sides of the market could bid?

In this section, we modify the basic model of a clock auction to accommodate supply that varies with price according to an increasing inverse supply function $P(q)$. Otherwise, the rules of the auction parallel those of the basic clock auction. A (reduced) strategy for bidder i in the game starting with reserve r is a continuous, nonincreasing function $q^i(p|r)$. The auction ends as soon as there is excess supply, that is, it ends at the lowest price $p \geq r$ for which $p \geq P(\sum_{j \in N} q^j(p|r))$. When the market clears at price p, bidder j's payoff is $V(q^j(p)) - pq^j(p)$. Recall that $\hat{q}(p)$ is the competitive demand of a bidder with valuation V.

For purposes of illustration, we assume a symmetric linear–quadratic model, scaling the supply according to the number of bidders N. Thus, let $P(q) = a + b(q/N)$ be the inverse supply function and suppose the bidder value functions are $V(q) = \alpha q - \frac{1}{2}\beta q^2$. Let q_N^* denote the symmetric Cournot quantity, and let $NS(p)$ be the total supply, so that

---

[21] The analysis in this section draws on Klemperer and Meyer (1989) and McAdams (2002). Klemperer and Meyer's analysis characterizes equilibrium in a model in which supply is both uncertain and elastic. They find no equilibria similar to the zero price equilibria. The McAdams analysis observes that very low price equilibria can be eliminated by modifying the rules of the auction in ways that resemble increasing the elasticity of supply.

$S(p) = (p - a)/b = P^{-1}(p)/N$ is the per-bidder supply function corresponding to P.

Theorem 7.10. Define $q(p, r) = \min(\hat{q}(p), \max(q_N^*, S(r)))$. Then, the the strategy $q(p, r)$ is a symmetric Nash equilibrium of the symmetric linear–quadratic[22] clock auction with reserve price r. Moreover, there is no symmetric equilibrium in which the price is less than the Cournot price p_N^*.

Proof. One can extend Theorem 7.6 to this model, so we may limit attention to deviations satisfying $q(p, r) \leq \hat{q}(p)$ and such that the price never exceeds the competitive price p^*. (The outcome in the case where $r > p^*$ is uninteresting and immediate.) On the remaining set of possible prices $[r, p^*]$, because the non-deviators play the equilibrium strategy, their quantities satisfy $q(p, r) = \max(q_N^*, S(r)) \leq \hat{q}(r)$.

To show that deviations are unprofitable, we consider two cases. First suppose $S(r) \leq q_N^*$. Then a bidder who deviates to win quantity q earns $V(q) - qP((q + (N-1)q_N^*)/N)$, his Cournot profit. So no deviation can lead to more than the Cournot profits, which are the equilibrium profits in this case. Hence, there exists no profitable deviation.

Next, suppose $S(r) \geq q_N^*$. Then, a bidder who deviates to win quantity $q \geq S(r)$ earns $V(q) - qP((q + (N-1)S(r))/N)$. Because the Cournot best reply curve slopes downward, if q were unconstrained in this bidder's objective, the bidder would optimally deviate to a quantity $q' < q_N^*$. By concavity, profits decrease in q' on the domain $q' \geq S(r) \geq q_N^*$, so there can be no profitable deviation to a higher quantity than specified by the proposed strategy. Hence, the best reply is some quantity $\bar{q} \leq S(r) \leq \hat{q}(r)$ at which the auction ends immediately at price r. So the best reply maximizes $V(q) - rq$. Because $\hat{q}(r) = \arg\max_q(V(q) - rq) \geq S(r)$, and because the objective is concave, the constrained optimum is at $S(r)$. Therefore, the proposed strategy is a best reply to itself, and so a symmetric equilibrium strategy.

Suppose, contrary to the theorem, that there is some equilibrium with prices below the Cournot price. Then there is some reserve price $r < p_N^*$

---

[22] In the proof of the theorem, we use the linearity to ensure that the bidders' optimization problems are concave and that the Cournot best reply function slopes downwards. The conclusion of the theorem remains true for any supply and value specifications that share these properties.

and some equilibrium such that the market clears immediately, and each bidder acquires his share $S(r)$ of the total quantity $NS(r)$. Because $r < p_N^*$ and supply increases with price, $S(r) < q_N^*$. Because the quantity $S(r)$ is not a Cournot quantity and because the Cournot best reply function slopes downward, the best reply in the Cournot game to the quantities $S(r)$ is some $q' > q_N^*$, which results in a price $p' > r$.

Let us verify that a deviator who demands q' at all prices in the auction increases his payoff by doing so. Indeed, if the other bidders continue to demand $S(r)$, then the deviator earns $V(q') - p'q' > V(S(r)) - rS(r)$, just as in the Cournot model. The only alternative is that the other bidders reduce their quantity demands, and in that case the bidder gets the same quantity q' at a price $p'' < p'$, so the deviation pays $V(q') - p''q' > V(q') - p'q'$.   ∎

A comparison of theorems 7.7 and 7.10 highlights several things. First, the equilibrium strategies are similar in the two theorems. Each bidder starts by demanding a quantity q_0 at the reserve price that is less than his competitive quantity $\hat{q}(r)$ and maintains that quantity demand until the price rises so high that $\hat{q}(p) < q_0$. In theorem 7.7, the quantity is $q_0 = S$, whereas in theorem 7.10 it is $q_0 = \max(q_N^*, S(r))$. In both cases, demand reduction occurs. Second, if the reserve price is less than the Cournot price, then the initially demanded quantities in the identified equilibrium are the Cournot quantities. Finally, there is no equilibrium with prices below the Cournot price.

We conclude that the lowest equilibrium price in the model with upward sloping supply is the Cournot price. Using the linear–quadratic specification, the Cournot price and quantity are

$$p_N^* = \frac{\left(\dfrac{\beta}{b} + \dfrac{1}{N}\right)a + \alpha}{\left(\dfrac{\beta}{b} + \dfrac{1}{N}\right) + 1} \quad \text{and} \quad q_N^* = \frac{\alpha - a}{\beta + b\left(1 + \dfrac{1}{N}\right)}. \tag{7.8}$$

For comparison, the competitive price and quantity are

$$p^* = \frac{\dfrac{\beta}{b}a + \alpha}{\dfrac{\beta}{b} + 1} \quad \text{and} \quad q^* = \frac{\alpha - a}{\beta + b}. \tag{7.9}$$

In both the competitive and Cournot cases, the equilibrium price is a weighted average of the supply and demand intercepts, a and α. The relative weight on the higher intercept a is β/b in a competitive equilibrium, and it is $\beta/b + 1/N$ in the N-bidder Cournot model. Thus, in the familiar fashion for Cournot models, the equilibrium price converges to competitive prices as the number of bidders grows.

This analysis clarifies the reasons for the low-price equilibria in the models of the preceding sections: the zero-price equilibria are Cournot equilibria. This result underlines the importance of making supply elastic to promote competitive auction outcomes. The combination of elastic supply and multiple bidders is especially effective for obtaining auction prices that are near the competitive market price.

7.3 Conclusion

This chapter has focused on auctions that promote uniform pricing. We studied three kinds of auctions. The first were sealed-bid auctions in which the price equates supply and demand. Such auctions have been used to sell Treasury bills in the United States and elsewhere, and also for certain power sales. The second were simultaneous ascending auctions, such as those used by the FCC. The third were clock auctions, which have been used for power sales and for the UK auction of emissions permits.

The three designs are closely related in theory. When a single divisible good is to be sold, the reduced normal form of a certain clock auction is identical to the normal form of the sealed-bid auction. We showed that clock auctions are equivalent to accelerated versions of the simultaneous ascending auction.

If goods are indivisible and unique but are nevertheless substitutes for the bidders, then a competitive equilibrium exists. That is, there exist prices at which the demand for each kind of good is equal to its unit supply. Conversely, if the set of possible bidder valuations includes any for which goods are not substitutes, then there is a profile of individual valuations such that no competitive equilibrium exists.

One can analyze two ascending auction designs with multiple kinds of goods as *tatonnement* processes. In this analysis, we set aside considerations of the bidders' incentives and assumed that all bid straightforwardly, according to their actual demands. We found that goods need to be substitutes for straightforward bidding even to be possible. Moreover, if goods are substitutes, then, despite the monotonicity restrictions imposed by the ascending auction process, straightforward bidding leads to approximately competitive outcomes, with the maximum approximation error proportional to the bid increments.

Practical concerns often dictate the choice of auction design. With a single homogeneous good, the sealed-bid form is quick and simple to administer. The simultaneous ascending auction and the clock auction better suit sales of multiple kinds of goods, because they allow the auction to determine relative prices. When there are a few homogeneous classes, each with many goods, the clock auction design can run much faster than the standard simultaneous ascending auction design, and it leads, with straightforward bidding, to the same near-competitive outcomes. However, to work effectively, clock auctions require more information than just a single bidder demand vector at each price vector. As of this writing, practical bidder interfaces to acquire the needed information have yet to be devised.

A key concern with all the auction designs discussed in this chapter is the possibility of extreme equilibrium prices. We found very general incentives for bidders (buyers) to reduce demand to keep prices low. In all three auction designs, in a variety of simple models, there are Nash equilibria in which prices are at or near the seller's reserve, even if that reserve is much lower than the competitive price. In the simplest models, these low-price equilibria rely on incompletely motivated choices by bidders, but attempts to eliminate the low-price equilibria by enriching the models in various ways have met limited success. Adding uncertainty sometimes (but not always) eliminates the most extreme equilibria. Eliminating weakly dominated strategies and attending to the dynamic structure of the auction both fail to eliminate the extremely low-price equilibria. The alternating-bid model of the clock auction generates the surprising conclusion that the unique equilibrium consistent with backward induction produces very low prices.

The most unfavorable results – those with prices far below the corresponding competitive prices – apply when the supply of goods for sale is fixed. In a model with positive supply elasticity, we found that the worst auction outcomes resemble the results of Cournot competition among buyers. With fixed supply, Cournot outcomes can entail very low prices. The analysis highlights the combined effectiveness for raising revenue of making supply elastic and ensuring that auction participants are numerous.

REFERENCES

Ashenfelter, Orley (1989). "How Auctions Work for Wine and Art." *Journal of Economic Perspectives* **3**: 23–36.

Ashenfelter, Orley and Kathryn Graddy (2002). "Art Auctions: A Survey of Empirical Studies." Center for Economic Policy Studies Working Paper 81.

Ausubel, Lawrence and Peter Cramton (2002). "Demand Reduction and Inefficiency in Multi-unit Auctions." www.cramton.umd.edu/papers1995–1999/98wp-demand-reduction.pdf.

Ausubel, Lawrence M. and Jesse A. Schwartz (1999). "The Ascending Auction Paradox." http://www.market-design.com/files/ausubel-schwartz-ascending-auction-paradox.pdf.

Back, Kerry and Jaime F. Zender (1993). "Auctions of Divisible Goods: On the Rationale for the Treasury Experiment." *Review of Financial Studies* **6**(4): 733–764.

Cramton, Peter and Jesse Schwartz (2001). "Collusive Bidding: Lessons from the FCC Spectrum Auctions." *Journal of Regulatory Economics* **17**: 229–252.

Demange, Gabrielle, David Gale, and Marilda Sotomayor (1986). "Multi-item Auctions." *Journal of Political Economy* **94**: 863–872.

Engelbrecht-Wiggans, Richard and Charles Kahn (1998). "Multi-unit Auctions with Uniform Prices." *Economic Theory* **12**: 227–258.

Gul, Faruk and Ennio Stacchetti (1999). "Walrasian Equilibrium with Gross Substitutes." *Journal of Economic Theory* **87**(1): 9–124.

Gul, Faruk and Ennio Stacchetti (2000). "The English Auction with Differentiated Commodities." *Journal of Economic Theory* **92**(1): 66–95.

Kagel, John H. and Dan Levin (2002). *Common Value Auctions and the Winner's Curse*. Princeton: Princeton University Press.

Kelso, Alexander and Vincent Crawford (1982). "Job Matching, Coalition Formation, and Gross Substitutes." *Econometrica* **50**: 1483.

Klemperer, Paul and Margaret Meyer (1989). "Supply Function Equilibria in Oligopoly under Uncertainty." *Econometrica* **57**(6): 1243–1277.

McAdams, David (2002). "Modifying the Uniform Price Auction to Eliminate 'Collusive Seeming Equilibria'." http://www.mit.edu/~mcadams/papers/mupa.pdf.

Milgrom, Paul (2000). "Putting Auctions Theory to Work: The Simultaneous Ascending Auction." *Journal of Political Economy* **108**(2): 245–272.

Postlewaite, Andrew and John Roberts (1976). "The Incentives for Price-Taking Behavior in Large Exchange Economies." *Econometrica* **44**(1): 115–129.

Swinkels, Jeroen (2001). "Efficiency of Large Private Value Auctions." *Econometrica* **69**(1): 37–68.

Weber, Robert (1997). "Making More from Less: Strategic Demand Reduction in the FCC Spectrum Auctions." *Journal of Economic and Management Strategy* **6**: 529–548.

Wilson, Robert (1979). "Auctions of Shares." *Quarterly Journal of Economics* **XCIII**(4): 675–689.

CHAPTER EIGHT

Package Auctions and Combinatorial Bidding

In chapter 7, we found that multi-object auctions that promote uniform prices raise new problems not found in single item auctions. One is that if the bidders do not regard the goods as substitutes, then market clearing prices can fail to exist. When goods are not substitutes, the conception of auctions as mechanisms to identify market clearing prices is fundamentally misguided. A second problem is that even when goods are substitutes, if the auction identifies uniform prices for each kind of good, there are generally incentives for bidders to bid for fewer units than they really want (*demand reduction*). That behavior can produce both inefficient outcomes and low revenue. So, even in those cases where the search for market clearing prices is not logically doomed to fail, mechanisms that might find market clearing prices when bidders are naïve may still perform poorly when bidders are sophisticated and strategic.

In this chapter, we explore another set of problems. When the auctioneer sells one indivisible good of fixed characteristics, she faces no question about how to package the goods offered for sale. If the characteristics of the good vary or if multiple buyers can divide it, we encounter that complex decision.

This decision can be complicated even in mundane sales, such as the sale of a farm estate after the death of a farmer. Although the whole estate could be sold as a single entity, it could also be divided into smaller pieces for sale to individual bidders with varying demands. For example, a farm auctioneer might sell the house and barn as one package, hoping to attract city dwellers seeking a weekend home. Another package might be the main field, which could attract bids from neighbors with nearby farms. Some of the farm equipment might be sold separately in a larger auction market, and an environmentally sensitive habitat near a forest or river might be sold to a nature conservancy.

Similar packaging decisions occur in spectrum auctions as well. Before the first US spectrum auctions, after regulators chose the portion of the spectrum to be used for PCS telephone service, a debate followed about how to divide that spectrum into licenses. Should the licenses cover the entire nation as European national licenses do? Or, should licenses be regional? Or should the government sell some of each? Should the spectrum bandwidth of the licenses be 10 MHz, or 20 MHz, or 30 MHz? The various spectrum users advocated a wide range of options, lobbying the FCC for licenses that fitted well with their own technologies, existing assets, and business plans, and poorly with their competitors' plans.

In Australia, which held its spectrum auctions soon after the US auctions, regulators considered whether the packaging decision could be "left to the market" by specifying *postage-stamp-size* licenses – tiny in both geographical coverage and bandwidth. That way, some argued, private spectrum users could put together any collections of licenses they liked. This finely divided spectrum could then be sold, it was proposed, using a simultaneous ascending auction.

Chapter 7 provides a foundation for the arguments I raised against the Australian proposal. Because of the fixed costs in establishing a wireless service, any small number of postage-stamp-size licenses would be useless by themselves, having a zero standalone value. A large collection of such licenses, however, might support a very profitable business. Such a pattern of values implies complementarities among the licenses, with all the problems complementarities entail: competitive equilibrium prices may not exist, and the exposure problem may vastly complicate bidding in the simultaneous ascending auction.

In chapters 6 and 7, we saw that when bidders vary in the packages they want to buy, the packaging decision involves trade-offs. Selling items individually when some bidders find some items complementary creates an exposure problem that can depress bidding. Selling items in large packages, however, can make it hard for small bidders to participate. Either way, if the chosen packages attract only a few bidders and participation in the auction is costly, then few bids may be submitted and the auction may produce low prices.

Solving the packaging problem is not always difficult. Dutch flower auctions solve the problem by allowing winning bidders to take as many lots as they wish at the winning price. This design allows competition among bidders who seek to buy one lot or many and encourages participation by a diverse set of bidders.

Packaging problems arise in procurement auctions as well as asset sales. A buyer may conduct a narrow procurement, buying different items in a series of auctions, or he may buy a comprehensive package in a single auction from a bidder who provides a discount for a high-value purchase. Either choice may exclude some bidders, leading to less competition and, presumably, higher prices for the buyer.

This chapter focuses on a set of auction designs that let the bidders choose the packages for themselves. These *package auction* or *combinatorial auction* designs have received only limited use in the past, partly because the auctions can quickly become complicated as the number of objects sold grows. With many bids for overlapping packages, just determining the identity of the winning bidder – the *winner determination problem* – is a hard computational problem that has become a hot topic in computer science. The very difficulty of the auctioneer's problem, however, makes it hard for bidders in a large package auction to forecast the consequences of their bids and hard to check that the seller ran the auction honestly.

Smaller package auctions are easier to run and have long been used for bankruptcy sales. Cassady (1967) reports examples from the mid-twentieth century in which some bidders bid on individual assets of the bankrupt business while others bid on the *entirety* of the assets. An entirety bid would typically take the form of a sealed bid before the individual assets were sold, whereas the individual assets might be sold by ascending auctions. The auctioneer would compare the sum of the winning bids for the individual items with the best entirety bid and choose the winning bid(s) to maximize the total revenue. Similar auctions are still common in bankruptcy sales.

Recently, several designs have been implemented that allow bidders much greater flexibility to name the packages on which they bid. The London Transportation Authority procures bus services from private operators in a sealed-bid auction that allows bids on all combinations of routes, and 46% of winning bids involve combinations.[1] That auction is relatively small and bids are processed manually. Between 1997

---

[1] Cantillon and Pesendorfer (2003).

and 1999, the Chilean government phased in a combinatorial auction for firms that supply meals to schoolchildren in various regions of the country. Proposed variations in the design weight both the bid amount and the supplier quality and include constraints to ensure that there are multiple suppliers in each region and that no firm obtains too dominant a share of the business. According to a recent study, costs have fallen by 22% since the adoption of this program.[2] Similarly, in 2002, IBM and Mars, Inc. collaborated on a combinatorial procurement auction to supply Mars' candy factories.[3] The IBM–Mars team designed two kinds of auctions. One was relatively simple for bidders and allowed them to offer volume discounts in conjunction with their bids. A second allowed suppliers to offer packages. In addition, the design allowed the buyer to impose constraints, for example to avoid allocating any one supplier too large a portion of the total procurement.

The ascending auction planned for Federal Communications Commission (FCC) Auction #31, which was supposed to sell spectrum licenses in the 700 MHz band, was designed to permit bids for any of the 4095 possible packages of the twelve licenses on offer. This is probably the most ambitious package auction designed for actual use. The FCC tested an early version of this design using laboratory experiments. The package design required a long training session for the bidders and took more rounds to run than the traditional FCC design. However, the experimenters report that the package design also led to more efficient outcomes, at least with complementarities among licenses.[4]

Another package design is one I tailored for the sale of the generating portfolio of Portland General Electric (PGE), an Oregon utility with contracts and interests in generating facilities in several states. The utility sought to divest its entire generating portfolio in order to free itself from regulation as a power generator. Complicating the situation was the fact that the contracts included long-term supply contracts with various California cities, which demanded the right to bid for their own individual contracts if the generating portfolio were to be sold. These cities had

---

[2] Epstein, Henríquez, Catalán, Weintraub, and Martínez (2002) and Weintraub (2003).

[3] Hohner, Rich, Ng, Reed, Davenport, Kalagnanam, Lee, and An (2002).

[4] Cybernomics (2000) summarizes the results. I report this claim with some skepticism, because Cybernomics has not fulfilled requests by the FCC, the author, and others to see raw data from these experiments.

considerable political clout and might have blocked a procedure that did not allow bidding on individual assets. PGE was equally insistent that all bids must cover the entire portfolio, because a sale of individual assets and contracts could leave some assets unsold, leaving it subject to continued regulation.

To accommodate this situation, I proposed an auction to take place in two stages. At the first stage, commercial bidders would make preliminary bids for the entire portfolio, and cities would bid for the particular contracts that they would name.[5] The investment banker running the auction would invite those that made the highest preliminary bids for the whole portfolio and those that made qualified bids for the individual contracts to participate at the second stage. All those that qualified would be invited to sign a confidentiality agreement and gain access to a data room where they could find detailed information about the assets and contracts offered at the auction. After a reasonable period for review of the data, the second-stage auction would be conducted. The cities would again be eligible to bid on their individual contracts, and the invited commercial bidders could again bid for the entire portfolio. What was novel in this design, however, is that the commercial bidders would also name *decrements* to apply to the relevant individual contracts. These decrements would be applied to reduce the commercial bidder's price in case it was an auction winner but some individual contracts were awarded to one or more other bidders. For example, if the winning bid for the portfolio specified a decrement of $1 million for contract A and if the highest individual bid for contract A were $2 million, then contract A would be awarded to the bidder that had made the $2 million bid, and the portfolio bidder would pay its bid minus $1 million.

Given all the bids at the second stage, the seller would then select the allocation that maximized the total revenue. The allocation would award the portfolio to a single commercial bidder, possibly with some of the individual contracts removed and awarded to the cities. This package auction design is simple to implement and promotes competition both among the commercial bidders seeking to acquire the PGE portfolio and between those bidders and the cities bidding for individual contracts. It enables competition for the individual contracts on the equal basis required by the cities and ensures that any auction sale would meet PGE's requirement that the entire portfolio must be sold.

---

[5] See chapter 6 for an analysis of preliminary bids and indicative bidding.

The granddaddy of applied package auction designs is the early proposal for a combinatorial auction sale of paired airport take-off and landing slots suggested by Rassenti, Bulfin, and Smith (1982). The authors also tested their proposal in an economic laboratory experiment, demonstrating that a package design could perform better than individual slot sales.

The IBM–Mars design confronts an important practical problem: how to incorporate policy constraints into an auction design. In procurement auctions, bidders may want to ensure that preferred suppliers or minority-owned firms receive a certain fraction of contracts, or that sources of supply are geographically dispersed to avoid disruptions, or that the suppliers have sufficient capacity to expand production, and so on. These complex constraints make deciding which set of bids to accept more complicated than just finding the highest or lowest prices.

The most novel aspects of some new auction designs are the ways they handle complex constraints. For example, Brewer and Plott (1996) designed an auction to allocate use of a single north–south railroad track in northern Sweden. The main constraint for their problem was that the trains must be scheduled to avoid crashes. In their auction design, a bid expresses a price the bidder will pay for a right to use the track under specific conditions, say, the right to a northbound departure at 10:00 A.M. using a train traveling at 50 km/h. Although such bids are simple in form, selecting the bids that maximize the total price requires the use of sophisticated optimization routines.

Brewer and Plott designed a simple ascending auction mechanism in which the auctioneer at each round selects the jointly feasible collection of bids that maximizes the seller's revenue. In their laboratory experiments testing the design, they found the design realized over 97% of the potential scheduling efficiencies.

Since the pioneering package auction experiment by Rassenti, Bulfin, and Smith (1982), several other experiments have also been influential. Banks, Ledyard, and Porter (1989) explored two kinds of iterative package auctions, in which bidders submit bids in a series of rounds and can raise their bids from round to round. In both versions, the winning bidders are those who submit the highest total package bid. In one version, prices follow the Vickrey pricing rule; in the other, each winning bidder pays his own bid. Experimental subjects bid in these ascending package auctions or participated in alternative procedures representing administrative processes and markets. The ascending package auctions outperformed the alternatives, on average realizing 80% of the available efficiencies.

In the run-up to the FCC's first spectrum auctions, Charles Plott ran a small set of experiments that confirm the superiority of the simultaneous ascending auction to simpler sequential designs. Later experiments by Ledyard, Porter, and Rangel (1997) confirmed the theoretical prediction that the FCC design degrades in the presence of complementarities, helping to spur interest in package auction designs at the FCC.

The three package auctions discussed in this chapter all permit bidders to place a different bid on each package without restricting relationships among the bids. As we shall see, this flexibility facilitates making a tractable analysis. However, such auctions require more bids and are more computationally complex than auctions with more restrictive package structures,[6] and they may impose a greater cognitive burden on the bidders.[7]

8.1 Vickrey Auctions and the Monotonicity Problems[8]

In chapter 2, we analyzed the advantages of Vickrey auctions and illustrated their disadvantages in simple package bidding environments. In this section, we explore the monotonicity problems of the Vickrey auction in greater detail. We show that these problems do not appear if goods are substitutes for all bidders, but that they are hard to rule out in other cases. If there is *any* bidder for whom it is not true that all goods are substitutes, then there exist additive valuations for the other bidders that create problematic examples similar to the ones of chapter 2, with low revenues, shill bidders, loser collusion, and so forth.

Before we can formally characterize the scope of the Vickrey auction's monotonicity problems, we need to state more precisely what we mean by "low revenues." Our example showed that it is possible for the Vickrey auction to yield *zero revenues* for valuable licenses, but would like to say revenues can be "too low" even under less extreme conditions.

Here, we will use the theory of the core to assess the adequacy of Vickrey payoffs (revenue for the seller, profit for the bidders). Associated

---

[6] Rothkopf, Pekec, and Harstad (1998) study designs that are simplified for ease of computation and for transparency. Lehmann, O'Callaghan, and Shoham (2002) study how to design auctions that perform well when the seller optimizes imperfectly.

[7] Parkes, Ungar, and Foster (1999) and Parkes and Ungar (2000) analyze the burdens of alternative package auction designs on the bidders. Nisan (2000) studies bidder interfaces, examining which *bidding languages* allow bidders to express all possible valuations and yet provide compact expressions for particular kinds of (presumably) common valuations.

[8] The theorems in this section are all drawn from Ausubel and Milgrom (2002).

with the outcome of any game is a payoff vector, or *imputation*. An outcome is a *core outcome*, and the corresponding payoff vector is a *core imputation*, if (1) the outcome is feasible and (2) no coalition can identify an alternative feasible outcome that its own members can implement and that strictly increases all coalition members' payoffs. If some coalition can identify such an alternative, then that coalition is said to *block* the proposed outcome and imputation.

The outcome of a second-price auction for a single good is always a core outcome. Also, it is well known that competitive equilibrium outcomes are always core outcomes, so an outcome outside the core can be labeled uncompetitive. By definition, core outcomes eliminate any incentive for any coalition to renege once the results of the auction are announced. This property can be quite important in practice, because execution of trades is a common problem in real-world transactions. Finally, because the seller is always a part of any blocking coalition in this model, the core implies a potentially interesting revenue standard, which we discuss below.

To characterize core outcomes for the Vickrey auction, we first define the game in coalitional form associated with the auction. That game is (N, w), where N is the set of players in the game and w is the *coalitional value function*. In our setting, for any coalition of players $S \subset N$, the coalitional value function is[9]

$$w(S) = \begin{cases} \max_{x \in X} \left\{ \sum_{l \in S} v^l(x^l) \right\} & \text{if } 0 \in S, \\ 0 & \text{if } 0 \notin S. \end{cases} \tag{8.1}$$

If the seller is not a member of coalition S, then the value of the coalition is zero, because the buyers in the model have nothing to trade among themselves. Otherwise, the value is the maximum value the coalition can obtain by trading with the seller.

Let $\pi^l = v^l(x^l) - p^l$ be the profit of agent l from any proposed transaction and set of transfers. Then the set of core payoffs is defined as follows:

$$\text{Core}(N, w) = \left\{ \pi \,\middle|\, \sum_{l \in N} \pi^l = w(N), \; (\forall S \subset N) \; w(S) \leq \sum_{l \in S} \pi^l \right\}. \tag{8.2}$$

---

[9] We limit attention here to transferable-utility games, so the payoff profiles that are feasible for a coalition are determined entirely by $w(S)$ – the total value available for sharing among the members of the coalition S.

If some payoff vector π is not in the core, then there is some coalition S for which the total payoff $w(S)$ is higher than the members' total payoffs in π. So there is some way to share the total that makes all members of S strictly better off.

To see how the core functions as a revenue standard, let us repeat our earlier low-price example. In that example, there were two items for sale. Bidders 1 and 2 had values of $1 billion and $900 million, respectively, for the package of two items, while bidders 3 and 4 each had values of $1 billion for a single item. Neither bidder 1 nor bidder 2 valued a single license alone, and neither bidder 3 nor bidder 4 valued a second license. In this example, the allocation is in the core if and only if bidders 3 and 4 acquire the items, neither pays more than $1 billion, and the seller's total revenue is at least $1 billion. The Vickrey auction does allocate the items to bidders 3 and 4, but at a price of zero; thus, the Vickrey allocation falls outside the core. This example verifies that the core does imply a minimum revenue standard and that the Vickrey auction sometimes fails that standard.

What is the precise relationship between the Vickrey outcome and the core? Are there situations in which we can reliably predict that the Vickrey outcome will lie in the core? Are there others in which we can predict that the Vickrey outcome will not lie in the core, because the seller's revenues are too low? Can we characterize the economic conditions under which the Vickrey outcome is most likely to fall outside the core?

A few cases contribute intuition. The Vickrey auction for a single good assigns the good to the bidder with the highest value for a price equal to the second highest value. No losing bidder has a value greater than that *Vickrey price*, so none can profitably offer to pay the seller more. Hence, the outcome in the one-good case lies in the core.

The same conclusion holds when each bidder's value for a package of goods is *additive*, meaning that the bidder's package value is the sum of the values of the individual goods in the package. In this case, a Vickrey auction for many goods operates effectively as a collection of second-price auctions. Each bidder in the Vickrey auction acquires an item when his value is the highest, and his total price is the sum of the second-highest values of all goods he buys.

We now extend this intuition with a series of theorems.

8.1.1 Bidders' Vickrey Payoffs Bound Their Core Payoffs

Our examples have shown that it is possible for revenues in a Vickrey auction to be lower than the seller's payoff at any core outcome. In the models we are studying, one can say more: each bidder's Vickrey payoff is equal to his highest payoff at any point in the core. To state this formally, let π_V^i denote participant i's payoff in a Vickrey auction.

Theorem 8.1. For each bidder i, the Vickrey payoff is

$$\pi_V^i = w(N) - w(N - i) = \max\{\pi^i | \pi \in \text{Core}(N, w)\}.$$

In addition, $\pi_V^0 = w(N) - \sum_{l \in N-0} \pi_V^l$.

Proof. Recall from chapter 2 that the pivot mechanism payment formula (suppressing the arguments of the functions $\hat{p}$ and $\hat{x}$) is $\hat{p}^i = V(X, N - i) - \sum_{j \in N-i} v^j(\hat{x})$, where $\hat{x}$ is the decision that maximizes the total payoff. Applying this formula, a bidder's Vickrey profit is $v^i(\hat{x}) - \hat{p}^i = \sum_{j \in N} v^j(\hat{x}) - V(X, N - i) = V(X, N) - V(X, N - i)$. By definition, $w(N) = V(X, N)$ and $w(N - i) = V(X, N - i)$, so the first equality is established.

By definition, for any $\pi \in \text{Core}(N, w)$, $\sum_{j \in N-i} \pi^j \geq w(N - i)$ and $\sum_{j \in N} \pi^j = w(N)$. So $\pi^i = \sum_{j \in N} \pi^j - \sum_{j \in N-i} \pi^j \leq w(N) - w(N - i) = \pi_V^i$. By inspection, the payoff profile π given by $\pi^i = \pi_V^i$, $\pi^0 = w(N - i)$, and $\pi^j = 0$ for other bidders j is a core payoff profile, so $\max\{\pi^i | \pi \in \text{Core}(N, w)\} \geq \pi_V^i$. Combining these proves that $\pi_V^i = \max\{\pi^i | \pi \in \text{Core}(N, w)\}$.

Because the Vickrey outcome is efficient, the total payoff to all participants must be $w(N)$, so the seller's payoff must be $\pi_V^0 = w(N) - \sum_{l \in N-0} \pi_V^l$. ∎

8.1.2 Vickrey Auctions and the Entry Puzzle

Next we study the most basic monotonicity problem of the Vickrey auction, which is that increased competition among bidders does not generally reduce bidder payoffs and increase seller revenues. That is, entry can harm the seller and benefit at least some existing bidders. To state this idea formally, let $\pi_V(S)$ be the Vickrey payoffs when only members of coalition S participate in the auction. We also introduce the following two definitions.

Definitions

1. A Vickrey auction displays *payoff monotonicity* if (1) $\pi_V^i(S - j) \geq \pi_V^i(S)$ for all S, and $i, j \in S - 0$, and (2) $\pi_V^0(S - j) \leq \pi_V^0(S)$.

2. The coalitional value function is *bidder-submodular* if for any coalitions S and T that include the seller,[10]

$$w(S) + w(T) \geq w(S \cup T) + w(S \cap T). \tag{8.3}$$

According to the first definition, payoff monotonicity means that adding bidders can only reduce the other bidders' payoffs and increase the seller's payoffs. The second of these two conditions is implied by the first,[11] so we omit it from the proofs below.

Theorem 8.2. The Vickrey auction satisfies payoff monotonicity for the coalitional game (N, w) if and only if w is bidder-submodular.

Proof. The payoff monotonicity inequalities can be rewritten as

$$w(S - j) - w(S - i - j) \geq w(S) - w(S - i). \tag{8.4}$$

If the coalitional value function is bidder-submodular, then applying (8.3) to the coalitions $S - i$ and coalition $S - j$ yields (8.4). So bidder submodularity implies payoff monotonicity. To show the converse, let $S' \subset S''$ be coalitions that include the seller. Observe that repeated applications of (8.4) imply that for any $j \notin S''$,

$$w(S' \cup \{j\}) - w(S') \geq w(S'' \cup \{j\}) - w(S''). \tag{8.5}$$

Then, for arbitrary S and T, let $T - S = \{i_1, \ldots, i_m\}$. We have

$$w(S \cup T) - w(S) = \sum_{j=1}^{m} (w(S \cup \{i_1, \ldots, i_j\}) - w(S \cup \{i_1, \ldots, i_{j-1}\}))$$

$$\leq \sum_{j=1}^{m} (w(S \cap T \cup \{i_1, \ldots, i_j\})$$

$$- w(S \cap T \cup \{i_1, \ldots, i_{j-1}\}))$$

$$= w(T) - w(S \cap T).$$

---

[10] Generally, submodularity is a property of functions defined on lattices. In the present application, the relevant lattice is the set of coalitions partially ordered by set inclusion.

[11] Formally, given the inequalities (1) in the definition of payoff monotonicity, $\pi_V^0(S - j)$ $= w(S - j) - \sum_{l \in S-0-j} \pi_V^l(S - j) = w(S - j) + [w(S) - w(S - j) - \pi_V^j(S)] - \sum_{l \in S-0-j} \pi_V^l(S - j)$ $\leq w(S) - \sum_{l \in S-0} \pi_V^l(S) = \pi_V^0(S)$. So the inequality (2) is redundant.

The equalities follow from summing the telescoping sequences, and the inequality follows by applying (8.5) to each term of the sum. We conclude that payoff monotonicity implies bidder submodularity. ∎

8.1.3 When Are Vickrey Outcomes in the Core?

Next, let us imagine the possibility that only some of the potential bidders will actually participate in the auction. We may then ask: Under what conditions on the coalitional value function w is the Vickrey outcome guaranteed to be a core outcome?

Theorem 8.3. The coalitional value function w is bidder-submodular if and only if for every coalition S with $0 \in S \subset N$, one has $\pi_V(S) \in$ Core(S, w).

Proof. Suppose the coalitional value function w is bidder-submodular, and let $S' \subset S$ be coalitions that include the seller. Number the bidders so that $S' = \{0, 1, \ldots, k\}$ and $S = \{0, 1, \ldots, n\}$ with $1 \leq k \leq n$. By bidder submodularity, for $1 \leq l \leq n$, $w(S) - w(S - l) \geq w(\{0, \ldots, l\}) - w(\{0, \ldots, l - 1\})$, so

$$\sum_{l \in S'} \pi_V^l(S) = w(S) - \sum_{l=k+1}^{n} \pi_V^l(S)$$

$$= w(S) - \sum_{l=k+1}^{n} [w(S) - w(S - l)]$$

$$\geq w(S) - \sum_{l=k+1}^{n} [w(\{0, \ldots, l\}) - w(\{0, \ldots, l - 1\})]$$

$$= w(S) - [w(S) - w(S')]$$

$$= w(S').$$

Hence, S' is not a blocking coalition. Because S' was an arbitrary coalition including the seller, there is no blocking coalition. Because the Vickrey outcome is efficient, $\sum_{l \in S} \pi_V^l(S) = w(S)$. It follows that $\pi_V(S) \in$ Core(S, w).

Conversely, suppose w is not bidder-submodular. Then by theorem 8.2, there exists a coalition S and bidders $i, j \in S$ such that $w(S - j) - w(S - i - j) < w(S) - w(S - i)$. But then $\sum_{l \in S-i-j} \pi_V^l(S) = w(S) - \pi_V^i - \pi_V^j = w(S) - (w(S) - w(S - i)) - (w(S) - w(S - j)) < w(S - i - j)$.

Because the core requires that $\sum_{l \in S-i-j} \pi_V^l(S) \geq w(S - i - j)$, we have $\pi_V(S) \notin \text{Core}(N, w)$. ∎

8.1.4 Substitute Goods and Core Outcomes

The previous sections have based the analysis on the coalitional value function w and highlighted the role of a condition on w, namely, that w is bidder-submodular. In most economic problems, it is goods valuations that are primitive and the coalitional value function is derived as in (8.1). In this section, we establish that the desired condition on coalitional values is closely related to the condition that the bidders regard the goods as substitutes.

To state the main result precisely, let $\mathbf{V}$ denote the set of possible bidder values of the M goods offered for sale in the auction. Let $\mathbf{V}_{\text{add}}$ denote the set of all additive value functions for goods such that all the individual goods' values are non-negative.

Theorem 8.4. Suppose that $\mathbf{V}_{\text{add}} \subset \mathbf{V}$. Then (i) the coalition value function w corresponding to every profile of goods valuations drawn from $\mathbf{V}$ is bidder-submodular if and only if (ii) at every valuation in $\mathbf{V}$, all goods are substitutes.

Remarks. With just two goods, the substitutes condition is equivalent to the condition that the goods valuations are submodular. With more than two goods, however, the substitutes condition is more restrictive. It implies that goods valuations are submodular,[12] but submodularity of goods valuations does not imply that the goods are substitutes.[13]

---

[12] If v is not submodular, then there exists $x \in \{0, 1\}^M$, some $\alpha > 0$, and some m and m' such that $v(1, 1, x_{-m,m'}) - v(0, 1, x_{-m,m'}) > \alpha > v(1, 0, x_{-m,m'}) - v(0, 0, x_{-m,m'})$, where the first and second arguments of v correspond to x_m and $x_{m'}$, respectively. Set prices as follows: let $p_m = \alpha$; and for $n \neq m$, m', $x_n = 0 \Rightarrow p_n = \infty$, and $x_n = 1 \Rightarrow p_n = 0$. These prices determine the demands for the goods besides m and m' to be $x_{-m,m'}$. Then one can verify that if $p_{m'} = \infty$, the demand for good m is zero (because the marginal value is less than the price: $v(1, 0, x_{-m,m'}) - v(0, 0, x_{-m,m'}) < \alpha$) and if $p_{m'} = 0$, the demand for good m is 1 (because the marginal value is greater than the price: $v(1, 1, x_{-m,m'}) - v(0, 1, x_{-m,m'}) > \alpha$). This contradicts the definition of substitutes.

[13] For example, suppose there are three goods, with $v(x_1, x_2, x_3) = x_1 + x_2 + x_3 - x_1 x_2 - x_2 x_3$, for $x \in \{0, 1\}^3$. This valuation is submodular, as one can check by verifying that $\partial^2 v / \partial x_i \partial x_j \leq 0$ for all $i \neq j$. Bidder demand is determined by solving $\max_{x_i \in \{0,1\}} (v(x_1, x_2, x_3) - \sum_{m=1}^3 p_m x_m)$. If goods prices satisfy $p \in (0, 1)^3$, then bidder demand is $(1, 0, 1)$ if $(1 - p_2) < (1 - p_1) + (1 - p_3)$, and $(0, 1, 0)$ if $(1 - p_2) > (1 - p_1) + (1 - p_3)$. In particular, an increase in the price p_1 can lead to reduction in demand for good 3, contrary to the definition of substitutes.

To prove that the coalition value function is bidder-submodular, we need the strong condition that goods are substitutes rather than the weaker condition that valuations are submodular. In the proof, we show how to use any failure of the condition that goods are substitutes (which we sometimes call the *substitutes condition*) to construct an example in which w is not bidder-submodular.

In outline, the proof proceeds as follows. First, we obtain a dual characterization of the substitutes condition that applies even though goods are indivisible. According to this characterization, goods are substitutes if and only if the corresponding indirect utility function is submodular. Using this characterization, we show that if goods are substitutes for every member of a coalition, then they are also substitutes in the coalitional value function, and that the opportunity cost to a coalition S of giving away any good or package of goods z increases as the coalition adds members. If a new member joins the coalition and the coalition gives him package z, the incremental value of the new member, which is the new member's value of package z minus the coalition's opportunity cost of that package, decreases in the coalition's size. Maximizing the new member's incremental value over z preserves the property that the member's incremental value decreases in the size of the coalition, so the coalitional value function is bidder-submodular.

Proof. We may assume without loss of generality that each bidder distinguishes all the goods, so for any bidder l and good m, we have $x_m^l \in \{0, 1\}$. Given bidder l's valuation v^l, the indirect utility function and its associated demand are defined by

$$u^l(p) = \max_z (v^l(z) - p \cdot z),$$

$$x^l(p) \in \arg\max_z (v^l(z) - p \cdot z).$$

As the maximum of a finite number of linear functions, u^l is continuous and convex. The envelope theorem (see chapter 3) further implies that at every point where demand is uniquely defined, the partial derivative is given by $\partial u^l(p)/\partial p_m = -x_m^l(p)$, where $x_m^l(p)$, the mth component of $x^l(p)$, is the quantity bidder l demands of the mth good at price vector p. By definition, the substitutes condition is satisfied if and only if $x_m^l(p)$ is nondecreasing in p_j for all $j \neq m$, or, equivalently, $\partial u^l(p)/\partial p_m$ is nonincreasing in p_j for all $j \neq m$. Therefore, goods are substitutes for l if and only if $u^l(p)$ is submodular.

Let S be a coalition that includes the seller. Coalition S's value for a package z is $v^S(z) \equiv \max_{x \in X(z)} \sum_{l \in S} v^l(x^l)$, where $X(z) \equiv \{x \geq 0 |$ $\sum_{j \in N} x^j \leq z, (\forall j, m)\; x_m^j \in \{0, 1\}\}$. The corresponding coalition indirect utility function is

$$u^S(p) = \max_z \{v^S(z) - p \cdot z\} = \sum_{l \in S} u^l(p). \tag{8.6}$$

As the function $u^S(p)$ is the sum of continuous, convex, submodular functions, it too is continuous, convex, and submodular. Also, for any z and p,

$$u^S(p) \geq v^S(z) - p \cdot z. \tag{8.7}$$

Let B be a large number that exceeds the incremental value of any good to any coalition. By inequality (8.7), for all z, $v^S(z) \leq \min_{p \in [0,B]^M} \{u^S(p) + p \cdot z\}$. Define $p = p(z)$ by $p_m = 0$ if $z_m = 1$ and $p_m = B$ otherwise. Then $u^S(p(z)) = v^S(z) - p(z) \cdot z$. Therefore, $v^S(z) = u^S(p(z)) + p(z) \cdot z \geq \min_{p \in [0,B]^M} \{u^S(p) + p \cdot z\}$. Combining the two preceding inequalities yields the *duality equation*:

$$v^S(z) = \min_{p \in [0,B]^M} \{u^S(p) + p \cdot z\}. \tag{8.8}$$

(This equation, which is familiar when goods are divisible, is thus proved to apply even though the goods are indivisible.)

The objective in (8.8) is continuous, convex, and submodular in p. Also, because each $u^l(p)$ is antitone (weakly decreasing), the function $u^S(p)$ has antitone differences in (p, S). The prices in (8.8) are constrained to lie in a compact interval, so the constraint set is a sublattice of $\mathbb{R}^M$. Hence, by the Topkis monotonicity theorem,[14] the set of minimizers has a maximum element $p(S|z)$, which is an isotone (weakly increasing) function of S.

If $z_m = 0$, then, by inspection of (8.8), $p_m(S|z) = B$.

Because $u^S(p(S|z)) = v^S(z) - p(S|z) \cdot z$ and $u^S(p) = \max_z\{v^S(z) - p \cdot z\}$, we have $z \in \arg\max_{z'}\{v^S(z') - p(S|z) \cdot z'\}$. Suppose $z_m = 1$. For $\varepsilon > 0$, set $p'_\varepsilon = p(S|z) + \varepsilon 1_m$, where 1_m is a vector with a 1 in the mth coordinate and zeros elsewhere. Because $p(S|z)$ is the maximum element among the set of minimizers, the demand for good m at price vector p'_ε is zero. By construction, the demand for good j for which $z_j = 0$ is zero at price vector

---

[14] See Topkis (1978) or Topkis (1998).

p'_ε, because $p'_{\varepsilon j} = B$. By the substitutes condition, increasing the price from $p(S|z)$ to p'_ε leaves the demand for the goods besides m undiminished. Hence, for all positive ε, we have $z - 1_m \in \arg\max_{z'}\{v^S(z') - p'_\varepsilon \cdot z'\}$. By Berge's theorem of the maximum,[15] the same must hold when $\varepsilon = 0$: $z - 1_m \in \arg\max_{z'}(v^S(z') - p(S|z) \cdot z')$. Therefore, $v^S(z - 1_m) - p(S|z) \cdot (z - 1_m) = v^S(z) - p(S|z) \cdot z$, so $p_m(S|z) = v^S(z) - v^S(z - 1_m)$.

Summarizing the main conclusion of the last two paragraphs:

$$p_m(S|z) = \begin{cases} B & \text{if } z_m = 0, \\ v^S(z) - v^S(z - 1_m) & \text{if } z_m = 1. \end{cases} \tag{8.9}$$

For any packages of goods $z' \leq z$, let $A = \{m | z'_m = 1\} = \{1, \ldots, n\}$. Then the opportunity cost to the coalition S of forgoing goods z' is $v^S(z) - v^S(z - z') = \sum_{m=1}^{n}(v^S(z - \sum_{j=1}^{m-1} 1_j) - v^S(z - \sum_{j=1}^{m} 1_j)) = \sum_{m=1}^{n} p_m(S|z - \sum_{j=1}^{m-1} 1_j)$. Because each summand is isotone in S, the function $v^S(z) - v^S(z - z')$ is isotone in S.

Because $w(S) = v^S(z)$, we have $w(S \cup \{l\}) - w(S) = \max_{z'}\{v^l(z') + v^S(z - z') - v^S(z)\}$. Because the maximand in this expression is nonincreasing in S, the maximum is nonincreasing in S as well. We conclude that w is bidder-submodular.

Next, suppose there is some valuation $v^1 \in \mathbf{V}$ for which the substitutes condition fails. Then there exist goods m and n, a price vector $(\bar{p}_m, p_{-m})$, and an $\varepsilon > 0$ such that (i) the buyer has unique demands (for all the goods) at price vector $(\bar{p}_m, p_{-m})$, and $x^1_m(\bar{p}_m, p_{-m}) = 1$, and (ii) the buyer has unique demands (for all the goods) at price vector $(\bar{p}_m + \varepsilon, p_{-m})$, and $x^1_n(\bar{p}_m + \varepsilon, p_{-m}) = 0$. As utility is quasi-linear, we infer that $1 = x^1_m(\bar{p}_m, p_{-m}) \neq x^1_m(\bar{p}_m + \varepsilon, p_{-m}) = 0$. By continuity, there exists $p_m \in (\bar{p}_m, \bar{p}_m + \varepsilon)$ such that at price vector $p = (p_m, p_{-m})$ the buyer's demand set contains a package including both goods, n and m, and one excluding both goods.

Thus, failure of the substitutes condition implies that there exist two goods, m and n, and a price vector, p, with $p_n, p_m > 0$, and with these two properties: (1) for all $\hat{p}_m \in [0, p_m)$, there is a unique maximizer x' of $v^1(x) - (\hat{p}_m, p_{-m}) \cdot x$, and it satisfies $x'_n = x'_m = 1$; (2) for all $\hat{p}_m \in (p_m, B]$, there is a unique maximizer x'', and it satisfies $x''_n = x''_m = 0$.

We use these prices to create bidder valuations that contradict bidder submodularity, as follows. Let $\hat{p}_m > p_m$, and suppose that bidders 2, 3,

---

[15] See Royden (1968).

and 4 have these valuations: $v^2(x) = \sum_{k \neq n,m} p_k x_k$, $v^3(x) = p_m x_m + p_n x_n$, and $v^4(x) = \hat{p}_m x_m$. Because x' is optimal for buyer 1 at the price vector p above, and because $x'_n = x'_m = 1$, there exists an optimal allocation for the coalition $\{0, 1, 2, 3\}$ that assigns no goods to buyer 3 and that is therefore feasible for the coalition $\{0, 1, 2\}$, so $w(0123) = w(012)$. Because x'' is the unique optimum for buyer 1 at the price vector $(p_{-m}, \hat{p}_m)$, the optimal allocation for the coalition $\{0, 1, 2, 3, 4\}$, which gives good n to bidder 3, is different from any optimal allocation for $\{0, 1, 2, 4\}$, so $w(01234) > w(0124)$. Therefore, $w(01234) + w(012) > w(0123) + w(0124)$. This proves that w is not bidder-submodular.   ∎

8.1.5 Substitute Goods and Vickrey Outcomes

The last result of this section combines and extends the preceding theorems. It shows that when the substitutes condition is satisfied, the Vickrey auction is immune to the various monotonicity problems identified in the earlier examples. However, when the substitutes condition is not satisfied, then one can always construct preference profiles that induce monotonicity problems.

Theorem 8.5. Suppose that the goods are unique and that bidder valuations are drawn from a set **V** such that $\mathbf{V}_{add} \subset \mathbf{V}$. Then the following statements are equivalent:

(1) For every valuation in **V**, the individual items are substitutes.
(2) For every profile of valuations drawn from **V**, the Vickrey outcome is in the core.
(3) For every profile of valuations drawn from **V**, the Vickrey outcome exhibits payoff monotonicity.
(4) For every profile of valuations drawn from **V**, losing bidders in the Vickrey auction have no profitable joint deviation.
(5) For every profile of valuations drawn from **V**, no bidder can gain by using shill bidders.[16]

Proof. Theorems 8.2–8.4 establish the equivalences of conditions (1)–(3).

---

[16] Yokoo, Sakurai, and Matsubara (2000) show that if the coalition value function is bidder-submodular, then there exists no shill bidding strategy that allows a bidder to win its equilibrium allocation at a lower price than its Vickrey price. The theorem reported here uses a stronger assumption (namely, that goods are substitutes) and reaches a stronger conclusion: participants have no profitable joint deviation of any kind.

To show (1)$\Rightarrow$(4), let $v^S(z)$ be as defined in (8.8); it is the value that the coalition S gets from the goods bundle z. As observed in the proof of Theorem 8.4, the dual profit function u^S associated with v^S is a submodular function, so v^S is a substitutes valuation. In particular, v^S is submodular. Let $\bar{x}$ denote the total bundle of goods offered for sale, and $X(\bar{x})$ the corresponding set of feasible allocations. Suppose a coalition S of losing bidders deviates, reporting values $(\tilde{v}^l)_{l \in S}$ and $\tilde{v}^l = v^l$ for $l \in N - S$. Suppose the Vickrey goods allocation after the deviation is $(\tilde{x}^l)_{l \in N}$. The Vickrey price paid by bidder l to acquire its bundle is then given by

$$
p^l = \max_{x \in X(\bar{x})} \left(\sum_{j \in S-l} \tilde{v}^j(x^j) + \sum_{j \in N-S} v^j(x^j) \right)
$$
$$
- \left(\sum_{j \in S-l} \tilde{v}^j(\tilde{x}^j) + \sum_{j \in N-S} v^j(\tilde{x}^j) \right). \tag{8.10}
$$

It follows that

$$
p^l \geq \max_{\substack{x \in X(\bar{x}) \\ x^j = \tilde{x}^j \text{ for } j \in S}} \left(\sum_{j \in S-l} \tilde{v}^j(x^j) + \sum_{j \in N-S} v^j(x^j) \right)
$$
$$
- \left(\sum_{j \in S-l} \tilde{v}^j(\tilde{x}^j) + \sum_{j \in N-S} v^j(\tilde{x}^j) \right)
$$
$$
= \max_{x \in X(\bar{x} - \sum_{j \in S-l} \tilde{x}^j)} \left(\sum_{j \in N-S} v^j(x^j) \right) - \sum_{j \in N-S} v^j(\tilde{x}^j)
$$
$$
= v^{N-S} \left(\bar{x} - \sum_{j \in S-l} \tilde{x}^j \right) - v^{N-S} \left(\bar{x} - \sum_{j \in S} \tilde{x}^j \right)
$$
$$
\geq v^{N-S}(\bar{x}) - v^{N-S}(\bar{x} - x^l)
$$
$$
= v^{N-l}(\bar{x}) - v^{N-l}(\bar{x} - x^l). \tag{8.11}
$$

The inequality in the first line of (8.11) follows from the extra constraints on the optimization. The third line follows by the definition of v^{N-S} and because $(\tilde{x}^l)_{l \in N}$ is the Vickrey allocation (in particular, $(\tilde{x}^l)_{l \in N-S}$ maximizes the payoff to the coalition $N - S$ given the total resources allocated to that coalition). The inequality on the fourth line follows because v^{N-S} is submodular. The last equation holds because the coalition S (which includes bidder l) is a coalition of losing bidders in the Vickrey auction using the actual valuations v.

Comparing the first and last members, we see that (8.11) establishes that the Vickrey price paid by a losing bidder l who deviates jointly with the coalition $S - l$ and wins the bundle x^l is higher than the price bidder l must pay to win the same bundle x^l without the other deviations. Because no individual bidder has a profitable deviation from his dominant strategy, no coalition of losing bidders has a profitable deviation.

For (1) $\Rightarrow$ (5), we denote the coalition of shills by $S = \{1, \ldots, n\}$. Then, given the shills' reports $\{\tilde{v}^j\}_{j=1}^n$, let $\tilde{x}$ denote the corresponding Vickrey auction allocation. The total price paid by the shills is

$$
\sum_{l=1}^n p^l \geq \sum_{l=1}^n \left[v^{N-S}\left(\tilde{x} - \sum_{j \in S-l} \tilde{x}^j\right) - v^{N-S}\left(\tilde{x} - \sum_{j \in S} \tilde{x}^j\right) \right]
$$

$$
\geq \sum_{l=1}^n \left[v^{N-S}\left(\tilde{x} - \sum_{j=1}^{l-1} \tilde{x}^j\right) - v^{N-S}\left(\tilde{x} - \sum_{j=1}^{l} \tilde{x}^j\right) \right]
$$

$$
= v^{N-S}(\tilde{x}) - v^{N-S}\left(\tilde{x} - \sum_{j=1}^n \tilde{x}^j\right).
$$

The first inequality follows from (8.11), and the second from submodularity of v^{N-S}. The sum telescopes to the last term, which is the Vickrey price the bidder would need to pay to acquire the same allocation without shill bidders. Hence, shill bidding is unprofitable.

To prove the converses, suppose that the set $\mathbf{V}$ includes values for which goods are not substitutes. Say that the goods for which the substitutes condition fails are goods 1 and 2. Then there is some price vector p at which demand is single-valued and such that increasing the price of good 1 from p_1 to $p_1 + \varepsilon$ reduces the demand for good 2.

As in the proof of Theorem 8.4, we utilize the following indirect value function for bidder 1: $\tilde{v}^1(x_1, x_2) = \max v^1(x) - \sum_{m \neq 1,2} p_m x_m$. As above, if goods 1 and 2 fail the substitutes condition for the original valuation v^1, then they also fail for the indirect valuation v, which allows us to focus on just the allocation of the two goods 1 and 2, if we can arrange for the prices of the other goods to be as prescribed by p. We accomplish that by introducing two bidders with linear valuations $v(x) = \sum_{k \neq 1,2} p_k x_k$.

Using the indirect valuation v, let the value of each good $i \in \{1, 2\}$ be v_i, and let the combined value be $\bar{v}$. If the goods are not substitutes, then $\alpha = \bar{v} - (v_1 + v_2) > 0$. Call the bidder with these values bidder A.

To analyze joint deviations by losing bidders, we introduce two additional bidders B_1 and B_2. Bidder B_i values good i at $v_i + \varepsilon_i > v_i$, where

$\varepsilon_1 + \varepsilon_2 < \alpha$. These bidders both lose at equilibrium and earn zero payoffs. However, the joint deviation in which each bidder i bids $v_i + \alpha$ makes each bidder i a winner at the respective prices v_i, earning a profit of ε_i. So, if the goods are not substitutes, then losing bidders have a profitable joint deviation.

To analyze shill bidding, we introduce a single bidder B that values each good i at $v_i + \varepsilon_i > v_i$, where $\varepsilon_1 + \varepsilon_2 < \alpha$. Bidder B values the pair at $v_1 + v_2 + \varepsilon_1 + \varepsilon_2$. Bidding honestly, this bidder earns a profit of zero. By bidding using two shills B_1 and B_2 and adopting the strategies of the previous paragraph, the two shills both win, and the total price is $v_1 + v_2$, earning a profit of $\varepsilon_1 + \varepsilon_2 > 0$. So, if the goods are not substitutes, then bidder B has a profitable deviation using shill bidders. ∎

Auctions in which bidders bid for packages of items are more complicated than simple auctions for separate items. Package auctions are most attractive when they can help bidders to avoid the problem of winning some assets without acquiring needed complementary assets, that is, when the substitutes condition may fail. In exactly these conditions, however, the preceding analysis indicates that the Vickrey auction has serious and possibly fatal defects as a practical mechanism.

8.2 Bernheim–Whinston First-Price Package Auctions

The simplest package auction design is the first-price design, in which bidders submit package bids and the seller selects the feasible combination of bids that maximizes the total price. Each bidder then pays the amount it has bid for the goods it acquires or, in a procurement auction, receives the amount it has bid in return for the promised performance. The IBM–Mars auction and the London bus auctions were procurement auctions that used the first-price design.

When implementing a package auction, it is important to design simple bidding procedures to keep the bidders' problems (and perhaps also the auctioneer's problem) manageable. For example, in the two auctions cited above, which are both procurement auctions, bidders bid individually for each item and, in addition, specified discounts for certain packages or quantities. Structuring the bidder interfaces can limit the complexity of bidding and the complexity of the winner determination problem.

Our analysis of first-price package auctions is developed in a series of subsections below. The first formulates the auction and illustrates the multiple equilibrium problem; the second describes profit-target strategies and the reasons to focus on equilibria using those strategies; and the third shows that the equilibrium payoffs of those equilibria coincide with the bidder-optimal frontier of the core of the associated coalitional game.

8.2.1 Formulation

The relevant theory for this auction has been worked out only for the full information case, so our model dispenses with bidder types. We assume that there is a set X of feasible allocations or, more generally, decisions $x = (x^1, \ldots, x^N)$ that the seller can make. The part of the allocation or decision relating to bidder i is the component x^i, and the set of possible decisions relating to i is $X^i = \{x^i | x \in X\}$.

The first-price auction proceeds as follows. Each bidder i makes a set of non-negative sealed bids $\{\beta^i(x^i)\}_{x^i \in X^i}$. The seller then maximizes the objective $\sum_{i=1}^N \beta^i(x^i) + v^0(x)$, which is the sum of the bids plus the seller's value for the allocation. Each bidder pays the amount of his own winning bid. Hence, if the seller chooses x, bidder i's payoff is $v^i(x^i) - \beta^i(x^i)$. Let $\Pi^i(\beta)$ denote i's payoff corresponding to bid profile β.

This model is general enough to encompass a wide variety of applications. For an FCC spectrum auction, X is the set of allocations in which each license is assigned to at most one buyer. In the train scheduling problem, X is the set of schedules for which the trains do not crash. In a public goods problem, we can specify that for all $x \in X$, $x^1 = \cdots = x^N$, so that everyone must get the same allocation. We are most interested in applying the model to auctions with voluntary participation, so we henceforth assume that for each bidder i, there is an outcome in which i does not participate, which we denote by $\emptyset$. We normalize so that $v^i(\emptyset) = 0$ for all i. In addition, we assume throughout this chapter that the seller has free disposal, as defined below.

Definition. The seller has *free disposal* if for all $x \in X$ one has $(x^{-i}, \emptyset) \in X$ and $v^0(x) \leq v^0(x^{-i}, \emptyset)$.

Bernheim and Whinston (1986) developed a theory of first-price package auctions with complete information. The assumption of full information is disturbing, but the theory nevertheless identifies some important strategic aspects of the auction.

Before beginning the analysis, we make an important observation about our modeling of *ties*, that is, bid profiles for which the seller's objective, $\sum_{i=1}^N \beta^i(x^i) + v^0(x)$, has multiple optima. If the auction requires

that bids be made in discrete units like dollars, then ties can be broken according to any criterion or even at random without creating any
technical difficulties. However, to obtain exact characterizations of equilibrium, it is convenient to model bids as non-negative real numbers.
Treating bids as real numbers raises problems with the existence of best
replies, because it implies that there is no bid that is "just" higher than
the highest opposing bid. The problem is the same as in the familiar
Bertrand model of sellers competing to sell a single item to a buyer.
Say the sellers' costs are 7 and 10, respectively. If bid units are discrete,
say whole numbers, then there is a pure strategy equilibrium in which
the low-cost seller offers to sell at a price of 10 and the other seller at
a price of 11. In equilibrium, the winning bidder bids just less than the
loser. This equilibrium has no exact analog in the continuous model. In
that model, it is a convenient but imprecise shortcut to say that there
is an equilibrium in which both sellers offer to sell at a price of 10 and
the low-cost seller wins the competition because he bids infinitesimally
less.

In this chapter, we adopt a similar shortcut based on a similar justification, but in auction models where the bidders are buyers and the
highest bids win. In the analyses to follow, when we say that a bid b is a
best reply and a winning bid, we mean that for all $\varepsilon > 0$, $b + \varepsilon$ is an ε-best
reply and a winning bid and that payments are to be determined as if the
bid b were winning. With this understanding, each bidder always has a
best reply to rivals' bids. To avoid distraction from economic issues, we
make no further comment about this understanding of best replies in
the proofs and discussions below.[17]

We begin our analysis of the model of first-price package auctions with
the observation that, generally, such auctions have many Nash equilibria.
To illustrate, consider an auction with two identical items for sale. Suppose that bidders 1 and 2 each want only a single unit of the good, which
they value at 10, while bidders 3 and 4 have no value for a single unit, but
will pay up to 16 for the pair. In one set of Nash equilibria, bidders 3 and
4 both bid 16 for the pair, while bidders 1 and 2 each make bids less than
10 that add up to 16. For convenience, we resolve this tie in favor of the
bidders with the higher total value. Then, in these equilibria, bidders 1
and 2 win at a total price of 16 and earn total profits of 4, but some Nash

---

[17] Reny (1999) provides a full formal analysis of this problem.

equilibrium supports any division of the total with non-negative profits for both bidders. The outcome in each of these equilibria is efficient.

In addition to the preceding equilibria, there are other equilibria in the same example with inefficient outcomes. In these equilibria, bidders 3 and 4 bid 16, but bidders 1 and 2 bid less than 6. The outcome is that bidder 3 or 4 wins. Bernheim and Whinston judged these equilibria to be intuitively less plausible, because bidders 1 and 2 fail to make serious bids.

8.2.2 Profit-Target Strategies

To isolate the equilibria they considered most plausible, they focused on *profit-target strategies*, which are defined as follows.

Definition.[18] The strategy β^i is the π^i-*profit-target strategy* if for all x, $\beta^i(x^i) = \max(0, v^i(x^i) - \pi^i)$.

Profit-target strategies have two kinds of appeal. First, they are simple. Given the bidder's value, the strategy is characterized by one single number, π^i – the profit the bidder requires from any winning bid. The bidder fixes his bids on each package by subtracting π^i from his package value. Second, regardless of the strategies played by the other bidders, each bidder's best reply set will always include a profit-target strategy.

Theorem 8.6. In a first-price package auction, for any bidder i and any bids β^{-i} by the other bidders, let $\bar{\pi}^i = \max_{\beta^i} \Pi^i(\beta^i, \beta^{-i})$. Then the $\bar{\pi}^i$-profit-target strategy is a best reply for bidder i in this auction.

Proof. Let β^i be a best reply, and let the corresponding decision by the auctioneer be $\hat{x}$. Then $\bar{\pi}^i = v^i(\hat{x}^i) - \beta^i(\hat{x}^i)$. Let $\bar{\beta}^i$ denote the $\bar{\pi}^i$-profit-target strategy. Then $\beta^i(\hat{x}^i) = \bar{\beta}^i(\hat{x}^i)$.

By the seller's selection rule, for any $x \neq \hat{x}$ we have $\sum_{i=1}^{N} \beta^i(x^i) + v^0(x) \leq \sum_{i=1}^{N} \beta^i(\hat{x}^i) + v^0(\hat{x})$. Then if $\bar{\beta}^i(x^i) = 0$ we have $\bar{\beta}^i(x^i) \leq \beta^i(x^i)$, so $\sum_{j \neq i} \beta^j(x^j) + \bar{\beta}^i(x^i) + v^0(x) \leq \sum_{j \neq i} \beta^j(\hat{x}^j) + \bar{\beta}^i(\hat{x}^i) + v^0(\hat{x})$. Hence, the auctioneer does not choose x when i bids $\bar{\beta}^i$. The auctioneer's choice $\bar{x}$ when i bids $\bar{\beta}^i$ therefore satisfies $\bar{\beta}^i(\bar{x}^i) > 0$, so $\bar{\beta}^i(\bar{x}^i) \equiv \max(0, v^i(\bar{x}^i) - \pi^i) = v^i(\bar{x}^i) - \bar{\pi}^i$. Hence, $\Pi^i(\beta^{-i}, \bar{\beta}^i) = v^i(\bar{x}^i) - \bar{\beta}^i(\bar{x}^i) = \bar{\pi}^i = \Pi^i(\beta^{-i}, \beta^i)$. ∎

---

[18] Bernheim and Whinston (1986) call these "truthful" strategies, and Ausubel and Milgrom (2002) call the corresponding proxy auction strategies "semi-sincere" strategies. The term "profit-target strategies," adopted here, seems more descriptive: the bidder makes the bids that, if they win, achieve the profit target.

The preceding theorem assumes that opposing bidders adopt pure strategies. If the opposing bidders adopt mixed strategies or if the bidder is uncertain about what pure strategies they may be adopting, then the best reply set does not generally include any profit-target strategy.

Theorem 8.6 indicates the difficulty of enforcing collusive behavior in equilibrium in the first-price package auction. It holds that, unlike in uniform price auctions, no bidder ever has any incentive to reduce her demand in the first-price package auction. For suppose that at some agreed strategy profile, bidder i wins the allocation x^i, paying some positive price. If a bidder uses a profit-target strategy and we increase his allocation by $\bar{x}^i - x^i$, he will increase his bid by $\beta^i(\bar{x}^i) - \beta^i(x^i) = v^i(\bar{x}^i) - v^i(x^i)$. Thus, the bidder offers to pay the seller his full marginal value for additional units. Profit-target strategies therefore involve no demand reduction at all. The fact that some profit-target strategy is always in the best reply set means that no pure strategy profile can deter a bidder from bidding aggressively for additional units. So there is no way to *enforce* a collusive bidding agreement using strategies in the auction itself.

8.2.3 Equilibrium and the Core

That consequence of Theorem 8.6 hints that the outcome of an equilibrium in profit-target strategies may resemble competitive equilibria; this intuition turns out to be correct. To characterize equilibrium in a first-price package auction, we compare equilibrium payoffs in the auction with points in the core of an associated coalitional form game.

We defined the coalitional value function and the core in (8.1) and (8.2). We may rewrite the latter as

$$\text{Core}(N, w) = \left\{ \pi \in \mathbb{R}^N \,\middle|\, (\forall S) \sum_{j \in S} \pi^j \geq w(S) \right\}$$
$$\cap \left\{ \pi \in \mathbb{R}^N \,\middle|\, \sum_{j \in N} \pi^j \leq w(N) \right\}. \tag{8.12}$$

A payoff vector $\pi \in \mathbb{R}^N$ is in the core if it is *unblocked* and *feasible*. The first set in the intersection in (8.12) expresses the restriction that the payoff vector π is unblocked: no coalition can earn more on its own than it does from the payoff vector π. The second set expresses the feasibility condition that the total promised payoff does not exceed what is available: $\sum_{j \in N} \pi^j \leq w(N)$. Because the reverse inequality is contained in the first set of inequalities, one may equivalently write the feasibility constraint as $\sum_{j \in N} \pi^j = w(N)$ to recover the form used in (8.2).

One may regard the core imputations in this context as *competitive prices* for the participants' services and resources. For imagine that there are several brokers who may hire the players. A broker who hires the coalition S can create a business of value $w(S)$. Suppose brokers bid for individual players in a perfectly competitive market, and let π^i be the price for the services of player i. For markets to clear, the brokers' maximum profits must be zero. This means that the prices must be such that for every coalition S, $w(S) - \sum_{j \in S} \pi^j \leq 0$. Because the efficient outcome entails forming the coalition N, the zero profit condition also implies $\sum_{j \in N} \pi^j = w(N)$. Thus, the condition that π is a competitive equilibrium price vector for the services and resources of the participants is the same as the condition $\pi \in \text{Core}(N, w)$.

A particular portion of the core is especially interesting for our analysis.

Definition. A payoff vector $\pi \in \mathbb{R}^N$ is *bidder-optimal* if $\pi \in \text{Core}(N, w)$ and there exists no $\pi' \in \text{Core}(N, w)$ with $\pi'_{-0} > \pi_{-0}$. The set of such points is called the *bidder-optimal frontier* of the core.

Recall our notation for vector inequalities, $\alpha > \beta \Leftrightarrow [\alpha \geq \beta, \alpha \neq \beta]$. Using this notation, a payoff vector is in the *bidder Pareto frontier* if there is no other payoff vector in $\text{Core}(N, w)$ that is Pareto-preferred. The emphasis on the Pareto frontier of the core is reminiscent of a similar emphasis in matching theory, but we do not develop that connection here.[19]

With these definitions, we can state our main theorem characterizing equilibrium in the first-price package auction.

Theorem 8.7. Suppose that π is bidder-optimal. Then the corresponding π^i-profit-target strategies constitute a Nash equilibrium of the first-price package auction. Conversely, if $\pi \in \mathbb{R}^N$ is an equilibrium payoff vector and the corresponding π^i-profit-target strategies constitute a Nash equilibrium of the first-price package auction, then π is bidder-optimal.

Proof. To demonstrate the first assertion, suppose that π is bidder-optimal. We must show that the corresponding profit-target strategies constitute an equilibrium.

---

[19] See Ausubel and Milgrom (2002).

We will show that no player i has a profitable deviation to any profit-target strategy. Then by theorem 8.6, no player has a profitable deviation of any kind.

Suppose some alternative profit-target strategy for i earns a payoff $\pi^i + \delta$, for some $\delta > 0$. Then the strategy must be the $\pi^i + \delta$-profit-target strategy.

Since π is bidder-optimal, $\pi \in \text{Core}(N, w)$ and $(\pi^0 - \delta, \pi^i + \delta, \pi^{-i-0}) \notin \text{Core}(N, w)$. So there exists some coalition S such that $\sum_{j \in S} \pi^j \geq w(S) > \sum_{j \in S} \pi^j - \delta 1_{\{0 \in S\}} + \delta 1_{\{i \in S\}}$. It follows that $0 \in S$ and $i \notin S$. The maximum value of the seller's objective if he excludes bids from bidder i is therefore

$$
\max_{\{x \in X | x^i = \emptyset\}} \left\{ \sum_{j \in N-0} \beta^j(x^j) + v^0(x) \right\}
$$

$$
\geq \max_{\{x \in X | x^{-S} = \emptyset\}} \left\{ \sum_{j \in S-0} \beta^j(x^j) + v^0(x) \right\}
$$

$$
\geq \max_{\{x \in X | x^{-S} = \emptyset\}} \left\{ \sum_{j \in S-0} \left(v^j(x^j) - \pi^j \right) + v^0(x) \right\}
$$

$$
= w(S) - \sum_{j \in S-0} \pi^j
$$

$$
> \pi^0 - \delta
$$

$$
= \max_{x} \left\{ v^0(x) + \sum_{j \in N-0} \beta^j(x^j) \right\} - \delta
$$

$$
\geq \max_{\{x \in X | x^i \neq \emptyset\}} \left\{ v^0(x) + \sum_{j \in N-0} \beta^j(x^j) \right\} - \delta. \tag{8.13}
$$

The first line of (8.13) holds because the second optimization is more constrained, the second because $\beta^j(x^j) = \max\left(0, v^j(x^j) - \pi^j\right)$, and the third by definition of $w(S)$. The strict inequality on the fourth line follows by selection of the coalition S, and the fifth line holds by definition of π^0. Finally, the last inequality follows because the last optimization is more constrained than the preceding one.

Comparing the first and last members in (8.13) indicates that, after the deviation, the seller does strictly better by excluding bidder i than by accepting one of i's bids. Hence, the deviation results in the bidder becoming a losing bidder. So there exists no profitable deviation for any bidder i.

To show the converse, suppose that the π^i-profit-target strategies constitute an equilibrium with payoff vector π. First, we show that $\pi \in \text{Core}(N, w)$. Because π is the payoff vector for these strategies, it is feasible. Hence, if $\pi \notin \text{Core}(N, w)$, then there exists some coalition S such that $\sum_{j \in S} \pi^j < w(S)$. Then

$$\pi^0 = \max_{x \in X} \left\{ v^0(x) + \sum_{j \in N-0} \beta^j(x) \right\}$$

$$\geq \max_{\{x \in X \mid x^{-S} = \emptyset\}} \left\{ v^0(x) + \sum_{j \in S-0} \beta^j(x) \right\}$$

$$\geq \max_{\{x \in X \mid x^{-S} = \emptyset\}} \left\{ v^0(x) + \sum_{j \in S-0} (v^j(x) - \pi^j) \right\}$$

$$= w(S) - \sum_{j \in S-0} \pi^j > \pi^0,$$

which is a contradiction. So $\pi \in \text{Core}(N, w)$.

Next, suppose that π is an equilibrium payoff vector and $\pi \in \text{Core}(N, w)$, but π is not bidder-optimal. Then there is some i and some $\delta > 0$ such that $\hat{\pi} \equiv (\pi^0 - 2\delta, \pi^i + 2\delta, \pi^{-i-0}) \in \text{Core}(N, w)$.

Suppose bidder i deviates to the $\pi^i + \delta$-profit-target strategy, which we denote below by $\tilde{\beta}^i$. If π is an equilibrium payoff vector, then there is a corresponding feasible allocation $\bar{x}$. So

$$\max_{x \in X} \left\{ \sum_{j \in N-i-0} \beta^j(x^j) + \tilde{\beta}^i(x^i) + v^0(x) \right\}$$

$$\geq \sum_{j \in N-i-0} \beta^j(\bar{x}^j) + \tilde{\beta}^i(\bar{x}^i) + v^0(\bar{x})$$

$$= \sum_{j \in N-0} (v^j(\bar{x}^j) - \pi^j) - \delta + v^0(\bar{x})$$

$$= \pi^0 - \delta > \pi^0 - 2\delta$$

$$\geq \max_{\{S \mid i \notin S\}} \left\{ w(S) - \sum_{j \in S-0} \pi^j \right\}$$

$$\geq \max_{\{S \mid i \notin S\}} \left\{ \max_{x \in X} \left\{ \sum_{j \in S} v^j(x^j) \right\} - \sum_{j \in S-0} \pi^j \right\}$$

$$= \max_{x \in X} \max_{\{S \mid i \notin S\}} \left\{ \sum_{j \in S-0} (v^j(x^j) - \pi^j) \right\} + v^0(x)$$

$$= \max_{x \in X} \left\{ \sum_{j \in N - i - 0} \max(0, v^j(x^j) - \pi^j) + v^0(x) \right\}$$

$$= \max_{x \in X} \left\{ \sum_{j \in N - i - 0} \beta^j(x^j) + v^0(x) \right\}.$$

The first line follows from maximization, the second from the definitions of the bid functions, and the third from the definition of $\bar{x}$. The fourth line holds because $(\pi^0 - 2\delta, \pi^i + 2\delta, \pi^{-i-0}) \in \text{Core}(N, w)$. The fifth follows from the definition of $w(S)$, and the sixth from reversing the order of optimization (and using free disposal). The seventh line follows from maximization over S, and the last by the definition of the bid functions.

Because the last term is less than the first term, the seller strictly reduces his profit by refusing all of i's bids after the deviation. So, according to the rules of the auction, the seller accepts one of i's bids, and i's deviation is profitable, contradicting the assumption that the original profit-target strategies constitute an equilibrium. ∎

According to our earlier interpretation, outcomes in the core pay the seller a competitive price for his resources. However, the core also includes the extreme payoff profile at which each bidder i earns $\pi^i = 0$ and the seller earns $\pi^0 = w(N)$. Intuitively, this extreme payoff reflects the fact that all the relevant coalitions include the seller (except the singleton coalitions, which ensure each bidder gets at least zero), so the core includes as one possibility that the seller is a perfect price discriminator. In an auction, however, it is the bidders who get to make the offers. Theorem 8.7 reflects the power the ability to make offers conveys: the bidders collectively bid just enough for the outcome to lie in the core. In terms of our competitive pricing interpretation, the theorem holds that the prices paid for the bidders' resources are as high as possible, consistent with paying the seller a competitive price for his resources.[20]

---

[20] In their analysis of first-price package auctions, Bernheim and Whinston (1986) also developed the concept of *coalition-proof Nash equilibrium* and showed that the equilibria identified in theorem 8.7 coincide exactly with the coalition-proof Nash equilibria of this auction. Their analysis, consistent with the discussion following theorem 8.6, further indicates the difficulty of creating incentives to sustain collusive outcomes, even when small groups of bidders can communicate privately.

8.3 Ausubel–Milgrom Ascending Proxy Auctions[21]

In this section, we introduce the Ausubel–Milgrom ascending proxy auctions, which incorporate many of the advantages of both the Vickrey and first-price package designs while avoiding some key disadvantages. We will show that this design essentially replicates the performance of the Vickrey design when all goods are substitutes and, like the Bernheim–Whinston first-price auction, has full information equilibrium outcomes that are bidder-optimal points in the core.

To develop the connection with the Vickrey auction, suppose that goods are substitutes for all bidders. Then, for every value profile, truthful bidding is a Nash equilibrium of the ascending package auction, and the allocation and payments coincide exactly with those of the Vickrey auction. The equilibrium payoff vector is then the unique bidder-optimal point in the core of the associated coalitional game. The ascending package auction thus matches the performance of the Vickrey auction when goods are substitutes – the condition under which the Vickrey auction performs best.

The ascending package auction performs quite differently from the Vickrey auction when goods are not substitutes. Whenever there is full information, the ascending package auction has profit-target Nash equilibria with strategies and equilibrium payoffs identical to those for the first-price package auction, as described by theorem 8.7. In addition, the ascending package auction duplicates the first-price package auction's resistance to collusion (described by theorem 8.6) – a property also shared by the Vickrey design.[22]

We model the proxy auction as a revelation game in which each bidder reports his values to a proxy agent who places bids in a multi-round auction on the bidder's behalf. We will study two versions of the proxy auction. The first assumes unlimited bidder budgets. Because tight budget constraints are a serious problem in some spectrum auctions, we analyze a proxy auction that respects budget constraints in the succeeding subsection.

---

[21] This section follows Ausubel and Milgrom (2002).

[22] Recall, though, that with even a small amount of outside enforcement, the Vickrey auction is vulnerable to collusive equilibria. The same is true of the ascending proxy auction when goods are substitutes.

8.3.1 The Proxy Auction with Unlimited Budgets

In this subsection we study the ascending proxy auction with unlimited budgets and negligibly small bid increments, showing three main results. First, the algorithm selects a core allocation with respect to the preferences reported to the proxies. Second, with full information, the Nash equilibria in target strategies induce bidder-optimal core allocations, and every bidder-optimal core allocation corresponds to some profit target equilibrium. Third, when goods are substitutes, truthful reporting to the proxy bidders is a Nash equilibrium.

Except where otherwise specified, we use the model of section 8.2, with quasi-linear preferences and valuation functions $(v^i)_{i \in N}$.

The proxies place bids in a multi-round auction. In each round, the auctioneer determines the feasible decision x that solves $\max_{x \in X} \{\sum_{j \in N-0} \beta^j(x^j) + v^0(x)\}$, where $\beta^j(x^j)$ is the highest bid j has ever made in any round for the package x^j. The bidders for whom the maximum specifies $x^i \neq \emptyset$ are called the *provisionally winning bidders*, and the set of all such bidders is called the *provisionally winning coalition*.

In each round, each bidder i faces a minimum bid $m^i(x^i)$ for every possible package. Initially, for every bidder and package, $m^i(x^i) = 0$. As the auction progresses, if the bidder has ever bid upon the package, then the minimum bid is the bidder's highest previous bid on that package plus one increment.

The proxy operates as follows. In each round, if bidder i is a provisional winner, then i's proxy makes no new bid. Otherwise, for every possible package, the proxy uses the reported value function $\tilde{v}^i$ to determine the package $\hat{x}^i$ with the highest potential profit $\hat{\pi}^i = \tilde{v}^i(\hat{x}^i) - m^i(\hat{x}^i)$. If $\hat{\pi}^i < 0$, then the proxy places no new bid, but if $\hat{\pi}^i \geq 0$, then i's proxy bids $m^i(\hat{x}^i)$ for the package $\hat{x}^i$. (It may be helpful to think of an exiting proxy's final bid as a bid of zero for the null allocation.) The auction terminates when there are no new bids. At that time, the provisional winners and the provisional allocation become the winners and the allocation of the auction.

We study the revelation game in which the bidders report values to their proxies, but to study that game, we first need to examine the ascending auction process. Given any values the bidders report to their proxies, one can reconstruct all of a bidder's bids in prior rounds from the potential profit $\hat{\pi}^i(t)$ associated with his most recent bid at time t. In particular (ignoring ties), by time t the proxy has made all legal bids on any package with potential profit of at least $\hat{\pi}^i(t)$. Let $\hat{\pi}^0(t)$ be the maximal value of seller's objective. Let the full vector of payoffs be $\hat{\pi}(t)$, which we sometimes denote simply by $\hat{\pi}$.

8.3.1.1 Proxy Outcomes Are Core Outcomes
We focus here on the limiting case of small bid increments and treat the rounds as continuous in time. Then bidder i's current minimum bid on any package x^i at time t is $\max(0, \tilde{v}^i(x^i) - \hat{\pi}^i(t))$. Let $\tilde{w}$ denote the corresponding coalitional value function computed according to (8.1). Then the seller's maximum payoff at time t is given by

$$\hat{\pi}^0(t) = \max_{x \in X} \left\{ v^0(x) + \sum_{j \in N-0} \max\left(0, \tilde{v}^j(x^j) - \hat{\pi}^j(t)\right) \right\}$$

$$= \max_{S \subset N} \max_{x \in X} \left\{ v^0(x) + \sum_{j \in S-0} (\tilde{v}^j(x^j) - \hat{\pi}^j(t)) \right\}$$

$$= \max_{S \subset N} \left\{ \tilde{w}(S) - \sum_{j \in S-0} \hat{\pi}^j(t) \right\}. \tag{8.14}$$

The first equality uses the definitions of $\hat{\pi}^0(t)$ and the proxy bids; the second follows because the maximum over S chooses exactly the positive summands; and the third follows the definition of $\tilde{w}$.

Remarkably, (8.14) suggests one can characterize the auction as a coalitional bargaining process. It is as if at any time t, each bidder demanded payoff $\hat{\pi}^i(t)$, and a manager for the coalition S, who planned to hire coalition members at prices $\hat{\pi}^i(t)$, bid the residual, $\tilde{w}(S) - \sum_{j \in S-0} \hat{\pi}^j(t)$, to buy the seller's resources. The winning coalition of bidders at any time is the coalition making the most generous offer, and losing bidders targeting positive payoffs reduce their demands and try again. Formula (8.14) and the story behind it arise repeatedly in the analysis below.

Formula (8.14) indicates that at any time t, no coalition S blocks the payoff vector $\hat{\pi}(t): \tilde{w}(S) \leq \sum_{j \in S} \hat{\pi}^j(t)$. When the auction ends, the payoff vector is also feasible, so we have the following result:

Theorem 8.8. When the auction ends at time $\tilde{t}$, the final decision $\tilde{x}$ maximizes the total of reported values, $\sum_{j \in N} \tilde{v}^j(\tilde{x}^j) = \tilde{w}(N)$, and the payoff outcome satisfies $\hat{\pi}(\tilde{t}) \in \text{Core}(N, \tilde{w})$.

Proof. Because $\hat{\pi}(\bar{t})$ is unblocked, it only remains to show that $\hat{\pi}(\bar{t})$ is feasible. Let W be the winning coalition at time $\bar{t}$, and let $\beta^j(\bar{x}^j)$ denote the final bid prices. By the rules of the auction,

$$\hat{\pi}^i(\bar{t}) = \begin{cases} \bar{v}^i(\bar{x}^i) - \beta^i(\bar{x}^i) & \text{for } i \in W, \\ v^0(\bar{x}) + \sum_{j \in W} \beta^j(\bar{x}^j) & \text{for } i = 0, \\ 0 & \text{for } i \notin W \cup \{0\}. \end{cases} \tag{8.15}$$

Writing $\bar{v}^0 = v^0$, we have $\sum_{j \in N} \hat{\pi}^j(\bar{t}) = \sum_{j \in N} \bar{v}^j(\bar{x}^j) \leq \max_{x \in X}$ $\sum_{j \in N} \bar{v}^j(x^j) = \bar{w}(N)$. That establishes feasibility. Hence, $\bar{w}(N) = \sum_{j \in N} \hat{\pi}^j(\bar{t})$ and $\hat{\pi}(\bar{t}) \in \text{Core}(N, \bar{w})$. ∎

8.3.1.2 Profit-Target Strategies and Equilibrium

Theorem 8.9. In the ascending proxy auction, for any bidder i and any reports $\bar{v}^{-i}$ by the other bidders, let $\bar{\pi}^i = \max_{\tilde{v}^i} \Pi^i(\tilde{v}^i, \bar{v}^{-i})$. Then the $\bar{\pi}^i$-profit-target strategy is a best reply for bidder i in this auction.

Proof. The conclusion is trivial if $\bar{\pi}^i = 0$, so suppose $\bar{\pi}^i > 0$. Let u^i be any report such that $\Pi^i(u^i, \bar{v}^{-i}) = \bar{\pi}^i$, and $\bar{x}$ be the associated final outcome. Then the price i pays is $v^i(\bar{x}^i) - \bar{\pi}^i$. Let $\delta = u^i(\bar{x}^i) - (v^i(\bar{x}^i) - \bar{\pi}^i)$. By the rules of the auction, the report $\bar{u}^i$ defined for each package by $\bar{u}^i(x^i) = u^i(x^i) - \delta$ leads to the same path of bids and the same auction outcome as the report u^i. According to theorem 8.8, the outcome is total-value-maximizing with respect to the reports $(\bar{v}^{-i}, \bar{u}^i)$, so there is no outcome x that excludes i and satisfies $v^0(x) + \sum_{j \in N-i-0} \bar{v}^j(x^j) > v^0(\bar{x}) + \sum_{j \in N-i-0} \bar{v}^j(\bar{x}^j) + \bar{u}^i(\bar{x}^i)$. Hence, again using theorem 8.8, any report by i that specifies the value $\bar{u}^i(\bar{x}^i)$ for $\bar{x}^i$ leads either to the outcome $\bar{x}$ or to some other outcome that does not exclude i.

Let $\bar{v}^i$ denote the $\bar{\pi}^i$-profit-target strategy. By definition, its report for $\bar{x}^i$ is $\bar{v}^i(\bar{x}^i) = v^i(\bar{x}^i) - \bar{\pi}^i = u^i(\bar{x}^i) - \delta = \bar{u}^i(\bar{x}^i)$, so the report $\bar{v}^i$ leads to some outcome at which i is a winning bidder. Because, by definition of the profit-target strategy, the lowest profit associated with any bid during the course of the auction using the report $\bar{v}^i$ is $\bar{\pi}^i$, it follows that $\Pi^i(\bar{v}^i, \bar{v}^{-i}) \geq \bar{\pi}^i$. ∎

Theorem 8.9 is closely analogous to theorem 8.6 and has a similar interpretation. In the ascending package auction with proxy bidders, no bidder has an incentive to withhold demand, so no strategy profile a ring of bidders could adopt protects an agreement about how to divide the items against aggressive deviations by the ring members.

The next theorem duplicates the first sentence, but not the second, of theorem 8.7.

Theorem 8.10. Suppose that π is bidder-optimal. Then the corresponding π^i-profit-target strategies constitute a Nash equilibrium of the ascending package auction.

Proof. Suppose π is bidder-optimal, and for each i let $\bar{v}^i$ denote the π^i-profit-target strategy. Suppose the strategy profile $\bar{v}$ is not a Nash equilibrium. In particular, suppose there is some player i with a profitable deviation to a $\hat{\pi}^i$-profit-target strategy. If $\hat{\pi}^i < \pi^i$ and i is a winner with this deviation, then either the auction outcome is unaffected or i earns a profit of less than π^i, so we restrict attention to the case $\hat{\pi}^i > \pi^i$.

Let T denote the winning coalition that results after the deviation, and let the payoff outcome be $\hat{\pi}$. Then $i \in T$ and $\hat{\pi}^i > \pi^i$. Also, the profit-target strategies imply that for all $j \in T$, $\hat{\pi}^j \geq \pi^j$ (because the bidder j makes no bids that involve a lower profit than π^j).

Because $\pi \in \mathrm{Core}(N, \bar{w})$, for every coalition S we have $\bar{w}(S) \leq \sum_{j \in S} \pi^j$. If there exists any $\varepsilon > 0$ such that for every coalition S we have $\bar{w}(S) + \varepsilon \leq \sum_{j \in S} \pi^j$, then $(\pi^0 - \varepsilon, \pi^i + \varepsilon, \pi^{-i-0}) \in \mathrm{Core}(N, \bar{w})$, which contradicts bidder optimality. So, there is some coalition S with $0 \in S$ and $i \notin S$ such that $\bar{w}(S) = \sum_{j \in S} \pi^j$.

Let $\beta(S)$ and $\beta(T)$ denote the highest total seller payoff associated with bids by the bidders in the coalitions S and T during the proxy auction, given the specified deviation by bidder i. Then

$$
\begin{aligned}
\beta(S) &\geq \bar{w}(S) - \sum_{j \in S-0} \max(\pi^j, \hat{\pi}^j) \\
&> \bar{w}(S) - \sum_{j \in S-0} \pi^j - \sum_{j \in T-0} \max(0, \hat{\pi}^j - \pi^j) \\
&= \pi_0 - \sum_{j \in T-0} \max(0, \hat{\pi}^j - \pi^j) \\
&\geq \bar{w}(T) - \sum_{j \in T-0} \pi^j - \sum_{j \in T-0} \max(0, \hat{\pi}^j - \pi^j) \\
&= \bar{w}(T) - \sum_{j \in T-0} \hat{\pi}^j \\
&= \beta(T).
\end{aligned}
\tag{8.16}
$$

The first step in (8.16) follows from the proxy rules: any losing bidders in S stop bidding only when their potential profits reach the specified levels. The strict inequality in the second step follows because $i \in T - S$ and $\hat{\pi}^i > \pi^i$. The third step follows by selection of S, the fourth because $\pi \in$ Core$(N, \bar{w})$, and the fifth and sixth by the definitions of T, $\hat{\pi}$, and $\beta(T)$.

We conclude that the coalition S offers a strictly higher total payoff to the seller than does T, which is impossible, because T is the winning coalition. This contradicts the hypothesis that bidder i has a profitable deviation. ∎

To highlight the theorem's scope and limits, consider a package auction with one unit of an indivisible good for sale. Suppose the good is worth 8 to bidder 1 and 4 to bidder 2. Then, in equilibrium in a first-price auction, both bidders bid 4 and bidder 1 wins. These are profit-target strategies; bidder 1 bids for a profit of 4, bidder 2 bids for a profit of 0, and the equilibrium payoff vector for the two bidders is $(4, 0)$. This equilibrium is consistent with theorem 8.7.

In the ascending auction, there exists a Nash equilibrium in which the bidders play the same strategies. Bidder 1 tells its proxy to bid up to 4, bidder 2 does the same, and bidder 1 wins. This equilibrium is one specified by theorem 8.10, but it highlights a problem with the equilibria identified by the theorem. In the ascending proxy auction, it is a dominant strategy for bidder 1 to report his value of 8 to the proxy. The identified equilibrium is inconsistent with bidder 1's dominant strategy.

This example indicates that the ascending auction performs better than theorem 8.10 might suggest. When bidders in the ascending package auction have dominant strategies, they have simpler optimization problems and less incentive to waste resources studying competitors' values and strategies than they might otherwise.

8.3.1.3 The Proxy Auction When Goods Are Substitutes
The next theorem shows that the simplicity of bidding in the proxy auction when there is just one item for sale also applies when there are several goods that are substitutes.

Theorem 8.11. Suppose that (1) for all $i \in N - 0$, $v^i \in \mathbf{V_{subs}}$ (all bidders regard the goods as substitutes) and (2) for all $x \in X$, $v^0(x) = 0$ (the seller has no value for unsold goods). Then the strategy profile in which every bidder reports $\tilde{v}^i = v^i$ is a Nash equilibrium. The corresponding payoff vector satisfies $\hat{\pi}^i = \pi_V^i = w(N) - w(N - i) = \max\{\pi^i | \pi \in \text{Core}(N, w)\}$. In particular, the equilibrium payoff vector is the unique bidder-optimal point in $\text{Core}(N, w)$.

Proof. By theorem 8.8, for any report by bidder i, the payoff outcome satisfies the core constraint: $\sum_{j \in N-i} \hat{\pi}^j \geq w(N - i)$. Moreover, for any report by player i, some feasible outcome results, so the total payoff necessarily satisfies $\sum_{j \in N} \hat{\pi}^j \leq w(N)$. Hence, regardless of i's report, his payoff is bounded above by $w(N) - w(N - i)$.

To show that truthful reporting is a best reply for i when all others report truthfully, it is therefore sufficient to prove that if the goods are substitutes for all the bidders, then i's payoff from truthful reporting is at least $w(N) - w(N - i)$. We do this by showing that during the auction, if there is any round t' at which $\hat{\pi}^i(t') \leq w(N) - w(N - i)$, then i is part of the provisionally winning coalition at every round $t \geq t'$.

By Theorem 8.4, because goods are substitutes, the coalitional value function w is bidder-submodular. Hence, for any coalition S with $i \in S$, we have $w(S) - w(S - i) \geq w(N) - w(N - i)$. We use this inequality below.

Suppose that $S - i - 0$ is the coalition excluding i that maximizes the seller's payoff at some round $t \geq t'$, where $0, i \in S$. By (8.14) (and using the fact that all bidders are reporting truthfully), the corresponding seller payoff is $w(S - i) - \sum_{j \in S-i-0} \hat{\pi}^j(t)$. If the seller were instead to select the coalition $S - 0$, which includes i, then his payoff would be $w(S) - \sum_{j \in S-0} \hat{\pi}^j(t) \geq w(S) - \sum_{j \in S-i-0} \hat{\pi}^j(t) - [w(N) - w(N - i)] \geq w(S) - \sum_{j \in S-i-0} \hat{\pi}^j(t) - [w(S) - w(S - i)] = w(S - i) - \sum_{j \in S-i-0} \hat{\pi}^j(t)$. So i must be part of any provisionally winning coalition.

Hence, by the mechanics of the auction, i's profit target never falls below $w(N) - w(N - i) = \pi_V^i$, so i eventually wins and earns $\hat{\pi}^i \geq \pi_V^i$. This proves that truthful reporting is a best reply for i. By theorem 8.8, truthful reporting leads to $\hat{\pi} \in \text{Core}(N, w)$. By theorem 8.1, $\pi_V^i = w(N) - w(N - i) = \max\{\pi^i | \pi \in \text{Core}(N, w)\}$, so $\hat{\pi}^i \leq \pi_V^i$. Hence, $\hat{\pi}^i = \pi_V^i$. ∎

8.3.2 The Non-transferable-Utility Proxy Auction

In this section, we extend the ascending proxy auction to accommodate limited budgets and more general valuations than the quasi-linear form used up to now. We show that an appropriate generalization of the auction algorithm still generates a core allocation with respect to reported preferences, but we do not identify equilibria in this more general case.

Suppose that each bidder i has a finite set Ω^i of feasible offers. (In the ordinary ascending proxy auction, offers are package–price pairs, and this analysis covers that special case.) Suppose that each bidder's feasible set includes a *null outcome*, $\emptyset \in \Omega^i$, which means that the seller does not select player i. Assume that i has a strict ordering over Ω^i represented by a utility function u^i.

The *feasible* combinations of offers are those in the set $\Omega^0 \subset \times_{j \in N-0} \Omega^j$. We assume that $(\emptyset, \ldots, \emptyset) \in \Omega^0$: the *null*, or no-trade, outcome is feasible. We also assume that the seller has a strict preference ranking over the set Ω^0 described by the utility function u^0. A non-null combination ξ is *feasible for the coalition S* if (1) $0 \in S$, (2) $\xi \in \Omega^0$ (the combination is feasible), and (3) $\xi^j = \emptyset$ for all $j \notin S$. For coalitions excluding the seller, the only feasible allocation is null.

The auction rules generalize those of the preceding section. Each bidder reports his preferences once and for all to his proxy. The report is a utility function $\tilde{u}^i : \Omega^i \to \mathbb{R}$ that strictly ranks the elements of Ω^i. The mechanism processes the reports in a series of rounds. The bidders' past bids and the seller's most preferred feasible allocation summarize the state of the auction after any round.

We describe the initial state of the auction with the collection of sets $\Psi^i(0) = \{\emptyset\}$ and the allocation $\omega^0(0) = (\emptyset, \ldots, \emptyset)$.

The process proceeds iteratively; the state of the process at round t is $(\{\Psi^i(t)\}_{i \in N-0}, \omega^0(t))$, where $\omega^0(t) = (\omega_i^0(t))_{i \in N-0}$ is the seller's currently most preferred feasible allocation and $\Psi^i(t)$ is the set of offers made by bidder i up to and including round t. The state evolves according to

$$\omega^0(t) = \arg \max_{\xi \in \Omega^0} u^0(\xi) \text{ subject to } \xi^i \in \Psi^i(t), i \in N-0,$$

$$\omega^i(t+1) = \arg \max_{\xi^i \in (\Omega^i - \Psi^i(t)) \cup \{\emptyset\}} \tilde{u}^i(\xi^i), \tag{8.17}$$

$$\Psi^i(t+1) = \begin{cases} \Psi^i(t) \cup \{\omega^i(t+1)\} & \text{if } \tilde{u}^i(\omega^i(t+1)) > \tilde{u}^i(\omega_i^0(t)), \\ \Psi^i(t) & \text{otherwise.} \end{cases}$$

The second line of (8.17) identifies a potential offer, $\omega^i(t+1)$, that a proxy may make at round $t+1$. According to the third line, the proxy actually offers $\omega^i(t+1)$ then if and only if bidder i strictly prefers that offer to its part of the provisional outcome, $\omega_i^0(t)$. Equivalently, the proxy makes the offer if and only if (i) the bidder is not a provisional winner at round t ($\omega_i^0(t) = \emptyset$) and (ii) the bidder prefers the offer $\omega^i(t+1)$ to the no-trade outcome.[23] Thus, just as in the preceding subsection, the set of offers made by any time t consists of the null offer plus all offers that are more profitable than the new offer $\omega^i(t+1)$ "planned" for $t+1$:

$$\Psi^i(t) = \{\emptyset\} \cup \{\tilde{\omega}^i \in \Omega^i | \tilde{u}^i(\tilde{\omega}^i) > \tilde{u}^i(\omega^i(t+1))\}. \tag{8.18}$$

The auction process terminates at a round $\bar{t}$ when there is a round with no new bids, that is, when $\tilde{u}^i(\omega^i(\bar{t}+1)) \le \tilde{u}^i(\omega_i^0(\bar{t}))$ for all i. At that time, the provisional allocation $\omega^0(\bar{t})$ becomes the final allocation.

The coalitional game corresponding to this auction generally may involve non-transferable utility, so we use the *non-transferable utility core* (or *NTU core*) to analyze the outcome. Recall that an allocation ω is *blocked* if there exists some coalition S and allocation $\tilde{\omega}$ feasible for coalition S such that all the members of S strictly prefer $\tilde{\omega}$ to ω. An allocation ω is in the NTU core is if it is feasible (satisfying $\omega^i \in \Omega^i$ for all $i \in N$) and unblocked. The main result of this section establishes that the identified auction process selects a core allocation.

Theorem 8.12. When the ascending proxy auction ends at time $\bar{t}$, the outcome $\omega^0(\bar{t}) = (\omega_i^0(\bar{t}))_{i \in N-0}$ is an NTU-core allocation with respect to the reported preferences $(u^0, (\tilde{u}^i)_{i \in N-0})$.

Proof. By construction, the final allocation $\omega^0(\bar{t})$ is feasible and Pareto-preferred to the null allocation. If $\omega^0(\bar{t})$ is not a core allocation, then there exists some coalition S and some non-null combination ξ feasible for S that blocks it. Feasibility requires that $0 \in S$, $\xi \in \Omega^0$, and $\xi^j = \emptyset$ for all $j \notin S$. Blocking additionally requires that (i) $u^0(\xi) > u^0(\omega^0(\bar{t}))$ and (ii) $\tilde{u}^i(\xi^i) > \tilde{u}^i(\omega_i^0(\bar{t}))$ for all $i \in S - 0$. Using (8.18), we have $\xi^i \in \{\tilde{\omega}^i \in \Omega^i | \tilde{u}^i(\tilde{\omega}^i) > \tilde{u}^i(\omega^i(\bar{t}+1))\} \subset \Psi^i(\bar{t})$ for all $i \in N - 0$. So, by the first line of (8.17), $u^0(\omega^0(\bar{t})) > u^0(\xi)$, contradicting (i). ∎

To illustrate the operation of this auction, suppose that offers are pairs of packages and corresponding money bids, as in the preceding

---

[23] In some versions of the ascending proxy auction, a bidder can revise the instructions to his proxy at certain times during the auction (Ausubel and Milgrom (2001)). In that extended design, the two descriptions of the proxy are not equivalent.

section, but that bidder budgets are limited. To adapt the ascending proxy auction to this situation, a bidder could report his package valuation function and budget to his proxy. Bidder i's budget would determine Ω^i. The proxy, behaving as prescribed by (8.17), would skip over bids that exceed the budget, but otherwise the auction would choose bids by the same criteria as in the ascending proxy auction with transferable utility. Theorem 8.12 asserts that the allocation resulting from such an auction is a core allocation with respect to the reported preferences and budgets. This means that no coalition has a feasible allocation that every coalition member prefers to the auction outcome, where *feasibility* includes the requirement that the allocation respect the bidders' budget limits.

This example establishes another advantage of the proxy auction design. Unlike the Vickrey auction, the ascending proxy auction can easily extend to the case of limited budgets.

8.4 Conclusion

In this chapter, we have discussed three leading designs in the new and burgeoning literature on combinatorial auctions. The three mechanisms have different advantages.

The Vickrey design is a dominant strategy auction mechanism that produces efficient outcomes. As we saw in chapter 3, it is the only such mechanism with the property that losing bidders pay nothing. The dominant strategy property is valuable in that it makes bidding easy and discourages unproductive research into competitors' values and plans.

Vickrey auctions suffer from a number of practical problems listed in chapter 2. Some of these, including the complexities of package bidding, are shared by all package auction designs. However, Vickrey auctions lose their performance advantages when budgets are limited, and they distort incentives for investment and mergers in ways that other package auctions do not. When goods are not substitutes, the Vickrey auction suffers from an important collection of *monotonicity problems*. As the set of bidders expands (for example through entry), it is possible that the existing bidders' payoffs rise and the seller's revenue falls. Whenever that happens, the outcome of the Vickrey auction ceases to be in the core. Losing bidders can sometimes collude profitably, raising their bids to become winners while reducing the prices they pay. A single bidder can sometimes profitably pretend to be multiple bidders. We showed that one can generally rule out these problems when all goods are substitutes,[24] but not otherwise.

One might summarize this discussion by saying that the Vickrey auction performs well when goods are substitutes and budgets are unlimited, but can encounter important theoretical and practical problems when goods may not be substitutes for some bidders and when budget constraints bind. (An additional disadvantage, associated with investments and mergers, is discussed in chapter 2.)

The advantages of the first-price package auction are very different. First, the auction itself is relatively simple and transparent: bidders need not perform difficult calculations to tell whether the auctioneer has calculated their prices correctly. When the bidders are fully informed about all values, the outcomes of *profit-target equilibria* identified by the theory lie in the core. Such equilibria therefore ensure a competitive price for the seller's goods. In addition, outcomes of such equilibria are *bidder-optimal* and thus lie on the bidder Pareto frontier of the core. Intuitively, this fact means that only competition – and not the seller's monopoly power – limits the bidders' earnings. These properties hold regardless of whether the goods are substitutes. In contrast, Vickrey outcomes are guaranteed to enjoy these properties only when goods are substitutes. In that case, the outcomes of the first-price auction in profit-target equilibria coincide exactly with the Vickrey outcomes.

A disadvantage of the first-price auction compared to the Vickrey auction is that bidders in the first-price package auction need to know a lot for the first-price auction to perform well. To choose their optimal bids, bidders need to set their profit targets accurately, and they need to be able to coordinate on one of the multiple equilibria. These observations suggest that the full information equilibrium outcomes are unlikely ever to hold exactly, although it remains possible that they may describe a central tendency for some kinds of environments.

The ascending proxy auction incorporates some of the advantages of each of the two preceding designs. When goods are substitutes, the ascending proxy auction has a Nash equilibrium in which each bidder

---

[24] The problems can also be characterized using the coalitional value function; we showed that most of the problems arise only when the function is not bidder-submodular.

reports his values truthfully, without regard to the other bidders' values. The outcome in that case is the unique bidder-optimal point, so it coincides with the Vickrey outcome. Thus, when the Vickrey design performs best, the ascending package auction exactly matches its performance. The two perform quite differently, however, when goods are not substitutes.

In the full information case, the ascending proxy auction has profit-target equilibria similar to those of the first-price package auction. The equilibrium payoffs are bidder-optimal points in the core of the associated coalitional game. The fact that the outcomes are in the core implies that the seller receives at least a competitive price for his goods. Because the payoff outcomes are bidder-optimal, the seller exercises no monopoly power, but accepts the prices dictated by competition alone.

Finally, the ascending proxy auction is adaptable to budget constraints and other extensions that frustrate the Vickrey design.

Besides the three auctions discussed here, several others based on different principles have also been proposed. Some of these auctions accept more than one bid from a particular bidder. These auctions are hybrids of the designs studied in chapters 7 and chapter 8. In the former class of auctions, bidders must bid on items individually; the latter auctions accept only one bid from each bidder and thus do not combine bids. These hybrid designs simplify some bidding problems and likely mix the advantages and disadvantages of the pure forms, but one cannot assess them confidently without more analysis. Other combinatorial auctions attracting interest include multi-stage or multi-round designs in which bidders effectively exchange information about which packages might be interesting before making their final bids. The cognitive challenge of bidding in a package auction is daunting, so developments of this kind are likely to be critical to successful use of these designs.

REFERENCES

Ausubel, Lawrence and Paul Milgrom (2001). "System and Method for a Dynamic Auction with Package Bidding." Patent Cooperation Treaty patent application.
Ausubel, Lawrence and Paul Milgrom (2002). "Ascending Auctions with Package Bidding." *Frontiers of Theoretical Economics* 1(1): Article 1.
Banks, Jeffrey S., John O. Ledyard, and David P. Porter (1989). "Allocating Uncertain and Unresponsive Resources: An Experimental Approach." *Rand Journal of Economics* 20: 1–25.

Bernheim, Douglas B. and Michael Whinston (1986). "Menu Auctions, Resource Allocation and Economic Influence." *Quarterly Journal of Economics* **101**: 1–31.

Brewer, Paul and Charles Plott (1996). "A Binary Conflict Ascending Price (Bicap) Mechanism for the Decentralized Allocation of the Right to Use Railroad Tracks." *International Journal of Industrial Organization* **14**: 857–886.

Cantillon, Estelle and Martin Pesendorfer (2003). "Combination Bidding in Multi-unit Auctions." Harvard Business School Working Paper.

Cassady, Ralph (1967). *Auctions and Auctioneering*. Berkeley: University of California Press.

Cybernomics (2000). "An Experimental Comparison of the Simultaneous Multi-Round Auction and the CRA Combinatorial Auction." http://wireless.fcc.gov/auctions/conferences/combin2000/releases/98540191.pdf

Epstein, Refael, Lysette Henríquez, Jaime Catalán, Gabriel Y. Weintraub, and Cristián Martínez (2002). "A Combinational Auction Improves School Meals in Chile." *Interfaces* **32**(6): 1–14.

Hohner, Gail, John Rich, Ed Ng, Grant Reed, Andrew Davenport, Jayant Kalagnanam, Ho Soo Lee, and Chae An (2002). "Combinatorial and Quantity Discount Procurement Auctions with Mutual Benefits at Mars, Incorporated." IBM Watson Labs Research Center Working Paper.

Ledyard, John O., David P. Porter, and Antonio Rangel (1997). "Experiments Testing Multi-object Allocation Mechanisms." *Journal of Economics and Management Strategy* **6**: 639–675.

Lehmann, Daniel, Liadan O'Callaghan, and Yoav Shoham (2002). "Truth Revelation in Approximately Efficient Combinatorial Auctions." *Journal of the ACM* **49**(5): 577–602.

Nisan, Noam (2000). "Bidding and Allocation in Combinatorial Auctions." http://www.cs.huji.ac.il/~noam/mkts.html.

Parkes, David and Lyle Ungar (2000). "Iterative Combinatorial Auctions: Theory and Practice." *Proceedings of the 17th National Conference on Artificial Intelligence*. AAAI. 74–81.

Parkes, David, Lyle Ungar, and David Foster (1999). "Accounting for Cognitive Costs in on-Line Auction Design." *Agent Mediated Electronic Commerce*. P. Noriega and C. Sierra. Heidelberg: Springer-Verlag.

Rassenti, S.J., R.L. Bulfin, and Vernon Smith (1982). "A Combinatorial Auction Mechanism for Airport Time Slot Allocation." *Bell Journal of Economics* **XIII**: 402–417.

Reny, Philip (1999). "On the Existence of Pure and Mixed Strategy Nash Equilibria in Discontinuous Games." *Econometrica* **67**(5): 1029–1056.

Rothkopf, Michael, Aleksandar Pekec, and Ronald Harstad (1998). "Computationally Manageable Combinatorial Auctions." *Management Science* **44**: 1131–1147.

Royden, H.L. (1968). *Real Analysis*. New York: Macmillan.

Simon, Leo K. and William R. Zame (1990). "Discontinuous Games and Endogenous Sharing Rules." *Econometrica* **58**: 861–872.

Topkis, Donald (1978). "Minimizing a Submodular Function on a Lattice." *Operations Research* **26**: 305–321.

Topkis, Donald (1998). *Supermodularity and Complementarity*. Princeton University Press.

Weintraub, Gabriel Y. (2003). "There is No Such Thing as a Free Lunch: Analysis of the Combinatorial Auction for School Meals in Chile." Stanford University, Working paper.

Yokoo, Makoto, Yuko Sakurai, and Shigeo Matsubara (2000). "The Effect of False-Name Declarations in Mechanism Design: Towards Collective Decision Making on the Internet." *Proceedings of the Twentieth International Conference on Distributed Computing Systems*. IEEE Computer Society. 146–153.

Bibliography

Akerlof, George (1970). "The Market for 'Lemons': Quality Uncertainty and the Market Mechanism." *Quarterly Journal of Economics* **84**: 488–500.

Alesina, Alberto and Allan Drazen (1991). "Why are Stabilizations Delayed?" *American Economic Review* **81**(5): 1170–1188.

Anton, James J. and Dennis A. Yao (1992). "Coordination in Split Award Auctions." *Quarterly Journal of Economics* **CVII**: 681–707.

Ashenfelter, Orley (1989). "How Auctions Work for Wine and Art." *Journal of Economic Perspectives* **3**: 23–36.

Ashenfelter, Orley and Kathryn Graddy (2002). "Art Auctions: A Survey of Empirical Studies." Center for Economic Policy Studies Working Paper 81.

Athey, Susan (2001). "Single Crossing Properties and the Existence of Pure Strategy Equilibria in Games of Incomplete Information." *Econometrica* **69**(4): 861–890.

Athey, Susan (2002). "Monotone Comparative Statics under Uncertainty." *Quarterly Journal of Economics* **117**(1): 187–223.

Athey, Susan and Kyle Bagwell (2001). "Optimal Collusion with Private Information." *Rand Journal of Economics* **32**(3): 428–465.

Athey, Susan, Kyle Bagwell, and Chris Sanchirico (2003). "Collusion and Price Rigidity." *Review of Economic Studies* (forthcoming).

Ausubel, Lawrence and Peter Cramton (2002). "Demand Reduction and Inefficiency in Multi-Unit Auctions." www.cramton.umd.edu/papers1995–1999/98wp-demand-reduction.pdf.

Ausubel, Lawrence M. and Jesse A. Schwartz (1999). "The Ascending Auction Paradox." http://www.market-design.com/files/ausubel-schwartz-ascending-auction-paradox.pdf.

Ausubel, Lawrence and Paul Milgrom (2001). "System and Method for a Dynamic Auction with Package Bidding." Patent Cooperation Treaty application Application.

Ausubel, Lawrence and Paul Milgrom (2002). "Ascending Auctions with Package Bidding." *Frontiers of Theoretical Economics* **1**(1): Article 1.

Avery, Christopher (1998). "Strategic Jump Bidding in English Auctions." *Review of Economic Studies* **65**(2, No. 223): 185–210.

Ayres, Ian and Peter Cramton (1996). "Deficit Reduction through Diversity: How Affirmative Action at the FCC Increased Auction Competition." *Stanford Law Review* **48**(4): 761–815.

Back, Kerry and Jaime F. Zender (1993). "Auctions of Divisible Goods: On the Rationale for the Treasury Experiment." *Review of Financial Studies* **6**(4): 733–764.

Bajari, Patrick and Steven Tadelis (2001). "Incentives versus Transactions Costs: A Theory of Procurement Contracts." *Rand Journal of Economics* **32**(3): 387–407.

Banks, Jeffrey S., John O. Ledyard, and David P. Porter (1989). "Allocating Uncertain and Unresponsive Resources: An Experimental Approach." *Rand Journal of Economics* **20**: 1–25.

Bergemann, Dirk and Juuso Valimaki (2002). "Information Acquisition and Efficient Mechanism Design." *Econometrica* **70**(3): 1007–1033.

Bernheim, Douglas B. and Michael Whinston (1986). "Menu Auctions, Resource Allocation and Economic Influence." *Quarterly Journal of Economics* **101**: 1–31.

Bertrand, Joseph (1883). "Théorie Mathématique de la Richesse Sociale." *Journal des Sawarts* **69**: 499–508.

Bikchandani, Sushil, Philip Haile, and John G. Riley (2002). "Symmetric Separating Equilibria in English Auctions." *Games and Economic Behavior* **38**: 19–27.

Board, Simon (2002). "Bidding into the Red." Stanford GSB Working Paper.

Brewer, Paul and Charles Plott (1996). "A Binary Conflict Ascending Price (Bicap) Mechanism for the Decentralized Allocation of the Right to Use Railroad Tracks." *International Journal of Industrial Organization* **14**: 857–886.

Bulow, Jeremy, Ming Huang, and Paul Klemperer (1999). "Toeholds and Takeovers." *Journal of Political Economy* **107**(3): 427–454.

Bulow, Jeremy and John Roberts (1989). "The Simple Economics of Optimal Auctions." *Journal of Political Economy* **97**(5): 1060–1090.

Cantillon, Estelle and Martin Pesendorfer (2002). "Combination Bidding in Multi-unit Auctions." http://www.people.hbs.edu/ecantillon/combination July2002.pdf.

Cantillon, Estelle and Martin Pesendorfer (2003). "Combination Bidding in Multi-unit Auctions." Harvard Business School Working Paper.

Cassady, Ralph (1967). *Auctions and Auctioneering.* Berkeley: University of California Press.

Che, Yeon-Koo (1993). "Design Competition through Multidimensional Auctions." *Rand Journal of Economics* **24**(4): 668–680.

Che, Yeon-Koo and Ian Gale (1998). "Standard Auctions with Financially Constrained Bidders." *Review of Economic Studies* **65**(1, No. 222): 1–21.

Clarke, E.H. (1971). "Multipart Pricing of Public Goods." *Public Choice* **XI**: 17–33.

Coase, Ronald (1959). "The Federal Communications Commission." *Journal of Law and Economics* **2**: 1–40.

Cramton, Peter, John McMillan, Paul Milgrom, Brad Miller, Bridger Mitchell, Daniel Vincent, and Robert Wilson (1997). "Auction Design Enhancements for Non-Combinatorial Auctions." Report 1a: Market Design, Inc and Charles River Associates, www.market-design.com/files/97cra-auction-design-enhancements-for-non-combinatorial-auctions.pdf.

Cramton, Peter and Jesse Schwartz (2001). "Collusive Bidding: Lessons from the FCC Spectrum Auctions." *Journal of Regulatory Economics* **17**: 229–252.

Cremer, Jacques and Richard P. McLean (1985). "Optimal Selling Strategies under Uncertainty for a Discriminating Monopolist When Demands Are Independent." *Econometrica* **53**(2): 345–361.

Cybernomics (2000). "An Experimental Comparison of the Simultaneous Multi-Round Auction and the CRA Combinatorial Auction." http://wireless.fcc.gov/auctions/conferences/combin2000/releases/98540191.pdf.

Dana, James and Kathryn Spier (1994). "Designing a Private Industry." *Journal of Public Economics* **53**: 127–147.

Dasgupta, Partha and Eric Maskin (2000). "Efficient Auctions." *Quarterly Journal of Economics* **95**: 341–388.

Demange, Gabrielle, David Gale, and Marilda Sotomayor (1986). "Multi-item Auctions." *Journal of Political Economy* **94**: 863–872.

Edlin, Aaron and Chris Shannon (1998a). "Strict Monotonicity in Comparative Statics." *Journal of Economic Theory* **81**: 201–219.

Edlin, Aaron and Chris Shannon (1998b). "Strict Single Crossing and the Strict Spence–Mirrlees Condition: A Comment on Monotone Comparative Statics." *Econometrica* **60**(6): 1417–1425.

Engelbrecht-Wiggans, Richard and Charles Kahn (1998). "Multi-unit Auctions with Uniform Prices." *Economic Theory* **12**: 227–258.

Engelbrecht-Wiggans, Richard, Paul Milgrom, and Robert Weber (1983). "Competitive Bidding with Proprietary Information." *Journal of Mathematical Economics* **11**: 161–169.

Epstein, Rafael, Lysette Henríquez, Jaime Catalán, Gabriel Y. Weintraub, and Cristián Martínez (2002). "A Combinational Auction Improves School Meals in Chile." *Interfaces* **32**(6): 1–14.

Fudenberg, Drew and Jean Tirole (1986). "Theory of Exit in Duopoly." *Econometrica* **54**(4): 943–960.

Fudenberg, Drew and Jean Tirole (1991). *Game Theory*. Cambridge, MA: MIT Press.

Goeree, Jacob and Theo Offerman (2002). "The Amsterdam Auction." http://ideas.repec.org/p/wpa/wuwpmi/0205002.html.

Graham, Daniel and Robert Marshall (1987). "Collusive Bidder Behavior at Single-Object, Second-Price and English Auctions." *Journal of Political Economy* **95**: 1217–1239.

Green, Jerry and Jean-Jacques Laffont (1977). "Characterization of Satisfactory Mechanisms for the Revelation of Preferences for Public Goods." *Econometrica* **45**: 427–438.

Griesmer, James H., Richard E. Levitan, and Martin Shubik (1967). "Toward a Study of Bidding Processes Part IV: Games with Unknown Costs." *Naval Research Logistics Quarterly* **14**(4): 415–433.

Grossman, Sanford (1981). "The Informational Role of Warranties and Private Disclosure about Product Quality." *Journal of Law and Economics* **24**(3): 461–483.

Groves, Theodore (1973). "Incentives in Teams." *Econometrica* **61**: 617–631.

Gul, Faruk and Ennio Stacchetti (1999). "Walrasian Equilibrium with Gross Substitutes." *Journal of Economic Theory* **87**(1): 9–124.

Gul, Faruk and Ennio Stacchetti (2000). "The English Auction with Differentiated Commodities." *Journal of Economic Theory* **92**(1): 66–95.

Hansen, Robert G. (1988). "Auctions with Endogenous Quantity." *Rand Journal of Economics* **19**(1): 44–58.

Harsanyi, John (1967–1968). "Games with Incomplete Information Played by Bayesian Players (Parts I–III)." *Management Science* **14**: 159–182, 320–334, 486–502.

Hazlett, Thomas (1998). "Assigning Property Rights to Radio Spectrum Users: Why Did FCC License Auctions Take 67 Years?" *Journal of Law and Economics* **XLI** (2, part 2): 529–575.

Hendricks, Kenneth, Robert Porter, and Charles Wilson (1994). "Auctions for Oil and Gas Leases with an Informed Bidder and a Random Reservation Price." *Econometrica* **63**(1): 1–27.

Hernando-Veciana, Angel (2003). "Successful Uninformed Bidding." *Games and Economic Behavior* (forthcoming).

Hohner, Gail, John Rich, Ed Ng, Grant Reed, Andrew Davenport, Jayant Kalagnanam, Ho Soo Lee, and Chae An (2002). "Combinatorial and Quantity Discount Procurement Auctions with Mutual Benefits at Mars, Incorporated." IBM Watson Labs Research Center Working Paper.

Hohner, Gail, John Rich, Ed Ng, Grant Reid, Andrew J. Davenport, Jayant R. Kalagnanam, Ho Soo Lee, and Chae An (2001). "Combinatorial and Quantity Discount Procurement Auctions with Mutual Benefits at Mars, Incorporated." IBM–Mars Report.

Holmstrom, Bengt (1979). "Groves Schemes on Restricted Domains." *Econometrica* **47**: 1137–1144.

Holmstrom, Bengt and Paul Milgrom (1987). "Aggregation and Linearity in the Provision of Intertemporal Incentives." *Econometrica* **55**(2): 303–328.

Hurwicz, Leonid (1973). "The Design of Mechanisms for Resource Allocation." *American Economic Review* **63**(2): 1–30.

Jehiel, Philippe and Benny Moldovanu (2001). "Efficient Design with Interdependent Valuations." *Econometrica* **69**(5): 1237–1259.

Jehiel, Philippe, Benny Moldovanu, and Ennio Stacchetti (1996). "How (Not) to Sell Nuclear Weapons." *American Economic Review* **86**: 814–829.

Kagel, John H. and Dan Levin (2002). *Common Value Auctions and the Winner's Curse.* Princeton: Princeton University Press.

Kagel, John H. (1995). "Auctions: A Survey of Experimental Research." *The Handbook of Experimental Economics.* J. H. Kagel and A. E. Roth. Princeton: Princeton University Press. Chapter 7, 501–585.

Kelso, Alexander and Vincent Crawford (1982). "Job Matching, Coalition Formation, and Gross Substitutes." *Econometrica* **50**: 1483.

Klemperer, Paul (1998). "Auctions with Almost Common Values: The Wallet Game and Its Applications." *European Economic Review* **42**: 757–769.

Klemperer, Paul (2002a). "What Really Matters in Auction Design." *Journal of Economics Perspectives* **16**(1): 169–190.

Klemperer, Paul (2002b). "Why Every Economist Should Learn Some Auction Theory." http://www.paulklemperer.org/.

Klemperer, Paul and Margaret Meyer (1989). "Supply Function Equilibria in Oligopoly under Uncertainty." *Econometrica* **57**(6): 1243–1277.

Kwerel, Evan and Alex Felker (1985). "Using Auctions to Select FCC Licensees." Washington: Federal Communications Commission. 32.

Laffont, Jean-Jacques (1997). "Game Theory and Empirical Economics: The Case of Auction Data." *European Economic Review* **41**: 1–35.

Laffont, Jean-Jacques and Eric Maskin (1980). "A Differentiable Approach to Dominant Strategy Mechanisms." *Econometrica* **48**: 1507–1520.

Laffont, Jean-Jacques, Herve Ossard, and Quang Vuong (1995). "Econometrics of First-Price Auctions." *Econometrica* **63**(4): 953–980.

Ledyard, John O., David P. Porter, and Antonio Rangel (1997). "Experiments Testing Multi-object Allocation Mechanisms." *Journal of Economics and Management Strategy* **6**: 639–675.

Lehmann, Daniel, Liadan O'Callaghan, and Yoav Shoham (2002). "Truth Revelation in Approximately Efficient Combinatorial Auctions." *Journal of the ACM* **49**(5): 577–602.

Levin, Dan and James L. Smith (1994). "Equilibrium in Auctions with Entry." *American Economic Review* **84**(3): 585–599.

Mas Colell, Andreu, Michael Whinston, and Jerry Green (1995). *Microeconomic Theory*. New York: Oxford University Press.

Maskin, Eric (1992). "Auctions and Privatisation." *Privatisation*. H. Siebert. 115–136.

Maskin, Eric and John G. Riley (2000a). "Equilibrium in Sealed High Bid Auctions." *Review of Economics Studies*. **67**(3): 439–454.

Maskin, Eric S. and John G. Riley (2000b). "Asymmetric Auctions." *Review of Economic Studies* **67**(3): 413–438.

Matthews, Stephen (1983). "Selling to Risk Averse Buyers with Unobservable Tastes." *Journal of Economic Theory* **30**: 370–400.

McAdams, David (2002). "Modifying the Uniform Price Auction to Eliminate 'Collusive Seeming Equilibria'." http://www.mit.edu/~mcadams/papers/mupa.pdf.

McAfee, R. Preston and John McMillan (1987). "Auctions with Entry." *Economics Letters* **23**: 343–348.

McAfee, R. Preston and John McMillan (1992). "Bidding Rings." *American Economic Review* **82**(3): 579–599.

McAfee, R. Preston and Philip Reny (1982). "Correlated Information and Mechanism Design." *Econometrica* **60**(2): 395–421.

McMillan, John (1994). "Selling Spectrum Rights." *Journal of Economics Perspectives* **8**: 145–162.

Milgrom, Paul (1979). "A Convergence Theorem for Competitive Bidding with Differential Information." *Econometrica* **47**: 670–688.

Milgrom, Paul (1981a). "Good News and Bad News: Representation Theorems and Applications." *Bell Journal of Economics* **12**: 380–391.

Milgrom, Paul R. (1981b). "Rational Expectations, Information Acquisition, and Competitive Bidding." *Econometrica* **49**(4): 921–943.

Milgrom, Paul (1986). "Auction Theory." *Advances in Economic Theory: Fifth World Congress of the Econometric Society*. T. Bewley. London: Cambridge University Press. 1–32.

Milgrom, Paul (1997). "Procuring Universal Service: Putting Auction Theory to Work." *Le Prix Nobel: The Nobel Prizes, 1996.* Stockholm: Nobel Foundation. 382–392.

Milgrom, Paul (2000). "Putting Auctions Theory to Work: The Simultaneous Ascending Auction." *Journal of Political Economy* **108**(2): 245–272.

Milgrom, Paul and Ilya Segal (2002). "Envelope Theorems for Arbitrary Choice Sets." *Econometrica* **70**(2): 583–601.

Milgrom, Paul and Chris Shannon (1994). "Monotone Comparative Statics." *Econometrica* **62**: 157–180.

Milgrom, Paul and Nancy Stokey (1982). "Information, Trade and Common Knowledge." *Journal of Economic Theory* **26**: 17–27.

Milgrom, Paul and Robert J. Weber (1982a). "A Theory of Auctions and Competitive Bidding." *Econometrica* **50**: 463–483.

Milgrom, Paul and Robert J. Weber (1982b). "The Value of Information in a Sealed-Bid Auction." *Journal of Mathematical Economics* **10**(1): 105–114.

Milgrom, Paul and Robert Weber (1985). "Distributional Strategies for Games with Incomplete Information." *Mathematics of Operations Research* **10**: 619–632.

Milgrom, Paul and Robert J. Weber (2000). "A Theory of Auctions and Competitive Bidding, II." *The Economic Theory of Auctions.* P. Klemperer. Cheltenham: Edward Elgar Publishing, Ltd. **2**: 179–194.

Mirrlees, James (1971). "An Exploration in the Theory of Optimal Taxation." *Review of Economic Studies* **38**: 175–208.

Mueller, Milton (1993). "New Zealand's Revolution in Spectrum Management." *Information Economics and Policy* **5**: 159–177.

Myerson, Roger B. (1981). "Optimal Auction Design." *Mathematics of Operations Research* **6**(1): 58–73.

Myerson, Roger B. (1991). *Game Theory.* Cambridge, MA: Harvard University Press.

Neeman, Zvika (2001). "The Relevance of Private Information in Mechanism Design." Boston University Working Paper.

Nisan, Noam (2000). "Bidding and Allocation in Combinatorial Auctions." http://www.cs.huji.ac.il/~noam/mkts.html.

Ockenfels, Axel and Alvin E. Roth (2002). "Last Minute Bidding and the Rules for Ending Second-Price Auctions: Evidence from Ebay and Amazon Auctions on the Internet." *American Economic Review* **92**(4): 1093–1103.

Ortega-Reichert, Armando (1968). "Models for Competitive Bidding under Uncertainty." Stanford, CA: Department of Operations Research, Stanford University.

Parkes, David and Lyle Ungar (2000). "Iterative Combinatorial Auctions: Theory and Practice." *Proceedings of the 17th National Conference on Artificial Intelligence* AAAI. 74–81.

Parkes, David, Lyle Ungar, and David Foster (1999). "Accounting for Cognitive Costs in on-Line Auction Design." *Agent Mediated Electronic Commerce.* P. Noriega and C. Sierra. Heidelberg: Springer-Verlag.

Perry, Motty and Philip Reny (1999). "On the Failure of the Linkage Principle." *Econometrica* **67**(4): 895–890.

Perry, Motty and Philip Reny (2002). "An Efficient Auction." *Econometrica* **70**(3): 1199–1212.

Pesendorfer, Wolfgang and Jeroen Swinkels (1997). "The Loser's Curse and Information Aggregation in Common Value Auctions." *Econometrica* **65**: 1247–1281.

Pesendorfer, Wolfgang and Jeroen Swinkels (2000). "Efficiency and Information Aggregation in Auctions." *American Economic Review* **90**(3): 499–525.

Postlewaite, Andrew and John Roberts (1976). "The Incentives for Price-Taking Behavior in Large Exchange Economies." *Econometrica* **44**(1): 115–129.

Rassenti, S.J., R.L. Bulfin, and Vernon Smith (1982). "A Combinatorial Auction Mechanism for Airport Time Slot Allocation." *Bell Journal of Economics* **XIII**: 402–417.

Reny, Philip (1999). "On the Existence of Pure and Mixed Strategy Nash Equilibria in Discontinuous Games." *Econometrica* **67**(5): 1029–1056.

Rezende, Leonardo (2002). "Biased Procurement." Stanford University Working Paper.

Riley, John G. and William S. Samuelson (1981). "Optimal Auctions." *American Economic Review* **71**(3): 381–392.

Riley, John G. and Richard Zeckhauser (1983). "Optimal Selling Strategies: When to Haggle, When to Hold Firm." *Quarterly Journal of Economics* **98**: 267–289.

Roth, Alvin E. (1991). "A Natural Experiment in the Organization of Entry-Level Labor Markets: Regional Markets for New Physicians and Surgeons in the United Kingdom." *American Economic Review* **81**(3): 415–440.

Roth, Alvin E. and Axel Ockenfels (2000). "Last Minute Bidding and the Rules for Ending Second-Price Auctions: Theory and Evidence from a Natural Experiment on the Internet." *NBER* Working Paper: 7299.

Rothkopf, Michael, Aleksandar Pekec, and Ronald Harstad (1998). "Computationally Manageable Combinatorial Auctions." *Management Science* **44**: 1131–1147.

Rothkopf, Michael, Thomas Teisberg, and Edward Kahn (1990). "Why Are Vickrey Auctions Rare?" *Journal of Political Economy* **98**: 94–109.

Royden, H.L. (1968). *Real Analysis*. New York: Macmillan.

Salant, David and Colin Loxley (2000). "Default Service Auctions." Mimeo.

Simon, C. and Larry Blume (1994). *Mathematics for Economists*. New York: W.W. Norton and Co.

Simon, Leo K. and William R. Zame (1990). "Discontinuous Games and Endogenous Sharing Rules." *Econometrica* **58**: 861–872.

Spence, A. Michael (1973). "Job Market Signaling." *Quarterly Journal of Economics* **87**(3): 355–374.

Swinkels, Jeroen (2001). "Efficiency of Large Private Value Auctions." *Econometrica* **69**(1): 37–68.

Topkis, Donald (1978). "Minimizing a Submodular Function on a Lattice." *Operations Research* **26**: 305–321.

Topkis, Donald (1998). *Supermodularity and Complementarity*. Princeton University Press.

Varian, Hal R. (1992). *Microeconomic Analysis*. New York: Norton.

Vickrey, William (1961). "Counterspeculation, Auctions, and Competitive Sealed Tenders." *Journal of Finance* **XVI**: 8–37.

Weber, Robert J. (1983). "Multiple-Object Auctions." *Auctions, Bidding, and Contracting: Uses and Theory*. R. Engelbrecht-Wiggans, M. Shubik, and R. M. Stark. New York: New York University Press. 165–191.

Weber, Robert (1997). "Making More from Less: Strategic Demand Reduction in the FCC Spectrum Auctions." *Journal of Economic and Management Strategy* **6**: 529–548.

Weintraub, Gabriel Y. (2003). "There is No Such Thing as a Free Lunch: Analysis of the Combinatorial Auction for School Meals in Chile." Working paper, *Stanford University*.

Weverbergh, Marcel (1979). "Competitive Bidding with Asymmetric Information Reanalyzed." *Management Science* **25**: 291–294.

Williams, Steven R. (1999). "A Characterization of Efficient, Bayesian Incentive Compatible Mechanism." *Economic Theory* **XIV**: 155–180.

Wilson, Robert (1967). "Competitive Bidding with Asymmetric Information." *Management Science* **13**: 816–820.

Wilson, Robert (1969). "Competitive Bidding with Disparate Information." *Management Science* **15**(7): 446–448.

Wilson, Robert (1977). "A Bidding Model of Perfect Competition." *Review of Economic Studies* **44**: 511–518.

Wilson, Robert (1979). "Auctions of Shares." *Quarterly Journal of Economics* **XCIII**(4): 675–689.

Wilson, Robert (1987). "Bidding." *The New Palgrave: A Dictionary of Economics*. J. Eatwell, M. Milgate, and P. Newman. London: MacMillan Press. **1**: 238–242.

Ye, Lixin (2002). "A Theory of Two-Stage Auctions." Ohio State University Working Paper.

Yokoo, Makoto, Yuko Sakurai, and Shigeo Matsubara (2000). "The Effect of False-Name Declarations in Mechanism Design: Towards Collective Decision Making on the Internet." *Proceedings of the Twentieth International Conference on Distributed Computing Systems*. IEEE Computer Society. 146–153.

Zheng, Charles (2001). "High Bids and Broke Winners." *Journal of Economic Theory* **100**(1): 129–171.

Author Index

Akerlof, George, 40
Alesina, Alberto, 117, 155
An, Chae, 253, 254, 299, 336
Anton, James. J., 238, 249
Ashenfelter, Orley, 90, 96, 255, 295
Athey, Susan, 89, 96, 182, 206
Ausubel, Lawrence, 57, 62, 252, 254, 258,
    287, 295, 302, 318, 320, 324, 332, 335
Avery, Christopher, 155, 188
Ayres, Ian, 235, 249

Back, Kerry, 295
Bagwell, Kyle, 89, 96
Bajari, Patrick, 213, 249
Banks, Jeffrey S., xx, 301, 335
Bergemann, Dirk, 62
Bernheim, Douglas B, 318, 323, 336
Bertrand, Joseph, 16, 33
Binmore, Ken, 2, 33
Bikchandani, Sushil, 197, 206
Blume, Larry, 65, 97
Board, Simon, 243, 249
Brewer, Paul, 301, 336
Bulfin, R.L., 301, 336
Bulow, Jeremy, 65, 96, 117, 142, 148, 155,
    192, 193, 206

Cantillon, Estelle, 253, 254, 298, 335
Cassady, Ralph, 298, 335
Catalán, Jaime, 299, 366
Che, Yeon-Koo, 132, 155, 245, 249
Clarke, E. H., 45, 62
Coase, Richard, 79, 96
Crampton, Peter, 30, 33, 235, 249, 258,
    295
Crawford, Vincent, 269, 295

Cremer, Jaques, 33, 162, 206
Cybernomics, 299, 336

Dana, James, 252, 254
Dasgupta, Partha, 22, 33
Davenport, Andrew, 253, 254, 299, 336
Demange, Gabrielle, 282, 295
Drazen, Allen, 117, 155

Edlin, Aaron, 107, 155
Englebrecht-Wiggans, Richard, 167, 206,
    258, 295
Epstein, Rafael, 299, 336

Felker, Alex, 3, 4
Foster, David, 302, 336
Fudenberg, Drew, 96, 117, 155

Gale, David, 282, 295
Gale, Ian, 132, 155
Gilbert, Richard, 249
Goeree, Jacob, 235, 249
Graddy, Katherine, 90, 96, 255, 295
Graham, Daniel, 87, 96, 251, 254
Green, Jerry, 56, 62, 65, 96, 186, 206
Griesmer, James H., 112
Grossman, Sanford, 176, 206
Groves, Theodore, 45, 62
Gul, Faruk, 252, 275, 282, 283, 295

Haile, Philip, 197, 206
Hansen, Robert G., 135, 155
Harsanyi, John, 40
Harstad, Ronald, 302, 336
Hazlett, Thomas, 12
Hendricks, Kenneth, 2, 167, 171, 206

Subject Index